Grounded in the Body, in Time and Place, in Scripture

Australian College of Theology Monograph Series

SERIES EDITOR GRAEME R. CHATFIELD

The ACT Monograph Series, generously supported by the Board of Directors of the Australian College of Theology, provides a forum for publishing quality research theses and studies by its graduates and affiliated college staff in the broad fields of Biblical Studies, Christian Thought and History, and Practical Theology with Wipf and Stock Publishers of Eugene, Oregon. The ACT selects the best of its doctoral and research masters theses as well as monographs that offer the academic community, scholars, church leaders and the wider community uniquely Australian and New Zealand perspectives on significant research topics and topics of current debate. The ACT also provides opportunity for contributors beyond its graduates and affiliated college staff to publish monographs which support the mission and values of the ACT.

Rev. Dr. Graeme Chatfield
Series Editor and Associate Dean

"This volume is one of the most inspiring books I have read in a long time. These Australian female scholars offer a theologically profound and biblically rich series of explorations into Indigenous peoples, biblical themes, human experience, embodied faith, land and place, and mission and witness. I cannot overstate the timeliness, quality, and importance of this book."

—**Graham Joseph Hill**, Principal and Director of Research, Stirling Theological College, University of Divinity, and author of *Holding Up Half the Sky*

"*Grounded* is an extraordinarily rich anthology of essays representing women's voices on a broad range of topics in relation to the Christian faith from an equally broad range of perspectives.... It is shot through with a welcome realism that is often lacking in scholarly essays. Although entirely penned by Australian women scholars, it would be a mistake to think this volume was written solely for women or for Australians.... I highly recommend this to scholars, students, and church people alike."

—**Lucy Peppiatt**, Principal, Westminster Theological Centre, United Kingdom

"This book dispels two myths: that there are very few women in Australian evangelical biblical and theological scholarship and that the Bible has little to say to the pressing issues of our day. *Grounded* showcases profound and practical theology at its best. A rich and rewarding read."

—**Brian Rosner**, Principal, Ridley College, Australia

"This eclectic, engaging collection of essays offers excellent exegetical insights into Scripture and pearls of wisdom for today's problems. The authors' wide range of experiences and confident humility enable them to address difficult issues head on. The book is a feast for the soul, a thoroughly enjoyable read that will shape future conversations about women's lives in Scripture and our modern world."

—**Lynn H. Cohick**, Provost/Dean, Denver Seminary

"It was enriching to read the diverse experiences of the women in this collection of essays. Informed by lived reality, each writer brings fresh insight into her area of expertise. What often stands out is a holistic view of the human person and spirituality, which is, of course, very biblical. Informative, stimulating, inspiring. Highly recommended."

—**Siu Fung Wu**, Lecturer in New Testament Studies, Whitley College, Australia

"*Grounded* recognizes the significance of our bodies, the land, our histories, and experiences for interdisciplinary biblical and theological scholarship. The contributors unabashedly bring their whole selves into the research and writing process. Consequently, this work is challenging and illuminating, directly addressing weighty topics with clarity and thoughtfulness while doing so in a refreshing and personal way. "

—**Christa McKirland**, Lecturer in Systematic Theology, Carey Baptist College, New Zealand

"*Grounded* is a landmark collection, showcasing the immense insight and expertise of Australian women doing theology in an evangelical tradition. From First Nations leaders to contemporary Pentecostals, close biblical exegesis to meditations on architecture and media, this is a stimulating set of engagements with the Christian Scriptures. At a moment when many people are seeking wiser ways of living in this particular time and place, *Grounded* is a great gift to the Australian church, and indeed to the wider nation."

—**Meredith Lake**, author of *The Bible in Australia: A Cultural History*

Grounded in the Body, in Time and Place, in Scripture

Papers by Australian Women Scholars in the Evangelical Tradition

Edited by
JILL FIRTH
and
DENISE COOPER-CLARKE

WIPF & STOCK · Eugene, Oregon

GROUNDED IN THE BODY, IN TIME AND PLACE, IN SCRIPTURE
Papers by Australian Women Scholars in the Evangelical Tradition

Australian College of Theology Monograph Series

Copyright © 2021 Wipf and Stock Publishers. All rights reserved. Except for brief quotations in critical publications or reviews, no part of this book may be reproduced in any manner without prior written permission from the publisher. Write: Permissions, Wipf and Stock Publishers, 199 W. 8th Ave., Suite 3, Eugene, OR 97401.

Wipf & Stock
An Imprint of Wipf and Stock Publishers
199 W. 8th Ave., Suite 3
Eugene, OR 97401

www.wipfandstock.com

PAPERBACK ISBN: 978-1-7252-8877-5
HARDCOVER ISBN: 978-1-7252-8878-2
EBOOK ISBN: 978-1-7252-8879-9

All Scripture quotations, unless otherwise indicated, are from the New Revised Standard Version Bible, copyright © 1989 National Council of the Churches of Christ in the United States of America. Used by permission. All rights reserved worldwide.

Scripture quotations marked (NIV) are taken from the Holy Bible, New International Version®, NIV®. Copyright © 1973, 1978, 1984, 2011 by Biblica, Inc.™ Used by permission of Zondervan. All rights reserved worldwide. www.zondervan.com. The "NIV" and "New International Version" are trademarks registered in the United States Patent and Trademark Office by Biblica, Inc.™

The Lord's Prayer in Woiwurrung, reproduced on the following page, is from:

Thomas, William. "Succinct Sketch of the Aboriginal Language." In *The Aborigines of Victoria: With Notes Relating to the Habits of the Natives of Other Parts of Australia and Tasmania. Compiled from Various Sources for the Government of Victoria.* Vol. 2, edited by R. Brough Smyth, 132. London: Trübner and Co, 1878. https://aiatsis.gov.au/sites/default/files/docs/digitised_collections/collectors_of_words/smyth/m0052799_a.pdf

01/07/21

The Lord's Prayer in Woiwurrung

Marmanellā Marman wellainer narlumboon karboit;
nerrīno murrumbinner koongee boundup;
woman trangbulk murrumbinner mongon tandowring beeker.
Umarleek nurnin yellenwă tanganan;
bar narlarnany nurnin nowdin murrumarter narlarnarny ungo;
bar kunark nurnin watticar koolin yellenwă nier nillam womeit.
Tindu Murrumbinner, Boundup Marman,
nulworthen nurnin netbo bar nanbo.
Amen.

Contents

Acknowledgements | xi

Contributors | xiii

1 Introduction | 1
 —Denise Cooper-Clarke and Jill Firth

Part I: Context

2 What Can the Birds of the *Land* Tell Us? | 19
 —Brooke Prentis

3 Grounded in Australia: Learning from our First Peoples | 31
 —Jude Long

4 Embodying Christ in the Neighborhood: A Reflection on Place, Home, and Mission | 43
 —Karina Kreminski

5 Purity: Guarding the Body Corporate | 60
 —Moyra Dale

Part II: Old Testament Explorations

6 The Transformation of Israel's Social Identity in the Book of Exodus | 79
 —Katherine M. Smith

7 Embodied Worship: The Psalms and the Senses | 92
—MELINDA COUSINS

8 "Descending from the Hills of Gilead": Undressing Descriptions of the Lover's Body, and How Australian Women Can Reclaim and Embrace Their Embodiment | 107
—ERIN MARTINE SESSIONS

9 Desert Spring, Dead Dog Waterhole, Disappointment Creek: Is the God of the Book of Jeremiah Bad for Women? | 121
—JILL FIRTH

Part III: New Testament Explorations

10 Grounded in His Lordship: Mary, Martha, and Me | 139
—THERESA YU LAU

11 Sensory Experience and the Gospel of John | 152
—LOUISE GOSBELL

12 At Jacob's Well: Re-grounding the Samaritan Woman | 167
—DEBORAH STORIE

Part IV: Applied Theology

13 "Wisdom Cries Out": Towards a Feminist Pentecostal Theology of (Dis)ability | 187
—TANYA RICHES

14 Grounding Our Discussion of Abortion | 203
—DENISE COOPER-CLARKE

15 Christianity in Contemporary Australian Media: "Get Your Rosaries Off My Ovaries" | 219
—ENQI WENG

16 Grounded yet Wandering: Church Architecture, Space, and Place | 235
—ELIZABETH C. CULHANE

17 Grounded in Work as Christians | 250
—KARA MARTIN

18 Tethered between Reality and Aspiration: Grounding and Formative Practices for Australian Leaders | 266
   —Monica O'Neil

19 Grandmothers of Intention: Women in Australian Theological Academia (1883–2003) | 282
   —Jill Firth

   Epilogue—Saam 151 | 301
   —Carol Robertson (translated by Kate Beer)

Acknowledgements

We would like to acknowledge the traditional custodians of all the lands on which these chapters were written, and especially the Wurundjeri people of the Kulin nation, upon whose land we have edited this book. We acknowledge their stewardship of this land on behalf of the Almighty Creator, and their generosity to all Australians. We pay our respects to Elders past, present, and emerging, and continue to learn from them.

Thank you to Brian Rosner for his encouragement to bring this book into being and to the leadership team of Ridley College (Brian Rosner, Tim Foster, Michael Petering, and Ruth Weatherlake) who graciously allowed us to use the profits from the 2019 Grounded conference to defray publishing expenses.

We thank our Ridley colleagues Diane Hockridge, Anthea McCall, Anne Ellison, Elizabeth Culhane, and Laura Paul for their contribution in conceptualizing the volume. Ridley's faculty, students, and staff, especially Katrine Bramley, Kathryn Shedden, Jane Ellison, Alison Foster, and Sarah Quinto, have given us unfailing support and encouragement.

We acknowledge the financial support of the Australian College of Theology for this book. We thank Graeme Chatfield for his encouragement, Megan Powell du Toit our Publishing Manager for her untiring help, and Gina Denholm our copyeditor for her advice and cheerful attention to detail.

Thanks also go to our chapter authors. And we also remember those who were unable to complete chapters for personal, health, or workflow reasons.

Our gratitude to the anonymous peer reviewers! Denise and I know who you are, and we are very grateful for your generosity with your expertise and time. The book is better for your work.

I (Jill) would like to acknowledge my co-editor, Denise Cooper-Clarke, who has been a delight to work with. Family and friends, my prayer group, and others have sat through a lot of random remarks on the book of Jeremiah, the editing learning curve, and Australian women's history. I especially thank my husband, Len, who has accompanied the Evangelical Women in Academia conferences and this project "in sickness and in health," and in the last days has rescued my crashed computer in the nick of time.

And I (Denise) give my thanks to Jill Firth for inviting me to be part of this project – you have the gift of encouragement in spades; to my husband David for allowing me to work all through the Easter weekend (though we were confined to home); to the staff team at St. Thomas Anglican Church Burwood, especially Rev. Ruth Newmarch for her lively interest in the project, and to my two small groups who prayed for the work.

Contributors

Rev. Kate Beer works as part of the Anglican Diocese Ministry Development Team to support Aboriginal church leaders in the Northern Territory. Kate is the Ministry Development Officer and works alongside women church leaders. She holds an MDiv and an MA and is investigating how ministry supervision can be applied with Indigenous community leaders.

Dr. Denise Cooper-Clarke is a graduate of medicine and theology with a PhD in medical ethics. She has special interests in professional ethics and the ethics of virtue. Denise is an occasional adjunct lecturer in Ethics at Ridley College Melbourne and voluntary researcher with Ethos Centre for Christianity and Society.

Rev. Dr. Melinda Cousins is the Director of Ministries for Baptist Churches South Australia and teaches Biblical Studies at Tabor. She completed her PhD in 2016 on the Psalms of Ascents (Psalms 120–134) looking at ideas of theological interpretation, pilgrimage, and performance.

Elizabeth C. Culhane is a tutor at Ridley College Melbourne and a PhD student at the University of Queensland. Her dissertation investigates the theological concept of revelation with respect to human artistic creations. Her work has been published in *Religion & Literature* and *Political Theology*.

Dr. Moyra Dale is an ethnographer who has worked for over two decades in the Middle East. Her research includes adult literacy in Egypt and the women's mosque movement in Syria through women's accounts and understanding of their own lives and realities. She writes and teaches on cross-cultural anthropology and Islam.

Rev. Dr. Jill Firth is a lecturer in Hebrew and Old Testament at Ridley College Melbourne. She completed her PhD on Psalms 140–143 in 2016. Jill is an ordained priest and has been a Canon of St. Paul's Cathedral, Melbourne. She is writing a monograph on Psalms and a commentary on Jeremiah.

Dr. Louise Gosbell is a lecturer at Mary Andrews College in Sydney and an Honorary Research Associate of the Sydney College of Divinity. Louise completed her PhD in 2015 at Macquarie University on the language of disability in the New Testament Gospels. Her thesis was published by Mohr Siebeck in 2018.

Rev. Dr. Karina Kreminski is Co-director of Neighbourhood Matters. She taught Missional Studies at Morling College Sydney. She was previously a senior pastor at a church in Sydney. She is a speaker, writer, mentor, and community worker in her local neighborhood. She is the author of *Urban Spirituality: Embodying God's Mission in the Neighborhood*.

Rev. Dr. Theresa Yu Lau currently serves as Dean of Faculty and Development at Melbourne School of Theology Chinese Department. She is also an ordained priest in the Anglican Church of Australia. She has been a missionary to Spain, serving as Academic Dean and Associate Professor in New Testament at International Chinese Biblical Seminary in Europe.

Dr. Jude Long is Vice Principal Academic at Melbourne School of Theology and Eastern College Australia. Prior to that, she was the Principal of Nungalinya College in Darwin for eight years. Jude has a passion for facilitating education that will transform the whole person and help learners to grow in their relationship with Christ.

Kara Martin has authored *Workship: How to Use your Work to Worship God*, and *Workship 2: How to Flourish at Work*. She lectures at Mary Andrews College and Alphacrucis College in Sydney and has worked in media and communications, human resources, business analysis, and policy development.

Rev. Monica O'Neil is an experienced minister, facilitator, and strategy consultant with a demonstrated history of working in professional training, supervision, and coaching. She is the Director at Vose Leadership and lectures in Ministry and Practice at Vose Seminary. Monica pastors Living Grace Dianella in Western Australia.

Brooke Prentis, BCom, BA, CA, GAICD, is a Wakka Wakka woman and Aboriginal Christian Leader. Brooke is the CEO of Common Grace and Co-ordinator of the Grasstree Gathering. Brooke is a founding board member of NAIITS Australia, a Scholar of the ACC&C, and a University of Divinity Masters student in partnership with NAIITS.

Dr. Tanya Riches is senior lecturer and MTh program coordinator at Hillsong College in Sydney. She co-led the research pillar at the Centre for Disability Studies, affiliate of the University of Sydney. Her monograph investigating urban Aboriginal-led Pentecostal Christian congregations was released with Brill's Global Pentecostal and Charismatic Studies series in 2019.

Rev. Carol Robertson and her husband Andrew are descendants of the first Ngukurr Christians. They were ordained as deacons in 2009 and as priests in 2011 at St. Matthew's Church, Ngukurr. Carol holds a Certificate of Theology from Nungalinya College (2008) and was part of the Bible translation team for the Kriol Baibul. She continues to work in translation.

Erin Martine Sessions is the recipient of the inaugural ACT Female Candidate Scholarship and is working toward her PhD on Song of Songs as a model for the primary prevention of Domestic and Family Violence. She is a lecturer in Integrative Studies at Excelsia and an Associate of Common Grace. Erin is an errant poet and arrant academic. She bends time and space to binge-watch Netflix.

Dr. Katherine M. Smith is the Principal and Lecturer in Old Testament at Mary Andrews College Sydney. She completed her PhD on Leviticus through Trinity College Bristol (University of Bristol).

Dr. Deborah Storie is a Baptist Pastor, lectures in Biblical Studies at Whitley and Stirling Colleges, and is an Honorary Postdoctoral Associate at the University of Divinity. She previously worked in community development in Afghanistan, served on the Board of TEAR Australia, and evaluated development projects in Africa and Asia.

Dr. Enqi Weng completed her PhD from the School of Media and Communications at RMIT University. Her monograph *Media Perceptions of Religious Changes in Australia: Of Dominance and Diversity* was recently published with Routledge. She was born in Singapore and has over seven years of industry experience in marketing communications.

I

Introduction

DENISE COOPER-CLARKE AND JILL FIRTH

"There Are No Women in My Bibliographies!"

IN 2015, MUSIC STUDENT Jessy McCabe observed that there were no women among the sixty-three composers featured on her UK school music syllabus. Five years later, another syllabus showed only 4 percent women composers.[1] Similarly, women's voices are underrepresented in the Australian media, as documented by Jenna Price and Anne Marie Price in their report, *2019 Women for Media: "You Can't Be What You Can't See."*[2] Theological college students can resonate with the experience of Marion Taylor, who asked her university professor if he could recommend a woman biblical interpreter as a topic for an upcoming essay. He replied succinctly that there were none. Marion's subsequent research identified many nineteenth-century women biblical interpreters, and later broadened out to her *Handbook of Women Biblical Interpreters* (2012), which introduces 180 women interpreters from Paula, associate of Jerome, and Macrina, sister of the Cappadocian fathers Basil and Gregory, in the fourth and fifth centuries, to Katharina Schütz Zell and Mary Sidney Herbert in the sixteenth and seventeenth centuries, to

---

1. Eleanor Busby, "Exam Board Criticised."
2. Jenna Price, "You Can't Be What You Can't See."

Florence Nightingale and Christina Rosetti (who wrote a commentary on the book of Revelation) in the nineteenth and twentieth centuries.[3]

Publishing, rather than public speaking, marks the "entry of women preachers into male dominated discourse," as early Methodist women observed.[4] Recent Australian research into women in theological education identified female representation in bibliographies and female role models as among key factors for encouraging women students.[5] In past decades, there were few or no women authors in many academic theology reading lists, and today there is still a dearth of women's writing, Australian women's writing, or evangelical women's writing in theology and biblical studies.

This book grew from a desire to offer accessible readings by Australian women scholars in the evangelical tradition, for students and lecturers in biblical studies, theology, and applied subjects. We invited chapters from established and emerging scholars from around Australia, and from a variety of theological colleges. Many of the chapters were first presented at the Evangelical Women in Academia conference, which took place at Ridley College in Melbourne on August 3, 2019. This conference was the third in a series of annual conferences, from 2017–2019. The inaugural Evangelical Women in Academia conference in 2017 featured speakers Lynn Cohick and Delle Matthews. The 2018 conference, *Finding Her Voice*, explored women's writing and public speaking with publisher Katya Covrett, Old Testament scholar Katy Smith, and missiologist Moyra Dale. At the 2019 conference, the theme *Grounded: in the Body, in Time and Place, in Scripture* was explored by featured speakers Paula Gooder and Jude Long and in around twenty academic papers that were presented by Australian evangelical women scholars. Alongside the conferences, Ridley has also developed women's writing groups and a women's preaching network.[6]

In this introduction, we consider what women, and Australian women in particular, bring to theological and biblical scholarship, then provide an overview of the chapters.

---

3. Taylor and Choi, *Handbook of Women Biblical Interpreters*; Rossetti, *Face of the Deep*.

4. Quote from Christine Kreuger in Pitman, *Prophets and Priests*, 253.

5. Martin et al., "Women in Theological Education," 172.

6 See Ridley College website (www.ridley.edu.au) for audio of conference keynotes and information on future conferences and the writing and preaching networks.

Women and Australian Women in Theological Scholarship

In considering the rationale for publishing a book by Australian women scholars in the fields of theology and biblical studies, it is reasonable to ask whether women have a particular contribution to make in these fields. We believe that they do. In 1889, over a century ago, Frances Willard, president of the Woman's Christian Temperance Union, issued this call: "We need women commentators to bring out the women's side of the book; we need the stereoscopic view of truth in general, which can only be had when woman's eye and man's eye together shall discern the perspective of the Bible's full-orbed revelation."[7]

Women's perspectives include the distinctive questions and concerns we bring to the text, arising from our distinctive experiences "of self and family, our relationship to institutions, the nature of our work and daily lives, and our spirituality."[8] As Amanda Benckhuysen notes, we need to acknowledge and consider the way gender affects the interpretation of texts.[9]

In 2016, an anonymous voluntary survey of women students and lecturers in the Australian College of Theology was undertaken to answer the question, "What do women bring to theological education as learners and teachers?"[10] Some of the students who responded said they valued a female perspective.[11] These respondents named dimensions frequently contributed by women to be "empathy, pastoral care, pragmatism, complex view of relationships, compassion, counselling, emotional engagement with Scripture, pastoral implications of biblical exegesis, experiential approach to spiritual formation, humor . . . serving God in the messiness of everyday life, and a holistic view."[12] Of course, none of these dimensions or qualities are exclusive to women, but some respondents drew attention to "the unique life experiences of women as daughters, sisters, mothers, wives, widows, and women in unpaid ministry"[13] that informed their understanding of discrimination and injustice, especially in relation to issues such as domestic violence and body image.

---

7. Frances Willard, *Woman in the Pulpit*, Chicago: Woman's Temperance Publishing Association, 1889, 21, in Newsom and Ringe, "Introduction," xxvii.

8. Newsom and Ringe, "Introduction," xxvii.

9. Benckhuysen, *Gospel According to Eve*, 5.

10. Martin et al., "Women in Theological Education," 161.

11. Martin et al., "Women in Theological Education," 165.

12. Martin et al., "Women in Theological Education," 165–66.

13. Martin et al., "Women in Theological Education," 166.

Even in this age of equality, women do experience the world differently to men in a number of ways, and so contribute a particular perspective. One aspect of this perspective is perhaps surprisingly captured in the teaching of 1 Peter: "Husbands, in the same way, show consideration for your wives in your life together, paying honor to the woman as the weaker sex, since they too are also heirs of the gracious gift of life—so that nothing may hinder your prayers" (1 Peter 3:7).

As women who take the authority of Scripture seriously, what are we to make of this text? Lucy Peppiatt has a helpful approach. She believes that few today would consider that women are weaker than men "intellectually, emotionally, spiritually" or in terms of physical stamina or ability to withstand pain.[14] It is true that that women are generally physically weaker than men, but Peppiatt points to another, albeit related, aspect of the weakness of women: their disempowerment in patriarchal societies. In the ancient world, the context in which Peter wrote, "on the whole women were socially, economically, politically, and educationally disadvantaged in comparison to men."[15] So we might paraphrase "weaker sex" as "disempowered or disadvantaged sex."

Whether to a greater or lesser extent, this is still the experience of women. There is a growing awareness, even among feminists who are wont to emphasize women's strength, of their vulnerability: "Women are almost universally at the mercy of a man's physical strength and in most cultures of the world at the mercy of men's economic and political strength."[16] On average, one woman a week is killed in Australia by her male partner or former partner. The #MeToo and #ChurchToo movements have made us more aware of the sexual harassment and assault experienced by so many women, including in Christian communities. Such violence is part of the reality for women and informs their perspective.

On the other hand, we should not speak of a "woman's perspective" as if this were distinct from an "objective" perspective (hitherto mostly understood as a male perspective, by default). What Lucy Peppiatt says of herself is true of every theologian and biblical scholar, male or female: "There cannot be any real objectivity in the task. I can only write as an insider of a particular world."[17] Or, as Maggi Dawn says, all theology is particular, not neutral: "There is theology done by people who happen to be male, by people who

---

14. Peppiatt, *Rediscovering Scripture's Vision*, 101.
15. Peppiatt, *Rediscovering Scripture's Vision*, 101.
16. Peppiatt, *Rediscovering Scripture's Vision*, 102.
17. Peppiatt, *Rediscovering Scripture's Vision*, 158.

may be white, black, or Asian, by people who may be disabled or not, poor or rich, Western or not."[18]

Nor can we speak of a single "woman's perspective":

> There is no single "woman's perspective" but a rich variety of insight that comes from the different ways in which women's experience is shaped by culture, class, ethnicity, religious community, and other aspects of social identity . . . People see things or are oblivious to them in part because of how they have been formed through their experiences. They ask certain kinds of questions and not others for the same reasons.[19]

Our authors are all Australian women, but they come from different geographical areas, different church traditions, and different ethnic backgrounds. Not all would identify as feminist, and only a few deal with what might be called "women's issues." Women in particular wish to hear women's voices on such issues, but Maggi Dawn observes that, unfortunately, when women do write about "women's issues," they may be dismissed for neglecting "serious theology." She also contends that "the most interesting women's voices in theology are not writing about 'women's issues' *per se*, they are simply writing theology . . . Certainly their experience of theology will be colored by the fact they are a woman."[20]

So, we believe that women *qua* women have a particular contribution to make to theology and biblical studies, yet their voices are not to be understood as an "optional extra," nor as a specialized—or, worse still, marginalized area—within these disciplines, but as integral to them, as is a rich variety of voices from diverse ethnicities and cultures. This seems to be increasingly the case, as Carol Newsom and Sharon Ringe observed in 1992:

> Over the last twenty-five years biblical scholarship by women has come into its maturity. Not only are women prominent in the discussions of traditional topics in biblical studies, but the new questions women have posed and the new ways of reading that women have pioneered have challenged the very way biblical studies are done.[21]

Evangelical women's voices have been hard to hear in Australia, as elsewhere. Along with the exclusion of women from universities until the 1880s, women have, until recently, formed a smaller cohort of students in Australian

---

18. Dawn, "There Are No Women," para. 3.
19. Newson and Ringe, "Introduction," xxix.
20. Dawn, "There are no women," para. 3.
21. Newsom and Ringe, "Introduction," xxviii.

theological colleges. In evangelical colleges, though women's numbers have increased, women have been less likely to graduate with a three-year degree than men and have formed a smaller percentage of students undertaking research degrees.[22] Female faculty numbers have been smaller, and there are fewer publications by women scholars in the evangelical tradition, though these are increasing in recent years.

Another reasonable question is whether Australian authors have a particular contribution to make in theology and biblical studies. It is helpful simply to hear Australian women scholars speaking with their own accents, addressing topics of general interest, while grounded in our own cultural setting and using Australian examples when discussing multiculturalism, church architecture, or the history of women as students and teachers of theology.

In finding its distinctive perspective, Australian scholarship needs to engage further with Australian history and Indigenous cultures. According to Aboriginal Anglican priest Glenn Loughrey,

> A major question for the church in Australia today is: how does it respond to its history with the Aboriginal people of this land? The church was and remains complicit in the genocidal colonial treatment of Aborigines as a result of massacres, destruction of language and culture, and the removal of children.[23]

In a 2017 public lecture, the Vice Chancellor of Melbourne's University of Divinity, Peter Sherlock, said "The most glaring omission in Australian theology is a sustained engagement with Aboriginal and Torres Strait Islander peoples. I think—I hope—that this is starting to change."[24]

This book makes a small contribution to such engagement. Brooke Prentis, a Wakka Wakka woman, writes on what non-Aboriginal people can learn from Aboriginal people's understanding of the Creator, stewardship, and sustainability. Jude Long's chapter, based on her key note address at the Evangelical Women in Academia conference in 2019, is a reflection on what she learned from the Aboriginal and Torres Strait Islander Christians with whom she worked at Nungalinya College, a Combined Churches Training College in Darwin. And our volume is bookended by Indigenous prayers. The Woiwurrung Lord's Prayer is from an 1878 compendium of Aboriginal language materials.[25] Woiwurrung is the language of the

---

22. Martin, et al., "Women in Theological Education," 161–65.
23. Loughrey, "The First Sin," 23.
24. Sherlock, "Why Australia Needs Theology," 16.
25. "The Lord's Prayer" in Thomas, "Succinct Sketch," 132.

Wurundjeri people, on whose land this book has been edited. We pray with those who used this prayer over a hundred and forty years ago, that God's ways will be established "as in heaven" in these lands of Australia, especially in redress of wrongs done to its original inhabitants, animals, plants, waterways, hills, valleys, and plains. Our book closes with "Saam 151," a recent song in Kriol about how our life is today, "*Song blanga wi laif, hau wi jidan tudei,*" written by the Aboriginal Anglican priest Rev. Carol Robertson of Ngukurr, who was part of the Bible translation team for the *Kriol Baibul*. In this song, Carol Robertson reflects on unhappiness and on drawing near to God, "the light that came into this world." Carol Robertson wrote this song after studying the Ridley Certificate Psalms Course, *A Journey through the Psalms*, with a group of Aboriginal Christians, led by Rev. Kate Beer, Ministry Development Officer for the Diocese of the Northern Territory, who works alongside women church leaders.

Overview of Chapters

The title of this volume is *Grounded in the Body, in Time and Place, in Scripture*. All the chapters are grounded in Scripture: some are topical, drawing on a number of texts, while others focus on a specific biblical text.

The first four chapters lay a foundation with reflections on the land and Indigenous peoples of Australia, neighborhood, and women's bodies. Four chapters of explorations in the Old Testament focus on biblical books (Exodus, Psalms, Song of Songs, Jeremiah) while three chapters on the New Testament consider Luke 10:38–42, the Gospel of John, and John 4:1–42. Six applied chapters consider disability, abortion, the media, church architecture, work, and leadership. A final chapter reviews our heritage as Australian women scholars of theology in the evangelical tradition.

Rather than introducing the chapters in order here, we have chosen to introduce them thematically, focusing on being grounded in the body, or in time and place. This shows the rich, overlapping nature of the contributions.

Grounded in the Body

Four chapters have a focus on women's bodies.

In "Purity: Guarding the Body Corporate," Moyra Dale points out that while we can all only meet God where we are, in our bodies, in space and time, women are more aware of our materiality in the everyday reality of our lives and the "earthy messiness of our bodily cycles." In the incarnation, God himself was grounded in a body, in a specific time and place. The individual body also functions as a map of the body corporate. Social ordering requires boundaries, and purity is a powerful organizing paradigm in societies around the world, as a way of guarding the corporate body and its values. Causes of defilement include body fluids, immoral behavior, disease, and death. Ritual and moral defilement find particular embodiment in women in many societies. Communities guard social boundaries through deterrents such as shame, isolating individuals. Control is also enforced through embodied standards of morality or desirability, such as Female Genital Mutilation or ideal body size. The socially powerless may seek control through their own body, through asceticism, anorexia, or cutting. But when we meet Jesus as God embodied, he redeems our bodies, individual and corporate, as he redefines and inverts social classifications.

Jill Firth, in "Desert Spring, Dead Dog Waterhole, Disappointment Creek: Is the God of the Book of Jeremiah Bad for Women?" addresses the criticism, found in some recent scholarly readings, that Jeremiah presents a distressing picture of Judah as a promiscuous woman, violently punished by God as an angry husband, who shames her through rape. This raises concerns about the impact of such deprecating imagery and masculine violence on present day misogyny, intimate partner violence, and weaponized rape. In the book of Jeremiah, God presents himself as a reliable spring of living water, but the people accuse him of offering them poisoned water, and Jeremiah himself questions whether God is untrustworthy like a seasonal brook. The drought setting of Jeremiah and the thirst for life-giving water resonate both as an external and an inner landscape in Australia. The chapter examines imagery in the early chapters of Jeremiah in the light of the genres of caricature, dystopia, heterotopia, and utopia, and in the context of the whole book.

The chapter from Erin Sessions, "'Descending from the Hills of Gilead': Undressing Descriptions of the Lover's Body, and How Australian Women Can Reclaim and Embrace Their Embodiment," presents the Song of Songs as an ecstatic exploration of love and of the bodies making it, and analyses the concentrated description of the lover's body in the fourth chapter of the Song of Songs. This enraptured depiction is grounded in pastoral, architectural, and military imagery. The chapter first explores what this poetic portrait might have meant in its original context, especially for the lover. And then, building on her research on Song of Songs and intimate partner violence, and using the same interdisciplinary approach combining feminist interpretation and Australian social research, the author applies these findings to the Australian context and explores their significance for women in Australia, the prevailing attitudes and beliefs about our bodies, their sexualization, and how we may reclaim and embrace our own embodiment.

In "Grounding Our Discussion of Abortion," Denise Cooper-Clarke notes that much of the discussion of abortion in evangelical circles is focused almost exclusively on the moral status of the unborn child and based on an assumption that the Scriptures are clear in relation to this. Both "pro-life" and "pro-choice" positions are usually framed in terms of the competing rights of the unborn child and of the woman. Both approaches are reductionistic and tend to abstract the discussion from the concrete realities of life for women and children. It might be assumed that adopting a feminist perspective will lead to a broadly "pro-choice" position. Yet a number of feminists now realize that abortion serves the interests of men more than of women, and that high abortion rates are a symptom of a society that devalues women and children. The author proposes an alternative evangelical approach that grounds the discussion in the Bible (specifically Genesis 3:16), but also in the lived experience of women and the unique bodily relationship between a mother and her unborn child.

Two chapters explore the way biblical texts engage with the body and its senses:

In "Embodied Worship: The Psalms and the Senses," Melinda Cousins notes that biblical studies have tended to engage with Scripture in predominantly intellectual ways. The Scriptures seek to transform by renewing the mind, but they also do so by evoking emotion, inspiring the imagination, and engaging the body. This is noticeably demonstrated in the book of Psalms, which is grounded in concrete communal experience. These poems, songs, and prayers of the people of God invite us into their engagement with God and the world, calling for worship as response to God that uses every aspect of who we are. This chapter reflects on the ways the Psalms do this through the embodied experience of sensation, using the framework of seven body parts through which we make sense of the world: eye, ear, nose, tongue, mouth, hand, and foot. It includes an exploration of how a contemporary Australian church could incorporate practices of seeing, listening, breathing, savoring, speaking, creating, and walking into community worship and life.

In "Sensory Experience and the Gospel of John," Louise Gosbell describes how the Gospel of John is filled with body and sensory related language right from its opening chapter, with the tactile emergence of God in human flesh. The chief steward at the wedding at Cana confirms the first miracle by tasting the wine. Lazarus's sister is afraid of the stench of his body when he is raised from the dead. The perfumes used to anoint Jesus fill the room with their scent. Those who encounter Jesus are encouraged to hear and see God while he likewise sees and hears them. Even the miracles themselves in John's Gospel are described by the visual term of "signs." Despite this abundance of sensory language, very little investigation has been done into the role the senses play in the Gospel of John or any of the New Testament texts. This chapter considers the role of the senses in the Gospel of John in light of current research into the senses in the ancient world and asks what it means to be embodied and sensory beings for believers today.

The focus shifts to (dis)abled bodies in Tanya Riches's chapter, "'Wisdom Cries Out': Towards a Feminist Pentecostal Theology of (Dis)ability." The author draws on Sarah Coakley's feminist pneumatology to reconstruct a "power-in-vulnerability" that decenters the normative able-bodied pastoral model of leadership. In the biblical wisdom literature, Sophia is depicted as crying out in the public square, or marketplace. Pentecostals today are critiqued in the mainstream press for embracing secular consumerism and individualism. However, at their origins they were known for their emphasis on ecstatic, embodied experience. Within Pentecostalism, God's wisdom was unmediated—a direct experience of the presence of God. With a liturgy gathered around Spirit-led prophetic prayer, the community practiced being attuned or attentive to hearing the voice of God who still cried out—with these vocalizations very often occurring via bodies relegated to the social margins. This contrasts with today's emphasis on brand, image, and performance. This chapter explores how the body becomes the site of the Spirit speaking, in order to move towards a feminist Pentecostal theology of (dis)ability.

Grounded in Time and Place

In "What Can the Birds of the *Land* Tell Us?" Wakka Wakka woman Brooke Prentis reminds us that the story of the Creator is embedded in the knowledge of Aboriginal peoples (sometimes called the Dreaming) and in the landscape of the lands now called Australia. There is a deep understanding of the connectedness of all creation, human and non-human, and the responsibility to care for it. Aboriginal people were not, as commonly portrayed, nomadic hunter-gatherers, but stewards, with sustainable agricultural practices developed over more than 65,000 years. Colonization led to deforestation and loss of many species, a land "out of balance," but Brooke argues that further destruction can be prevented if non-Aboriginal Australians are willing to humble themselves and learn from this ancient wisdom. The chapter then focuses on what three birds of the land, the Ostrich (Job 39:13–18), the Emu, and the Southern Cassowary, can tell us about the Creator and about being grounded since time immemorial.

Jude Long reflects on the eight years she spent as Principal of Nungalinya College, an Aboriginal and Torres Strait Islander Theological College in Darwin, in "Grounded in Australia: Learning from our First Peoples." She worked as a teacher, but says that more accurately she should be described as a learner. While only claiming to have glimpsed the richness of the contributions Indigenous Christians can make to the Australian Church, she discusses three of their central concerns—land, kinship, and suffering. These are key ideas as we explore what it is to be grounded in this country and in relationships of all kinds. However, she believes that perhaps even more significant is what we can learn from our Indigenous brothers and sisters about keeping Jesus at the center and being grounded in him alone.

Karina Kreminski, in "Embodying Christ in the Neighborhood: A Reflection on Place, Home and Mission," says that for too long the church has been internally focused and neglected its missional role in the community where it lives and breathes. Mission can be seen as not primarily about activity but about embodying the values of Jesus. The gospel must always be fleshed out rather than captured in creeds, propositions, and theologies. What does it look like if we specifically apply this to our local communities and contexts? If we ask, "What is the Spirit of God doing in our local neighborhood?" then we have an opportunity to think about the intersection between place, embodying the gospel, and fleshing out the way of Jesus in our local community. The church has given little attention to reflecting on a theology of place and often practices a disembodied expression of the gospel. This detrimentally affects God's missional call on our lives as it hinders us from grounding ourselves in a specific place and time. Due to a subtle Gnosticism and a preference for an "other-worldly" spirituality, Christians have preferred to see the "life to come" as home. She challenges us to consider the possibility that this world is home, even though most importantly and ultimately, it will be renewed at the restoration of all things.

In "Grounded yet Wandering: Church Architecture, Space, and Place," Elizabeth Culhane also notes that the theological significance of place is contested in contemporary Protestant thought, but focuses on how this is manifested in ideas about church buildings. For some, they are deemed a means of attracting newcomers and extending hospitality. For others, they are judged a frivolous distraction from the real work of disciple-making. Such beliefs about church buildings have been shaped by the notion of the church as God's homeless people, a community that lacks material and visible contours as it journeys toward its true eschatological home. This chapter defends the theological importance of the church as an entity grounded in material reality and time, existing alongside its identity as a peripatetic community that is performed. Drawing on William Dyrness and John Inge, the author argues that place is situated in God's good creation, where created entities point to God and God meets with humanity. This provides a basis for understanding how church buildings can signify invisible realities and orientate humans toward their maker. Such an understanding is illustrated using the example of St. Paul's Anglican Cathedral, Melbourne.

Katherine Smith traces the formation of Israel's social identity through the particular time and place of the events of the Exodus. In "The Transformation and Re-Formation of Israel's Social Identity in the Book of Exodus," she describes the formation of Israel as a covenant community whose social identity is grounded in YHWH's presence with, and in the midst of, his people. In the opening chapters of the book of Exodus, the Israelites' social identity is based on being descendants of the Patriarchs yet belonging to Pharaoh. However, the text's presentation of Israel's social identity is transformed as soon as the name YHWH is introduced into the Exodus narrative in the context of divine presence in chapter 3; the Israelites are now YHWH's people and YHWH is now present with them. By taking a literary approach, this chapter explores the implications of Israel's transformed social identity in Exodus and offers observations about how these implications may be contextualized for the church in a different time and place, in Australian secular culture.

Deborah Storie's chapter, "At Jacob's Well: Re-grounding the Samaritan Woman," is informed by her experiences in Australia, Afghanistan, Nepal, India, and Africa. It explores what happens if we re-ground the famous encounter at Jacob's well in time and place, in community, and in the rest of Scripture—in particular, if we invite the experiences of contemporary women who navigate similarly precarious situations to guide our encounters with this text. Until recently, dominant traditions of interpretation focused on the woman's dubious reputation, shady past, and alleged immorality, sometimes associating her personal failings with the alleged idolatry of her people. More recent interpretive traditions valorize the woman. Missiologists claim her as "the first evangelist" or "missionary." Few interpreters seem to appreciate how profoundly power, privilege, and life experience, as well as time, geography, culture, and language, estrange us from the worlds of and behind the text. This chapter offers a "discipleship reading" of Jesus' encounter with the Samaritan woman and explores what types of discipleship response a re-grounded encounter with this text might motivate and generate in our time and place.

In a similar way, Theresa Lau grounds her reading of the story of Jesus at the home of Martha and Mary (Luke 10:38–42) in her own time and place as a Malaysian Chinese Australian woman in "Grounded in His Lordship: Mary, Martha, and Me." She recognizes the particularity of her response;

she does not speak for all Chinese, and yet she finds a resonance between the social context of the Lukan story, where men's and women's spaces were divided and women expected to respect the boundary, and attitudes within traditional Chinese culture. Honoring of work and hospitality also contributes to a Chinese reading of the text that sees Martha as the one who behaves virtuously and Mary as bringing shame to the family. An alternative reading of this passage that links it with the pericopes immediately preceding (the parable of the Good Samaritan) and following it (Jesus' teaching on prayer) is that it is primarily about the Lordship of Christ. Martha does not submit to his Lordship, whereas Mary does, and it is this that Jesus commends as the "better part" and the one thing that is necessary.

Enqi Weng also writes from a Chinese perspective, as a Singaporean Chinese Australian. In "Christianity in Contemporary Australian Media: 'Get Your Rosaries Off My Ovaries,'" she demonstrates a particular sensitivity to the "narrowly informed institutional, gendered, and racialized perspectives" that repeatedly inform discussions of religion in the Australian media. She outlines the way that Christianity has adapted to changes in media, from the Apostle Paul's use of written letters, through the invention of the printing press, to today's digital technology and social media. The author describes key theories of the relationship between the intersecting fields of religious and media studies, then she draws on her analysis of selected episodes of the Australian Broadcasting Corporation's Q&A current affairs program. She notes an over-representation of Catholic, white, male participants in the panel discussions, and that Christianity was frequently identified with moralism, which she traces to Australia's British colonial history. She ends with a challenge to Australian churches to engage carefully with the new media.

In "Tethered between Reality and Aspiration: Grounding and Formative Practices for Australian Leaders," Monica O'Neil explores the possibilities and difficulties raised by the tension for leaders of aspiring to be good while simultaneously being grounded in the "gutsy reality" of life. She identifies shalom (which encapsulates love and justice) as the human *telos* or aspiration point. As director of a leadership center, Monica developed a charter of formation that explicates three virtues required to achieve this *telos*: mercy, humility, and endurance. Challenges to leaders include both the personal conflict between the flesh and the spirit, and external factors such as either hyper-positivity or hypercriticism from others. But hypercriticism can also come from within: "Imposter Phenomenon," which is more commonly experienced by women than men. The chapter then describes Peter Senge's model of transformation as process, and Joseph Kotya's approach to transforming practices (based on virtue theory): prayer habits, friendship habits, and intentional relating habits, such as supervision. Through such practices, leaders may be grounded in both reality and in a vision of what might be.

A more literal sense of "ground" and the idea of being grounded is the basis for Kara Martin's chapter "Grounded in Work as Christians." God is the first worker; his work is the work of creation, and then God invites humankind to join him in the work that needs to be done: He tells Adam to work or "till the ground," and to "keep the garden." So work is a good gift of God, though because of sin, all work becomes harder and more painful. We can become overwhelmed by the "curse" or burden of working, as we experience weariness, frustration, conflict or a sense of futility in our workplaces, whether we are in paid or unpaid work. As city dwellers, many of us have lost connection to the ground, and this may be linked to our lack of appreciation for our vocation to care for the earth and all creation. Reclaiming a sense of the goodness of work also involves understanding it as participation in the repair of the brokenness of creation—whether "through medicine, or plumbing, or mothering, or counselling, or as a police officer; we are used by God to mend and solve and rescue."

Jill Firth's "Grandmothers of Intention: Women in Australian Theological Academia (1883–2003)" is not a systematic or comprehensive survey, but rather a collection of snapshots in a gallery of women's theological scholarship in Australia. We had originally intended to include a few paragraphs about women pioneers in Australian theological colleges in the book's Introduction, but crowdsourcing led to the names of more than a hundred women students and lecturers from Australian history from all around Australia, justifying a separate chapter. Women's participation in Australian theological college education is placed in the context of study in homes and communities, in missionary training, and in women's departments. Though most of the names in this chapter will be unknown, these women are our grandmothers, mothers, and sisters in theological study, who have blazed the trail for today's women scholars in theology and biblical studies.

The extreme Australian bushfire season and coronavirus pandemic in 2020 have given new depth and significance to reflection on the body, time and place, and Scripture. We are more aware of the fragility of the body, our embodiment, and our neighborhoods, and are reconsidering our attitudes to the environment, to work, and to leadership. Our hearts have grieved as many in the international community suffer from illness, death, and loss of work and livelihood. This grief has been compounded by the death of George Floyd in Minneapolis and the ensuing "Black Lives Matter" protests, which have raised global awareness of systemic racism. In Australia, protests have centered on Aboriginal deaths in custody, for example those of Ms. Dhu

(2014), David Dungay (2015), and Tanya Day (2017), rendering acute the need to address the ongoing injustice and deadly harm resulting from our history of dispossession and genocide of Aboriginal peoples and to stand with them in solidarity with their pain and grief.

At the time of finalizing the compilation of this volume, we, like many throughout the world, have found ourselves "grounded" in yet another sense. We have been confined to our homes by government regulations designed to curb the spread of COVID-19. How long this situation will last is uncertain, but there is a real possibility we will not be able to launch the book with a public event as we had planned. The irony of having a "virtual" launch of this book will not, we trust, be lost on the reader.

Bibliography

Benckhuysen, Amanda. *The Gospel According to Eve*. Downers Grove, IL: InterVarsity, 2019.

Busby, Eleanor. "Exam Board Criticised for Failing to Include More Works by Female Composers on Piano Syllabus." https://www.independent.co.uk/news/uk/female-composers-piano-grades-music-exam-board-abrsm-gender-imbalance-a9256901.html

Dawn, Maggi. "There Are No Women on My Theology Bookshelf." https://maggidawn.net/2015/08/11/there-are-no-women-on-my-theology-bookshelf-2/

Loughrey, Glenn. "The First Sin and Inherited Responsibility." *Zadok Perspectives* 138 (2018) 23–25.

Manne, Robert. "The Sorry History of Australia's Apology." *The Guardian* May 27, 2013. https://www.theguardian.com/commentisfree/2013/may/26/sorry-history-australia-apology-indigenous

Martin, Kara, Megan Powell du Toit, Jill Firth, and Moyra Dale. "Women in Theological Education in the ACT in 21st Century Australia." in *Theological Education in Australia: Foundations, Current Practices and Future Options*, edited by Andrew Bain and Ian Hussey, 160–74. Eugene, OR: Wipf & Stock, 2018.

Newsom, Carol A., and Sharon H. Ringe. "Introduction to the First Edition." In *Women's Bible Commentary*, third edition, edited by Carol A. Newsom and Sharon H. Ringe, xix–xxv. Louisville, KY: Westminster John Knox, 2012.

Peppiatt, Lucy. *Rediscovering Scripture's Vision for Women: Fresh Perspectives on Disputed Texts*. Downers Grove, IL: InterVarsity, 2019.

Pitman, Julia. *Prophets and Priests: Congregational Women in Australia 1919–1977*. Unpublished PhD diss., University of Adelaide, 2005.

Price, Jenna. "You Can't Be What You Can't See: The Invisible Women in Our Media." https://www.smh.com.au/national/you-can-t-be-what-you-can-t-see-the-invisible-women-in-our-media-20190404-p51av6.html

Rossetti, Christina G. *The Face of the Deep: A Devotional Commentary on the Apocalypse*. London: SPCK, 1911.

Sherlock, Peter. "Why Australia Needs Theology." https://www.trinity.unimelb.edu.au/getmedia/6ce2f214-cbbe-40da-8a75-cda1cbea55c8/Why-Australia-Needs-Theology.aspx

Taylor, Marion Ann, and Agnes Choi (eds). *Handbook of Women Biblical Interpreters: A Historical and Biographical Guide*. Grand Rapids, MI: Baker Academic, 2012.

Thomas, William. "Succinct Sketch of the Aboriginal Language." In *The Aborigines of Victoria: With Notes Relating to the Habits of the Natives of Other Parts of Australia and Tasmania. Compiled from Various Sources for the Government of Victoria*. Vol. 2, edited by R. Brough Smyth, 118–33. London: Trübner and Co, 1878. https://aiatsis.gov.au/sites/default/files/docs/digitised_collections/collectors_of_words/smyth/m0052799_a.pdf

Part I

Context

2

What Can the Birds of the *Land* Tell Us?

Brooke Prentis

Aboriginal peoples of these lands now called Australia have been walking, for millennia, with the Creator. The story of the Creator is embedded in our knowledge, passed down from generation to generation. The story of the Creator is embedded in our landscape—the lands, the waters, the mountains, the rivers, and the desert. The story of the Creator is embedded in us—our minds, our bodies, our spirit, our dance, our song. The story of the Creator keeps us grounded.

For over 65,000 years, according to science—and for some who hold a particular theological position, for over 6,000 years—Aboriginal peoples of these lands now called Australia lived sustainably. Australia was once abundant with life, human and non-human, God's wondrous creation. God had determined the boundaries for over three hundred nations of Aboriginal peoples of these lands now called Australia[1] and had given us, the Aboriginal peoples, the God-given role of stewards of these lands and waters. In 1770, with the invasion of the British, and then later in 1788, this God-given role was diminished, and nearly destroyed, by outsiders who imported their understanding of stewardship into a household that was not theirs.

---

1. "When the Most High gave the nations their inheritance, when he divided all mankind, he set up boundaries for the peoples according to the number of the sons of Israel." Deut 32:8 (NIV).

Since 1788, fifty-five species of fauna[2] and thirty-six species of flora[3] have become extinct, with Australia now having one of the highest loss of species anywhere in the world. The colonial invaders failed to live out the biblical mandates to care for creation, to see Aboriginal peoples as made in the image of God, and to love their neighbor as themselves. This resulted in ecological and relational destruction.

While we cannot undo that which has been destroyed, we can work together to prevent further destruction by learning from Aboriginal peoples as leaders, ecologists, environmentalists, theologians; learning from millennia of practices of stewardship and sustainability; learning from the God-appointed ancient hosts[4] of these lands now called Australia, including our knowledge of the Creator.

The Indigenous Worldview

There are many Bible passages that resonate deeply with the Indigenous worldview. One such passage is Job 12:7–10:

> But ask the animals, and they will teach you,
>   or the birds in the sky, and they will tell you;
> or speak to the earth, and it will teach you,
>   or let the fish in the sea inform you.
> Which of all these does not know
>   that the hand of the Lord has done this?
> In his hand is the life of every creature
>   and the breath of all mankind.[5]

The Indigenous worldview has no separation between human and non-human. Uncle Reverend Graham Paulson and Mark Brett, in *Five Smooth Stones*, use land, one of five cultural practices of Aboriginal peoples, to describe this interconnectedness: "'Country' in this particular Aboriginal sense includes the animals and plants, along with lands and waters, all of which must be cared for by their traditional owners."[6]

---

2. http://www.environment.gov.au/cgi-bin/sprat/public/publicthreatenedlist.pl

3. http://www.environment.gov.au/cgi-bin/sprat/public/publicthreatenedlist.pl?wanted=flora

4. Prentis and Crowden, "Learning to be Guests of Ancient Hosts on Ancient Lands," 79.

5. NIV translation.

6. Paulson and Brett, *Five Smooth Stones*, 201.

Job 12:7–10 reminds us that the animals, the birds, the earth, the fish, and indeed the oceans, sky, land, and rivers—all of God's wondrous creation—are connected, precious, are to be cared for, and can teach, tell, speak, and inform us. Aboriginal peoples have always known this and been living out our Creator-appointed roles. We have lived sustainably, using only what God provided and not taking too much, being grounded since time immemorial.

This knowledge has been called the Dreamtime or the Dreaming. The use of Dreamtime and Dreaming was coined by anthropologists, particularly white male anthropologists, to document our knowledge of the Creator, our stewardship of creation, and our practices of living sustainably. Today, Dreaming is a better word, as it represents the cyclical, non-linear, Indigenous worldview and brings past, present, and future into relationship with each other. But it is still problematic. As I described in the paper, "Learning to be Guests of Ancient Hosts on Ancient Lands,"

> Our Dreaming is not "myths" as some historians, anthropologists, and sociologists have called it, but are teachings from our Elders, passed down from one generation to the next that tell us who the Creator is, how to care for creation, and how to live in right relationship. These principles of course strike a chord with our Biblical principles.[7]

Dreamtime or Dreaming are not words from any Aboriginal languages,[8] and the English language does not have a word to correctly identify what is in fact a whole system of law and living.[9] To better understand this, we look at the example of the Yolngu peoples of Arnhem Land:

> All (Yolngu) clans would agree that life started in Arnhem Land at the dawn of creation, when the Great Creator Spirit, *Wanarr*, sent women as creators from the spirit land of *burralku*, an island to the east of Arnhem Land. They moved across the land creating fresh waterholes, the features of the land and the Yolngu themselves (the peoples). As they created, they gave the people the gifts of language and the way to live. This way is called the *Madayin*.[10]

---

7. Prentis and Crowden, "Learning to be Guests of Ancient Hosts on Ancient Lands," 80.
8. There are over six hundred dialects of Aboriginal languages.
9. Mala, *Why Warriors Lie Down and Die*, 13.
10. Mala, *Why Warriors Lie Down and Die*, 12–13.

The *Madayin* includes details of the practices of stewardship and sustainability that include, but are not limited to,

> all the property, resource, criminal, economic, political, moral and religious laws of the people; . . . the protected production sites (hatcheries and nurseries) for different animals, fish and birds; the correct conservation and production of plants and food such as yams; the husbandry of fish, turtles, animals, birds and so on; . . . [and] protection of the clans assets. . .[11]

This is a whole system of law and living, grounded in the knowledge of the Creator, since time immemorial.

Aunty Reverend Denise Champion, an Adnyamathanha woman, articulates this further in *Yarta Wandatha*:

> It's the way we relate to creation and to nature, to all other living things. It doesn't matter whether you are a person, a human being, a bird, an animal, whether you are this peak or that peak. In all of life that's the framework that we operate on. That's our very foundation of our Adnyamathanha understanding of the world . . . This is created to try and keep balance in our world.[12]

While these are only two examples from among the more than three hundred nations of Aboriginal peoples in these lands now called Australia, this is a consistent understanding throughout all Aboriginal peoples and nations in these lands. And while Dreaming is still a problematic word, to the extent where the word is not known in each Aboriginal language, it is the best word we have today to describe the systems of law and living, including spirituality, that have been used since time immemorial to stay grounded and keep balance right across these lands now called Australia.

A Land out of Balance

Colonization, including the rapid loss of Australia's fauna and flora, and deforestation, has resulted in Australia being a land out of balance.

One of the first acts with the arrival of the Europeans was to cut down a tree. "After the first permanent European settlement was established in Sydney Cove in 1788, vegetation clearing for agriculture followed almost immediately."[13] One can only imagine the distress of the peoples of the Eora

---

11. Mala, *Why Warriors Lie Down and Die*, 13.
12. Champion, *Yarta Wandatha*, 15.
13. Bradshaw, "Little Left to Lose," 109.

nation.[14] For Aboriginal peoples, this was more than a clash of culture, it was disobedience to the Creator and a destabilization of millennia of balance.

In the last two hundred and thirty years there has been further destabilization and unbalance. Today Australia, one of the world's wealthiest nations and with a relatively small population,[15] is responsible for extensive deforestation and forest degradation, with Australia's native forests now only 1.474 million km^2, representing a total loss of ~38 percent since European settlement (invasion).[16]

Bruce Pascoe in *Dark Emu* explains two hundred and thirty years of cultural conflict in spiritual and religious terms:

> In Aboriginal life, the spirit and the corporeal world are wedded; but in European society, the economy operates independently of the spirit, and, as modern examples illustrate, almost in defiance of the religious moral code. The financial crash of 2008 and the oil spill in the Gulf of Mexico in 2010 occurred because the Christian morality of most participants had been excluded from their business dealings . . . The ability of the planet to survive such cavalier (practices) . . . is being sorely tested.[17]

In 2020, we are still experiencing this cultural clash and witnessing these cavalier practices that disobey the Creator, where profit, wealth, and greed are sought at the expense of caring for creation. The Wangan and Jagalingou peoples fight to protect creation from the proposed coal mine in Queensland's Galilee Basin,[18] the Mirning peoples fight to protect creation from deep sea oil drilling in South Australia's Great Australian Bight,[19] and the Adnyamathanha peoples fight to protect creation from the proposed Nuclear Waste Dump in South Australia's Flinders Ranges.[20] This is a fight of stewardship, a fight for sustainability, and a fight for stability and balance.

Further destruction will only be prevented if we look at ourselves closely, our words and our actions, our treatment of the earth and all creation. If non-Aboriginal peoples can humble themselves to learn from Aboriginal peoples, there is hope—hope for peace with all creation—human and non-human. This is not a new idea, but rather a return to learning and understanding of over 65,000 years of stories—not myths, but oral lore and

14. The Eora nation is the Aboriginal peoples of the Sydney Cove area.
15. Bradshaw, "Little Left to Lose," 110.
16. Bradshaw, "Little Left to Lose," 120.
17. Pascoe, *Dark Emu*, 207–8.
18. http://wanganjagalingou.com.au/our-fight/
19. https://www.fightforthebight.org.au/
20. https://www.nodumpalliance.org.au/

law passed down through generations from the Creator. As Aunty Reverend Denise Champion says,

> Aboriginal people in general have a very strong sense of connection with the Creator and with all our creation . . . Muda (worldview) are showing us how we can live peacefully with our world—with each other, with our environment, and with God. Not only living peacefully with those three things but how to find the way. The stories actually give us a pathway, the Good Road, Wandu Yapa. This is not about new discovery. It's about rediscovery.[21]

Mick Pope, in his book *A Climate of Justice*, implores non-Aboriginal peoples to use the Bible to challenge the Western Christian mindset, to help create a better future for the Earth and our world, through rediscovery of Jesus' call to love our neighbor:

> Can we embrace the non-human as our neighbour as well, as an object of our love? You needn't think this way to care about climate change, we know the impacts that are happening now, and the possible impacts in the future if we do nothing. And yet can we go further? We know that humans are made in the image and likeness of God, and so to love God means we must love our neighbour. But what if loving God means also treasuring what he has made and takes delight in (Psalm 104:24–25, 31)? . . .
>
> We can spend so much time drawing a line between humans and non-humans, that we forget that there is only one line to be drawn, between creator and creatures. We might be more valuable to God than sparrows, but sparrows are also valuable to God (Matthew 10:28–31)."[22]

So how do we deal with the Western cultural line between human and non-human and Aboriginal cultures' absence of a line? The sparrows are indeed also valuable to God; returning to Job 12:7–10, Job encourages us to listen to the birds of the sky, for they will tell us.

The Birds of the Sky

One bird of the sky appears in the first two verses of the Bible in another passage that resonates deeply with Aboriginal peoples—Genesis 1:1–2. *The*

---

21. Champion, *Yarta Wandatha*, 29.
22. Pope, *A Climate of Justice*, 136.

Message version says, "First this: God created the Heavens and Earth—all you see, all you don't see. Earth was a soup of nothingness, a bottomless emptiness, an inky blackness. God's Spirit brooded like a bird above the watery abyss." This resonates with some Aboriginal Dreaming stories, in particular that of Bunjil the Eagle, from the Wurundjeri people, depicted in the painting, "Heaven Came Down"[23] by Aboriginal and Torres Strait Islander Christian Leader, Wuthathi and Mabuiag Island woman, Safina Stewart.

As Stewart describes: "Outlined silhouette of Bunjil, the wedge tail eagle, represents the One who formed and gave life to all creation."[24] The top of the painting shows the different shades of dark blues of the night sky with the stars, then transitions into lighter blues of the oceans, showing the shoreline, which then flows into the rivers, and the mountains, which are depicted in the dot painting style using ochre colors of browns, oranges, and reds. Bunjil is centered in the sky and visually appears to be hovering over the oceans, rivers, mountains, and lands, and with each element of creation seemingly flowing into every other, this is another way to show the interconnectedness of all creation with each element of creation and with the Creator.

It is not difficult to draw a comparison between Genesis 1:2, especially *The Message* version, and Aboriginal Dreaming, by looking upon Stewart's painting "Heaven Came Down." As an Aboriginal Christian leader myself, with a knowledge of the Dreaming, it is easy to describe Genesis 1 as the greatest Aboriginal Dreaming story ever told.

When I think of the birds of the sky, my mind, heart, and spirit, are filled with the knowledge of the Creator, but my ears are filled with the deafening screech of the Sulphur Crested Cockatoos as they circle the skies of Brisbane after the destruction of the forests, their homes, to make way for roads.

There are many lessons to learn from the birds of the sky. But as we focus on the ground, in being grounded, there are also lessons to learn from the birds of the land.

The Birds of the *Land*

The birds of the land have much to tell us. This chapter focuses on three birds of the land—the Ostrich, the Emu, and the Southern Cassowary. These birds of the land, as ratites, are all cousins, and have several commonalities: they are the largest flightless birds in the world, fast runners, and the male bird is the one that tends the nest and raises the young. The Emu and

---

23. Stewart, *Heaven Came Down*.
24. Stewart, *Heaven Came Down*.

Cassowary also share that they cannot walk backwards. But what specifically can these birds of the land tell us about the Creator and about being grounded since time immemorial?

The Ostrich

The Ostrich appears in Job, in chapter 39.[25] This bird of the land tells us about the Creator's role in creation.

In Job 39:13–18 God talks to Job and refers to the Ostrich, not to point out the failings of the Ostrich, but to declare God's role in creation. God created the Ostrich this way, and while wisdom was withheld from the Ostrich, it can run faster than the horse and rider.

The Emu

The Emu appears in many Dreaming stories. This bird of the land tells us who the Creator is and about the Creator's protection and love.

Science now suggests Aboriginal peoples are the first astronomers.[26] In linking science and the Dreaming, we look to the night sky.

> Baiame, the creator Spirit Emu, left the earth after its creation to reside as a dark shape in the Milky Way. The emu is inextricably linked with the wide grasslands of Australia, the landscape managed by Aboriginals. The fate of the emu, people, and grain are locked in step because, for Aboriginal people, the economy and the spirit are inseparable. Europeans stare at the stars, but Aboriginal peoples also see the spaces in between where the Spirit Emu resides.[27]

Aboriginal Christian Leader, Uncle Reverend Ron Williams, rewrote Psalm 23 in an Aboriginal style, assisting in acknowledging the father Emu's role in caring for its chicks just as Father God loves and protects all peoples as his children:

---

25. "The wings of the ostrich flap joyfully, though they cannot compare with the wings and feathers of the stork. She lays her eggs on the ground and lets them warm in the sand, unmindful that a foot may crush them, that some wild animal may trample them. She treats her young harshly, as if they were not hers; she cares not that her labor was in vain, for God did not endow her with wisdom or give her a share of good sense. Yet when she spreads her feathers to run, she laughs at horse and rider." Job 39:13–18 (NIV)

26. http://www.abc.net.au/science/articles/2009/07/27/2632463.htm

27. Pascoe, *Dark Emu*, Frontispiece.

My big fella boss up in the sky is like the father Emu.

He will always look after me and take me to green grass,

and lead me to where the water holes are full and fresh all the time.

He leads me away from the thick scrub and helps me keep safe from the hunters, dingoes and eagles.

At night time when I am very lonely and sad,

I will not be afraid,

for my Father covers me with his feathers like a father emu.

His spear and shield will always protect me.

My big fella boss always give me a good feed in the middle of my enemies.

In hot times he makes me sit down in a cool shade and rest.

He gives me plenty of love and care all of my life through.

Then I will live with my big fella boss like a father emu:

that cares for his chicks in good country,

full of peace and safety

For evermore and evermore.[28]

The Emu can therefore tell us that when we look to the stars and when we look at the bird Emu, we see the Creator and understand the interconnectedness of creation.

Recently, we saw distressing images of a mob of Emus wandering into the urban area of Broken Hill searching for water to quench their thirst[29] from the impacts of the worst drought in four hundred years.[30] In the grip of drought, climate disruption, thirst, and hunger, these emus tell us of the Creator and the need for stewardship of creation.

---

28. Aunty Jean Phillips shared Uncle Reverend Ron Williams's rewriting of Psalm 23 at the Salvation Army Indigenous Gathering held at The Salvation Army's The Collaroy Centre, Sydney, in 2013. It was subsequently published in a web booklet as Psalm 23 (Aboriginal Style). See Williams, "Psalm 23."

29. https://www.msn.com/en-au/video/lifestyle/thirsty-emu-mob-wanders-the-streets-of-broken-hill/vp-BBMc814

30. Bedo, "Current Drought the Worst in Centuries."

The Southern Cassowary

There are three species of Cassowary, but only the Southern Cassowary appears in these lands now called Australia and only in the Eastern Far North of Queensland. This ancient bird of the land tells us, and in fact warns us, of the consequences of not caring for creation and not fulfilling our role as stewards of God's creation.

Cassowaries play an important role in the rainforest ecosystem. The Southern Cassowary is listed as endangered under the *Environment Protection and Biodiversity Conservation Act 1999*.[31] It is estimated there are only about 2,000 Southern Cassowaries left in the world with the main threats to survival being vehicle traffic, dogs, and feral pigs. They have not been successfully bred in captivity.

Lack of hope for the survival of the Southern Cassowary and lack of human stewardship of creation has greater consequences than just for the bird itself:

> What of the large-fruited species, the big "plums," satinashes, walnuts, silky oaks and certain gardenias? . . . For them the cassowary is the main agent of dispersal. The size of a fruit that a cassowary can swallow is phenomenal. It has no trouble with a good sized apple, and few rainforest fruit are that large. Cassowaries are rare now and have disappeared from large areas of their former range. Will the large-fruited trees now also disappear from those places?"[32]

The rainforest in Far North Queensland is approximately 7,500 km^2, approximately 0.5 percent of Australia's native forests. Though such a small area, it is home to over one thousand species of trees, with half of these only found in Australia.[33]

We, as humans in these lands now called Australia, both Aboriginal and non-Aboriginal peoples, have been given unique and ancient creation to care for. The question is, will we humble ourselves to realize humans' role in destroying creation—and then, embracing Aboriginal peoples and our knowledge of the Creator since time immemorial, enact our role of stewardship and sustainable practice of God's wondrous creation?

---

31. http://www.environment.gov.au/biodiversity/threatened/publications/factsheet-southern-cassowary

32. Breeden, *Visions of a Rainforest*, 39.

33. Breeden, *Visions of a Rainforest*, vii.

The Birds of the Land Telling Us into the Future

Together we have explored the stories of three birds of the land (flightless)—the Ostrich, the Emu, and the Southern Cassowary. These three cousins have told us much about the past and present, about the Creator, creation, and how to live in right relationship. They have told us about being grounded since time immemorial. Their stories give us principles into which to live into a better future for all creation with the Creator—but we must learn how to listen and how to take action.

The impacts of colonization cannot be underestimated, and we can only grieve for a time where plains were rich with life, skies dark with birds, seas black with fish,[34] and the land filled with Emus and Southern Cassowaries in healthy abundance. But grief should drive us to action.

Just as the stories of the Ostrich, Emu, and Southern Cassowary have been reframed in this paper, non-Aboriginal people must reframe their knowledge of Aboriginal peoples, and these lands now called Australia, with the story of the Creator, which ties us all together today and into the future. One important reframe is the non-Aboriginal perception and knowledge of who Aboriginal peoples are and Aboriginal peoples' contribution to these lands now called Australia.

The first action is to correct the non-Aboriginal perception of Aboriginal peoples—no longer viewed as nomadic hunter-gatherers but correctly identified as the Almighty Creator's stewards, living sustainably for over 65,000 years. This correction is not only important to sustainability but even to prosperity in today's—and future—Australia, as Bruce Pascoe says:

> The start of the journey is to allow the knowledge that Aboriginal people did build houses, did cultivate and irrigate crops, did sew clothes, and were not hapless wanderers across the soil, mere hunter-gatherers. Aboriginal and Torres Strait Islander people were intervening in the productivity of this country, and what has been learned during that process over many thousands of years will be useful to us today. To deny Aboriginal and Torres Strait Islander agricultural and spiritual achievement is the single greatest impediment to intercultural understanding and, perhaps, to Australian moral wellbeing and economic prosperity.[35]

Australian Christians have much work to do to practice stewardship in the household of God—Australia—in order to return to right relationship. While we have focused on the relationship between human and non-human, we are reminded that Australia is a land without Reconciliation, or even

---

34. Pascoe, *Dark Emu*, 208.
35. Pascoe, *Dark Emu*, 229.

Conciliation, between Aboriginal and non-Aboriginal peoples. Perhaps, through what these birds of the land can tell us, through an embracing of Aboriginal wisdom founded in Great Creator Spirit, and through the reminder of Job 12:7–10, we will learn how to close the gap in equality, justice, and relationship, which will lead to true healing in these lands now called Australia. My prayer is that, through truth and friendship with Aboriginal peoples, and particularly truth and friendship with Aboriginal Christian Leaders, past, present, and future, we, all peoples, will learn to be grounded—not just in a colonial history of two hundred and fifty years, which has seen Australia become a land out of balance, but grounded with Creator, Spirit, and Jesus, who have been with us here since time immemorial.

Bibliography

Bedo, Stephanie. "Current Drought the Worst in Centuries as Cost of Feed Sends Farmers Broke." *News.com.au.* August 3, 2018. https://www.news.com.au/technology/environment/climate-change/cost-of-hay-to-feed-animals-sending-farmers-broke/news-story/013ef510afc617d4d329722fc2f3ad8a

Bradshaw, Corey J. A. "Little Left to Lose: Deforestation and Forest Degradation in Australia since European Colonization." *Journal of Plant Ecology* 5.1 (2012) 109–20.

Breeden, Stanley. *Visions of a Rainforest: A Year in Australia's Tropical Rainforest.* East Roseville: Simon & Schuster, 1992.

Champion, Denise. *Yarta Wandatha.* Salisbury: Uniting Aboriginal and Islander Christian Congress, 2014.

Mala, Djambatj. *Why Warriors Lie Down and Die: Towards an Understanding of Why the Aboriginal People of Arnhem Land Face the Greatest Crisis in Health and Education Since European Contact.* Parap: Aboriginal Resource and Development Services Inc., 2010.

Pascoe, Bruce. *Dark Emu: Aboriginal Australia and the Birth of Agriculture.* Broome: Magabala, 2018.

Paulson, Graham, and Brett, Mark G. *Five Smooth Stones.* Melbourne: Whitley College, 2013.

Pope, Mick. *A Climate of Justice: Loving Your Neighbour in a Warming World.* Reservoir: Morning Star, 2017.

Prentis, Brooke, and Sandra Crowden. "Learning to be Guests of Ancient Hosts on Ancient Lands." *Thought Matters* 7 (2017) 79–85. The Journal of The Salvation Army Tri-Territorial Forum, held 29 September—1 October 2017. Edited by Coralie Bridle.

Stewart, Safina. *Heaven Came Down*, 2013, Acrylic on canvas, Wonthaggi, Victoria. http://artbysafina.com.au/portfolio/spirit/heaven-came-down/ accessed 10 April 2020.

Williams, Rev. Ron. "Psalm 23 (Aboriginal Style)." In *We Value the Vision.* Web booklet, July 2013. http://my.salvos.org.au/scribe/sites/my.salvos.org.au/files/indigenous/Booklet_Web.pdf

3

Grounded in Australia

Learning from Our First Peoples[1]

JUDE LONG

I HAD THE PRIVILEGE of working for eight years as the Principal of Nungalinya College, a Combined Churches Training College for Aboriginal and Torres Strait Islander Christians located in Darwin. When I started in my role, I had very little experience of Aboriginal peoples or their cultures. I did have some tools to process what I was learning, thanks to my studies in anthropology and missiology. However, it was a steep learning curve. It was also life changing, and I am now very aware of the great contributions Aboriginal Christians can make to our understanding of what it means to be Christians in this place, Australia.

I need to be clear that I am not attempting to speak from an Indigenous perspective, but rather from my context as a white, dominant culture woman sharing what I have learned from Aboriginal people through my time at Nungalinya. I also wish to clarify that the perspectives of Aboriginal peoples vary significantly depending on the history of their people group and location in Australia. Most of the students I learned from at Nungalinya were from remote communities, mainly in the top end and central areas of Australia. Most spoke English as a second or third or fourth language, and

---

1. This paper was originally given as a keynote at the Evangelical Women in Academia conference at Ridley College, Melbourne, on August 3, 2019.

many were still very much in touch with their traditional cultures. More particularly, because I was adopted into the kinship structure of the Yolngu people of Elcho Island, much of what I learned was through these relationships. Aboriginal cultures and their experiences of colonization are diverse, and their expression of their cultures and faith is equally diverse. I am aware that my perspective is only one of many that could emerge in connecting with this diversity. I also need to express that I have only glimpsed the depths and richness of those cultures as I shared with people in the context of study and in visiting a number of remote communities.

Being Grounded

Being "grounded" is an interesting idiom. It is certainly an unusual theme for reflections from women in academia. In fact, the two words grounded and academia seem something of a mismatch.

What do we actually mean by the term grounded? It depends on your point of view. From a tradesperson's point of view, it means making electrical circuits safe by connecting them to the earth; from a contemporary culture perspective, it is being real, authentic; from a theological perspective it is being connected to the "ground of our being," God—Father, Son, and Holy Spirit; and from a teenager's perspective it probably means you can't go out for a month! It is a curious coincidence that the theme for Reconciliation Week in 2019 used the term grounded. The theme was "Grounded in Truth: Walk Together with Courage." This carries the idea that you must face and connect with the truth of the past if there is going to be the possibility of walking together in the future. This could also be a good way to understand what it is for women in academia to be grounded.

Often the world of academia seems to relate primarily to ideas rather than life. It is one of the accusations people make about theological colleges. They are ivory towers, out of touch with reality, a place where you lose your faith. The accusation is that academic work isn't grounded, and there is a real danger of losing your way. For me personally, this has long been an issue. As a theology student and then lecturer, one of my frustrations has been the disconnection between theological reflection and the world of ideas, and our real-life contexts. This was reflected in my choice of topic for a doctoral thesis, which was about how to study theology for personal transformation. How can our learning actually build up our relationship with God, the world, and each other? As women in academia, we have the opportunity to present a different way of doing theology. When our theology is grounded, it has the ability to be transformational for individuals, for church, and for society.

My experience of going to Nungalinya College in Darwin was certainly a big change from working in a theological college in Melbourne. First, as Aboriginal and Torres Strait Islanders, all the students were from totally different cultures to me. Secondly, we were operating in the Vocational Education Training (VET) sector rather than Higher Education. Students were studying at Certificate I through to Certificate IV level. Doing theology in the VET sector is quite a different proposition to Higher Education and inherently requires you to make the connections between learning and practice. Lastly, I was confronted by the huge inequities present in our country and the generational trauma experienced by the students as an ongoing and painful reality. It was a very rich and challenging time. I was learning many things about what it is to be a Christian in this country. I use the past continuous tense, "was learning," because I certainly hadn't mastered anything and was only just beginning to understand. Nor have I completed my learning; what I share is part of my continuing journey.

The Aboriginal students had a very different way of learning to that of the traditional theological college method of research, lectures, critical thinking, and debate. Once you experience something different, you realize that the Western model expressed in academia is quite adversarial. You must defend against attack and demonstrate the validity of your ideas based on a particular rationalistic model of logic and particular models of biblical exegesis. The topics and outcomes may vary from college to college depending on the nature of the college's theology, but they have a similar methodology. I would question whether this methodology is helpful for Christian formation, especially for the emerging generation who view the world quite differently due to the changes in culture and particularly the influence of technology.

Traditionally, Aboriginal learning is accumulated very slowly over many years in small increments, and a person is not entrusted with the next piece of knowledge until they have mastered the previous one. This is quite an alien concept for a world based on free access to information through technology. Learning is also always done in a communal context. Tyson Yunkaporta,[2] in his thesis, "Aboriginal Pedagogies at the Cultural Interface," very helpfully articulates a model of Aboriginal pedagogy incorporating eight aspects of learning that relate dynamically in the connection between Aboriginal and Western learning. This is expressed as a graphic that mirrors the way kinship

---

2. Yunkaporta, "Aboriginal Pedagogies."

relationships are expressed. One of the key aspects of Aboriginal learning is that it is embedded in story, place, and relationship.

In reflecting on what I have learned from Aboriginal people about being grounded, it seems appropriate to use many stories to illustrate these learnings. The three key loci of my reflection will be land, kinship, and suffering. I will start with a story.

One time I was taking a student with me as I was driving down to Katherine Christian Convention. I was trying to chat with her and learn more about her culture (which in itself is not a culturally normal thing to do). As we went along I noticed a tree, and we were talking about the tree. I asked her what the tree was called in her language, which was Kunwinku. She just looked at me pityingly, and said gently, "That is too hard for you." That comment effectively shut me up, and we continued the journey in silence. But it was true. Much of Aboriginal language, culture, and understanding was just too hard for me—and continues to be so. One of my coworkers at Nungalinya, who had lived and worked in the small community of Gäwa on Elcho Island, said how when she came across something she didn't understand (which happened regularly), she would mentally put it into a dilly bag to see if it came out again later.[3] Some things did, and she grew in understanding; but many things stayed in the dilly bag.

Land

For Aboriginal people, land has a significance that those of us from Western cultures can only begin to glimpse. However, as Christians, we should not be surprised. Land was one of the keys for God's people in the Old Testament. Land was a key aspect of God's covenant with Abraham:

> God took him outside and said, "Look up at the sky and count the stars—if indeed you can count them." Then he said to him, "So shall your offspring be." Abram believed the LORD, and he credited it to him as righteousness. He also said to him, "I am the LORD, who brought you out of Ur of the Chaldeans to give you this land to take possession of it." (Gen 15:5–7, NIV).[4]

We know the promised land was an essential part of the people of Israel's understanding of God's covenant with them. For Indigenous peoples throughout

---

3. A dilly bag is a bag made of woven pandanus traditionally used by Aboriginal people to carry food.

4. New International Version used for all Scripture quotations in this chapter.

the world, connection to the land is one of the common threads.⁵ It is not just about ownership and anti-colonialism. It is about identity.

Modern Australian society is very different, and probably different to how most cultures have viewed the land in the past. We are highly mobile and disconnected from land. Most Australians live in cities, and many no longer even live in houses with gardens, but in apartments. Many are migrants or children of migrants. The connection to this land may be very recent, or perhaps one or more generations. Personally, the longest time I have lived anywhere in my life is twelve years, growing up in Brisbane, and I don't think I am unusual for that. Our society is becoming increasingly mobile, and our disconnection from land, local communities, and family is also growing, partly as a result.

In spending time with Aboriginal people and visiting their home communities, I was struck by how important land was to them. Neville Naden says, "Land for the majority of my people is everything about them, and they are everything about land. Land will survive without people, but our people need land to remind them of who they are. Land is not just a place we occupy, it is also what gives us meaning and belonging."⁶

This connection to land is not about ownership, or productivity, or about somewhere to live. Many Aboriginal people would describe the land as their mother, or even say that the land owns them. It is a deeply spiritual relationship that affects everything about them. For them, there is also a deep sense of God's presence in Australia long before the arrival of the Christian gospel with colonization.

Intellectually, we would accept that God reveals himself through the land. Romans 1:20 says, "For since the creation of the world God's invisible qualities—his eternal power and divine nature—have been clearly seen, being understood from what has been made, so that people are without excuse" (Rom 1:20 NIV). In academia, we would call that general revelation. But as our society, and we as part of it, are becoming more and more disconnected from the land, that ability to see and hear God through his creation becomes muted. We are using the term "grounded" in this book, and here is a key lesson for us. We need to connect with God through the ground—through creation.

So how can we connect better with God through the land? Miriam Rose Ungunmerr-Baumann, an Aboriginal woman from Daly River, has expressed her understanding of this very powerfully in her theology of *Dadirri*.

---

5. See the Introduction in Longchar, *Returning to Mother Earth,* for a discussion of the importance of land for Indigenous people throught out the world.

6. Naden and Havea, "Colonization Has Many Names," 1.

She says, "There are deep springs within each of us. Within this deep spring, which is the very Spirit of God, is a sound. The sound of Deep calling to Deep. The sound is the word of God—Jesus."[7] We hear that sound as we deeply listen, away from the distractions, connected to the land.

Often when I visited a remote community, I would spend a lot of time just sitting with Aboriginal people. We probably wouldn't talk all that much. We would just sit on the ground together—something that became more challenging as arthritis set in. It was really hard not to feel that I needed to talk, or to get enrolments, or be up and moving on to this group or that group. I confess that I really struggled to sit, to listen, to be.

How can we learn from this literally grounded view of the world and God? Obviously, time is one of the most significant challenges. We need to be willing to take the time to sit, to be in a place, and connect with it. To sit, to listen deeply, to allow God to speak to us in this quiet, still way.

Kinship

The second key thing I learned from the students at Nungalinya was about the importance of kinship. We often use the word family in our society and the church, but in my culture, family is a very small word, usually referring to the nuclear family. Using the word kinship helps to understand the wider interconnected relationships we have. For Aboriginal people, everything is about relationship. Relationship with each other, with the land, and with God. I have heard the distinction made between a Western view of family, expressed in a family tree, and an Indigenous view of kinship, which is more like a bowl of spaghetti where there are connections everywhere.

Western culture has a highly individualized understanding of the human person. However, many other cultures including Aboriginal cultures, have a corporate worldview. It is interesting that this includes the biblical cultures. In Aboriginal cultures, to be truly human you have to be in relationship, kinship. It is a way of defining who you are as a person, how you should be related to, where you fit into the land and the community.

In order to be able to engage with non-Indigenous people, many Indigenous people have the practice of adopting people into their kinship system. Without being adopted, the non-Indigenous person is almost not really a person. I was privileged to be adopted by a woman from Elcho Island as her sister, and I have a skin name, Gamanydjan. This meant that when I met Aboriginal people I would explain I had been adopted, what my skin name was, and they would immediately be able to say, "You call

---

7. Ungunmerr-Baumann, "About Dadirri", para. 29.

me daughter," or grandmother, or various other relationship names for which we have no English equivalent. I could fit into their worldview, and we had a basis for relationship.

The Indigenous kinship systems are highly structured and have significant responsibilities and areas of respect built into them. The details of kinship structures vary across the different Indigenous nations, but they are common to all. Aboriginal people can negotiate the connections from one people group to another and work out how you are related across cultures. Once you are adopted into the kinship structure, you are family.

I find this a beautiful picture of how God adopts us into his family through his Son Jesus. Once part of the family, you have responsibilities and privileges. However, I think sometimes we impose our own cultural values on this idea of God's family: that it is only a small family, perhaps sometimes just me, Dad, and big brother Jesus. But we are actually part of a worldwide family that includes people of all ages, genders, ethnicities, political persuasions, denominations, and theologies. Many people describe feeling this connection when they meet someone who is a Christian in a non-Christian environment such as a secular workplace, or a meeting, or at the shops. There is kinship there. There is often a feeling of connectedness, even between strangers. This is actually expressing a deep biblical truth that as God's children we are all family with each other.

How does this relate to being *grounded*? For many individuals, being grounded often means looking within oneself, or into an individual relationship with God. However, that is fraught with peril. It is so dependent on oneself. This perhaps relates especially to that idea of authenticity as an expression of being grounded. Brian Rosner argues that "the appeal to authenticity can be just an excuse for questionable behavior."[8] When we seek to create our own authenticity, even as we seek to relate to God, the dangers of selfishness, pride, and blindness are almost impossible to avoid. It is very rare that a person successfully describes themselves as a grounded person, or an authentic person; it is usually an observation from others and demonstrated by that person's character and connectedness.

Aboriginal kinship reminds us of the importance of being grounded in the church, God's family. Many Christians today struggle with the church, often with good reason. It has been tainted by issues of abuse and domestic violence, as well as intellectualism, sexism, moralism, and cultural imperialism. Yet this is God's family. It is a bit like saying "blood is thicker than water," an idiom used to express that despite the dysfunction or broken relationships, there is something special in a family relationship.

---

8. Rosner, *Known by God*, 25.

How much more does this apply when we are talking about the blood of Jesus! Aboriginal kinship relationships are not utopian either. There are problems and abuse, particularly as those cultures have changed through contact with dominant culture.

In thinking about land, I identified that our society is a highly mobile one, and this has implications in the area of kinship as well. As people move locations, they often disconnect from friends, neighbors, biological family, church. Isolation and loneliness are common, even for Christians. How can we become more grounded in God's family? The first thing is to be intentional about it. It is not enough to just attend church, to fulfil all righteousness by being part of an established church. If church is family, that then entails relationships and responsibility. One of the key things is to intentionally build relationships. Sometimes we hear that churches are not friendly, or we feel we don't fit in. I have certainly experienced both these things. However, if we are grounding ourselves in the church, that involves a significant commitment. It is much more than attendance. Prayerfully seeking wisdom about how we can be involved should be a part of that connectedness. Staying a significant period of time is also a major factor. Relationships take time.

When I was in Darwin one of the distinctive features of church life was the high turnover of people. Darwin is an extreme example of the mobility in Australia today. The statistics show that in 2017–18 the turnover was 16.4 percent of the population, compared to 6.3 percent in Victoria. Most of that turnover occurs at the end of each year. Perhaps people have had enough of the hot, humid weather before the wet season and decide to leave. However, at our church at the beginning of each year we would have probably lost about a third of our members, and new people would arrive. After a while this constant churn of people made it very hard to build relationships. For me personally, knowing that I wasn't going to stay forever always affected my ability to really commit to the church and connect with people. I was not grounded there. Perhaps others can relate to that experience. It is particularly a challenge if you are in some sort of employed ministry in the church, as that significantly affects the sorts of relationships you end up having.

The reality for many of us is that our lives will be mobile. How can we become grounded in God's family with that as a given? Paul is a great example. He was a highly mobile person in ministry, traveling and visiting churches all the time. Yet he was very intentional in maintaining contact with the churches as a whole and people as individuals, as we see through the letters we have preserved in the New Testament. We know that these were not all of Paul's letters. He was an intentional correspondent. In our day of instant communication, we have much greater opportunities to maintain relationships from a distance. Once again our Aboriginal sisters and brothers are a great example. They have embraced the mobile phone as a wonderful means of maintaining relationships. I remember one lovely time when I took an Aboriginal friend for her first look at snow. She spent the rest of the day on the phone. I couldn't understand most of what she was saying, but the word snow was present in every conversation!

I am now a grandmother with four lovely granddaughters, and I love it. It is interesting that for the Yolngu people of Arnhem Land, one of the most important relationships is the *mari–guthara* relationship, the grandmother-grandchild relationship. Even connections between tribes are expressed as *mari–guthara*. Being a grandmother is very grounding. Suddenly instead of running a college, you are changing nappies, delighting in first smiles and steps, sharing the same stories over and over again. One of the main reasons I left Darwin and Nungalinya was to return to Melbourne to be close to my daughter. We made a conscious decision to shape our lives around those close kinship relationships. After we made the decision, we found out she was expecting twins. We bought a house in Gembrook, the same township she lives in, and our other daughter moved to Cockatoo, the next township. We all go to the same church again for the first time since the girls were teenagers. We get to share life together. I have the joy of being part of a small congregation plant in the Primary School in Gembrook.

We recently had a visit from a group involved in drug rehabilitation, and several of the recovering addicts shared their stories of being transformed by Jesus. The director of the group gave a challenge to our little congregation. We could grow by attracting Christians moving to the area or unhappy with their own churches, and become a church like all the others, or we could continue to be different, to be reaching out to those in our community desperately in need of the gospel, and grow slowly, messily, into something different and authentic. This really resonated with me. Too often church has been an obligation, going through the motions, putting up with exclusion from ministry because of my gender, rather than being family, kin. This leads to my final topic: being grounded in kinship means really sharing in one another's joys and sorrows.

Suffering

Land and kinship are two traditional aspects of Indigenous cultures, and probably the ones I was expected to focus on when invited to write this chapter. At Nungalinya I was facilitating a class on Indigenous expressions of faith. In the class we went through a process to help students develop contextual theologies, using land and kinship as the two areas we focused on. This worked well, and the students resonated with reflecting theologically on these topics. However, at the end of the intensive we had the opportunity for the students to select another area to apply their learning to. It was interesting and confronting that most students wanted to reflect theologically about the problem of pain.

In my time at Nungalinya, during every single intensive, we mourned with at least one student about the loss of a family member either through ill-health, suicide, or accident. Very rarely was it a death that came at the end of a long life. Many had to wait months for funerals to happen because there were so many funerals booked up, which led to an extended period of grief. Many students struggled themselves with issues of ill-health or domestic violence. Yet in the midst of ongoing trauma most also clung on to God.

Suffering is not a topic that we enjoy discussing and we find experiencing it even less attractive. But it is very much a part of the Christian life and it is modeled on Jesus. In the incarnation Jesus came as a weak and fragile human being, emptying himself of his glory (Philippians 2). He came not to rule as a king in comfort and luxury, but to be homeless, itinerant, and eventually to be executed by the colonizing Roman powers at the request of his own people. And he says, "Follow me!" I have been studying the book of Ephesians for my personal devotions all this year, and one commentator repeatedly referred to the call for us to live a "cruciform" life characterized by weakness and vulnerability.[9] My Aboriginal sisters didn't necessarily choose to live in weakness and vulnerability, but they demonstrated the reality of this cruciform life.

How does this relate to being *grounded*? It seems to me that being grounded relates to who we are when everything else is stripped away. Who are we when our jobs, our homes, our security, our health, our reputation, are stripped away? This is what Jesus experienced. He even experienced separation from God as he bore humanity's sins on the cross—a mystery I find hard to fathom. But for us, we have the promise that he will be with us. When all is stripped away from a human perspective, we are still God's children dearly loved. We are in the process of becoming more like Jesus.

But suffering is not just individual. Corporate suffering is very real. Kinship involves being truly affected by the joys and sufferings of our family. Do we really feel the pain of dispossession, trauma, and powerlessness of our Aboriginal sisters and brothers for example? Or those who have come to this country fleeing persecution in their own country? What about those whose biological family has fractured and disintegrated, or those who are

---

9. Gombis, *The Drama of Ephesians*.

just plain lonely? We don't have to look far within our church family to find suffering. How do we respond?

As women in academia, it might be tempting to write a paper about the "Problem of Pain," and that may well be helpful for us, even if not for others. But I think one of the challenges of being grounded is being truly connected with those who are suffering, not to solve their problems, but to be with them in their suffering. Paul says in Romans 5,

> Therefore, since we have been justified through faith, we have peace with God through our Lord Jesus Christ, through whom we have gained access by faith into this grace in which we now stand. And we boast in the hope of the glory of God. Not only so, but we also glory in our sufferings, because we know that suffering produces perseverance; perseverance, character; and character, hope. And hope does not put us to shame, because God's love has been poured out into our hearts through the Holy Spirit, who has been given to us. (Rom 5:1–5, NIV).

As part of the Australian church, God's family in this land, our individual sufferings will not disappear, and our corporate suffering will probably only increase until Jesus returns. We can see the thunderclouds of change on the horizon as our society moves further and further away from its Christian roots. There is the temptation to tone down our distinctiveness, to seek to be politically correct, to bend a bit here and there. But this is how we can lose our groundedness.

The whole image of being grounded is to be firmly rooted, connected, centered. This means coming back to Jesus. He is the center and foundation of our faith. To be grounded means to be connected to him. To be connected to him means to be connected to each other. To be connected to each other means to be connected to our place. To be connected to place means to be connected to Jesus. It is circular, organic, incremental learning that involves the whole of our person, not just our mind or our spirit.

Conclusion

The Australian church has much to learn from Aboriginal Christians about what it means to be Christian in this place. An understanding of land and kinship and the challenges of spending time listening to God through creation and investing in relationships in God's family can lead us to become more grounded in our faith. However, the reality of being truly grounded in Jesus as we experience suffering is perhaps the greatest lesson of all. As we look to the future, the comfort and complacency of being Christian in

Australia will disappear. It is time for the church and for individual Christians to become grounded in this place, in our kinship, and through the suffering that is so evident in our churches and society.

Bibliography

Dhamarrandji, Maratja. "Receive, Touch and Feel Raypirri." In *Indigenous Australia and the Unfinished Business of Theology: Cross-Cultural Engagement*, edited by Jione Havea, 9–16. New York: Palgrave MacMillan, 2014.

Gombis, Timothy G. *The Drama of Ephesians: Participating in the Triumph of God*. Downers Grove, IL: InterVarsity, 2010.

Kowal, Emma. *Trapped in the Gap: Doing Good in Indigenous Australia*. New York: Berghahn, 2015.

Longchar, A. W. *Returning to Mother Earth: Theology, Christian Witness and Theological Education an Indigenous Perspective*. West Bengal: Sceptre, 2012.

Naden, Neville, and Jione Havea. "Colonization Has Many Names." In *Indigenous Australia and the Unfinished Business of Theology: Cross-Cultural Engagement*, edited by Jione Havea, 1–8. New York: Palgrave MacMillan, 2014.

Rainbow Spirit Elders. *Rainbow Spirit Theology: Towards an Australian Aboriginal Theology*. Cairns: Wontulp-Bi-Buya College, 2007.

Rosner, Brian S. *Known by God: A Biblical Theology of Personal Identity*. Grand Rapids, MI: Zondervan, 2017.

Thompson, David (ed). *Milbi Dabaar: A Resource Book for Teachers, Leaders, Pastors and Students for Use in Christian Ministry Among Aborigines of Australia*. Cairns: Wontulp-Bi-Buya College, 2004.

Ungunmerr-Baumann, Miriam Rose. 1988. "About Dadirri." Miriam Rose Foundation. Accessed August 12, 2019. https://www.miriamrosefoundation.org.au/about-dadirri.

Yunkaporta, Tyson. "Aboriginal Pedagogies at the Cultural Interface." Professional Doctorate (Research) diss., James Cook University, 2009.

4

Embodying Christ in the Neighborhood

A Reflection on Place, Home, and Mission

Karina Kreminski

Do you think very much about the physical aspects of the built environment? What is the relationship you have with the space where you live? Is it merely a space you inhabit for a portion of the day? Do you think the spaces where you live and work are important? Do they influence your daily rhythms and routines? Is your neighborhood a place or simply a space? What is the difference between the two? How does God work in the ecology of the neighborhood?

From the moment we wake up, get ready for work, drive, walk, or take public transport, and walk into our workplaces or neighborhoods, our physical environment is affecting us as we affect it. Our physical environment matters. There is also a way we can look at the physical spaces we inhabit from a theological perspective that can frame our thinking on this topic. In other words, *God* thinks our physical environment matters.

We need first to explore what we mean by a theology of place and the built environment. How do we think theologically about our physical spaces, places, and buildings where we live and work? Why is this important? Secondly, we can think about how those places impact us, and then—most importantly—how we can impact those spaces as a people of God who work for good in this world and want to embody kingdom values in our contexts.

In his book *Where Mortals Dwell*, Craig Bartholomew takes an in-depth look at what the Bible has to say about place and our physical environment. What is most interesting is his analysis of Genesis from the perspective of a theology of place. He argues that in the creation narrative, the move from Genesis 1 to 2 is a move that takes us from the broad to the particular. He writes:

> Narratively, therefore, the move from Genesis 1 to 2, rather than indicating a juxtaposition of two unrelated sources, involves a movement of progressive implacement culminating in the planting of Eden as the specific place in which the earthlings Adam and Eve will dwell. It is important to note just how illuminating place is at this point. Genesis 1 presents the world as a potential place for human habitation, but the nature of Adam and Eve as embodied earthlings means that the human story itself must begin in a specific place, in this case Eden. As [philosopher Edward Casey] notes, "Implacement itself, *being concretely placed*, is intrinsically particular."[1]

When we read Genesis, we see that to be human means to be located and placed. Adam and Eve's story becomes particular by the fact that they are placed in Eden.

The name of the place is Eden. This conveys that the names of places are important, they are pointers to our humanity. Bartholomew exegetes Genesis from the perspective of a theology of place and says that Genesis shows us that firstly, creation is the basis of place and not some neutral concept of nature. Secondly, humans are always placed. Thirdly, implacement is a gift to humans by God; in other words, place is a dynamic concept bringing forth the creative engagement of humans with their contexts. Fourthly, place is never fully a place without God as co-inhabitant, so place is always a theological concept. Lastly, after Eden we see the challenge of implacement and the constant threat of *dis*placement to human beings. Implacement is, then, a core human quality, and displacement—a constant threat in a fallen world—is dehumanizing.[2]

How relevant is Bartholomew's theology of place, seen through his exegesis of Genesis, to our view of the place where we live—our neighborhoods? What does it mean to be placed in the neighborhood, for instance? What does it look like to engage creatively with our communities where we live? What does displacement look like in the neighborhood? What are some physical factors that can cause dehumanization in that context? Do we view

---

1. Bartholomew, *Where Mortals Dwell*, 25. Emphasis original.
2. Bartholomew, *Where Mortals Dwell*, 31.

God as a co-inhabitant in our habitations? I will explore these questions later, but first we need to explore further a theology of place.

Undergirding this theology of place is our core belief in the incarnation. God who is Spirit (John 4:24) chose to be embodied, limited, and placed as a human being in a particular time and physical context. God put on flesh. God was implaced. This should make us realize and accept that all matter is holy. The physical matters to God, as God enfleshed has made it so. Therefore nothing is secular. God became flesh and it follows that we can imitate this incarnational strategy by embodying the gospel in the places where we live and work. This is not about proclamation but about fleshing out the values of beauty, truth, love, peace, and reconciliation in our contexts.

Ross Hastings, in his book *Missional God, Missional Church,* says that the incarnation has a few implications when it comes to Christians impacting their environment. First, the gospel is justified as holistic and therefore an unhealthy dualism between spirit and matter is nullified. Secondly, there must now be the "solidarity of the Christian with all humanity in light of the fact that through the Incarnation God became a neighbor to all humanity." Thirdly, contextualization becomes a legitimate way of applying the gospel in different situations. Fourthly, the church must then be committed to being church in a localized manner.[3] They are all points worthy of our attention, but his first point is interesting for our purposes. The incarnation means that the gospel is justified as holistic; therefore, an unhealthy dualism between spirit and matter is nullified.

Part of the problem we have around understanding and absorbing the importance of a theology of place is this unhealthy dualism that sees the spiritual as more important than the material. We separate the spiritual from secular and find it hard to see how God could be at work in the so-called secular spaces. Roger Helland and Leonard Hjalmarson, in their book *Missional Spirituality,* say:

> Christians today regularly refer to their culture as the secular world. It's where one holds a secular job, attends a secular university, listens to secular music and watches secular movies and TV. Even though all cultures express religion and spirituality in one form or another, the so-called secular world is often wrongly perceived as a separate realm disenchanted from the sacred realm where the God way up there and Christian faith reside. Some Christians place culture in one realm and place the

---

3. Hastings, *Missional God, Missional Church,* loc 3021.

institutional church, Christian faith and their personal spiritual life in another realm.[4]

Do we have an inherent form of Gnosticism within our evangelicalism? Are we living out a spirituality that prioritizes spirit over matter? Is our spirituality escapist, other worldly, and consumeristic? This is the opposite of a holistic and incarnational spirituality that expresses its faith for the sake of the world.

Paula Gooder gives an example of how this other-worldly view affects our attitudes to the environment:

> For many years . . . Christians have displayed an ambivalence to creation and the environmental disaster that is approaching with ever-growing rapidity. This ambivalence emerges, at least in part, out of an emphasis on the "good" of the spiritual to the exclusion of the physical. If we believe that our ultimate fate is a spiritual existence in heaven with God and that the physical world is coming to an end then it is much harder to feel motivated to act for the good of the planet.[5]

Craig van Gelder agrees and says that in the perspective of many Christians,

> Creation is viewed either as lacking God's presence or as the mere object of missionary work. In either case, it is understood largely as being without God-given worth and agency. Most striking is the lack of imagination of the Spirit's ongoing movement within creation, especially outside the church. A more robustly Trinitarian framework invites us into a deeper, more theological view of the world and God's continuing work of creation within it.[6]

So his question is, do we believe that the Spirit is not only at work in the church but equally in the world?

In her comment, Gooder makes a crucial observation that our spirituality is affected by our eschatology. Our eschatological view will affect whether we value the material in our world as full of God's affirmation and presence. In *Travail of Nature*, Santmire asks the pertinent question:

> Is the final aim of God, in his governance of all things, to bring into being at the very end a glorified kingdom of spirits alone who thus united with God may contemplate him in perfect bliss,

---

4. Helland and Hjalmarson, *Missional Spirituality*, loc 331.
5. Gooder, *Body*, 4–5.
6. Zscheile and Van Gelder, *Missional Church in Perspective*, loc 2404.

> while as a precondition of their ecstasy all the other creatures of nature must be left by God to fall away into eternal oblivion? Or is the final aim of God, in his governance of all things, to communicate his life to another in ways that call forth at the very end new heavens and a new earth in which righteousness dwells, a transfigured cosmos where peace is universally established between all creatures at last, in the midst of which is situated a glorious city of resurrected saints who dwell in justice, blessed with all the resplendent fullness of the earth and who continually call upon all creatures to join with them in their joyful praise of the one who is all in all?[7]

Will our ultimate existence be embodied or disembodied? Orthodox Christian faith says embodied, but often we live out a faith today that betrays a Gnosticism rather than a belief in the goodness of material things that will last for eternity. It is clear that these issues can stop us from developing a robust theology about place. This means that we struggle, for instance, to see how God could be active in our neighborhoods and contexts. N. T. Wright says:

> The early Christians saw Jesus' resurrection as the action of the creator God to reaffirm the essential goodness of creation and, in an initial and representative act of new creation, to establish a bridgehead within the present world of space, time and matter . . . through which the whole new creation could now come to birth . . . the resurrection, in the full Jewish and early Christian sense, is the ultimate affirmation that creation matters, that embodied human beings matter.[8]

The incarnation and the resurrection tell us that material things matter to God.

One consequence of the ambivalence around and separation of the sacred and secular has been that Christians tend to give little focus to the built environment as a place of God's presence and activity. That space is relegated to the secular or profane. Notably, this also has to do with our eschatology. What are our thoughts around the consummation of all things? If we believe that the world will in the end times be destroyed by God rather than restored, and if we as a result live out an "escape from the world" theology, we will not be interested in our buildings, land, workspaces, or neighborhoods.

---

7. Santmire, *The Travail of Nature*, 175.
8. Wright, *Resurrection*, 729–30.

Thankfully, many scholars and practitioners are increasingly focusing more on the intersection between spirituality and the built environment by developing a theology of place. Timothy Gorringe writes that our Augustinian heritage has influenced us to believe that the "true Christ of history" tells us to "turn away from the preoccupations of human society," our ancient spiritual fathers encouraged us to "disentangle (ourselves) from all things created," and architects of the past wanted to evoke a sense of the "unearthly" in their buildings.[9] All of this leads to a very displaced and disembodied view of our geography. Therefore, we must today rediscover a more positive approach to a theology of the built environment. Do we ignore the built environment as a space that is secular and fading away as we sing "Turn your eyes upon Jesus" who makes the "things of earth grow strangely dim"? Or do we input and shape our inner-city neighborhoods with reign of God values? These are crucial considerations for the practice of our faith.

Once we start thinking of the built environment as just as spiritual as natural landscapes, and also important in the framework of God's renewal of all things, this impacts the way that we think about the shape of our contexts. Philip Sheldrake in *The Spiritual City* says, "In urban environments we cannot separate functional, ethical and spiritual questions. If a city is to be more than merely efficient, it needs to embrace some sacred quality—above all it must affirm and promote the sacredness of people and the human capacity for transcendence."[10] An incarnational spirituality will seek to actively build an environment that will promote sacred spaces, compassion, and respect for humanity. Our physical contexts, neighborhoods, and cities can be impersonal, inhumane, and places of fragmentation, but as we embody the gospel we will seek to encourage values that are in line with the kingdom of God. This will happen as we take more of an interest in things such as urban planning, local politics, and environmental care in the spaces that we inhabit.

Christians seem more comfortable in finding God in nature, the mountains, hills, valleys, and oceans rather than in the spaces, places, and buildings of urban spaces. Not many worship songs are written about finding God in the city or thinking about the buildings that are erected in our local urban neighborhoods. We retreat to the mountains for an encounter with God but we find it hard to locate God in the busyness and mess of the city.

Four biblical images of the city capture our imagination as Christians: the tower of Babel, Nineveh, Babylon, and Jerusalem. Most of these images

---

9. Gorringe, *Built Environment*, 9-10.
10. Sheldrake, *Spiritual City*, loc 3121.

are seen in a negative—or at least a confused—light. If we look at the story of Babel in Genesis 11, we notice a few things that cast a dark shadow on cities. The intention of the people of "the whole earth" (v.1) was to build a city and a tower in order to "make a name for ourselves" (v.4). Putting that into the context of the ancient world, this desire is an indication of a darker drive than the simple desire for acknowledgment. The parent or ancestor named a relative, so to name oneself meant ultimately to reject and usurp the authority of that ancestor. We know the tower of Babel to be a story that symbolizes pride, hubris, the "self-made" person, and rebellion towards God. The story of Jonah and the city of Nineveh also brings up negative images in our minds. In Jonah 1:2 God describes the city as a "great city," but he also says, "Its wickedness has come up before me." It is a city that has inhabitants who are so confused in their thinking because of evil that "they do not know their right hand from their left" (4:11). By the time we get to the book of Revelation in the New Testament, the city of Babylon becomes a metaphor for all that is evil, that stands contrary to God (Revelation 18). Lastly, while the city of Jerusalem in the Bible is a picture of the presence of God, it has a checkered history perhaps best summarized by Jesus' sigh of exasperation, "O Jerusalem, Jerusalem, the city that kills the prophets and stones God's messengers! How often I have wanted to gather your children together as a hen protects her chicks beneath her wings, but you wouldn't let me. And now, look, your house is abandoned and desolate" (Matt 23:37–38).

For whatever reasons, this skewed appropriation of the city has persisted in Christian culture. I think that this impacts how we see our workplaces and the built environment. The built environment is a place to escape from as it is human-made, fallen, corrupted, and prideful rather than a place which can be redeemed as a place of rest, beauty and reconciliation for instance. Work is seen as a curse rather than a gift from God, albeit marred by sin (Gen 3:17).

We need to recover a more balanced view if we are going to live in, love, and redeem our contexts. Timothy Gorringe presents a more nuanced view, which can correct our unhelpful bias. He points to counter perspectives that also can be found in the Bible. Nineveh was an evil city, but it was able to be redeemed. In other words, reconciliation with God can happen in the city (Ps 87:4). Moreover, cities were refuges for protection of the vulnerable (Numbers 35, Joshua 20). Therefore, Gorringe says, the city in Scripture "is both a center of violence and protection against it."[11] In other words, we must see the dialectic of the good and bad within the city and therefore within the built environment. Stemming from a robust theology of place,

---

11. Gorringe, *Theology of Place*, 145.

this is a much more positive approach to the built environment that will influence how we see our neighborhoods.

As we diminish the artificial separation between sacred and secular and begin to see the material as worthy of God's attention and presence, we then see God in ordinary daily things and start to practice an everyday spirituality.

Barbara Brown Taylor reminds us of the daily challenge of doing this, saying,

> The last place most people look is right under their feet, in the everyday activities, accidents, and encounters of their lives . . . my life depends on ignoring all touted distinctions between the secular and the sacred, the physical and the spiritual, the body and the soul. What is saving my life now is becoming more fully human, trusting that there is no way to God apart from real life in the real world.[12]

We become more human, embodied beings and less "other worldly" by living out this kind of incarnational spirituality. Crucially, what our calling then means is that we work with God in our environments to discern God and create, with him, this new habitation where we will be at home in this world as fully restored and fully embodied human beings. How can we do this and especially in our neighborhoods? I want to look at four ways we can think through how we can contribute to our communities creatively, using this perspective of a theology of place that reinforces an incarnational spirituality, to work with God as he grows his kingdom.

The Practice of Placemaking

Walter Brueggemann makes an insightful distinction between space and place:

> Space means an arena of freedom, without coercion or accountability, free of pressures and void of authority. Space may be imaged as a weekend, holiday, a vocation and is characterized by a kind of neutrality or emptiness waiting to be filled by our choosing . . . But "place" is a very different matter. Place is space that has historical meanings, where some things have happened that are now remembered and that provide continuity and identity across generations.

---

12. Taylor, *Altar in the World*, xiv–xv.

> Place is space in which important words have been spoken that have established identity, defined vocation, and envisioned destiny. Place is space in which vows have been exchanged, promises have been made, and demands have been issued. Place is indeed a protest against the compromising pursuit of space. It is a declaration that our humanness cannot be found in escape, detachment, absence of commitment, and undefined freedom.[13]

Spaces wait to be made places. Placemaking is simply the process of making a space a place.

If we are making a space a place—that is, placemaking—we will intentionally or unintentionally shape that place with particular values and the vision we hold. The built environment is nothing in and of itself unless it displays and fosters virtues that hopefully help create a flourishing place that is good and beautiful for all. For example, a context or space like a city needs a vision or some kind of direction in order for it to become a flourishing place. We as Christians can have a crucial role in an activity like placemaking in our contexts. Philip Bess, a Catholic professor of architecture, says that there are four orders that constitute the city: the ecological, the economic, the moral, and the formal. However, he also points to the sacred order (as opposed to the "secular") for the city.[14] Although new urbanists would not usually think about a sacred or moral vision to bring cities together, more and more we see cities being designed according to a moral vision. The question is, what are the virtues or values that ground this vision. As Christians we have a crucial role to play here. Edward Casey says,

> We must question the presumption that building is an exclusively Promethean activity of brawny aggression and forceful imposition . . . building is also and just as crucially Epimethean . . . In this latter capacity building is most effectively cultivational in character, for it seeks not to exploit materials but to care for them. In building-as-cultivating, the builder respects the already present properties of that form which building begins.[15]

While some visions of creating places can tend towards the Promethean or aggressive, as people who embody kingdom values, we can instead have a leaning to create places out of spaces that is more Epimethean—that is, cultivational. Instead of exploiting, we create places that build community and character and we respect the materials we use as gifts from God.

---

13. Brueggemann, *The Land*, 4.
14. Bess, *Till We Have Built Jerusalem*, 65–77.
15. Casey, *Getting Back into Place*, 152.

How could we, with an Epimethean spirit, cultivate a place in our neighborhoods? Al Gore famously once asked the question "Why do our children believe that the Kingdom of God is up, somewhere in the ethereal reaches of space, far removed from this planet?"[16] The kingdom of God is in our workspaces also "down here" not only "up there" (Matt 10:7). If the kingdom of God is around us in our neighborhoods, what does it look like to cultivate a flourishing environment there?

I believe that it is our role as God's stewards to create places out of spaces where we live and work. Bartholomew makes a point that instead of favoring wilderness we must favor placemaking.[17] This is an interesting comment. We see the good themes and images of wilderness in Scripture (Luke 4:1), however the notion of ordering that wilderness, carefully, with a view to creating spaces that flourish must be prioritized by us as we live out our faith daily. We are called as stewards (Gen 1:28) to humbly order nature and spaces so they reflect the virtues of the kingdom. How could we do this in our local contexts?

Two ways we can do this, which perhaps might be surprising, are through art and gardening. If we read Revelation, the picture of the new creation given there is of a city. However, this city is a garden city. There is a river running through the center of the city, not off on a tangent (Rev 22:2). Robert Harrison in his book *Gardens: An Essay on the Human Condition*, says that gardens have "a way of slowing time down—allowing its flow to gather in placid ponds as it were, but that is part of their power of enchantment not their power of endurance," and also he says, "Gardens are not memorials . . . if anything they exist to reenchant the present."[18] Imagine planting a community garden in your neighborhood. In neighborhoods that are busy, often stressful, and can be dehumanizing due to fragmentation, a garden could help slow down that busyness; it could allow what is called a "third space" for enchantment in places that are sometimes more about consumerism, control, efficiency, and pragmatism that can leave us feeling dehumanized. It could be a place where people take time to reflect. This is the practice of an incarnational spirituality. What we are doing is taking our built environment seriously. We are placemaking, making spaces into places through a vision for human flourishing according to godly virtues. This is similar to the role that art plays in contexts like the workspace. Instead of art that is thoughtless, sterile, and commercial, what

---

16. Bartholomew, *Where Mortals Dwell*, 235.
17. Bartholomew, *Where Mortals Dwell*, 245.
18. Harrison, *Gardens*, 39.

about creating and establishing art in the neighborhood that fosters community, reflections, even creative activism?

Curator Emilya Colliver says that the enemy of public art is "plonk art":

> What is plonk art?
>
> Plonk art is an afterthought.
>
> Plonk art is there to tick a box.
>
> Plonk art is forgettable and not engaging.
>
> Plonk art is a bad investment and a waste of money.
>
> Plonk art is a public art piece that is just there.[19]

Can you think of any examples of plonk art? This has to be counter to values like beauty and life, which are kingdom of God values. Do we think this is just as important as creating an efficient or functional workplace?

In her book *Placemaking and the Arts*, Jennifer Allen Craft says:

> The arts are a form of placemaking, they place us in time, space and community in ways that encourage us to be fully and imaginatively present, continually calling us to pay attention to the world around us and inviting us to engage in responsible practices in those places. The arts help us to live locally and to know the places we are a part of. And this is a matter of supreme theological significance. . . . Art in a unique way can cultivate a theological imagination and Christian sense of place so that we may become people who better participate with Christ and his church to bring about the kingdom of God in our places.[20]

What would it look like for people in neighborhoods to create art or gardens that help to stimulate beautiful, just, peaceful, life-giving, kind, thoughtful, and community-oriented neighborhoods? Is this not the work of the kingdom to which we have been called? As Craft says, this is a matter of supreme theological significance.

Homemaking

James Davison Hunter has coined the term "faithful presence" to describe our posture in the world as Christians. It means that our impact is the greatest when we commit to being present to others as God was and is present

---

19 Colliver, "Plonk Art." Link no longer available.

20. Craft, *Placemaking and the Arts*, 42.

with us. If we embody the gospel and become present to our world's needs, this what is needed to "change the world"[21]—though his use of that phrase is ironic in that Hunter does not ultimately believe that we can change the world. What would it look like to be a faithfully present people of God who practice a theology of place in order to work with God's Spirit to make this world our home? We know all things will be restored in the new creation (Col 1:20), but we are to work today with God to make this place our home because while it will be transformed, it is where we will permanently live. How can we be good "homemakers" in our world? This is the work of living and bringing shalom to our world. In her book *The Very Good Gospel: How Everything Wrong can be Made Right,* Lisa Sharon Harper says that in Scripture, shalom means wellbeing, wholeness, the perfection of God's creation, abundance, and peace. Good relationships are a crucial part of shalom. Harper explains how cultivating shalom looks:

> The peace of self is dependent upon the peace of the other. God created the world in a web of relationships that overflowed with forceful goodness. These relationships are far-reaching: between humanity and God, between humanity and self, between genders, between humanity and the rest of creation, within families, between ethnic groups or races, and between nations. These relationships were very good in the beginning. One word characterized them all: *shalom* . . . Shalom is the stuff of the kingdom.[22]

We are to practice and flesh out shalom in our contexts as we work to make this world our home. Brian Walsh also outlines this posture well, but then describes the tension we have between being transient sojourners and permanent residents in this world. For as Christians, we are both pilgrims and residents. He writes:

> So the sojourner is a homemaker, but a homemaker who is potentially on the move. And the homeland for which the sojourner yearns is not some other world, but this world redeemed and transfigured. The contrast is not ontological but eschatological. Because the kingdom of God is not yet realized in its fullness, the sojourner yearns for its consummation. And that is why Christian sojourners are *aching visionaries* who bear witness to and work for a future of shalom . . . we are not immigrants or refugees, exiles or migrants, tourists, post modern nomads. If we understand ourselves properly, then in contrast to all of them we are, in a real sense, at home. But this being at home is

---

21. Hunter, *To Change the World*, 241.
22. Harper, *The Very Good Gospel*, 12. Emphasis original.

a posture, a way of being in the world. It is a journeying home-making characterized by . . . permanence, dwelling, memory, rest, hospitality, inhabitation, orientation and belonging.[23]

If we believe that this world is our ultimate home, how do we view the places where we live? It means we view those places with a sense of permanence, not transience. We work to build community, create beauty, and bring light to the places where we live. Our places are a gift from God yet fallen, so what can we do to be homemakers in our local communities, creating a sense of safety, comfort, humanity, and justice there? This means thinking about design and beauty, for example, with a theology of the built environment in mind and seeing this as just as important as sharing the gospel with someone. Our bias towards the latter again shows our tendency to over-spiritualize by preferencing the immaterial over the physical, revealing what a truncated view of the gospel we have.

Exegeting Place

A practice that we can regularly engage in is to exegete our places where we work and live. It is amazing the extent to which we neglect our physical environments as Christians when we could be reading our places in the same way we carefully exegete Scripture in order to understand and embody godliness. We can read our places and then more fully understand our contexts for better engagement and placemaking. Simon Holt in *The God Next Door* advocates walking around our neighborhoods and asking questions such as "Where is there a sense of hope in this place?", "Where are there signs of death here?", and "Where do people gather and connect?"[24] We could easily devise some more questions to ask about our neighborhoods: "What is the history of the land on which this building is built?", "How are the buildings designed to foster life?", "Which objects are dehumanizing?", "Are there places where people can congregate to build community?", "Do I feel that my built environment is beautiful?", "What does the art say about our community?", "Does the built environment show that this community cares?", and "What are the stories and memories that this place holds?"

This last question is important if we are going to take place seriously. How do stories and memories get embedded in the places where we live? If we think about places where terrible things have happened, for example, is there even a possibility that the place can be redeemed? Think

---

23. Boumer-Prediger and Walsh, *Beyond Homelessness*, 297.
24. Holt, *The God Next Door*, loc 404.

of particular places that have experienced the horrors of genocide. Can those physical places and lands ever be redeemed? Memories and stories can shape places and people. Alternatively, are there sacred spaces? If a place has experienced deep spiritual engagement and practices, does this impact people in any tangible way?

Once we engage in this act of deep listening to our contexts, we are better poised to start up tangible projects that will make our spaces places that emanate the values of the kingdom.

Discerning the Spirit—Sacred Spaces

This last point leads us to thinking about practices like discerning the Spirit in our environments. Once we start asking questions such as "What is God doing in my neighborhood?" rather than "God, what are you doing in my church?", this shifts our attention from being ecclesiocentric to clearly seeing God at work in our world and in the local places that we inhabit daily. Do we then believe in sacred spaces? If we look at the Old Testament story of Jacob, who saw angels descending and ascending a ladder at Bethel (Gen 28:12), we can discern a theology of place with an emphasis on sacred events happening at particular places. Have we over-spiritualized the New Testament so that we cannot even conceive of sacred spaces anymore?

Reflecting on this Jacob story, Barbara Brown Taylor says, "The last place most people look (for God) is right under their feet, in the everyday activities, accidents, and encounters of their lives."[25] Should we be taking a more sacramental approach to our workplaces if we are thinking about practicing a theology of place? Inge, in his book *A Christian Theology of Place*, says "Places are the seat of relations or the place of meeting and activity in the interaction between God and the world," and that "the biblical narrative leads us to expect God's self-revelation and that the world is a possible place of sacramentality."[26] Bartholomew says that "once God discloses himself in a particular place it is possible for his disclosure to continue to be associated with that place. Time and history are central components of place, and just as places can be desecrated, so they can be redeemed."[27] Can this apply to our neighborhoods at all? Do we discern the sacred places in our environments? Can we create those spaces in a community to be more open to the presence of God and welcoming of the values of the kingdom?

Jennifer Allen Craft says in her book, *Placemaking and the Arts*:

25. Taylor, *Altar in the World*, xiv-xv.
26. Inge, *Theology of Place*, 251.
27. Bartholomew, *Where Mortals Dwell*, 239.

> Places don't just exist; places must be made. American author and essayist Wallace Stegner writes: "At least to human perception a place is not a place until people have been born in it, have grown up in it, lived in it, known it, died in it—have both experienced and shaped it, as individuals, families, neighborhoods, and communities, over more than one generation . . . it is made a place only by slow accrual, like a coral reef."[28]

Places are made, therefore, through social relationships that shape them. A place becomes what it is by a long history of actions performed there. As we perform and reperform actions in a place, we are drawing on a place's history and memory for our own understanding of ourselves as well as adding back to the value of that place, remaking it over and over again in a sort of dynamic conversation and liturgy.

So sacred places can potentially be created if we perform and reperform spiritual acts in a place. It's a kind of conversation and liturgy that occurs, as Craft says.

If we believe that God values the physical and material as much as the spiritual, then we will develop a robust theology of place and the built environment. Rather than maintaining an otherworldly spirituality, we will practice a this-worldly spirituality. It will be a faith that is holistic rather than compartmentalized and dualistic. We will discern God in all places, and this will influence how we think about our neighborhoods. They will not be secondary to God's mission and restoration of the world. Places are full of the presence of God. What we need to do is discern and then work "with" God, not "for" God, as he grows his kingdom. It won't be easy to change the current practice of evangelical Christianity, which is skewed towards a functional Gnosticism. We have also become too enamored with our consumeristic, driven Western culture. But deep within we cry out for good practices such as slowing down, attentiveness, faithfulness, stability—this is true Christian spirituality, which is the foundation for a theology of place that grounds us. Bartholomew says, "If placemaking is part of our journey out into the world, then it needs to be funded by a deep journey in engagement with God, engagement with ourselves and engagement with one another."[29] This is Christian spirituality.

As Bartholomew goes on to say,

> Implacement ultimately means that by the Spirit we have the Father and Son as our co-inhabitants. Such at-homeness is the key to being at home in our particular places in God's good but

---

28. Craft, *Placemaking and the Arts*, 45.
29. Bartholomew, *Where Mortals Dwell*, 320.

fallen world, and is the place from which we derive the vision and resources for birthing Christ again and again in our world.[30]

May we "birth Christ" again and again in the neighborhoods and workspaces where God has placed us to live.

Bibliography

Bartholomew, Craig. *Where Mortals Dwell: A Christian View of Place for Today*. Grand Rapids, MI: Baker Academic, 2011.

Bess, Phillip. *Till We Have Built Jerusalem: Architecture, Urbanism and the Sacred*. Wilmington, DE: ISI, 2006.

Bouma-Prediger S., and Brian Walsh. *Beyond Homelessness: Christian Faith in a Culture of Displacement*. Grand Rapids, MI: Eerdmans, 2008.

Brueggemann, Walter. *The Land: Place as Gift Promise and Challenge in Biblical Faith*. Minneapolis: Augsburg, 2002.

Casey, Edward S. *Getting Back into Place: Towards a Renewed Understanding of the Place-world*. Bloomington and Indianapolis: Indiana University Press, 1993.

Colliver, Emilya. "Design Excellence: How to Avoid 'Plonk Art.'" Blog post. 2019. https://www.artpharmacyconsulting.com/ideas-source/design-excellence-how-to-avoid-plonk-art?utm_source=Art+Pharmacy+Consultancy&utm_campaign=d80e71e064-EMAIL_CAMPAIGN_2019_04_17_05_45_COPY_01&utm_medium=email&utm_term=0_a99c32a2bd-d80e71e064-356642513

Craft, Jennifer Allen. *Placemaking and the Arts: Cultivating the Christian Life*. Downers Grove, IL: IVP Academic, 2018.

Gooder, Paula. *Body: Biblical Spirituality for the Whole Person*. London: SPCK, 2016.

Gorringe, Tim. *A Theology of the Built Environment: Justice, Empowerment, Redemption*. Cambridge: Cambridge University Press, 2002.

Harper, Lisa Sharon. *The Very Good Gospel*. New York: WaterBrook, 2016.

Harrison, Robert Pogue. *Gardens: An Essay on the Human Condition*. Chicago: University of Chicago Press, 2010.

Hastings, Ross. *Missional God, Missional Church*. Downers Grove, IL: InterVarsity, 2012. Kindle Edition.

Helland, Roger, and Leonard Hjalmarson. *Missional Spirituality: Embodying God's Love from the Inside Out*. Downers Grove, IL: InterVarsity, 2011. Kindle Edition.

Holt, Simon Carey. *God Next Door: Spirituality and Mission in the Neighborhood*. Brunswick East: Acorn, 2007. Kindle Edition.

Hunter, James Davison. *To Change the World: The Irony, Tragedy and Possibility of Christianity in the Late Modern World*. Oxford: Oxford University Press, 2010.

Inge, John. *A Christian Theology of Place*. Aldershot, UK: Ashgate, 2003.

Santmire, H. Paul. *The Travail of Nature: The Ambiguous Ecological Promise of Christian Theology*. Minneapolis: Fortress, 1985.

Sheldrake, Phillip. *The Spiritual City: Theology, Spirituality and the Urban*. Chichester, West Sussex: John Wiley and Sons, 2014. Kindle Edition.

---

30. Bartholomew, *Where Mortals Dwell*, 320.

Taylor, Barbara. *An Altar in the World: A Geography of Faith*. New York: HarperCollins, 2009.
Wright, N. T. *The Resurrection of the Son of God*. London: SPCK, 2003.
Zscheile, Dwight J., and Craig Van Gelder. *The Missional Church in Perspective: Mapping Trends and Shaping the Conversation*. Grand Rapids, MI: Baker Academic, 2011. Kindle Edition.

5

Purity: Guarding the Body Corporate

Moyra Dale

I. Encountering the World, Encountering God

We are embodied beings. Life is earthed, lived, in the physical. Each of us encounters the world in our bodies in real space and time:

> [Each person] exists in the body in the place in which it is. This is also then the place of his sensory organization of immediate experience; the place where his coordinates of here and now, before and after, are organized around himself as center; the place where he confronts people face to face in the physical mode in which he expresses himself to them and they to him as more and other than either can speak. This is the place where things smell, where the irrelevant birds fly away in front of the window, where he has indigestion, where he dies. Into this space must come as actual material events—whether as sounds of speech, scratchings on the surface of paper, which he constitutes as text, or directly—anything he knows of the world. It has to happen here somehow if he is to experience it at all.[1]

Our bodies ground us where we are, in the space and time occupied by our skin, flesh, and bones. Most immediately, there is the floor under our feet, the surfaces that press against our bodies, the noises and sights around

---

1. Smith, *Practices of Power*, 17.

us that invite our attention. We are in time, coming from the events that we have participated in today up till this moment, in our lives as we have experienced them to bring us to this point, in the wider history of our families, communities, cultures. We live in time and space in and through our bodies: our bodies are repositories of our histories and geographies, and so shape our current experience and future.

We experience the world in present time and space, as part of the communities in which we live, hewn by our collective histories, geographies, cultures, and struggles. Our experiences of the world are inevitably affected by class interests, by the gender or ethnic standpoints from within which we speak. Hence Parker Palmer describes knowing as "a profoundly communal act . . . In order to know something, we depend on the consensus of the community in which we are rooted."[2]

For each community this includes consensus about what belongs in their world and what corrupts or pollutes it: how communal purity is both defined and protected, together with the consequences of pollution. Purity and defilement are also defined and enacted in the physical world. It is precisely because of this that the very physical categories of purity and defilement are so influential in the lives of women and men around the world.

It is also in our bodies that we meet with God. The situated world where we are, the place where we experience daily life, is also where God meets us now, just as we are—not as the people we wish we were or aspire to become. This is the place where God calls us to follow him, where we live out each day our beliefs about who God is and who we are. The Bible summonses us to bring our lives and stories into God's story, to become part of a history of people that is recounted as it is grounded in the material realities of daily life, of birth and death, of war and food production. We worship God in our bodies, where we sit or kneel or prostrate ourselves, in silence or song. Robert Alter notes how the psalms

> exhibit an intensely spiritual inwardness. Yet that inwardness is characteristically expressed in the most concretely somatic terms.
> God, my God, for You I search.
> My throat thirsts for You,
> my flesh yearns for You
> in a land waste and parched, with no water. (Ps 63:2)[3]

---

2. Palmer, *As We Are Known*, LOC 134.
3. Alter, *The Hebrew Bible*, Vol. 3:16.

This chapter explores the connection between physical and social bodies and how relationships are shaped and guarded by categories of appropriateness or inappropriateness, purity and defilement. An examination of categories of purity and defilement will draw out their impact on women and men in Western societies and other cultural/religious groups. We then consider how it is that we can meet with God as embodied beings.

II. Relationship between the Individual Body and the Body Corporate

Our individual experience of life in the world, through our bodies, has social implications. Fiona Bowie describes how:

> All experience of the world is mediated through our perception of it—via biological, psychological, and spiritual mechanisms, or senses. As the world acts on our bodies, so our experience of being in the world affects and shapes the phenomena we perceive. There is a continual interaction between the embodied individual and the social and natural world of which the individual is a part.[4]

Social values are inscribed in our bodies, in how we move, speak, and situate ourselves in social space. Given that we experience the world through our bodies, it is no surprise that we use our bodies to orient ourselves in the world, to map and impose meaning on what is around us and also to relate to the other bodies who surround and interact with us. Anthropological theory describes how the individual body functions as a map of the body corporate. We interpret location and orient ourselves in space through our physical body which becomes the center of our coordinates, the basis for symbolic hierarchies of in front or behind, on our left or right hand, above or below. This orientation is fundamental to our existing in the world. At the same time, it is also socially constructed, derived from social relations of the historical community within which we live. Social distance is expressed through two dimensions: front-back, and spatial. Front signifies respect and dignity, in contrast to back. More distance indicates formality, and intimacy is expressed by nearness.[5]

This cartographic process is bi-directional. We use our bodies to map and orient to the physical and social world around us. And society maps

---

4. Bowie, *Anthropology of Religion*, 39.
5. Douglas, *Natural Symbols*, 78–80.

itself onto the body. The social world uses the physical body as an image or microcosm of society. Mary Douglas explains how:

> The social body constrains the way the physical body is perceived. The physical experience of the body, always modified by the social categories through which it is known, sustains a particular view of society. There is a continual exchange of meanings between the two kinds of bodily experience so that each reinforces the categories of the other.[6]

Douglas was drawing on the work of Marcel Mauss, who took the term *habitus* to describe the social-cultural dimension of all human actions, including how people walk or swim, sit, sleep or eat. Social values are imprinted on individual bodies in the way they move in space, whether learned through being constrained to perform tasks in a specific way or by imitating admired individuals.[7] So too, changing from one social group to another involves relearning both the group values and how to move within their embodied expression in everyday actions, ways of walking or eating or talking.

The categories of social and bodily experience are mutually reinforcing. A significant dimension of this reciprocity is in the area of control: bodily control is an expression of social control. The more important that rules, control, and categories are in society, the more constraints and formality are required of its members in their bodily expression, whether dress, hairstyle, or comportment. For example, the closer one approaches to the monarchy in Britain, the more conventions and regulations govern behavior. This contrasts with a more informal style in Australia, which has far less social hierarchy.

III. Social Control Reflected in Purity Regulations

Concerns for the community, the body corporate, are expressed in how we view our bodies. As noted, the emphasis on bodily control signifies the importance of social control. Control depends on classification, through which we make meaning of our world. Social control requires boundaries and classification of appropriate and inappropriate elements (objects or behavior), as a way of guarding the corporate body, the community and its values. Social disruption occurs through "dirt"—substances or actions that cross socially determined boundaries.

---

6. Douglas, *Natural Symbols*, 72.
7. Mauss, "Techniques of the Body," 70–88.

Mary Douglas has famously summarized this principle in her definition of "Dirt as matter out of place." So physical dirt has its right place in the garden, as an appropriate habitat for plants: however, on the kitchen floor, it is dirty and needs removing. Shoes belong on people's feet or in a shoe stand, but not on the kitchen bench or dining table. Food is not dirty, but it becomes so if it is dribbled on someone's clothing. Swimming costumes can be skimpily worn on the beach: but equivalent underwear is inappropriate for clothing on the street. Dirt/pollution is the by-product of a system of ordering and classifying matter and behavior: social control therefore involves rejecting and dealing with inappropriate, or polluting, elements.[8]

Concerns around social structure, control, and borders are expressed particularly through purity restrictions. Purity is a powerful organizing paradigm in societies around the world, which provides a way of guarding the corporate body and its values. Pollution is what confuses or contradicts our patterns of classification. Matter out of place (dirt) or disorder (social disruption) is perceived as putting the body corporate at risk. Here the relationship between the individual body and the body corporate means that the body boundaries can represent external boundaries that are insecure or at risk: social danger is reproduced in rituals or restrictions around body boundaries and the substances extruded from them. Margins are places of danger where the risk of boundary crossing may occur.

> All margins are dangerous . . . Any structure of ideas is vulnerable at its margins. We should expect the orifices of the body to symbolize its specially vulnerable points. Matter issuing from them is marginal stuff of the most obvious kind. Spittle, blood, milk, urine, faeces or tears by simply issuing forth have traversed the boundary of the body. So also have bodily parings, skin, nail, hair clippings and sweat.[9]

Because female life experience is often involved with perceived sources of pollution (e.g., menstruation, caring for sick relatives) the danger zones or boundaries for community defilement can be associated more with women.

Understandings of purity and pollution are intimately connected to holiness and defilement. "To be holy is to be whole, to be one; holiness is unity, integrity, perfection of the individual and of the kind." Reflecting on the laws of cleanness and uncleanness in Leviticus, Douglas suggests that "holiness is exemplified by completeness. Holiness requires that individuals shall conform to the class to which they belong. And holiness requires that different classes of things shall not be confused . . . Holiness means keeping

---

8. Douglas, *Purity and Danger*, 36–37.
9. Douglas, *Purity and Danger*, 116, 122.

distinct the categories of creation. It therefore involves correct definition, discrimination and order."[10] This understanding of purity and holiness undergirded the system of sacrifice and access to deity in New Testament times within both the Greco-Roman and Jewish worlds. Only those who were pure and whole could be close to God. As David deSilva describes, "most sources of defilement or pollution, moreover, stem from some condition that betrays the unwholeness of a person or creature (skin diseases, bodily discharges, corpses), and it is essential to contain and eliminate pollution before entering the presence of the divine."[11]

Purity restrictions have an important role in defining group boundaries and also the order, including hierarchy and structures, within a community. They help to maintain group ethos and morality. The boundary lines of clean and unclean enable the individual to know her or his place within the cosmic order, together with appropriate behavior in relation to divinity and to other community members.

These two dimensions of relationship are evident in a little-discussed distinction within the Levitical rules of purity. This divide is between the food laws of Leviticus 11:1–23, and the following purity guidelines from Leviticus 11:24—15:32, which deal with conditions or substances that render the worshipper unclean.[12] The intriguing difference between the food laws and other purity regulations is that for the former, there is no process offered for purification. Food laws were primarily about horizontal/*communal* relations. Like circumcision, they served to maintain the distinction or boundary between the nation of Israel and the surrounding nations. The following purity regulations in Leviticus, which include detailed processes for purification when defilement was incurred, concern the vertical/*celestial* relationship between the worshipper(s) and God. The arguments around purity that occupy a prominent place in the gospel accounts and the Pauline letters are primarily around the 'horizontal' regulations: food laws and circumcision. These are the laws that maintained the separation between Jews and Gentiles, which was overcome in Jesus Messiah's reconciling work on the cross (Eph 2:11–22).[13]

---

10. Douglas, *Purity and Danger*, 54–5.

11. deSilva, *Honor, Patronage*, 248.

12. These include corpses (Leviticus 11, also Numbers 11:19–22), childbirth (Leviticus 12), skin eruptions (Leviticus 13), spreading mold in clothing or house walls (Leviticus 13, 14), penile discharge and sexual intercourse, and menstruation or other vaginal bleeding (Leviticus 15).

13. See Dale, "Ritual Purity," for further discussion.

IV. Pollution Defined, Controlled—and Gendered?

There are five categories of sources of pollution that occur across most societies. They are:

a. Defilement (body fluids)
b. Depravity (moral pollution)
c. Disfigurement
d. Disease
e. Death

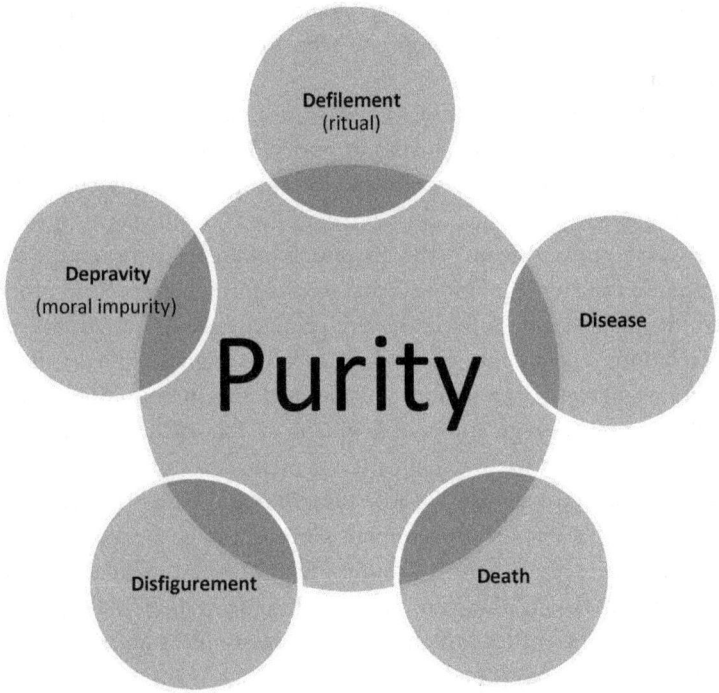

Communities have their own definitions of pollution within these groupings, with social mechanisms to control pollution or restore purity. In exploring these categories, we see that often the source of pollution and means of control find particular focus in the female body.

In the Bible we see these categories reflected, and also challenged and inverted through the revelation, life, death, and resurrection of Jesus Messiah.

A. Defilement

Ritual defilement is most often caused by body substances outside the boundary of the body. It is "matter out of place" that was in or attached to the body and is now outside. To understand this category, we may think of the substances where, having touched them, we cannot think of doing anything until we have washed our hands—and even then, we don't feel really clean. When I ask a group for examples, the discussion typically elicits body substances such as nasal mucus, blood (and in particular, menstrual blood), vomit, sexual fluids, urine, and fecal matter.[14]

Ritual defilement is more often associated with the female body. In Islam, the category of major defilement, which requires complete body washing to regain purity, includes menstrual flow, emission of sexual fluid, sexual intercourse, childbirth, and post-birth bleeding.[15] The unclean individual is prohibited from performing the required daily prayers, from fasting, from holding or reading the Qur'an, and from circumambulating the sacred *Kaaba* stone at Mecca as part of the prescribed pilgrimage. Notably, four fifths of the conditions of major defilement apply to women, and only two fifths to men. Hence, we may estimate that for at the very least a quarter of their lives between about thirteen and sixty years of age (menarche to menopause), Muslim women are in a state of ritual pollution, and thus proscribed from participating in pious duties just described. And that is for women who are not engaged at all in sexual relations or childcare. The daily activities of caring for young children involve contact with defiling substances.[16] Marjo Buitelaar notes that although "this only means that women are more often impure but certainly not inherently more impure than men, in practice women tend to be more strongly associated with impurity than men."[17]

---

14. While excrement is not included in the Levitical list of substances that make the individual unclean, it finds spatial expression in Deuteronomy 23:12–14, which specifies that excrement must be expelled and buried outside the camp because the camp is holy.

15. Minor defilement is incurred through any solids, liquids, or gas leaving body boundaries, or through sleep or unconsciousness.

16. The urine of a male child is also less impure than that of a female child; defilement is further gender-specific. Gauvain, "Ritual Rewards," 354, n. 68.

17. Buitelaar, "Space," 542.

Menstrual fluids in particular are linked with pollution or danger across many cultures.[18] Traditionally, Hindu women are barred from entering temples to offer prayer when they are menstruating. The tradition of using menstrual huts to confine women during menstruation extends over diverse geographical regions, including the Dogon people in West Africa, the Haualu of Indonesia, and tribes in the Highlands of Papua New Guinea, with parts of India and Nepal.[19] Within Christianity today, in many Eastern churches menstruating women may not take communion or enter behind the iconostasis. Kristin De Troyer et al. discuss issues of bleeding and purity for women in Jewish and Christian traditions; and Diamant's compelling narrative of Dinah's story deals with defilement and fertility in the context of the Genesis records.[20] In the Western New Age movement, some of the promoted treatments such as "steaming the vagina" link back to old ideas of the uterus as unclean and women as "dirty" inside.[21]

B. Depravity

Moral depravity is attributed to those breaking a society's ethical code. Transgressions occur across society, attracting the punishment deemed appropriate within the community. In this dimension, particularly around sexual impurity, it is helpful to ask to whom shame is ascribed most in different communities and social groups.

In sexual misdemeanors, the female typically carries more shame or blame.[22] This has also been true of rape, where the victim may be cross-examined about her clothes or sexual habits, rather than the perpetrator,[23] and in domestic violence ("What did you do to provoke him?"). In divorce, the woman may carry the associated stigma more than the man, regardless of responsibility for the breakdown of relationship. Some societies still consider the wife responsible for childlessness, rather than admitting the possibility of a husband's contribution, such as male infertility.

18. Dale, "Women's Shame 3."

19. For example, Ratcliffe, "Young Woman Dies"; Preiss, "Ban the Menstrual Shed."

20. Crumbley, "Patriarchies, Prophets, and Procreation," 584–606; De Troyer, *Wholly Woman*; Diamant, *The Red Tent*.

21. Wiseman, "Jennifer Gunter."

22. See also Dale, "Women's Shame 1" and "Women's Shame 2."

23. Is this the reason that some commentators prefer to ascribe blame to Bathsheba for David's actions? While they might question the power imbalance between a woman and the king, the Bible is clear in attributing responsibility to David (2 Sam 12:1–14, 1 Kgs 15:5, Matt 1:6).

Around the world, women are made to carry the responsibility for men's desire or violent actions. This is used to justify some of the required rules of women's covering in different cultures. In the West also, by preferring language that describes a woman as "hot" rather than talking about his own sexual desires, the man is placing the locus of control within the woman's body, thus absolving him of responsibility for his sexual feelings, making her responsible, so that it is "her fault" if he gets turned on—or if he doesn't.

The embodiment of shame in women has consequences in communal cultures, where extended family honor rests precariously on what happens to women's bodies. The proverb that "the honor of a man lies between the legs of a woman" is quoted in the Middle East, Central Asia, and also Latin America.[24] When family honor is compromised by violence against a woman, it can then be restored by killing the woman. It is estimated that 5–6,000 women die annually in so-called "honor killings."[25] Another consequence is what can be termed "honor rapes," where a woman's rape is used as a weapon to disgrace the victim's family, clan, or nation. Militias in many countries have recognized that the most effective way to terrorize a civilian population is to commit brutally savage rapes. Rape, formally recognized as a "weapon of war" by the United Nations in 2008, is now so widely used that one army commander suggests "it has probably become more dangerous to be a woman than a soldier in an armed conflict."[26]

This understanding of family/national shame embodied in women finds an important counter-narrative in the book of Judges, which instead measures the descent into dishonor of a nation in part by its (mis)treatment of women.

C. Disfigurement

Discussing the link between wholeness and holiness, David deSilva describes how:

> Defilement and unwholeness separated people from contact with the pure and whole God. Thus the blemished and deformed persons are barred from access to the sanctuary, since it would affront holiness to be presented with unwholeness. The blemished or deformed animal is likewise barred from sacrifice,

---

24. Hudson, *Sex and World Peace*, 8.

25. Kristor and WuDunn, *Half the Sky*, 82. They suggest that many of the executions are disguised as accidents or suicides.

26. Kristor and WuDunn, *Half the Sky*, 84.

since such unwholeness would provoke rather than please the holy deity.[27]

This is exemplified in the Old Testament lists of those who were forbidden proximity to God's altar or entry to the Temple. They included the blind, lame, disfigured, deformed, the hunchbacked and dwarfs, those with defective eyes, skin sores or scabs, and eunuchs (Lev 21:18–20).[28]

Many communities control this dimension of perceived "impurity" through isolation. Those categorized as "disfigured" or "deformed" may have restricted access to places of worship or other community gatherings. In societies around the world, family members can be hidden away if they are perceived to have a form of mental or physical impairment.

"Wholeness" is also defined by community definitions of what a body should look like. This is often linked to ideal body types—particularly for women. This aspect of wholeness finds control through body modification or mutilation. Female Genital Mutilation is found through parts of sub-Saharan Africa, the Middle East, and Asia, and is associated with concepts of purity. Another form of body mutilation was the custom of foot-binding in China, where girls' feet were bound so tightly that they became misshapen and damaged, making it almost impossible for the women to walk. This was tied to an ideal of feminine beauty demonstrated by small feet.[29] The link between women's feet and freedom of movement is similarly evident in the edict from the medieval Egyptian Caliph al-Hakim bi-Amr Allah, which restricted women from leaving their homes; he enforced it by forbidding cobblers to make women's shoes.[30] In a more contemporary context, how many Western women have limped home blistered and footsore after an evening in "fashionable" shoes? Other modifications in pursuit of the ideal body type include corsets, where women could be laced so tightly that it was difficult for them to breathe. Many body modifications said to be in the quest of female beauty have the real impact of limiting women's movement or experience. This is the difference between FGM and male circumcision: the former limits female experience in the sexual encounter. Other female body ideals have led

---

27. deSilva, *Honor, Patronage*, 248.

28. For the latter category, see also Deut 31:1.

29. It has also been linked to keeping girls sitting at looms to weave textiles (Reuell, "Economics of Foot-Binding").

30. Mernissi, viewing the disruptions of the Gulf War, asks about the impact on women's movements: "Traditionally women were the designated victims of the rituals for re-establishing equilibrium. As soon as the city showed signs of disorder, the caliph ordered women to stay at home. Will it be we, the women living in the Muslim city, who will pay the price . . . ?" (*Islam and Democracy*, 9). Her question recalls the experience of many women post-World War I in the West.

to women pursuing super-thin bodies, emulating airbrushed photographic models that leave girls feeling ashamed of their own bodies; or alternatively, breast implants, with all the consequent health risks.

The other side of body modification in pursuit of the ideal female body type is the use of disfiguration and deformity to punish women. This is exemplified in throwing acid in women's faces or cutting off lips or noses.

Self-administered means of body modification include hair-removal, tattoos, and piercings. Notably, those who are socially powerless seek a way of control through their own body, through asceticism, anorexia, bulimia, or cutting.

The dimension of disfigurement is complex, including socially-enforced or self-administered ways of body modification or mutilation, which can find particular focus across societies around the bodies of women.

D. Disease

Both the disease and the sufferer may be viewed in some sense as "unclean." People with diseases associated with ritual impurity (usually skin diseases) are commonly described as "cleansed" rather than "healed" in Biblical accounts. Contagious diseases today are similarly viewed as making the patient in some sense "unclean" and needing to be isolated. Contemporary Western societies seek control over disease through eradicating germs as far as possible.[31] Lifestyle becomes another form of control: through eating the right food or having the right sleep patterns, one may become more immune. Conversely those who have the "wrong" lifestyles can be stigmatized: a recent article discusses how "clean eating became an excuse to judge 'bad' people."[32]

As a non-smoker with lung cancer, I am familiar with the inclination of people to blame the patient for the disease. It is not only lung cancer: people with other forms of cancer have told me of being interrogated about their eating habits and lifestyle, with the implication that they brought it on themselves. Blaming the victim is an effort to protect the other—if it can be tied to smoking or eating or lifestyle, maybe others can somehow avoid contracting cancer.

Cancer itself is due to cell growth that is so rapid it becomes abnormal. In Genesis, fertility is both gift and commandment of God, exemplified in the term to swarm, or teem (*sh-r-tz*, שרץ) (Gen 1:20, 21; and again

---

31. There is some discussion whether overprotection from germs can make the body more at risk when it does encounter germs, or more susceptible to allergies.

32. Blueprint for Living, "Pure Food."

in 9:7). Mary Douglas, reflecting on Leviticus 13 and 14, which describe an eruptive condition on skin or clothing or in a house, "each with the same tests and same periods of testing, and the same pronouncements," notes that the condition is also characterized by teeming fecundity, but here the "blossoming and erupting are morbid."[33] The description is an apt encapsulation of cancer: are there more parallels with "ritually impure" skin diseases than we realize?

E. Death

Dead bodies are breakers of the ultimate boundary, that between life and death. They are that which was alive and is now dead. Dead bodies, and also graveyards, are associated with pollution across many societies.[34]

People may seek some control of death through trying to protect themselves against it as long as possible. Western societies control death by hiding it. The occurrence of death is well concealed in society—how many people have never seen a dead body? Death is further camouflaged in the move to memorial services, where there is not even a coffin: the dead body of the person we mourn is not present.

Death is the one category which can never be conclusively controlled but comes to us all: to be in a body is eventually to die. As Judith Wright describes it poignantly and paradoxically, time pursues eternity, but flesh toils towards its termination.[35]

V. Meeting God

As women and men embodied in our physical, social context, how do we encounter God? Here we can turn to Jesus as both model of human embodiment and revelation of God embodied.

The story of Jesus' encounter with the woman of Samaria forms, alongside Jesus' conversation with Nicodemus, a prominent male-female pair in John's Gospel. The account is located in specific geography and history (the Samaritan village of Sychar, near the field that Jacob gave to his son Joseph), within the context of domestic duties (buying food, drawing water) and physical details of body state and position (Jesus was tired, sitting by the

---

33. Douglas, *Leviticus as Literature*, 191, 185. Douglas adds, "Nowhere does Leviticus say that the disease can be attributed to sin of the victim."

34. See Leviticus 11:24–28, 39–40; Numbers 19:11–20; and 1 Chronicles 22:7–8.

35. Wright, "The Morning of the Dead," 195.

well). The metaphor of living water is found in both Old and New Testament. But here it is drawn from the immediate context and experience of the woman to whom Jesus is talking, and she responds to it instinctively in terms of the place and history that surrounds them as they talk. Jesus continues the conversation to engage with the woman's own life and family experience. While deep theological issues are canvassed in the conversation—even including, unusually, Jesus' self-revelation as Messiah—the theological discussion of how to live and worship is earthed in the woman's daily life and immediate family relationships.

In Jesus, God reveals himself to humanity grounded in specific time, place, relationships—as carpenter and itinerant teacher, a Galilean member of a small occupied nation in a corner of the sprawling Roman Empire. We meet him in the context of his relationships with his mother, siblings, his own townsfolk, with religious leaders and the civil (occupying) authorities, in the political and social realities within which the Gospel narratives are brought to us. When we realize that all our knowledge is mediated through our own experiences, realities, through our own bodies, we are taken aback again at both the unexpectedness and also the inevitability of God and flesh meeting ultimately in the incarnation, where God calls us to know God.[36]

Thus, we meet God by meeting Jesus as God embodied, who restores holiness/wholeness in the individual body and body corporate.

First, the individual body is redeemed in Christ. God comes to us in Jesus, taking on human flesh, in specific history and space. God present in the incarnation is a denial of the dualism between body and spirit, for Jesus is fully present as both God and human. This denial of body-spirit dualism also challenges other good-evil dualisms such as mind-body, male-female.

Across cultures, menstrual and birth fluids are seen as dangerous and defiling. Yet Jesus took human form in a woman's womb. Woman's body, with all the ritual uncleanness of menstrual fertility and birth, is made the vehicle of God's incarnation—*theotokos*. Through God's inhabiting, women's bodies are made holy and honored forever.

Jesus redeems us by taking our place at the cross in his own body, stripped naked and exposed, broken and deformed, bodily pierced/invaded (nails and spear), uncontrolled (thirst, hunger, loss of bodily functions).

---

36. All knowing is situated. Esther Lightcap Meek suggests that we think of knower and known as in relationship, where knowing is the relationship. "To know is to love; to love will be to know." (Meek, *A Little Manual*, 5: and *Loving To Know*, Loc 874.) This situated interconnected view of knowledge recalls the relational dimensions and use of the Hebrew word "to know" (*ydʿ*, ידע), encompassing knowing or being acquainted with something or someone, through to the intimacy of sexual relationship.

God's power is revealed in impotence.[37] Through the very pollution of his spilt blood and death, he brings cleansing and wholeness.

Across religions, defilement is contagious. In Jesus it is reversed, and purity becomes contagious. Dead bodies come back to life, lepers are cleaned, unclean spirits are cast out. Jesus meets each one of us and purifies our unwholeness, unholiness, through his own contagious purity, and so restores us to society.

Second, the corporate body is redeemed in Christ. Those who are considered polluted are restored to society. Jesus does not collude with the hiddenness of shame, but brings public vindication, forgiveness (when needed), allowing the communal restoration of relationships and status.[38]

Jesus breaks down social barriers and divisions, redefining and inverting social classifications as presaged in Mary's song.[39] In his teaching, Jesus takes the woman, the child, the unclean outsider, as exemplar disciples.[40] On the cross in his own flesh, he broke down the walls of communal boundaries that divided us.[41]

Finally, the final defilement of death is defeated in Christ. As God embodied and resurrected, Jesus invites us now to become children of God who are born of Spirit, so that we are not bounded finally by the death of our bodies, but destined to live in resurrection bodies in eternal life with the Triune God.

Conclusion

To be human—to know this world, one another, God—is to be grounded in our physical existence. We encounter the world and God in our bodies. Communal relationships in the body corporate become mapped onto our individual bodies; our physical and social bodies reciprocally map how we make meaning of the world. Relationships, horizontal and vertical, or human and celestial, are defined through prescriptions of purity and defilement. As we have seen, requirements of bodily control reflect rules of social control. Each community has rules of purity and pollution, where dirt or disorder incur social danger. The sources of pollution we have explored include ritual defilement, moral depravity, disfigurement, disease, and death. The first three categories find particular embodiment in

---

37. Wilson, *Unmanly Men*, 262–3.
38. Matt 8:1–4; 9:20–22; Luke 7:36–50; 19:1–9; John 8:1–8.
39. Luke 1:51–53.
40. Luke 21:1–4; 18:15–17; 10:25–42; 11:29–32.
41. Eph 2:14–18.

women: defilement is more associated with women's bodily fluids; women carry community shame; and disfigurement can be linked to ideal body shapes for women, and to control.

We meet Jesus as God embodied, who restores us, individually and corporately, to wholeness and purity. Jesus takes on our humanity, our physicality, and in doing so calls us all to wholeness, both women and men, reordering pervasive social categories of purity and defilement (whether underlying or overt), and inviting us into at-one-ment with each other and God.

Bibliography

Alter, Robert. *The Hebrew Bible: A Translation with Commentary*. 1st ed. New York: Norton, 2018.

Blueprint for Living. "Pure Food and the Magic Pill: How Clean Eating Became an Excuse to Judge 'Bad' People." *ABC News*. July 14, 2018. https://www.abc.net.au/news/2018-07-14/clean-eating-food-purity-and-the-quest-for-a-magic-pill/9985506.

Bowie, Fiona. *The Anthropology of Religion*. Oxford: Blackwell, 2000.

Buitelaar, Marjo. "Space: Hammam—Overview." In *Encyclopedia of Women & Islamic Cultures*, 4:541–43. Leiden: Brill, 2007.

Crumbley, Deidre Helen. "Patriarchies, Prophets, and Procreation: Sources of Gender Practices in Three African Churches." *Africa* 73/4 (2003) 584–606.

Dale, Moyra. "Ritual Purity and Defilement: What Place Does It Have?" *When Women Speak . . . Webzine* 2/1 (2018) 35–66.

———. "Women's Shame 1." *When Women Speak . . .* Blog post. May 28, 2017. https://whenwomenspeak.net/blog/womens-shame-1/.

———. "Women's Shame 2." *When Women Speak . . .* Blog post. November 6, 2017. https://whenwomenspeak.net/blog/womens-shame-2/.

———. "Women's Shame 3." *When Women Speak . . .* Blog post. June 25, 2017. https://whenwomenspeak.net/blog/womens-shame-3/.

Dale, Moyra, Cathy Hine, and Carol Walker, eds. *When Women Speak . . .* Oxford: Regnum, 2018.

De Troyer, Kristin, et al. *Wholly Woman, Holy Blood: A Feminist Critique of Purity and Impurity*. Harrisburg, PA: Trinity, 2003.

deSilva, David A. *Honor, Patronage, Kinship and Purity. Unlocking the New Testament Culture*. Downers Grove, IL: IVP Academic, 2000.

Diamant, Anita. *The Red Tent*. Crows Nest, Australia: Allen & Unwin, 1998.

Douglas, Mary. *Leviticus as Literature*. Oxford: OUP, 1999.

———. *Natural Symbols: Explorations in Cosmology*. 2nd edition. London: Routledge Classics, 1996.

———. *Purity and Danger. An Analysis of the Concepts of Pollution and Taboo*. London: Routledge, 1966.

Gauvain, Richard. "Ritual Rewards: A Consideration of Three Recent Approaches to Sunni Purity Law." *Islamic Law and Society* 12/3 (2005) 333–93.

Hudson, Valerie, Bonnie Ballif-Spanvill, Mary Capriolo, and Chad Emmett. *Sex and World Peace*. Columbia University Press, 2012.

Kristor, Nicholas D., and Sheryl WuDunn. *Half the Sky. Turning Oppression into Opportunity for Women Worldwide*. New York: Alfred A. Knopf, 2010.

Mauss, Marcel. "Techniques of the Body." *Economy and Society* 2/1 (1973) 70–88.

Meek, Esther Lightcap. *A Little Manual for Knowing*. Eugene, Oregon: Cascade, 2014.

———. *Loving To Know. Covenant Epistemology*. Eugene, Oregon: Cascade, 2011.

Mernissi, Fatima. *Islam and Democracy. Fear of the Modern World*. Translated by Mary Jo Lakeland. Lakeland, Massachusetts: Addison-Wesley, 1992.

Palmer, Parker J. *To Know as We Are Known*. Reprint edition. San Francisco: HarperCollins Religious-US, 1993.

Preiss, Danielle. "Why It's Hard to Ban the Menstrual Shed." *Goats and Soda Newsletter, Heard on National Public Radio*. May 13, 2019. https://www.npr.org/sections/goatsandsoda/2019/05/13/721450261/why-its-so-hard-to-stop-women-from-sleeping-in-a-menstrual-shed.

Ratcliffe, Rebecca. "Young Woman Dies in Fourth 'Period Hut' Tragedy This Year in Nepal." *The Guardian*. June 2, 2019. https://www.theguardian.com/global-development/2019/feb/06/young-woman-dies-fourth-period-hut-tragedy-this-year-nepal.

Reuell, Peter. "Uncovering the Economics of Foot-Binding." *The Harvard Gazette*, October 19, 2018. https://news.harvard.edu/gazette/story/2018/10/study-foot-binding-was-driven-by-economics-not-sex-and-beauty/.

Smith, Dorothy E. *The Conceptual Practices of Power. A Feminist Sociology of Knowledge*. Boston: Northeastern University Press, 1990.

Wilson, Brittany E. *Unmanly Men: Refigurations of Masculinity in Luke-Acts*. Oxford, New York: Oxford University Press, 2015.

Wiseman, Eva. "Jennifer Gunter: 'Women Are Being Told Lies about Their Bodies.'" *The Guardian*. August 9, 2019. https://www.theguardian.com/lifeandstyle/2019/sep/08/jennifer-gunter-gynaecologist-womens-health-bodies-myths-and-medicine.

Wright, Judith. *Collected Poems*. Sydney: HarperCollins, 1994.

Part II

Old Testament Explorations

6

The Transformation of Israel's Social Identity in the Book of Exodus

Katherine M. Smith

Within the narrative context of the Pentateuch, the book of Exodus focuses upon the formation of Israel as a nation under the kingship of YHWH. The events that form Israel into a nation within Exodus transform Israel's social identity. These events are the new reference point by which Israel is to define itself and the social group to which the individual Israelite belongs. Social order is maintained when the Israelites have a positive view of their transformed social identity, but disorder threatens this social order when Israel rejects a part, or the whole.

In this chapter, I will trace the transformation of Israel's social identity and its implications for the covenant nation as depicted in the book of Exodus through the lens of social identity theory. I will explore how the covenant nation is grounded—or, conversely, becomes ungrounded—in direct relationship to their attitude towards their transformed social identity as "a people belonging to YHWH" and to YHWH's presence among them. I will then offer some brief observations on how the evangelical church in Australia seeks to ground itself and how this exploration of Exodus may provide timely correctives for us within an Australian secular culture.

Central to social identity is the observation that when individuals are placed in situations where there is interaction between groups, individuals will act as members of their group and so align their behavior towards their group's patterns, values, and characteristics.¹ Thus, a social group can "define the individual's place in society." Turner and Tajfel observe:

> Social groups understood in this sense provide their members with an identification of themselves in social terms. In this theory, social identity is defined as "those aspects of an individual's self-image that derive from the social categories to which he perceives himself as belonging."²

Social identity theory is an intriguing lens through which to view Exodus's narrative, because the perspective of the narrative from the beginning establishes the Israelites as a distinctive "in-group" set within the wider context of an "out-group" (i.e., the Egyptians). The narrative is shaped by conflict between these two groups, revealing that central to God's purpose in rescuing is the intent to form and transform Israel's identity within a global context.

Exodus 1–2: A People Belonging to Pharaoh and Social Identity

The prologue to the book of Exodus (Exod 1:1–7) focuses upon the familial relationship of those who came to Egypt with Jacob, namely his eleven sons and their households.³ The rhetoric of the prologue accentuates how this family group continued to thrive beyond the first generation who came to Egypt as resident foreigners. In this context, the first use of the phrase "sons of Israel" in v. 1a precedes the list naming the eleven sons of Israel and purposefully uses the name "Israel," rather than "Jacob," to remind the hearer of Jacob's covenant name from Genesis 32.⁴ In this first instance, "the sons of Israel" refers specifically to Jacob's eleven sons who came to Egypt with him.⁵ In the second instance in v. 7a, however, the use of the same expression "sons of Israel" refers to the future generations of Jacob's family group

---

1. Tajfel and Turner, "Social Identity Theory," 281–83.
2. Tajfel and Turner, "Social Identity Theory," 283.
3. All English translation provided in this chapter are the author's translation of the Hebrew text. The choice to translate, rather than providing the Hebrew text, is to enable a greater accessibility for a broader range of readers.
4. Contrary to Sarna, *Exodus*, 3, who views this use of the name Israel as referring to "national identity."
5. In this chapter, I use gender exclusive language such as "sons of Israel" when the Hebrew text does so as to maintain a close reading to the Hebrew text. Propp, *Exodus 1–18*, 129, notes the inclusive use of the term "sons" and the text's preference for masculine language is due to "Israelite identity descend[ing] through the male line."

that flourished in Egypt beyond the death of this first generation.[6] The repetition of the phrase "sons of Israel" suggests that their social identity is derived from belonging to this family group, which in turn brings social cohesion to the Israelites as a people in a foreign land.

Within the first scene of the Exodus narrative (1:8–22), the new Egyptian king, who has no relational ties of loyalty to this family group (v. 8), strategizes to control the Israelites because he fears that their growth would upset the power dynamic in the land (vv. 9–10). As the Egyptian king invites his people to observe the Israelites, he describes the flourishing people group as "the people of the sons of Israel" (v. 9), which is significant in this context for two reasons. From a rhetorical perspective, the Egyptian king's use of the term "people" places the Israelites as having the same power status as "his people," that is, the Egyptian people. By clearly distinguishing the two groups, "his people" and the "people of the sons of Israel," the speech is seeking to introduce inter-group conflict where the Egyptians must act "wisely" for the sake of their own self-preservation.[7] Second, the description being spoken by the Egyptian king reinforces the group's primary identification marker as being descended from the sons of Israel, that is, from the eleven sons of Jacob who came to Egypt (1:1–7).[8]

As the king's strategies are enacted in 1:11–22, the Egyptians conscript the Israelites against their will, and so the power dynamic changes between the two distinct people groups (v. 11). The Israelites who once enjoyed favor and hospitality in Egypt are now forced into Pharaoh's service as slaves with great cruelty (vv. 13–14). Curiously, the text repeats that the Israelites were enslaved and how they were oppressed—with cruelty—but the status of this family group as now belonging to the Egyptian king as they build storehouses for him is implied, never stated explicitly. As the Israelites' social status as resident foreigners changes, their social identity as a people descended from Israel, as being Hebrews, is reinforced. This is evident in 2:12–15 where, although there was initial interpersonal conflict between the two Hebrew men, this conflict was redirected when Moses intervened (v. 13).[9] There was immediate cohesion between the two Israelite

---

6. See also Stuart, *Exodus*, 58, for the view that the first use of "the sons of Israel" in v. 1 refers specifically to the eleven sons listed in vv. 1–4, while the reference in v. 7 takes "its usual post-Genesis meaning," which is the people group that will become the nation. Also, Bruckner, *Exodus*, 19; Dozeman, *Exodus*, 63; Houtman, *Exodus Volume 1*, 110; Stargel, *Construction of Exodus Identity*, 1406.

7. See also Alexander, *Exodus*, 44; Stargel, *Construction of Exodus Identity*, 1582.

8. See also Kürle, *Appeal of Exodus*, 208.

9. See also Houtman, *Exodus Volume 1*, 302. Contrary to Dozeman, *Exodus*, 87, vv. 13–14 suggests that both Israelite men are still alive after Moses intervened in the

men when confronted with Moses who is, in their eyes, an Egyptian.[10] Although Moses may view his social identity as being one of the Hebrews, he is not accepted as being an Israelite but is associated with being Egyptian. Thus, the intergroup conflict between the Egyptians and Israelites overrides, for the two Hebrew men, their own interpersonal conflict.

Exodus 2:23–25 forms a bridging transition between the Israelite plight in Exodus 1–2 and its resolution in Exodus 3–18. Within this bridging summary, the narrator relates that the "sons of Israel" finally cry out from their slavery (v. 23). However, there is no indirect object suggesting that they are crying out towards God, only that their cries rise up to the place that God is residing and that he heard, he remembered the covenant, he saw, and that he knew (vv. 24–25).[11] After the prominent use of the name YHWH throughout Genesis 12–50, the absence of this same name from Exodus 1–2 is conspicuous given the continuity emphasized between the Genesis narrative and that of Exodus in its beginning (1:1–7). Within the eight times (1:17, 1:20a, 1:21a, 2:23e, 2:24a, 2:24b, 2:25a, 2:25b) that the narrator refers to God in Exodus 1–2, the text only uses the title *hā ʾĕlōhîm* (or *ʾĕlōhîm*). Furthermore, while the patriarchal covenant is finally recalled explicitly in 2:24, at no point in Exodus 1–2 does God take ownership of the Israelites as his people. Their identity is depicted predominantly as being "a people of the sons of Israel" and so their social cohesion, as depicted in Exodus 1–2, is still based primarily on their shared family heritage and, as the narrative develops, being resident foreigners oppressed by Egyptian power.

Exodus 3–18: A People Belonging to YHWH and a Transformed Social Identity

One of the great ironies of Exodus is that God is motivated to contend on behalf of the Israelites and battle against Egypt, which results in the Israelites leaving (Exodus 3–18), because of the very strategies purposed by the Egyptian king to constrain the Israelites to Egypt within Exodus 1–2. This irony is also one of the great reversals within the Exodus narrative. This great reversal is previewed first in 3:1—4:26, and it is not a coincidence that within this immediate context, the text suddenly uses God's personal name, YHWH, when he first appears to and reveals his identity to Moses.[12] In

---

conflict, rather than Moses contending with only the guilty Israelite.

10. See also Dozeman, *Exodus*, 88; contrary to Propp, *Exodus 1–18*, 167–68.

11. See also Brueggemann, "Exodus," 706; Dozeman, *Exodus*, 93; Houtman, *Exodus Volume 1*, 329.

12. See also Schmid, *Genesis and the Moses Story*, 179.

3:2–5 in particular, the name YHWH is related to divine presence as God restricts Moses stepping further onto the ground sanctified by his presence. In 3:7–10, the divine presence announces his identity in 3:6b as the God of "your fathers," preceding the divine speech in 3:7–10 where YHWH announces his intent to rescue the Israelites.

Again, it is not coincidental that the name YHWH first emerges in the Exodus narrative in the context where he describes the Israelites for the first time as "my people" (v. 7b), and where he announces his intent to rescue them (v. 8). Where v. 7 notes first that YHWH has seen the plight of his people and second that he has heard their cries, v. 9 parallels v. 7, but reverses the focus: first noting the cries of the "sons of Israel" coming to YHWH and second that he has seen their oppression.[13] These parallel lines in v. 7 and v. 9 connect the identity that YHWH now gives to the Israelites—"my people"—with their familial identity "the sons of Israel."

This relationship between the Israelites as a people belonging to YHWH and their family identity is then repeated again in 3:10 as God commands Moses to go to Pharaoh and to bring "my people, the sons of Israel out from Egypt." Thus, from the first preview of the exodus event that will play out in Exodus 5–14, it is evident that this great reversal will transform their social identity; no longer a family group enslaved by Egypt, their transformed social identity is a people belonging to YHWH.[14]

While the exodus event, both its hope (Exodus 3–12) and its realization (Exodus 13–15), is the vital experience that will bring cohesion to the Israelite people as a nation belonging to YHWH, there is a second reversal anticipated too. As noted previously, the name YHWH is absent from Exodus 1–2, and the only point within Exodus 1:1–2:22 where God's activity is explicitly commented upon is where he acts in favor to the two midwives who fear him rather than fearing Pharaoh and his command (1:15–21). Suspending the use of God's name, and the avoidance of explicitly attributing the Israelites' numerical growth to his work, has the rhetorical effect of distancing God from the events unravelling in Egypt within 1:1—2:22 until the time at which he chooses to intervene (i.e., Exodus 3 onwards).

This distance is further evinced in 2:23 where the cries of the Israelites need *to go up* to God, which is the turning point for the sequence of actions where God heard, remembered, saw, and knew (2:24). For this reason, YHWH breaking his silence in Exodus 3:1–10 is significant, and so too is his declaration that he will overcome the distance between himself and the

---

13. See also Alexander, *Exodus*, 85.

14. Stargel, *Construction of Exodus Identity*, 1307, states, "the primary exodus story ultimately constructs the ingroup 'as the people whom God brought up out of Egypt'" but does not connect this observation with their people group identity as Israelites.

Israelites in 3:8. Reactivating the action sequence from 2:23–24, the repetition that God has seen and heard at the beginning of the YHWH's direct speech to Moses in 3:7 highlights that God is now very much active. The direct consequence of YHWH having seen, heard, and known the Israelites' sufferings in 3:7 is that he *has* come down with the purpose of effecting the major reversal—rescuing the Israelites from slavery (3:8).[15]

This first mention of God being present with and contending for the Israelites is further developed throughout 3:12–22, where YHWH affirms that his presence is with Moses as he uses him as his agent to rescue the Israelites and to battle against Pharaoh. This theme is then accentuated later in 13:17–22, where God is said to be the one leading the Israelites (v. 18) with his presence visibly in front of the people—never departing (vv. 21–22). While YHWH's work of rescuing the Israelites from Egypt is the experience that will bring cohesion to the Israelites as a people who now belong to YHWH, it is God's presence with his people that provides groundedness, stability, and certainty.

This stability and groundedness is sustained when the Israelites have a positive view of their transformed social identity. For instance, when the Israelites saw YHWH's victory over the Egyptians in Exodus 14, their response was fear and belief in YHWH and Moses (14:31). This positive alignment is given further expression in the thanksgiving song in 15:1–18, which attributes unparalleled sovereignty and majesty to YHWH, acknowledging his work in rescuing the Israelites from Egypt.

Conflict occurs, however, which threatens this stability, when the people distort a key belief central to their transformed social identity. Only three days after expressing their positive alignment to YHWH and Moses, Israel's grumblings begin when water is scarce in the wilderness of Shur and then, upon finding water, it is bitter (15:22–25). Notably, in this first instance, the Israelites do not question the exodus event. However, their second grumbling in 16:1–3 is expressed as a desire to have died in Egypt, where they had access to abundant food. Their complaint attributes their hardship in Egypt to YHWH's hand rather than the Egyptian king's and also blames Moses for bringing the people into the wilderness to die.[16] By distorting their memory of their oppression in Egypt and attributing wrong motive to both YHWH and Moses, they express a negative view of their transformed social identity.[17] In turn, this causes conflict between the people, Moses,

---

15. See Alexander, *Exodus*, 86; Bruggemann, *Exodus*, 712–13.

16. See also Childs, *Exodus*, 285; Fretheim, *Exodus*, 181; Hamilton, *Exodus*, 250–51. This is a different understanding of the Israelite's complaint in comparison with Alexander, *Exodus*, 322.

17. See also Kürle, *Appeal of Exodus*, 219–20.

and YHWH. The tension is resolved solely by YHWH's abundant provision of manna and quail, and eventually when Israel learns to hear and obey God's voice (16:4–36). YHWH's listening to Israel's complaint in Exodus 16 preserves relational order.

Similarly, in 17:1–3, the Israelites articulate their grumbling again through an interrogative question against Moses, asking why he brought them out of Egypt to kill their households with thirst. Once more, their complaint suggests a negative view of their transformed social identity as they attribute wrong motive to Moses and YHWH. Again, this conflict is relieved by YHWH providing water (17:5–7). Significantly, though, the narrator presents the problem of their grumbling in 17:1–7 as a questioning of YHWH's presence among them (v. 7). Alexander notes the significance of this question: "The whole movement within the book of Exodus is towards God constantly in the midst of his people. To ask the question 'Is YHWH among us or not?' runs counter to all that God is seeking to achieve by bringing the Israelites out of Egypt."[18] Where there is doubt about whether YHWH is present and contending for them, Israel tends towards a negative view of their social identity and so conflict arises.

Thus, where previously in Exodus 1–2 the Israelites' social identity as a people group was grounded in being descendants of Israel's sons, Exodus 3–18 marks a transformation in their social identity through two reversals; the first is YHWH bringing the Israelites out of slavery to become "his people" and second, YHWH overcoming distance between himself and "his people" so that his presence is with them. While the exodus event transforms how Israel defines who the people are, it is God's presence among the people that grounds the people as they move out from Egypt and journey towards Sinai. During this journey, the people's tendency towards a negative perception of their transformed social identity is evident when they question YHWH's and Moses' motive for the exodus event. This negative view leads to interpersonal conflict and rejection, which is resolved solely through YHWH hearing and providing life-sustaining provision to the Israelites.

Exodus 19–40: Implications of Israel's Transformed Social Identity

While Israel's social identity is transformed through the exodus event, their formation as a nation is not yet complete until Israel becomes YHWH's

---

18. Alexander, *Exodus*, 336.

covenant nation in Exodus 19–24.[19] In 19:4, YHWH describes how he brought the Israelites to himself, but 19:5 is equally clear that their formation as a nation is established by their agreement to be a covenant nation. Thus, an implication of Israel's transformed social identity is that covenant obedience is critical to sustain interpersonal social order between God and the people whom he treasures as his nation. To this, we can add a further two implications; first, Israel is formed into a nation whose function is to mediate God to the nations (i.e., "a holy priesthood").[20] Second, Israel will be sanctified by God's presence with his nation (i.e., "a holy nation," 19:6).[21] While the emphasis so far has been upon Israel being YHWH's people, a further implication of this transformed social identity is that YHWH also belongs to Israel as their God. Thus, their transformed social identity is intrinsically connected to YHWH being their God. The function of the Decalogue and the Book of the Covenant is to expound clearly these four implications of Israel's transformed social identity so that there can be positive alignment and interpersonal order preserved between the newly-formed nation and YHWH.

The preface to the Decalogue in 20:2 begins YHWH's self-declaration of his identity and relationship to Israel—"I am YHWH your God." This declaration of YHWH's relationship with Israel is then modified by the relative clause "who has brought you out from the land of Egypt, from the house of slavery." The Israelites are no longer a family group belonging to the Egyptian king; on the basis that YHWH has rescued the Israelites, they are now formed into a nation where YHWH is their covenant-king.[22] The principles of the Decalogue, both the commands and the prohibitions, clearly expound the implications of God's social identity as belonging to Israel and Israel's social identity as belonging YHWH. The Decalogue's logic progressing from the sustaining of relational order between Israel and himself (vv. 2–11), to relational order within the family household (v. 12), to relational order within the wider covenant community (vv. 13–17), accentuates that YHWH belonging to Israel and Israel belonging to YHWH now shapes relational order and what is considered relational disorder within the covenant community.

19. Contrary to Fretheim, *Exodus*, 208–9.

20. See also Alexander, *Exodus*, 367–68; Childs, *Exodus*, 367; Durham, *Exodus*, 263; Kürle, *Appeal of Exodus*, 232; Sarna, *Exodus*, 104.

21. I understand the two phrases "a kingdom of priests" and a "holy nation" to be distinct in meaning i.e., not synonymous. For a similar understanding of Israel being a "holy nation" as presented here, see Alexander, *Exodus*, 369–70. Contrary to Kürle, *Appeal of Exodus*, 229–31.

22. See also Dozeman, *Exodus*, 479–80; Durham, *Exodus*, 284.

The function of the following Book of the Covenant in 21:1—23:33 is to communicate concrete examples of relational order and disorder as the Decalogue is applied to everyday life within the covenant community.[23] Israel's responsibility to uphold relational order within the community is grounded in the nation's transformed social identity as being a covenant nation belonging to YHWH and whose presence is with, although now distant from, his people. Where these instructions explicitly use the memory of being rescued from slavery as the rationale for how they are to treat a resident foreigner in 23:9, the focus is upon ensuring that the Israelite nation offers hospitality rather than mirroring the actions of Egypt done to them (see also 23:9).[24] This is an essential part of sustaining social cohesion derived from their transformed social identity.

Once Israel's covenant obedience is affirmed and the relationship sealed through the blood rite and feast in Exodus 24, Exodus 25–31 focuses upon how the divine presence that provides stability for Israel's transformed social identity is now to be resident in the midst of his covenant nation. As soon as Israel arrived at Sinai, the divine presence that visibly led them to the mountain descended onto the mountain top, and so there has been spatial separation between divine presence and the people (see 19:7–25). In 25:1–9 however, YHWH's presence that was present but geographically separate is now intended to be present and in the midst of his covenant nation with the tabernacle separating divine presence from the camp.[25] The ensuing instruction in Exodus 25–31 that focuses upon the establishing of the tabernacle and the priesthood is intended to help Israel negotiate the holy presence that will now reside in their midst.

However, between the instructions in Exodus 25–31 and Israel's obedience to those instructions in Exodus 35–40, an event in 32:1–12 threatens the social cohesion and relational order essential to the covenant relationship, and thus to Israel's transformed social identity. By Aaron serving the desire of the Israelite people by creating a golden calf and attributing Israel's rescue from Egypt to this hand-made image, Israel rejects their transformed social identity by displacing the holy God to whom they belong with a hand-formed image of a calf. In contrast with their positive alignment in the victory song in Exodus 15, this attribution of the exodus event to the golden calf expresses a negative view of their transformed social identity and about the divine presence that, to this point, has grounded the nation. The consequence of their actions threatens their status as a people belonging

---

23. Dozeman, *Exodus*, 478; Sprinkle, *Book of the Covenant*, 21–25.
24. See also Kürle, *Appeal of Exodus*, 237–39.
25. See also Alexander, *Exodus*, 570.

to YHWH. YHWH no longer describes Israel as "my people" but rather "your people" as he speaks to Moses in Exodus 32:7–10.[26] This choice to use the second person pronoun suggests that there is now interpersonal conflict between Israel and YHWH, which compromises Israel's social identity. Furthermore, Israel's rejection of YHWH as the nation's God also jeopardizes the very presence that provides groundedness to Israel and the fledgling nation's transformed social identity.

A consequence of Israel's negative alignment to their transformed social identity is YHWH's declaration to withdraw his presence from the people as they travel to and conquer the land of promise (33:1–6). This causes a crisis in Exodus 32–34; how can Israel continue into the land if YHWH is not present among them? Moses' appeal in 33:14–16 highlights that it is YHWH's presence among the people that distinguishes the nation from all other people groups (v. 16). As Durham observes, without YHWH's presence, Israel cannot even begin traveling to the land because they would have "lost their identity . . . what they had seen, what they had been given, what they had the chance of becoming, all were the direct result of the Presence in their midst of Yahweh."[27] Thus, YHWH withdrawing his presence would diminish Israel's social identity. This crisis suggests once more that it is the YHWH's presence that grounds Israel's social identity as a people belonging to YHWH; without the divine presence being present, they would be like every other nation.

While YHWH relents from his intent to withdraw his presence (33:17) and he renews his covenant with Israel (34:10–27), at no point in the Exodus narrative is there an explicit statement about YHWH's forgiveness of their rebellion.[28] This causes a second crisis to emerge by the conclusion of the book of Exodus. With YHWH's glory filling the tabernacle, how can YHWH's presence continue to dwell among a people who will reject the nation's transformed social identity time and again? While Exodus does not provide resolution, the book of Leviticus—as it bridges the end of Exodus and the beginning of Numbers—provides the means for Israel to maintain and restore relational order through sacrifice and by embodying the nation's distinctiveness as a people belonging to YHWH and who is sanctified by YHWH's presence.

YHWH's provision of the Sabbath, feasts, and festivals—such as the feast of unleavened bread and the Passover—at critical points throughout

---

26. Boda, *Severe Mercy*, 41; Moberly, *At the Mountain of God*, 49–50.

27. Durham, *Exodus*, 447.

28. Please note that the only mention of forgiveness in 34:9 is spoken by Moses as a petition. YHWH's response affirms the continuity of the covenant relationship but does not yet make explicit provision for forgiveness (see Leviticus 4:1—5:13).

the Exodus narrative, purposefully connect the first Israelite generation, who experienced the transformative event of being brought out of slavery in Egypt, with future generations.[29] For example, in Exodus 12:14–17, the feast of unleavened bread is to be a feast of remembrance for all generations that YHWH is the one who brought them out of Egypt. Similarly, YHWH instructs the Israelites in 12:24–17 to observe the Passover within the family so as to remember how YHWH passed over Israelite households and displayed his justice within Egyptian households. By enacting these feasts and festivals at key points throughout the year, future generations are to remember the key events in their past that shape their social identity as being a people belonging to the YHWH in their present.[30] So too it could be said that the whole book of Exodus was orally passed on and written for these future generations so the memory of how their social identity was transformed shapes who they are in the midst of the world's nations and so that they sustain social cohesion as a distinctive nation belonging to YHWH. The inherent warning for future generations is that if they reject the core beliefs at the center of their social identity—belonging solely to YHWH, being a holy priesthood and a holy nation—then they jeopardize the presence of God that grounds their social identity as they reside in the land of promise.

Groundedness in our Social Identity within the Australian Church

In a Western culture that values self-identity based on self-discovery, the idea that our identity can be formed by our relationships external to ourselves clashes with the culture that the Australian church seeks to live within and engage. Yet identity for the Christian believer is a social identity, and our identity is transformed through the second great reversal foreshadowed by the first—the rescue of humanity from being enslaved by the power of evil, sin, and death, through the death and resurrection of the Lord Jesus. Belief in this memory transforms our identity in the present when we whole-heartedly repent. Like the pattern of Israel's transformed social identity where there is a distinction between Israel as God's people and the other nations, there is a distinction inherent in our transformed social identity too. This distinction is between those who are still enslaved to the power of sin, death, and evil, and so are still part of the world, and those whose belief in Jesus as Savior and Lord leads to membership in the

---

29. See also Kürle, *Appeal of Exodus*, 218.
30. See also Stargel, *Construction of Exodus Identity*, 1406, 1841.

new covenant community, of which our local church gatherings in Australia are only but a small part.

Presently within the Australian evangelical church, there is little cohesion sustained through our transformed social identity in Christ. The Australian evangelical church is divided into tribes where additional core values other than a proclamation of Jesus as Savior and Lord are identity defining and determine whether an individual is accepted, or not. Yet within the Australian church more broadly, there is pressure to remain in an uneasy unity while some seek to change core values and beliefs contrary to the distinctiveness that is central to our transformed social identity in Christ.

The Australian evangelical church needs to recover a biblical distinctiveness of belonging wholly to God in Christ. Reflection upon Israel's transformed social identity in Exodus and its implications for the nation as a covenant community provides three critical correctives for the church in such a time as this.

The first corrective is to put away tribalism that reinforces division and to seek cohesive unity in our shared participation of dying and rising with Christ. This does not mean embracing theological broadness that seeks inclusion and unity at any cost, but rather restoring a cohesive unity among those still standing firm in the Lord Jesus through core doctrinal beliefs, such as the five *solas* of the Reformation—by Scripture alone, by faith alone, by grace alone, through Christ alone, and for the glory of God alone.

The second corrective is recovering courage to be a distinctive people shaped by our transformed social identity. In my estimation, the Australian evangelical church is seeking distinctiveness by challenging culture that is still in bondage to sin, death, and evil, rather than seeking distinctiveness as a covenant community by ensuring our actions, desires, decisions, and speech are shaped by the character of our Lord and Savior. The reason that the Australian evangelical church can take courage is that the God in whom we have our transformed social identity is sovereign and can be trusted to preserve and provide for us, just as he demonstrated trustworthiness to Israel in the book of Exodus. If we blame Australian Western culture, seek to be antagonistic towards it, or make demands of it, we show to the detriment of the church's mission that we are more fearful of culture's impact than trusting of the goodness of the sovereign God who hears and knows.

The third corrective, then, is that our transformed social identity does make the Australian evangelical church distinctive from the world, but for the purpose that we engage with and show Christ to the world. When under pressure in the world, and perhaps even from the world, the temptation is to mirror the world's antagonistic behavior towards us. God's desire for Israel as they remembered their experience of slavery and then rescue was that they were then motivated to show compassion and hospitality towards outsiders; so too, our experience of living in bondage to sin and death, then knowing how marvelously we have been rescued in Christ, is to shape how we relate to our neighbor in the world around us in compassion and hospitality.

Bibliography

Alexander, T. Desmond. *Exodus*. AOTC 2, London: Apollos, 2017.
Boda, Mark J. *A Severe Mercy: Sin and its Remedy in the Old Testament*. Siphrut. Winona Lake: Eisenbrauns, 2009.
Bruckner, James K. *Exodus*. NIBC. Peabody, MA: Hendrickson, 2008.
Brueggemann, Walter. "Exodus." In *NIB Volume 1*, 677–981. Nashville: Abingdon, 1994.
Childs, Brevard S. *Exodus*. OTL. London: SCM, 1974.
Dozeman, Thomas B. *Exodus*. EEC. Grand Rapids, MI: Eerdmans, 2009.
Durham, John I. *Exodus*. WBC. Grand Rapids, MI: Zondervan Academic, 1987.
Fretheim, Terence E. *Exodus*. Interpretation. Louisville, KY: John Knox, 1991.
Hamilton, Victor. *Exodus*. Grand Rapids, MI: Baker Academic, 2011.
Houtman, Cornelius. *Exodus Volume 1*. HCOT. Leuven: Peeters, 1993.
Kürle, Stefan. *The Appeal of Exodus: The Characters God, Moses and Israel in the Rhetoric of the Book of Exodus*. PBM. Milton Keynes: Paternoster, 2013.
Moberly, R. W. L. *At the Mountain of God: Story and Theology in Exodus 32–34*. JSOTSS. Sheffield: JSOT, 1983.
Propp, William C. *Exodus 1–18*. Anchor 2a. New Haven: Yale, 1999.
Sarna, Nahum M. *Exodus*. JPS Torah. JPS: New York, 1991.
Schmid, Konrad. *Genesis and the Moses Story: Israel's Dual Origins in the Hebrew Bible*. Siphrut 3. Winona Lake: Eisenbrauns, 2010.
Sprinkle, Joe M. *The Book of the Covenant: A Literary Approach*. JSOTSS. Sheffield: JSOT, 1994.
Stargel, Linda M. *The Construction of Exodus Identity in Ancient Israel: A Social Identity Approach*. Eugene: Pickwick, 2018. Kindle edition.
Stuart, Douglas K. *Exodus*. NAC 2. Nashville: B&H, 2006.
Tajfel, Henri and John C. Turner. "The Social Identity Theory of Intergroup Behavior." In *Key Readings in Social Psychology: Political Psychology*, edited by John T. Jost & Jim Sidanius, 276–91. New York: Psychology Press, 2004.

7

Embodied Worship

The Psalms and the Senses

Melinda Cousins

Biblical studies, as a field, has tended to engage with Scripture in predominantly intellectual ways. We learn and study the word of God, analyze, exegete, interpret, and decipher it. We write books and theses about it, debate and explain it. All these can surely be noble and useful activities. The Scriptures seek to transform us by renewing our minds. But that is not their only goal. As James K. A. Smith says, we human beings are not simply brains on sticks.[1]

The ancient invitation of the Shema is to love God with all our mind, strength, and soul (Deut 6:4–5)—with all of who we are. All of who we are includes our bodies, emotions, imaginations, and relationships. The Scriptures seek to transform us by renewing our minds *and* by evoking our emotions, inspiring our imaginations, and engaging our bodies. Importantly, they do all these things grounded in concrete communal experience. They are a community document, given by, to, and for a people, the people of God.

---

1. Smith, *You Are What You Love*, 3.

The Psalms

My own entry point into a rediscovery of these dimensions of the impact and engagement of Scripture has been through the book of Psalms, the communal songbook of the people of Israel. The psalms are unique in the Bible. They started life as the words of people to God; they are the songs, prayers, and poems of the people of Israel as they responded to the God who had revealed himself to them. The psalms are then given to the community of faith to be used, generation after generation, as their responses to God making himself known to them. In doing so, they discover that these words are inspired; this is the word of God. The psalms become part of the Holy Scriptures, through which God speaks to us his people. Through them we are taught, inspired, corrected, and transformed. The words of the people to God have become the word of God to us.

How do the psalms work as Scripture? I believe they invite us to take on their words as our words and in so doing to hear God speak to us through them. The psalms call us to step in: to voice what they say, feel the emotions they evoke, imagine the pictures they paint, embody the actions they enact, inhabit their relationship with God, and make that our own divine encounter. To pick up a Bible and merely scan these poems with my eyes as words on a page, to then put them down and think I have understood what they say, is to miss their purpose and invitation. They have been given to be sung, prayed, heard, walked in, recited, remembered, lived, loved, known, used, embodied, and enacted. The psalms have been given to the community of faith to be used in every generation, in every experience, expression, and dimension of life.

We can consider first the relational dimensions of the psalms. While some theological approaches to the book of Psalms have approached the text primarily as a source of information *about* God, with the intent of arriving at an accurate description of the God they present, this is simply not enough. As Harry Nasuti argues, an understanding of "the way these texts *make available a relationship* between God and the believing individuals and communities" is at least equally as important.[2] The psalms have a significant relational dimension, a role as an encounter with the divine. This encounter is "mediated by the faith community and is informed by the history of God's people,"[3] inviting an approach in which the interpreter's own stance before God is recognized and celebrated as a significant dimension of

---

2. Nasuti, "God at Work in the World," 29. Emphasis added.
3. Jacobson, "Christian Theology in the Psalms," 505.

interpretation and use of the text. This is a way of doing theology grounded in a present encounter between God and his people.

Secondly, the psalms have a substantial emotional dimension. The range of emotions *expressed* in the psalms has often been noted, with many commentators referencing John Calvin's comment that "there is not an emotion of which any one can be conscious that is not here represented."[4] However, scholarly treatments of the psalms have rarely provided sustained analysis of the emotions *generated* by the psalms. What emotions do they evoke? What is their affective impact on those who read and use them? By recounting situations and expressions that generate an emotional response, the text actually elicits those emotions. The wide range and breadth of emotions generated by the psalms allows for embodied exploration of the emotional range of what it means to be human.

A third dimension of the psalms is their imagination. They are poetry, filled with imagery. Again, they do not merely describe the imaginings of other people; they evoke imagination in us as we engage with them. Walter Brueggemann defines imagination as "the capacity to picture (image!) the world out beyond what we take as established given. Imagination is an ability to hold loosely what the world assumes and to walk into alternative contours of reality, which we have only in hint and trace."[5] How do the psalms, and indeed the Scriptures as a whole, invite us to imagine anew all that could be?

Fourthly, the psalms have a notable kinesthetic dimension. They engage within physical space, with our bodies, and with embodied movement. In recent years, spatiality has become a key area of interest in social-scientific perspectives more broadly and biblical studies more particularly.[6] Edward Soja's work delineating space into geophysical realities (firstspace), ideas about space (secondspace), and lived space (thirdspace) is commonly cited.[7] The psalms describe spatial dimensions and invite us to take up space as we use them. As we participate in them, we enter into and move within their understanding of space. The psalms also employ significant body vocabulary. Body part terms contribute much more than physical reference in many languages,[8] including our own (e.g., "foot in mouth," "get off my back," "cold feet"). However, simply focusing on the more metaphorical meanings overlooks the visceral impact of the connection to embodied

---

4. Calvin, *Commentary on the Book of Psalms*, 23.
5. Brueggemann and Sharp, *Disruptive Grace*, 296.
6. See Matthews, "Physical Space, Imagined Space, and 'Lived Space,'" 12.
7. Soja, *Thirdspace*.
8. Warren-Rothlin, "Body Idioms and the Psalms," 204.

sensation. Some translations entirely remove any such association. Even when body imagery is used for God, which can be assumed to be idiomatic or metaphorical, the effect of the anthropomorphism is its connection to our own embodied experience. Warren-Rothlin calls it "naïve" to translate these literally,[9] but perhaps this is an instance where what Ricoeur calls the "second naïveté"[10] is entirely appropriate.

A framework that brings some of these dimensions together is to consider the senses of the psalms. Where do they connect with the use of our bodies in emotive, imaginative, and kinesthetic ways, as they engage us with God, his word, and his world?

The Senses

The idea that we have five senses (sight, hearing, taste, smell, and touch) goes back to the Greek philosophers, including Plato who popularized it, and Aristotle who established a hierarchy.[11] It was picked up by writers in Middle English and used by Chaucer and Shakespeare. It is commonly taught to children and perhaps understood as a universal truth that these are the ways we make sense of the world. However, a number of modern thinkers have questioned this taxonomy and added extra senses to it. Of course, this depends on what one defines as a sense, with some saying it is any action based on a receptor, and others limiting it to the ability to absorb content that reaches consciousness.[12] There are lists of nine, seventeen, or even thirty-three different senses including our sense of balance, sense of movement, ability to feel pain, or how we sense the passing of time.[13]

The categorization and hierarchy of the senses can also vary between cultures. The language we use can limit our understanding and reflection on our experience, or it can lead us to assume ethical preferences. Western thinkers have also tended to separate the senses from the mind—part of a larger body-mind dichotomy—so that what we "'feel" from our senses does not have to be connected to what we "think." Smith observes that we have become so accustomed to a "Cartesian or Platonic diminution of the body"[14] that we can be "scandalized" by the embodiedness of our faith. At the same time, the practices and rituals of the marketplace are tactile and

---

9. Warren-Rothlin, "Body Idioms and the Psalms," 210.
10. See for example, Roberts, "Conceptual Blending," 30–31.
11. See Sorabji, "Aristotle on Demarcating the Five Senses," for a thorough overview.
12. Avrahami, *The Senses of Scripture*, 14.
13. See Macpherson, "Individuating the Senses," 14–20.
14. Smith, *Desiring the Kingdom*, 146.

visceral, capturing our imaginations through engagement with our senses.[15] A purely rational or intellectualized faith cannot compete with such appeals. We need practices and rhythms that are embodied and grounded to engage all our senses.

Yael Avrahami's study of the Old Testament, *The Senses of Scripture*, asks how sensory perception was defined by the ancient Hebrews. She points out that the Israelites speak more concretely about the parts of the body than about the abstract senses as we tend to name them. There is no Hebrew word for "sense" in the Bible, nor nouns for "sight" or "smell." The focus is on the part of the body and how it engages with the world around it. Sensation is an embodied experience, which is quite obvious but can be lost in our use of more abstract language. She writes,

> In our modern perception, we imagine the senses as figurative abilities that are differentiated from the sensory body organs and limbs. Yet in the biblical perception, where the embodiment is taken for granted, there is no real differentiation between touching and holding—both of which are associated with the hand. There is no real differentiation between mobility and posture—both of which are actions associated with the foot . . . the Hebrew Bible treats the senses as a category of experiencing the world through body organs.[16]

The Old Testament names at least seven sensory organs: eyes, ears, mouth, tongue, nose, hand/arm, and foot/leg. Psalm 115 uses a similar list to speak about idols, who lack the ability to engage with the world: they have mouths but cannot speak, eyes but cannot see, ears but cannot hear, noses but cannot smell, hands but cannot feel, feet but cannot walk, throats but cannot make a sound. The use of these seven organs throughout the Scripture has some clear resonances with how we may be familiar with exploring our senses, but also nuances and adds to our experience and understanding.

The eye sees. It therefore becomes the source of knowledge, perception, and judgment. The eyes are central in the Hebrew Scriptures for both what God does and what we do.

The ear hears. It therefore becomes a symbol for understanding: for something to be made known, it must be heard by another.

The mouth and tongue are used across the Old Testament for both speech and taste. As the organs of speech, they make sense of the world by use of words and language. This is much more prevalent than the eating/tasting mouth.

---

15. Smith, *Desiring the Kingdom*, 95.
16. Avrahami, *The Senses of Scripture*, 127.

The nose in the Hebrew Bible is linked to smell but also—perhaps more significantly—to breathing. Thus, the nose can take in scents by inhaling but also spread them by exhaling.

The hand symbolizes the feeling limb and is used with the verb to touch. It can be an agent of support or harm.

The foot walks. It is the organ of movement and posture. It is used with the verbs for walking and going, but also for standing and stopping.

> It seems that in the culture reflected in the Hebrew Bible there was a septasensory model which included the senses of sight, hearing, kinaesthesia, speech, touch, taste, and smell . . . Moreover, sensory perception was perceived to include various types of experience, including cognitive, emotional, and social experiences. Using the senses was a symbol for autonomy, subjectivity, and sovereignty. This symbol was based on the derived experience attributed to the senses as well as to the perception that God had created the senses.[17]

The Psalms and the Senses

How do we see this septasensory model reflected in the psalms, and how might the psalms help us engage with our senses to make our worship more embodied?

As we turn to examine the use of these sensory organs within the psalms, it is worth noting that many English translations take the concrete, grounded, and embodied words for these sensory organs and translate them with the more theoretical sensation, or at other times completely remove the connection to the body and replace it with an abstract idea. For this reason, the following analysis is based on the Hebrew text.[18] Undoubtedly, body language in Hebrew is also often used metaphorically. However, significant recent work on metaphor theory has helped us understand that images are more than mere literary ornaments, but in fact means of "cognitive mediation."[19] In order to generate associations beyond words, metaphors draw on our familiarity with what they name. In this chapter, the focus is on the grounded, sensory implications of this language, while also noting some of the further implications of these images beyond embodied sensation.

---

17. Avrahami, *The Senses of Scripture*, 278.

18. All verse numbers, however, are to the English text, as the Hebrew verse numbers often differ due to the treatment of the superscriptions.

19. Brown, *Seeing the Psalms*, 5.

The language of the psalms reminds us that our worship is grounded in embodied practice and engagement with sound, sight, taste, and touch. They are a "language training manual—an affective, embodied means of training our speech, which is so centrally constitutive of who we are and how we imagine ourselves."[20] As we speak their words *about* our senses, we intuitively and formatively engage God and the world *with* our senses. The psalms are also brimming with references to God's bodily senses, particularly sight and hearing. While a modern intellectual approach may seek to challenge the idea of a spiritual being having senses, in the psalms it is only the enemies of God who question his sensory perception. The psalmists argue that without bodily senses, God would be indifferent.[21]

The eyes (*'ayin*) are named sixty-six times in the book of Psalms, with twenty references to God's eyes, and the remaining to the eyes of the psalmist, the community, or other people. God's eyes watch over his people, and over their enemies too, observant and aware of all they do. In their responses to God, his people seek to fix their eyes on him and be aware of all he is doing. Metaphorically, they look to God as the source of all things, waiting, expecting.

This preponderance of sight activity and imagery in the psalms resonates in our context. We live in a highly visual culture, with ubiquitous screens, constant images, and the pervasive idea that something must be seen to be real; that is, "pics or it didn't happen." The danger is that this might make us think we are good at seeing. Perhaps it is culturally our dominant sense. When asked to choose, a majority of people would rather lose their smell, taste, or even hearing than their sight.[22] We have a breadth and range of words we use for what we do with our eyes—from a long gaze to a quick glance, a wide-eyed stare to a peering squint. So we might wonder what these ancient texts have to teach us about seeing. But James says we can look without really seeing (Jas 1:23–24). Jesus reminds us we can see but yet not perceive (Matt 13:14). The psalms encourage us to consider what we do with our eyes in various ways and to practice using them to engage with God, his word, and his world in grounded and embodied ways.

Psalm 119 provides a representative example of the range of ways the psalms speak about our eyes. It includes the prayer "Open my eyes . . ." (v. 18), a prayer to physically take in and appreciate the sources of joy and beauty God has given and by extension to be aware and gain insight from God in all situations. There is also a cry to close our eyes, to turn our eyes

---

20. Smith, *Desiring the Kingdom*, 172.
21. See Brown, *Seeing the Psalms*, 172.
22. See Noll, *Principles of Modern Communication Technology*, 81.

(v. 37) from worthless things. At first glance this is a simple encouragement to be careful with what we actually choose to spend time looking at. But this physical action also points to the importance of "turning away" in wise perception and judgment more comprehensively. The psalmist speaks of his eyes being full (*kālāh*) or straining for what they cannot yet see (v. 82), a prayer of anticipation to look beyond what is to what could be, engaging our imaginations. He later speaks of weeping eyes (v. 136), reminding us that our senses and emotions come together, with tears an appropriate and godly response to seeing—or more broadly being cognizant of—brokenness and distortion in our world. Finally, he speaks of eyes staying open long into the night (v. 148), choosing to stay watchful, paying attention well after others might stop noticing. This physical diligence is linked to the act of meditation. The psalms call us to use our eyes to look, observe, notice, reflect, consider, and ponder—and to then respond with our hearts as we see things the way God sees them.[23]

The ears (*'ozen*) are named twenty-two times in the psalms, with twelve references to God's ears, inclined to pay attention to the cries of his people. The embodied imagery portrays a God who is attentive, engaged, and responsive to the community. Created in his image, his people incline their ears to listen to God, to the passing on of ancient wisdom, and to community reports of God's work in the world. This is a posture of participation. Eugene Peterson has noted the graphic imagery of Psalm 40:6, which could be translated "my ears you have dug," with the Creator forcefully shaping our bodies so we might hear and respond,[24] suggesting this receptiveness does not come easily.

The call to listen (*šamaʿ*) is found seventy-nine times in the book of Psalms, again both as an action of God and the response of his people. The ears become the sensory organ not only of receiving information but of obedience, for to truly listen is to act upon what is heard. In a world full of noise, of competing sounds and siren calls, what does it look like for the worshiping people of God to turn their ears toward his voice?

The mouth (*peh*) is named sixty-seven times in the book of Psalms, with the overwhelming majority of references connected to human speech. Likewise, the tongue (*lāšon*) is named thirty-five times and the lips (*śāpāh*) twenty-eight, with almost all occurrences used for speech. We might think of our mouth as the sensory organ for taste, but we actually use it far more often to speak than we do to eat. The idea of speech as a sense resonates with

---

23. The word pair eye-heart occurs about forty times in the Hebrew Bible. See Avrahami, *The Senses of Scripture*, 56.

24. See Peterson, *Eat This Book*, 92.

me personally as an external processor, someone who thinks out loud. I often make sense of things by talking through them. The psalms offer an invitation to explore how using our voices can help us connect with, respond to, and engage with God, his people, and his world.

Most obviously, we use our voices to praise God. The psalms affirm there is power in declaring aloud what we believe. In speaking the words of the psalms, we discover we can also hear God speak his words through our voices. Psalm 40 provides a number of representative examples of how the voice acts as a sensory organ in the psalms. The poem starts with a cry to God (v. 1), as his ears listen to the words of our mouths. We use our voices to ask for help, expressing and experiencing vulnerability and power in articulating our needs, placing us in a position of dependence. Then, God places a new song in the mouth (v. 3). We receive words from God himself to give back to him in praise. The psalms invite us to speak out God's storying and re-storying of the world so that we might live out of his articulation of the way things are. As is common in the psalms, the activity of speaking God's deeds to others is named (v. 5). Proclamation has always been understood as an important calling of the church and key to our mission. Perhaps it is also key to our sense of identity and community. There is a fascinating expression as the psalmist speaks to himself words of truth about his identity (v. 7)—that God's word speaks about him. If we step into this psalm and enact its words and actions as our own, we find ourselves naming aloud a truth that God's words are for and about us. I want to explore this expression more, but as a preacher who has the privilege at times of hearing the words of the Holy Spirit come unbidden from my mouth, this is a sensory and spiritual experience I have not often heard named. Then, the psalmist proclaims God's saving acts in the assembly (v. 9), speaking aloud in the gathered community what God is saying. He next refers to speaking from the heart (v. 10), with words, groans, tongues, overflowing from the depths of the spirit within. Finally, the psalm ends with an articulated desire for other mouths to join in speaking God's praise (v. 16), inviting others into the sensory experience of worship and pointing to the power of speech to affirm and even generate what it declares (Rom 10:9).

The savoring senses, taste and smell, are less common in the psalms. These senses from which we are used to deriving much pleasure do not find dominant expression in these texts. The verb "to eat" (*ʾākal*) appears thirty times, but most of these references are used metaphorically for consuming and devouring, and those that do refer to food focus on sustenance rather than sensation. Psalm 81:16 hints at embodied perception, with God's provision for his people including the finest and sweetest foods, but again the focus is on nourishment rather than sensory delight. Perhaps more well-known is Psalm 34:8, the call to taste and see that God is good. The verb "taste" (*ṭāʿam*) is found eleven times in the Hebrew Scriptures, with nine concretely connected with food. Here, the usage is metaphorical, with the experiential perception and appreciation of God himself in view, but the body imagery still triggers in the reader emotive and kinesthetic dimensions in this theological truth.

The nose (*ʾap̄*) is named thirty-five times in the book of Psalms, however this is commonly understood and almost always translated metaphorically as anger, with the physical body part connected to this expression of emotion. The physical sensation has been almost entirely subsumed by its symbolic use, and yet an awareness of this connection can ground how we feel and respond to these texts.

Although the idea of scent and smell is found in the Old Testament, Avrahami notes that the nose is more commonly connected to breath. In the creation story, God breathes the breath of life into the human nose. In Psalm 18:7, God breathes out from his nose and the earth trembles. Slowing down and breathing in and out through the nose calms, stills, and silences us and the use of this language can encourage a physical response. Metaphorically, a number of psalms connect the image of breath to the shortness of our lives before God (e.g., Pss 39:5, 11; 62:9; 144:4). In our fast-paced world, the invitation of the psalms to simply breathe, reflecting on the breath of life placed within us, grounds us in myriad ways.

Far more common in the psalms are the two final sensory organs: the hand and the foot. Grounded in the physical body and its movement in time and space, these senses connect people to place, land, community, and family. The hand (*yād*) is named ninety-four times. God's hands create (8:6), sustain (89:21), provide (145:16), and save (17:14). Human hands can be taken up in battle (18:34) or outstretched in praise (28:2), enacting violence (58:2) or extending in favor (123:2). Our hands work with strength and generosity (90:17), but also need to be emptied in order to be raised in submission and worship (134:2). God opens his hands in generosity to his people (104:28), and his people are likewise called to be openhanded to the poor (see Deut 15:11). In a culture where many of us do not think of our vocations as "working with our hands," how does this reminder of the psalms ground us in our practice, our calling, and our communities?

Finally, the foot (*regel*) is named thirty-one times in the book of Psalms, perhaps far more than those of us who travel predominantly by other modes of transport might imagine. A couple of these speak of God's feet, but most are in reference to humanity. Add to these thirty-two references to standing (*ʿāmad*) and sixty-eight to walking (*hālak*), and perhaps the psalms calls us to pay more attention to the actions of these sensory organs that ground us in time and space. It appears that like my Indigenous Australian sisters and brothers, the Hebrew people were familiar with the idea of making sense of the world by walking on country. Where do the rest of us need to pay more attention to the steps of our feet?

Psalm 8 reminds us that God has placed his good gift of creation beneath our feet. Our Creator God has grounded us, placed us upon the earth, placed the dirt under our feet. Perhaps we need to take our shoes off more often. Psalm 26 speaks of the gathering of God's people as level ground to stand upon. Do we notice our stance in community? Psalm 25 pictures salvation as having our feet released from a trap. We have been set free to walk, run, jump, and dance. Psalms 18 and 31 speak of this freedom of our feet as like that of prancing deer or wild animals set free to run and run. Psalms 56 and 121 name God as the one who guards and guides the steps our feet take, keeping us from stumbling. Throughout the whole book of Psalms, walking with God and in his paths is a dominant image for the life of faith. Is this just a metaphor, as it appears we have frequently taken it to be, or do we need to take more seriously the reality of a God who walks with us and invites us to walk with him, so that we might turn our feet to heed his call, following him into the places and spaces where he is wanting to ground us?

A Practical Example

Below is an outline of a series on the psalms and the senses I prepared for my church. Each week included a sermon exploring a particular sense and its associated body imagery in the book of Psalms, followed by a time of practice, inviting the community to use their senses together to respond to God. We used social media during the subsequent week to provide ideas for daily practices using the senses. This was a six-week series, combining the nose and tongue together given the lesser usage of these senses in the psalms and an assumption that the practices of smelling and tasting would go well together.[25]

Hearing: We used a soundscape to listen together to the noises of nature, city, people, and silence. We asked people to close their eyes and focus particularly on what they were listening to, seeking to encounter God within it. We made shorter clips from the soundscape available each day for people to spend time listening to at home.

Seeing: We put together an art gallery and gave people time to explore. Artists within our community shared their work; we printed copies of Christian artworks from across the centuries; we borrowed significant pieces from

---

25. See Macpherson, "Individuating the Senses," 14.

collections to include indigenous artwork and art from other cultures. We also had a series of photographs of nature and another of our community doing life together. Instead of descriptions, we put questions next to different artworks, asking people to reflect on what they saw and where they saw God at work in it. On social media, we posted a picture each day with questions to reflect on. We invited people to share photos of what they noticed as they opened their eyes to God's presence around them.

Speaking: We spoke prepared words aloud together as a community. We asked a simple question about what we were hearing God say and gave each person time to write their own response. We asked them to share this aloud with two others. Each group developed one shared answer, which they spoke aloud to another group; then each group of six articulated their shared answer aloud to another group. Finally, each group of twelve spoke their shared answer to the whole gathered community. Using social media, we encouraged people to use their voices in different ways each day: crying out to God, singing a new song, telling someone about Jesus, speaking to themselves a truth from God, speaking God's word to someone else, speaking from the heart, and inviting others to speak.

Forming: We had a child teach us origami together as a community. We then provided art and craft supplies for people to spend time working with their hands, including sculpting clay, painting, and textiles. Throughout the following week, we invited people to draw, find something to touch, hold, and connect hands with others as daily practices.

Walking: A dancer prepared and shared a piece with us, focused on the use of her feet. We walked our neighborhood in small groups, paying attention to where our feet trod. One group went barefoot in a park; another crossed a major traffic intersection. We walked to significant community locations and prayed for those who walk and live in those spaces. Throughout the following week, we reminded people to pay attention to where they placed their feet and how they used them in various ways.

Savoring: We prepared an abundant grazing table at the front of our gathering space, which could be seen and smelled throughout our time together. We practiced simple breathing exercises and passed around strong-smelling scents. Finally, we joined around the table to feast together. Throughout the following week, we shared breathing and meditation exercises, invited people to find and share different scents, and encouraged them to take time over food and share meals with one another.

# 7 Senses: An Expressions Series (Richmond Baptist Church)

Sense	Psalms	Communal Practices	Daily Practices
Listening: We will use our ears to listen to God through music and in silence. What does a posture of listening look like and how can we practice listening?	17:6: Turn your ear to us 40:6: My ears you have dug 44:1: We have heard 78:1: Turn our ears to your words	Soundscape: nature, city, people, silence	Short clips of various sounds to reflect on
Seeing: We will use our eyes to perceive and appreciate God's beauty. How do we learn to see kingdom beauty?	119:18 Open our eyes 119:37: Close our eyes 119:82: Fill our eyes 119:136: Flood our eyes 119:148: Keep our eyes open	Art gallery: created art, borrowed art, printed art, photos, reflection questions	Pictures to reflect on, invitation to share photos of what we are seeing
Speaking: We will use our mouths to speak of who God is and what he has done. How do we hear God as we think out loud?	40:1: Cry out to God 40:3: Sing a new song 40:5: Proclaim what God has done 40:7: Speak God's words myself 40:10: Speak from the heart 40:16: May others speak too	Shared spoken word poem, individual written and spoken response to question, shared aloud and adapted with progressively larger groups	Using your voice to cry out, sing a new song, tell someone about Jesus, remind yourself of truth, speak life to someone else, invite others to speak

Sense	Psalms	Communal Practices	Daily Practices
Crafting: We will use our hands to participate in God's creativity. There's something spiritual that can happen as we engage and touch and create.	8:6: God's creating hand 10:14: God's caring hand 145:16: God's providing hand 18:34: Our hands trained 28:2: Our hands lifted 90:17: Our hands creating	Origami lesson, sculpting clay, painting, fabric, Lego	Drawing, find an object to hold, connect with someone else using touch
Walking: We will unpack our sense of place. Does where our feet are matter? What does it mean for us to be connected to land, and how does our environment shape us?	8:6: Creation beneath our feet 26:12: Our feet on level ground 25:15: Our feet set free 18:33: Our feet dancing 121:3: Our feet guided	Watch a dancer's feet, walk the neighborhood together, pray for those who walk in these spaces	Pay attention to where you place your feet, go barefoot, run, jump, dance
Savoring: We will use our noses and tongues to smell and taste God's goodness. Taste and smell are connected to memories and experiences. How do we practice those connections and enjoy the tastes of what is to come?	22:26 Eat and be satisfied 128:2 Enjoy the fruit of our labor 81:16 Feed us the best 34:8 Taste and see that the Lord is good	Grazing table, breathing exercises, smelling strong scents, feasting together	Breathing and meditation exercises, find and share scents, take time to savor food, share meals together

Bibliography

Avrahami, Yael. *The Senses of Scripture: Sensory Perception in the Hebrew Bible*. LHBOTS 545. London: Bloomsbury/T&T Clark, 2012.

Brown, William P. *Seeing the Psalms: A Theology of Metaphor*. Louisville, KY: Westminster John Knox, 2002.

Brueggemann, Walter and Carolyn Sharp. *Disruptive Grace: Reflections on God, Scripture, and the Church.* Minneapolis: Fortress, 2011.

Calvin, John. *Commentary on the Book of Psalms Volume I.* Translated by James Anderson. Edinburgh: Calvin Translation Society, 1845.

Jacobson, Rolf A. "Christian Theology in the Psalms." In *The Oxford Handbook of the Psalms*, edited by William P. Brown, 499–512. Oxford: Oxford University Press, 2014.

Macpherson, Fiona. "Individuating the Senses." In *The Senses: Classic and Contemporary Philosophical Perspectives*, edited by Fiona Macpherson, 3–46. New York: Oxford University Press, 2011.

Matthews, Victor H. "Physical Space, Imagined Space and 'Lived Space' in Ancient Israel." *Biblical Theology Bulletin* 33 (2003) 12–20.

Nasuti, Harry P. "God at Work in the World: A Theology of Divine-Human Encounter in the Psalms." In *Soundings in the Theology of the Psalms: Perspectives and Methods in Contemporary Scholarship*, edited by Rolf A. Jacobson, 27–48. Minneapolis: Fortress 2011.

Noll, A. Michael. *Principles of Modern Communications Technology.* Boston: Artech House, 2001.

Peterson, Eugene. *Eat This Book: A Conversation in the Art of Spiritual Reading.* Grand Rapids, MI: Eerdmans, 2006.

Roberts, Jason P. "Conceptual Blending, the Second Naïveté, and the Emergence of New Meanings." *Open Theology* 4 (2018) 29–45.

Smith, James K. A. *Desiring the Kingdom: Worship, Worldview, and Cultural Formation.* Grand Rapids, MI: Baker Academic, 2009.

———. *You Are What You Love: The Spiritual Power of Habit.* Grand Rapids, MI: Brazos, 2016.

Soja, Edward W. *Thirdspace: Journeys to Los Angeles and Other Real-and-Imagined Places.* Oxford: Basil Blackwell, 1996.

Sorabji, Richard. "Aristotle on Demarcating the Five Senses." In *The Senses: Classic and Contemporary Philosophical Perspectives*, edited by Fiona Macpherson, 47–63. New York: Oxford University Press, 2011.

Warren-Rothlin, Andy L. "Body Idioms and the Psalms." In *Interpreting the Psalms: Issues and Approaches*, edited by David Firth and Philip S. Johnston, 195–212. Downers Grove, IL: InterVarsity, 2005.

8

"Descending from the Hills of Gilead"

*Undressing Descriptions of the Lover's Body,
and How Australian Women Can Reclaim
and Embrace Their Embodiment*

Erin Martine Sessions

WOMEN HAVE BEEN REDUCED to the sum of our parts. We have only to look to the Headless Women of Hollywood project to see the advertising trope that sexualizes women's body parts and makes them interchangeable.[1] Depictions of women and girls have become more objectifying and sexualizing over time, to a point of relentless saturation. Women are fragmented and fetishized the world over, and Australia is certainly no exception. The objectification and sexualization of women have reached such proportions that Women's Health Victoria commissioned a study into gender inequality in advertising and the impacts of sexist advertising on women's health and wellbeing. Some key findings of the study are: these depictions of the female form have "helped to perpetuate inequalities based on gender in broader society"; "objectifying and sexualized media content is associated with attitudes that support violence against women"; and "women's body satisfaction is negatively affected by sexualized portrayals."[2] However, it is only recently that government initiatives "have paid attention to the

---

1 The Headless Women Project, "Headless Women of Hollywood."
2. McKenzie, "Advertising (In)Equality," 4–5.

critical role of advertising . . . for preventing violence against women and promoting gender equality."[3]

But what does this have to do with being grounded in time, in our bodies, and in Scripture? First, this is timely. Not only are we—women and men—pointing out the problems with prevailing attitudes towards women and the ways in which women's bodies are portrayed, we've also reached a watershed moment—post #MeToo, post Royal Commission—where our collective consciousness has woken up to women as reliable witnesses to our own experiences. Second, to be grounded in our bodies, women must be respected as whole embodied (and agential) persons, rather than mere objects. Third, and perhaps most important, contained within Scripture is a book that foregrounds a woman's embodied experience. As much as the psalms encourage us to imagine ourselves in the place of the psalmist, the Song of Songs invites us to step into the particular world of a woman who stands for all women.

So how can we undress attitudes, advertising and everyday media messaging, expose it for what it is, and reclaim our embodiment, thereby joining in the work of gender based violence primary prevention? Strangely enough, we can look to a segmented description of a woman's body in Song of Songs, that is, the first *waṣf* at 4:1–7.[4]

What is a *Waṣf*?

A *waṣf* is a poem which describes and celebrates its subject, piece by piece. After the woman—the lover—speaks in 2:3—3:11, chapter four opens with the man—her beloved—illustrating and lauding her body, in a concentrated, part by part description. The seven verses of the poem are structured around seven of the lover's bodily features and seven similes.[5] This lyric is the backbone of the beloved's enraptured depictions of his lover's body, grounded in pastoral, animal, architectural, and military imagery.

The poem opens and closes with the beloved exclaiming his lover's beauty. She is so beautiful, in fact, that the word יָפָה (*yph*) is repeated, and the description of her wow-factor[6] intensifies until the climax of the description in verse seven: an emphatic "all of you is beautiful, my love."[7] The structure,

---

3. McKenzie, "Advertising (In)Equality," 5.
4. Of four: Song 4:1–7; 5:9–16; 6:4–10; 7:1–6.
5. More accurately: one metaphor and six similes, but allow me the alliteration.
6. Dobbs-Allsopp, "The Delight of Beauty," 262.
7. The adjective is also used to describe male beauty. E.g. Ps 45 and 2 Sam 14:25.

or framing of the poem, mirrors the "fearful symmetry" of her frame.[8] This symmetrical, chiastic, formation is a frequent standard of beauty.[9]

But how can we be sure this fragmenting poem is not doing the exact same objectifying and sexualizing that permeates Australian society and culture, particularly advertising, today?

Helpfully, F. Scott Spencer identifies three possible interpretations which problematize my feminist reading: universal idealism; surgical grotesquerie; and somatic objectification.[10] Idealism seems unlikely given Song of Songs is literary, not literal. The man is not describing a real woman. But neither is she a fictionalized ideal woman; the *inclusio* is sealed in hyperbole[11]—her body is not, in fact, perfect. It is her particularity that makes her beautiful. Fiona Black has made a strong case for the grotesque: "an unsettling quality, making the body ridiculous, conflicted, even alienating."[12] However, the man does not see his love as an assemblage of limbs—a monster akin to Frankenstein's; "he views her . . . as an embodied person—a glorious 'you/thou' (4:1,7) incarnation."[13] And, more tellingly, he appreciates her body "altogether" (4:7), not as dismembered parts. Objectification is "when a person's body or body parts are separated from them as a person so that they are reduced to the status of a mere object."[14] And the text clearly tells us this is not what the man is doing: he wants to go to her (4:6), not remain at an objectifying (dismembering) distance. Here, remembering genre can be humanizing: the point of the *waṣf* is not to prescribe the ideal body, to dismember, or objectify, but to incite and evoke in the (original) audience the intended emotion—the joy of love.[15]

We are all too aware that a focus on beautiful bodies can serve a "cultural pathology,"[16] as is well evidenced in Australian advertising. But it doesn't have to, if kept in proper perspective, and so we turn to a closer reading of 4:1–7, exploring how women can begin to reclaim our bodies

---

8. A nod to William Blake's *The Tyger* in Spencer, *Song of Songs*, 85.
9. Etcoff, *Survival of the Prettiest*, 15–17.
10. Spencer, *Song of Songs*, 86–90.
11. Compare the hyperbolic praise of Absalom's beauty in 2 Sam 14:25.
12. Black, *Artifice of Love*, 2.
13. Spencer, *Song of Songs*, 88.
14. McKenzie, "Advertising (In)Equality," 9. WHV have used a popular definition. For a philosophical exploration see Nussbaum, "Objectification," 249–91. Nussbaum brings nuance to the term "objectification" and here we would do well to note that Song of Songs is *literature,* and that there is a difference between established relationship (e.g. Song of Songs) and public representation (e.g. advertising).
15. Zhang, *I, You and the Word "God,"* 91.
16. Dobbs-Allsopp, "Delight of Beauty," 266.

from the ways in which we are misrepresented, objectified and sexualized in advertising and society, and embrace our embodiment.

Song of Songs 4:1–7

In the opening verse of chapter four, the beloved commences by praising his lover's features with a seemingly simple pastoral and animal metaphor he has used before—her eyes are doves—except the metaphor is not simple at all and he quickly eschews the familiar metaphor for stranger similes. While the gazelle is the animal particularly associated with the man, the dove is the animal most often associated with the woman.[17] Much has been made of the dove signifying a "coy reserve,"[18] but just as the lover's eyes being veiled "hints there is much more to them than meets his eye,"[19] there is much more to this metaphor than a facile modesty or gentleness. In a hallmark of Hebrew poetry, this line is extremely terse, yet it is laden with allusion. Doves are also known to coo.[20] Fox explains that "her eyes are like doves calling to [her beloved]."[21] I would add, as much as the woman invites consent in the opening verse of Songs of Songs,[22] here she is inviting and consenting to the loving appraisal of her body from her beloved. And the imagery is associated with her face and head, evoking a communicative relationship with an agential person—the antithesis of the Headless Women of Hollywood. Moreover, Fox refers to a body of evidence from Egypt and Western Asia for the "motif of doves as news-bringers."[23]

What news does the dove bring to this encounter and what good news might it be for Australian women today?

First, since her dove-eyes coo from behind her veil, it seems the beloved is less interested in segmenting his lover's body and desires "to hear her voice and to see her face (cf. 2:14cd)."[24] Second, her veil is not simply signifying modesty but also autonomy. The veil means, similarly to a dove in the cleft of a rock (2:14), "she is not automatically available to his beck and

---

17. Munro, *Imagery*, 155.
18. Munro, *Imagery*, 96. See Keel's range of interpretive options (*Song of Songs*, 69–71).
19. Spencer, *Song of Songs*, 85.
20. Song 2:12. See also Ezek 7:16; Isa 38:14; 59:11; Nah 2:8.
21. Fox, *Song of Songs*, 129.
22. Sessions, "Do Not Arouse or Awaken Love," 6.
23. Fox, *Song of Songs*, 129.
24. Munro, *Imagery*, 96.

call or his look or gaze."²⁵ Dobbs-Allsopp argues that "this woman betokens a vibrant, knowing agency—one who knows her mind and acts on it."²⁶ This metaphor, and the two similes which immediately follow, constitute pastoral imagery with animals not normally considered "powerful," yet each "appears in a setting that enhances not only their descriptive power but also, by analogy, the woman's power."²⁷ So, despite the advertising that pervades Australian culture being far more likely to portray men than women as powerful,²⁸ Song of Songs shows not only are women not disembodied from our voices—and indeed our heads—which communicate our autonomy and agency, we are also powerful.

Continuing the powerful animalistic and pastoral description, the first of six similes likens the lover's hair to a flock of goats descending from the hills of Gilead. Both the collective noun and the moving image viewed from a distance are key, because comparing one's love to a singular goat up close "was probably no more romantic in the Song of Song's ancient Near Eastern (ANE) world than in our own."²⁹ The image is most often understood to be "flowing tresses of black hair . . . [that] resemble lines of black goats seen from afar as they wend their way down the mountainside."³⁰ But what is often missed is the Hebrew poetic device of comparing "a person to a place which adds that place's attributes to the person."³¹ While Gilead was rugged and remote, evoking "energy, vitality, and perhaps even a degree of wildness,"³² the "luxuriant grasslands of Gilead . . . were [also] the most important sheep-raising regions in biblical times."³³ This hints at both the next sheep-simile, and the strength to bear and sustain life, which is more overtly explored later. Here, the woman is imbued with Gilead's power to sustain life.

But what does this mean for women today? Allow me to refer to the other Gilead with which we should be familiar—that of *The Handmaid's Tale*. The fictional Gilead—avidly watched by record numbers of Australians—abuses reproductive ability, where the biblical Gilead evokes

---

25. Spencer, *Song of Songs*, 92.
26. Dobbs-Allsopp, "Delight of Beauty," 269–70.
27. Spencer, *Song of Songs*, 91.
28. McKenzie, "Advertising (In)Equality," 2.
29. Spencer, *Song of Songs*, 92.
30. Fox, *Song of Songs*, 129.
31. Hunt, *Poetry*, 52. This is the poetic device of topographia (or *shem maqom* in Hebrew).
32. Spencer, *Song of Songs*, 92.
33. Moller-Christensen and Jorgensen, *Encyclopedia of Biblical Creatures*, 98.

fertility, sustenance, growth, and flourishing as part of an image that is also extolling the woman for her beauty, vitality, and even (wild) freedom. While in the fictional Gilead women are fungible and are mere vessels—bodies that incubate babies—the biblical Gilead reference is part of a whole *waṣf*, just as her different features are lauded as part of a whole. And not only a whole beautiful body, but a whole beautiful, embodied woman. "A body is an assemblage of body parts; an embodied person is a free being revealed in the flesh. When we speak of a beautiful human body we are referring to the beautiful embodiment of a person, and not to a body considered merely as such."[34]

It is not only the fictional worlds Australians watch, but also the advertising we are exposed to while watching them, that stereotypes women and reduces us to a reproductive role, or defines us only in relation to children or a male partner. Australian social research shows that "women continue to be portrayed in stereotypical roles such as . . . mothers, wives and girlfriends."[35]

How do we descend from the hills of Gilead to reclaim our bodies—our embodied selves—as our own? Perhaps looking to the interpretive tradition of Songs of Songs, which asserts "there is no male dominance, no female subordination, and no stereotyping of either sex."[36] In particular, we may turn to this goat-Gilead simile, which is not sentimental about nature,[37] but recognizes its creative strength and lauds its freedom and vitality. And in the process, woven into this *waṣf*, praises the whole embodied woman, including her beauty, energy, agency, creative capacity, strength and power. Here we have a (somewhat subversive) biblical reminder that women are more than our appearance, or our parts, or our "capacity for motherhood,"[38] and we are not to be narrowly defined or described in relation to with whom we might reproduce.

Moving on to verse two, but not quite yet moving away from the biblical and fictional Gileads, this next simile compares teeth and sheep. And just as there are sound resonances in the English, so too, in the Hebrew. Along with chiasm, hyperbole and punning, there is a "striking assonance,"[39] in the last line of the verse drawing attention to a verb which can mean to "miscarry" (שַׁכֻּלָה, šklh). Perhaps tellingly, I have not been able to find any comment on

34. Scruton, *Beauty*, 40.
35. McKenzie, "Advertising (In)Equality," 4.
36. Trible, "Love's Lyrics Redeemed," 161.
37. Munro, *Imagery*, 151.
38. Munro, *Imagery*, 152.
39. Fox, *Song of Songs*, 129.

the word "miscarry" in this verse, only the translational offering from Fox.[40] Commentators generally agree the meaning of this simile is that the woman's teeth are white like freshly sheared sheep[41] and that she is not missing any. It seems commentators are comfortable discussing how common missing teeth would have been in ancient Israel, but not miscarriage. Miscarriage is an all-too-common embodied experience in Australia with two hundred and eighty-two women experiencing miscarriage a day,[42] and it was all the more common—and dangerous—in the ANE.[43] While miscarriage is arguably not the focus of this verse, it does add another layer of meaning to what is a complex and "stunning pastoral-dental image."[44] Miscarriage was largely unavoidable, and dental issues were an inescapable reality. So perhaps what is to be (additionally) admired here, along with her wholeness and completeness, is that chance—or YHWH—has favored her.

In applying this to our Australian context, we learn that one in four women under the age of thirty-five will experience miscarriage.[45] Yet miscarriage is taboo. I would suggest that part of reclaiming and embracing our embodiment is encouraging public discourse about such a grievous and prevalent embodied experience. But, with the recent backlash against showing menstrual blood in Australian advertising, we are a far cry from making miscarriage mentionable.[46] However, the writer of the Song did not shy away from using the desolate but powerful language of miscarriage and bereavement. And with studies suggesting that thirty to fifty percent of women who miscarry experience post-partum anxiety and ten to fifteen percent experience postnatal depression, we should not shy away from it either.[47] This is but one part of a simile which conveys the coalescence of "elements of purity, symmetry, fecundity ("bearing") and security

---

40. Fox, *Song of Songs*. The verb is more often translated as "bereave (of children)" (one of the most common ways to lose a child, of course, being miscarriage) and it is derived from a primitive root meaning "to miscarry."

41. This is significant because: "the shearing of the sheep was, like the harvest, a great festival in Israel, one so highly regarded that even royalty were invited to partake in the celebration." (Moller-Christensen and Jorgensen, *Encyclopedia of Biblical Creatures*, 99.)

42. Franks, "Taboo topic."

43. Note metaphors of miscarriage in the Psalter (Psalm 35:12; Psalm 58:9; Psalm 144:14).

44. Spencer, *Song of Songs*, 92.

45. Franks, "Taboo Topic."

46. BBC, "Menstrual blood ad complaints dismissed in Australia."

47. Pattanayak, "Improving Psychological Wellbeing after Miscarriage."

("not one . . . is bereaved")"[48] reminding us once again that we are more than sum of our parts.

Turning to verse three and the third simile, we are presented with the contour and color of the lover's lips, which are compared to a red thread, weaving its way into the following simile through hue and haberdashery, evocative of both her pomegranate-temples and the veil they are behind. The following line, *your mouth is lovely*, extends the image to her whole mouth, but to our English-hearing ears is a strange "adjectival predication"[49] seemingly not as dexterous or as brilliant as the metaphor and similes surrounding it. Though, it serves a number of functions: it is a linguistic link to the *inclusio* of the opening and closing verses of the *waṣf*; but it is also a clever punning homophone—the chosen hapax legomenon word for (your) mouth (מִדְבָּרֵךְ, *mdbrk*) sounds like the word for wilderness, *midbar* (מִדְבָּר), and the word *lovely* (נָאוֶה, *nʾwh*) sounds like the word for habitation *naah* (נָאָה).[50] And so a subtle metaphor or paranomasia emerges: the lover's mouth becomes an oasis.[51] In the delicately woven cloth of this *waṣf*, we find an abstraction—an ambiguity—that alludes to a savoring beyond words (cf. Song 1:2, 4:6). This polysemy—the double reference to lips/mouth—and the *inclusio* ferment the image and elicit the idea that *all* of her is to be savored, like a fine wine, not quickly consumed, moving onto the next interchangeable part. And it is well worth noting the intersectionality here: we know that the woman of the Song is black but beautiful (1:5) and that objectification and sexualization often intersect with racism. "Studies in the US have found that African-American women are portrayed in advertisements as having the least facial prominence."[52] This makes the relishing focus on the woman's face good news for black women.[53]

In the fourth simile, form once again mirrors content, encasing parallelism and chiasm within the *inclusio,* reflecting the segments within a pomegranate, and the woman's fragmented features forming an embodied whole. While some have argued that her pomegranate-temples (רַקָּה) *raqqah* should be translated as cheek(bone)s,[54] outside of the Song the word is only

---

48. Spencer, *Song of Songs*, 92.
49. Fox, *Song of Songs*, 130.
50. Spencer, *Song of Songs*, 93. See also Fox, *Song of Songs*, 130.
51. Also playing into v. 12: "a garden . . . a spring . . . fountain."
52. McKenzie, "Advertising (In)Equality," 16. Note also Asian women are more likely to be depicted as "exotic."
53. See Laurence's essay "Beautiful Black Women and the Power of Love (Song 1:5)" in Spencer, *Song of Songs*, 10–14. See Sessions, "Do Not Arouse or Awaken Love," 11–12, for a brief exploration of intersectionality and Song 1.
54. E.g., Alter following Rashi, *Hebrew Bible*, 598.

used to mean temples.[55] Even more interesting than temples and bones is the pomegranate, and its function and position in this verse. Here and in 6:7, the open pomegranate is the image used for the appearance of flushed temples/cheeks behind a veil. This repeated simile is placed either side of an extended image of a garden (4:12—5:1). Pomegranates were considered to be a sign of life and fertility in the ANE due to their clusters of seeds.[56] And this garden had a vast orchard of pomegranates, symbolizing the lover's fruitfulness and the power of potential. Her fruitfulness and potentiality are not limited to reproduction. Pomegranates also symbolized abundant and flourishing life that comes from obedience in the promised land. The woman of the Song represents our potential to flourish. And turning to our Australian context, advertising that accurately portrays women as whole, embodied humans "has the potential to positively transform gender norms and to support and normalize gender equality."[57]

The volta (a poetic device for a turn in thought) of the *waṣf* is at verse four, where a startling military simile disrupts the pleasant pastoral pattern but also finally makes explicit what has been implicit from the first metaphor—the woman of the Song is strong. The lover's neck is likened to the Tower of David, a fitting image, since "a long neck was considered graceful in [other ANE cultures like] Egypt,"[58] and since "height is an important dimension of the *waṣf*."[59] The first part of this two-part simile—the neck and the Tower of David—also solicits pride and respect because "Hebrew associates the neck with an attitude,"[60] and because the tower is "inviolable,"[61] connoting a "proud dynasty and David as a great warrior."[62] Now, if a reference to Gilead imbues the woman with the qualities of Gilead, then would not a reference to a tower do likewise? Curiously, the record, until recently, has remained relatively quiet.

Though the Hebrew is unclear, (mostly male) scholars tend to agree that the second part of this simile—courses of stones hung with warrior shields—refers to the woman's necklace.[63] Fox even makes so much of

---

55. Spencer, *Song of Songs*, 93. In fact, the only other usage is in Judges (4:21f and 5:26) when Jael struck Sisera.

56. Munro, *Imagery*, 168. Also Hess, *Song of Songs*, 133; Keel, *Song of Songs*, 143–7.

57. McKenzie, "Advertising (In)Equality," 6.

58. Fox, *Song of Songs*, 130.

59. Munro, *Imagery*, 121.

60. Keel, *Song of Songs*, 147.

61. See Ps 48:12–13; Keel, *Song of Songs*, 147.

62. Zhang, *I, You and the Word "God,"* 36.

63. Alter, *Hebrew Bible*, 599; Fox, *Song of Songs*, 130; Hess, *Song of Songs*, 134; Hunt, *Poetry*, 254; Keel, *Song of Songs*, 147; Longman, *Song of Songs*, 146, etc.

this unmentioned necklace that he has suggested it is "the main point of the simile."⁶⁴ I am less concerned with whether the woman was wearing a necklace and more interested in the imagery of the warrior shields. Usually if military might is deployed in an image, it is to signal strength. Surely the main point of the simile is thus her strength! But not until fairly recently has anyone recognized that this simile is describing and praising the woman's strength.⁶⁵

And we shouldn't be shocked that it has also taken Australian society a long time to realize women—including our diverse bodies—are strong in many and varied ways and to depict and describe us so. The research also discusses the impact gendered portrayals are having on our culture: "Girls learn that they are expected to be attractive, cooperative and caring, while boys learn that they are expected to be strong, active and independent. Both boys and girls learn that activities and behaviors associated with masculinity have a higher social status."⁶⁶ So how do women reclaim our embodied selves as strong and powerful?⁶⁷ I think we can look to this often-missed-and-misunderstood simile of staunch strength and safeguarding skill. The woman of the Song is a royal armory upholding a thousand warrior shields. "This is no weak woman to be trifled with or scanned up and down with leering lust. While she may welcome admiring looks, especially from her lover, her bearing demands that she be treated with respect, even fear."⁶⁸ Perhaps that necklace is actually a "No Trespassing" sign.⁶⁹

From the warrior woman's neck, we move to the heart of the matter—or the chest and breast of the matter—with the final similes likening the lover's breasts to twin gazelle fawns. It is well established that gazelles were associated with love in the ANE.⁷⁰ And commentators have tended to focus on the appearance of her breasts: "they are perfectly balanced, and dappled,"⁷¹ with a few managing to move on to an idyllic, nurturing image

---

64. Fox, *Song of Songs*, 130.

65. Hess, Hunt, Keel and others come close, but as best I can tell, it is not until Spencer that the simile is explicitly linked to her strength.

66. McKenzie, "Advertising (In)Equality," 5.

67. Note that I don't mean femvertising, nor do I wish to be ableist.

68. Spencer, *Song of Songs*, 85.

69. Spencer, *Song of Songs*, 94.

70. Keel demonstrates this point with reference to iconography (*Song of Songs*, 89–94); Pope with reference to Mesopotamian magical spells (*Song of Songs*, 386); and various others via Egyptian love poetry.

71. Munro, *Imagery*, 154, providing a rare example from a woman. See also Alter, *Hebrew Bible*, 599; Fox, *Song of Songs*, 131; Hess, *Song of Songs*, 136; Hunt, *Poetry*, 155; Longman, *Song of Songs*, 147; Murphy, *Song of Songs*, 155; Pope, *Song of Songs*, 470, etc.

of their "maternal function."[72] I do wonder if these (mostly male) commentators are aware of what having breasts and breastfeeding is actually like? Neither they nor those who perpetuate the stereotyped roles for women in Australian advertising seem to grasp that sustaining life from our bodies is hard work and requires health and strength (not to mention a pain threshold for toddler teeth)! And why be limited to a choice between form and function? The Hebrew thought-world associates breasts with "notions of blessing (Gen 49:25), kindness, nourishment, and trust building (Ps 22:9; Job 3:12)."[73] Much like the pomegranate of verse three, breasts evoke "full participation in life and life's renewal."[74]

While it has also been established that gazelles are "associated with the hunt and with the royal park"[75] and that the gazelle is emblematic of speed[76] and surefootedness,[77] some commentators have tended to refer to qualities like beauty and grace when the gazelle is used to describe the woman.[78] But when the gazelle is used to describe the man, commentators apply motifs of virility and strength.[79] Does it not take fertility, energy, and strength to bear and care for a child? Furthermore, the description of the Daughters of Jerusalem being "as free as the gazelles and hinds of the field"[80] should also evoke the lover's freedom, and freedom to move. So, the lover also has a kind of "kinesthetic beauty"[81] like the movement of gazelles. And in reclaiming our embodied movement, women can improve not only our physical health, but also our mental health and body image,[82] since there is a proven link between participating in sport/movement and our body image. After all, a gazelle does not worry about what it looks like when it leaps. It just leaps.

The remainder of this verse is concerned with lilies and whether browsing among them has more to do with the form or function of breasts (or even whether the simile refers to breasts like the rumps of gazelles, with nipples

---

72. Munro, *Imagery*, 154. Spencer, *Song of Songs*, 96. Hunt, *Poetry*, 154.
73. Keel, *Song of Songs*, 150.
74. Keel, *Song of Songs*, 150.
75. Munro, *Imagery*, 151.
76. Moller-Christensen and Jorgensen, *Encyclopedia of Biblical Creatures*, 3–6.
77. Hunt, *Poetry*, 148.
78. Fox, *Song of Songs*, 131 See also Hess, *Song of Songs*, 136; Alter, *Hebrew Bible*, 599.
79. Alter, *Hebrew Bible*, 593; Fox, *Song of Songs*, 112; Hunt, *Poetry*, 157.
80. Munro, *Imagery*, 155.
81. Hunt, *Poetry*, 141.
82. Hausenblas, "Exercise and Body Image," 6.

like tails!)[83] Given I have already argued we are not limited to a choice between appearance and operation, we shall turn to the question of the lilies. These are the most frequently mentioned flower in the Song, but we're not entirely sure what they are. On the basis of the LXX's "lilium", the word שׁוֹשַׁנִּים (*shoshanim*) has traditionally been associated with the Madonna lily. But it could just as easily be a waterlily or lotus. Going as far back as Herodotus may help here: "What is known in the Greek world as a lily, is called a lotus in Egypt."[84] We also know that similar imagery appears in Egyptian love poetry, which favored fawns feeding on lilies suggestive of breasts.[85] But, as we transition away from the seven segmented similes and into verse six, which we know is about the beloved wanting to go to his lover, perhaps the lotuses also herald that a change is coming: "Flowers are often used in the OT to evoke the transitory nature of human life."[86]

Verse six is both evocative of the transformation of night into day, but also of traversing the space between them, as the beloved repeats his lover's words from 2:17; he is responding to her invitation to come to her. He "is less specific with regard to the body part or parts in question,"[87] and "the distance is eliminated, as the man puts himself in the picture"[88] as he clearly wants to be with her. Again, it is not entirely clear what is meant by "the mountain of myrrh," with some scholars arguing for breasts, though the mountain is singular. Others suggest it may be her pubic mound.[89] What *is* clear is that the beloved aims "no more to reduce her to this one erogenous zone than to any other body part. Ultimately it is her beautiful embodied person that overwhelms him 'altogether.'"[90] And it is the "altogether" of verse seven that is key: Women are whole, complete, beautiful embodied humans altogether, not an assemblage of interchangeable parts.

Conclusion

We know from the work of Women's Health Victoria that "sexualized and objectifying . . . representations in advertising and other media can cause

83. Longman, *Song of Songs*, 148.

84. Munro, *Imagery*, 163–4, quoting Herodotus.

85. Fox, *Song of Songs*, 32.

86. Munro, *Imagery*, 161. See: Ps 103:15; Job 14:2; Isa 28:1; 40:6, 7, 8.

87. Exum, *Song of Songs*, 167.

88. Exum, *Song of Songs*, 167. Cf. Longman, *Song of Songs*, 147.

89. Alter, *The Hebrew Bible*, 599; Longman, *Song of Songs*, 147; Spencer, *Song of Songs*, 97.

90. Spencer, *Song of Songs*, 97.

women and men to have a diminished view of women's humanity, competence, and morality. Women are perceived as less capable, less intelligent and are dehumanized when we are portrayed in sexualized ways."[91]

And so, by way of a conclusion, we turn to the closing verse of the *waṣf*, which forms an *inclusio* by not only repeating her beauty but stating that *all* of her is beautiful. And in between we have experienced animal and pastoral images which convey the woman's autonomy, agency, creative power, and flourishing, which builds to the display of her strength in architectural and military imagery and transitions into a display of her skill—skill not only to sustain life but to confidently and freely move.

If we are to descend from the hills of Gilead and reclaim our bodies from contemporary advertising, perhaps we may look to the woman of the song to encourage us to embrace our embodiment. "*All* of you is beautiful." It is stressed in the final verse and is woven throughout the *waṣf* by "a perfect cycle of seven"[92]—the Hebrew number for wholeness. Seven verses, seven similes, seven body parts, all working together to convey not only all her features but all her qualities converging to form a comprehensive completeness.

Each one of us is a comprehensive completeness.

Bibliography

Alter, Robert. *The Hebrew Bible: A Translation with Commentary*. New York: Norton, 2018.
BBC. "Menstrual Blood Ad Complaints Dismissed in Australia." *BBC News* website. September 18, 2018. www.bbc.com/news/world-australia-49736708
Black, Fiona. *The Artifice of Love: Grotesque Bodies and the Song of Songs*. London: T&T Clark, 2009.
Dobbs-Allsopp, F. W. "The Delight of Beauty and Song of Songs 4:1–7." *Interpretation* 59 (2005) 260–77.
Etcoff, Nancy. *Survival of the Prettiest: The Science of Beauty*. New York: Anchor, 1999.
Exum, J. Cheryl. *Song of Songs: A Commentary*. The Old Testament Library, Louisville: Westminster John Knox, 2005.
Fox, Michael, V. *The Song of Songs and the Egyptian Love Songs*. Madison: University of Wisconsin Press, 1985.
Franks, Rebecca. "Taboo Topic: 'No One Talks about It.'" *The Morning Bulletin* website. July 2, 2018. https://www.themorningbulletin.com.au/news/the-taboo-topic-affecting-282-aussie-women-a-day-t/3456419/
Hausenblas, Heather, A., and Elizabeth A. Fallon. "Exercise and Body Image: A Meta-Analysis." *Psychology & Health* 21/1 (2006) 33–47.

---

91. McKenzie, "Advertising (In)Equality," 5.
92. Zhang, *I, You and the Word "God,"* 37.

The Headless Women Project. "Headless Women of Hollywood." Website. https://headlesswomenofhollywood.com/?ref_url=http://headlesswomenofhollywood.com/post/151367596158/headlesswomenofhollywood-wife-material-a/embed

Hess, Richard. *Song of Songs*. Baker Commentary on the Old Testament Wisdom and Psalms. Grand Rapids: Baker Academic, 2005.

Hunt, Patrick. *Poetry in the Song of Songs: A Literary Analysis*. New York: Peter Lang, 2008.

Keel, Othmar. *The Song of Songs: A Continental Commentary*. Philadelphia: Fortress, 1994.

Longman, Tremper. *Song of Songs*. NICOT. Grand Rapids: Eerdmans, 2001.

Mehta M., and R. D. Pattanayak. "Follow-up for Improving Psychological Well-Being for Women after a Miscarriage." *The WHO Reproductive Health Library*. Geneva: WHO, 2013.

McKenzie, M. et al. "Advertising (In)Equality: The Impacts of Sexist Advertising on Women's Health and Wellbeing." Women's Health Victoria Issues Paper. Women's Health Victoria: December 2018. https://whv.org.au/resources/whv-publications/advertising-inequality-impacts-sexist-advertising-women%E2%80%99s-health-and

Moller-Christensen, V., and Jordt J Jorgensen. *Encyclopedia of Biblical Creatures*. Philadelphia: Fortress, 1965.

Munro, Jill. *Imagery of the Song of Songs*. PhD diss., University of Edinburgh, November 1991: https://pdfs.semanticscholar.org

Murphy, Roland E. *The Song of Songs*. Philadelphia: Fortress, 1990.

Nussbaum, Martha. "Objectification." *Philosophy & Public Affairs* 24/4 (1995) 249–91.

Pope, Marvin. *Song of Songs*. Anchor Bible Commentary. New York: Doubleday, 1977.

Scruton, Roger. *Beauty: A Very Short Introduction*. Oxford: Oxford University Press, 2011.

Sessions, Erin Martine. "Do Not Arouse or Awaken Love until It So Desires: How Songs of Songs Speaks to Australia's Problem with Intimate Partner Violence." *Crucible* 9/1 (2018) 1–16.

Spencer, F. Scott. *Song of Songs*. Wisdom Commentary 25. Edited by Barbara E. Reid. Collegeville: Liturgical, 2017.

Trible, Phyllis. "Love's Lyrics Redeemed." In *God and the Rhetoric of Sexuality*, 144–65. Overtures to Biblical Theology 2. Philadelphia: Fortress, 1978.

Zhang, Sarah. *I, You and the Word "God": Finding Meaning in the Song of Songs*. Indiana: Eisenbrauns, 2016.

9

Desert Spring, Dead Dog Waterhole, Disappointment Creek

Is the God of the Book of Jeremiah Bad for Women?

JILL FIRTH[1]

UNCOMPLIMENTARY FEMININE METAPHORS, DEPICTION of masculine violence, and distressing imagery about God are disturbing to many readers of the early chapters of Jeremiah.[2] Jerusalem is imaged as an immoral woman (Jeremiah 2), who is threatened with violence and shamed by her enemies (chs. 4–13). Some scholars have further developed the images into a narrative of Judah as God's promiscuous wife (chs. 2–4) who is violently punished by God in his role as angry husband (chs. 4–6) and then publicly raped by him (Jer 13:20–26).[3] We may ask how our attitudes to God and to women can be grounded in this Scripture today. In Australia, we are conscious of the sexualization of women in the media, the frequency of sexual harassment of women and girls, the appalling statistics of domestic and family violence, and the tragic and violent rapes of women, such as those

---

1. A summary of this chapter was given at ETS in San Diego, California on 22 November 2019 in the section Evangelicals and Gender. "Is the God of the Book of Jeremiah Bad for Women?: Clarifying Genres, Metaphors, and Contexts."

2. Weems, *Battered*, 1–3; Seibert, *Violence*, 130, 142; Scholz, *Introducing*, 85.

3. Scholz, *Introducing*, 101, 101 n45, 104, 106; O'Connor, *Jeremiah*, 54, 107.

of Melbourne women Jill Meagher and Euridice Dixon. In our history, this violence is also horrifyingly prevalent against Aboriginal women, as seen in the 1896 attitude of Mounted Constable William Willshire, who believed that "God meant Aboriginal women to be used by white men, 'as He had placed them wherever the pioneers go.'"[4] In this season of greater awareness of #MeToo and domestic violence, we can wonder if God is a reliable ally for women and question God's claim to be a reliable source of refreshing water (2:13).[5] The people of Jeremiah's time accused God of offering them poisoned water (8:14), and Jeremiah himself questioned whether God was an unreliable brook (15:18). We too may ask if God is always trustworthy, like a waterfall in Dyambrin, or sometimes unavailable, like an intermittent stream in the Wimmera, or if he is a harmful figure, standing by, or even complicit in domestic violence and the degradation of women, like a polluted waterhole in Kuwarra country.[6]

In this paper, I explore whether the God of Jeremiah is bad for women by examining the rhetorical use of feminine metaphors within various genres in the context of the whole book of Jeremiah, as the genre of prophecy is "timefull,"[7] persuasive, and complex. I distinguish four genres: *caricature* (2–3), *dystopia* (4–13), *heterotopia* (24, 29, 40), and *utopia* (30–33).[8] I conclude that the God of the book of Jeremiah was good for women in the time of Jeremiah, and is still good for Australian women today.

Prophecy: Timefullness, Persuasion, and Complexity

The book of Jeremiah is "timefull," persuasive, and complex. Many people read prophecies as timeless, but the messages were spoken at a specific time and place, and a specific time of Israel's history. Prophecy brings us truth that is timefull, not timeless. The early chapters of Jeremiah suggest that

---

4. Quote from unpublished paper by Judy Atkinson, cited in Thomas, "Sexual Assault," 140.

5. References are to Jeremiah unless otherwise noted.

6. Dyambrin is the original name of Mount Tamborine in Queensland. The Wimmera is in Western Victoria. Kuwarra land is in the eastern Goldfields region of Western Australia.

7. I adapt the term "timefull" from Swinton, *Becoming*, 1, 183–84, 207.

8. Dystopia and utopia in Jeremiah are treated in O'Connor, "Two Visions," and Carvalho, "Drunkenness." The concept of heterotopia is from Foucalt, "Of Other Spaces," see West, "Between," 219. Feminine imagery in Jeremiah 2–13 has been viewed through the lens of various genres including pornography (Brenner, "Response," 305), horror (Kalmanofsky, "Monstrous," 190), trauma (O'Connor, *Jeremiah*, 35–36), and lament (Claassens, "Calling," 65).

foreign invasion is not far away, and the text repeatedly expresses amazement and disbelief that Israel could be so blind to God's goodness and their own danger (2:10–12, 14, 31, 32). Jeremiah's preaching over previous decades has not led to repentance, and Nebuchadnezzar will soon approach the gates of Jerusalem (25:3, 9). It seems that the Jewish leaders were trusting in a prophecy of Isaiah to Sennacherib from a hundred years earlier (Isa 37:21–35), rather than hearing God's voice through Jeremiah concerning Nebuchadnezzar in their own day.

Prophecy is typically *persuasion* rather than prescription or prediction.[9] I propose that the use of harsh female imagery in Jeremiah is part of a rhetorical strategy where Jeremiah builds an "affective charge" into his message,[10] to awaken the nation from apathy, and emphasizing the appalling consequences if people do not turn from their wicked ways. The uncomplimentary feminine imagery in Jeremiah has attracted accusations of misogyny,[11] but a critical portrayal does not necessarily imply a negative view of women. Tim Winton, a well-known commentator on toxic masculinity, depicts monstrous men, such as Max in "The Turning," not from misanthropy, but to challenge men to be the best they can be.[12] In seeking to get the attention of his people, God uses harsh feminine imagery in invitation, not in denigration.[13] God exposes Israel's blindness in the past and present, concerning covenant unfaithfulness. The danger is urgent, and forceful pleas are appropriate. In a shock tactic to gain the attention of those who are not listening to subtle messages, Jeremiah features a ridiculous and grotesque caricature of Jerusalem as a promiscuous woman (2:23–25, 32–37). Later in the book (chs. 30–33), Jeremiah uses tender female imagery to represent future hope. As very positive images of women are also found in the Old Testament in the Song of Songs, Proverbs 31, and narratives including Hannah, Deborah, and Huldah, the rhetorical purpose of the negative feminine metaphors in the early chapters of Jeremiah can be examined further.

Some assign God sole responsibility for the violence of the fall of Jerusalem, but "God is, finally, not the sole subject of verbs of violence."[14] Rather than aligning God's preferences with historical outcomes, a

---

9. Carvalho, "Challenge," 109; Siebert, *Violence*, 134.

10. Ivakhiv, "Cinema," 187.

11. Weems, *Battered*, 85; Shields, *Circumscribing*, 1; Kalmanofsky, "Monstrous," 207–8.

12. Winton, "The Turning," 160–61.

13. Hays, *Message*, 63.

14. Fretheim, "Violence," 118.

complex account of the causation of disaster is required, as "when dealing with the things of God, one can hardly but expect paradox, nuance, subtlety and multi-facetedness."[15] God has limited himself in his direct control of human history, as God committed himself to the use of means in our world (Gen 1:11). In the creation, he gave agency to human beings and allowed choices that forever impacted the course of history (Gen 1:28; 2:16-17; 3:6).[16] After the flood, he committed himself to "never again" (לֹא אָסֵף, *lʾ ʾsp*) curse the ground, nor to destroy every creature (Gen 8:21). God's decision to use Nebuchadnezzar as his agent included the possibility of violence, for God's agents may exceed their commission (Zech 1:15), and may cause God regret (Jer 42:10).[17]

With this reminder of timefullness rather than timelessness, persuasion rather than prediction or prescription, and complex causality, we turn to the use of feminine imagery in the rhetorical strategies in Jeremiah, which include alternating masculine and feminine metaphors and the use of various genres including caricature, dystopia, heterotopia, and utopia.

Masculine and Feminine Metaphors

Masculine and feminine imagery are used in Jeremiah to convey both positive and negative messages. Marriage and sonship, two major family metaphors for the covenant in the Old Testament, are used in Jeremiah's early chapters, where Judah is imaged as a son (masculine) and as a wife (feminine). The past is introduced with a positive feminine image of Jerusalem as a bride in the wilderness (2:2) and a positive masculine image of Israel as holy first-fruits (2:3), before castigating their ancestors (masculine plural) for defiling the land and failing to know him (2:4-8).

Using feminine imagery, Jeremiah presents an exaggerated metaphor of an out of control, promiscuous wife (2:16-25, 32-37) in contrast with the earlier covenant faithfulness of Jerusalem as a bride (2:1). Judah forsakes the LORD for political alliances with Egypt and Assyria (2:16-19) and rebelliously engages in idolatry (2:20-22). She becomes ridiculous, like a skittish young camel and a wild ass eagerly seeking male partners, risking thirst and discomfort, proclaiming, "It is hopeless!" (נוֹאָשׁ לוֹא, *nwʾš lwʾ*),

---

15. Paul A. Barker, cited in Martens, "Toward," 140.

16. Fretheim, "Violence," 113-14.

17. Fretheim, "Violence," 117, 121-22, responds to Brueggemann, *Commentary*, 54, "the real agent is Yahweh" (see also, Brueggemann, *Commentary*, 70, 176, 193, 428, 430, 439, 460).

and determined to pursue strangers (זרים, *zrym*) whether these represent political allies or other gods (2:23–25, see also 2:32–37).

Using masculine terms, the present generation is critiqued for their unnatural substitution of false gods for the true God (2:9–13) and for behaving like a slave (masculine singular) instead of as son (2:14–15). Original readers would have been as shocked by the characterization of themselves as a son who has forgotten his father (2:14) as by the image of themselves as a promiscuous wife (3:1). Jeremiah further challenges the complacency of Israel with uncomplimentary masculine images throughout the book, including a thief (2:26; 5:26), den of robbers (7:11), treacherous hunters (7:27), neighing lustful stallions (5:8), a horse foolishly plunging into battle (8:6), a foolish bird (8:7), a wild vine (2:21), fruitless fig tree (8:13), chaff (13:24), bad figs (24:1), a filthy linen loincloth (13:10–11), and dung on the ground (8:2; 9:22; 16:4; 25:33).

Myopia and Caricature

The genre of caricature is fronted in the book for rhetorical purposes, employing exaggeration and grim humor to invite Judah's leaders to review their behavior. Gérard Genette includes "grandiloquent hyperbole" as an aspect of caricature.[18] The cartoonist Peggy Bacon (1895–1897) explains the exaggeration of caricature:

> The aim of a caricature is to heighten and intensify to the point of absurdity all the subject's most striking attributes; a caricature should not necessarily stop at ridiculing the features but should include in its extravagant appraisal whatever of the figure may be needed to explain the personality, the whole drawing imparting a spicy and clairvoyant comment upon the subject's peculiarities.[19]

Modern commentators use devices such as animal imagery and gender switching to sharpen and heighten their statements through caricature. George Orwell wrote *Animal Farm* as a satire on the Russian Revolution.[20] Gender reversal is used effectively by Naomi Alderman in her novel, *The Power*, which exposes gender violence by describing a dystopia where women have become physically stronger than men and treat men with contempt. The locating of powerful feminine images in the beginning of the book of

---

18. Genette, *Palimpsests*, 90.
19. Bacon, "Untitled."
20. Davison, "George Orwell."

Jeremiah may be intended to get under the guard of male leaders.²¹ By experiencing distaste and contempt for the antics of wife Jerusalem, they may become more open to examining their own unfaithful behavior.

The sexualized feminine descriptions of sinful Judah in chapters 2–3 do not single out the sexual behavior of women for critique. The people as a whole are castigated for forsaking the LORD and the covenant (2:13), idolatry (2:26–27), violence and exploitation of the needy (5:28), adultery (9:2), and child sacrifice (7:30–31). The book of Jeremiah focuses on the sins of male leaders, especially priests, rulers, and prophets who rebelled against the LORD (2:8; 16:11–12; 23:11; 26:23; 32:32; 36:29), priests who committed adultery and told lies (23.14), and prophets who were ungodly (23:15). *There is no specific mention of sexual sins of women in the poetry, sermons or narratives in Jeremiah.*²² Women are directly critiqued for baking cakes for the Queen of Heaven, but are not sexualized in the text.²³ The sins of women are mentioned only in company with their husbands and families (7:18; 44:9). The purpose of these feminine metaphors must be explored further.

In the ancient Near East, feminine imagery was traditionally used to denote a city or land. Throughout the Old Testament, cities including Jerusalem are usually "she." In Hebrew, the words for city (עיר, *ʿyr*), land (ארץ, *ʾrṣ*), and ground (אדמה, *ʾdmh*) are all grammatically feminine. In Mesopotamian city laments of the second and first millennium BC, a female figure utters lament for the fallen city.²⁴ In Hebrew prophetic literature, a feminine figure is often used to represent nations including Israel. Such depictions can be sympathetic, such as Jerusalem receiving respect as a beloved mother figure (Isa 60:14–16), or critical, as where virgin daughter Egypt (בתולת בת־מצרים, *btwlt bt-mṣrym*) needs healing (Jer 46:11) or Jerusalem's abominations are judged (Ezek 5:5–12).

The shock value of displeasing feminine imagery in the early chapters of Jeremiah may have been specifically chosen to counter Judah's myopia based on an earlier prophecy of Isaiah, when Sennacherib was besieging Jerusalem a hundred years earlier.²⁵ Judah's leaders may have clung to a past portrait of daughter Jerusalem tossing her head at the Assyrians, "She despises you, she scorns you—virgin daughter Zion [בתולת בת־ציון, *btwlt bt-ṣywn*] . . . I will defend my city to save it, for my own sake and for the sake

---

21. As in the well-known strategy in Amos 1–2, where other nations are critiqued before turning to Israel in the following chapters.

22. Carvalho, "Challenge," 111. Allen, *Jeremiah*, 48, says there is "no evidence" for "Canaanite orgiastic rites of sexual prostitution."

23. Carvalho, "Challenge," 119.

24. Gwaltney, "Biblical," 202, as in the biblical book of Lamentations.

25. The term "myopia" is adapted from Boda, "Dystopia," 210.

of my servant David" (Isa 37:22, 35), rather than seeing their true current status as seedy adulterers rejected by God.

In summary, the rhetorical strategy using the genre of caricature in Chapters 2–3 sought to elicit disgust and shame at Israel's rejection of the LORD. The exaggerated depiction of women in chapters 2–3 is directed to male leaders. It is not misogyny, and does not reflect a critique directed to women. We now turn to chapters 4–6, which undertake a different rhetorical strategy focusing on fear and pity using the genre of *dystopia*.

Future Dystopia

In chapters 4–6, the time moves from the present to the future, the genre shifts from *caricature* to *dystopia*, and the feminine metaphor changes from representing Israel as God's wife, and mother of his children (3:20–21), to daughter imagery (4:31; 6:2).[26] Dystopias are typically set in the future and may evoke fear, horror, or pity. Dystopia has become a familiar category through novels and movies including George Orwell's *Nineteen Eighty-Four* (1949), Margaret Attwood's *The Handmaid's Tale* (1985), and Suzanne Collins's *The Hunger Games* (2008). Modern dystopias are not intended to invite imitation of the violence or abuse that they describe, but to help to avoid them.[27] A dystopia is irreal, a presentation of what might happen if a current trajectory is continued. George Orwell said of *Nineteen Eighty-Four*,

> I do not believe that the kind of society I describe necessarily *will* arrive, but I believe (allowing of course for the fact that the book is a satire) that something resembling it *could* arrive . . . I have tried to draw these ideas out to their logical consequences.[28]

In a recent example, modelling of the *coronavirus* (COVID-19) exemplifies what might happen under alternative scenarios of mitigation, suppression, and intermittent social distancing.[29] Some government strategies have been impacted by reflecting on the possible outcome of doing nothing compared with listening to expert advice.[30]

---

26. O'Connor, "Two Visions," 87, looks back at dystopia from the exile: "the dystopic world . . . has already come." Carvalho, "Drunkenness," 598, focuses on "the twenty-first century gendered world."

27. Carvalho, "Drunkenness," 612.

28. Orwell, quoted in O'Flinn, "Rereading," n. p.

29. Ferguson et. al., "Impact of Non-Pharmaceutical Interventions," 1–2.

30. Van Elsland and O'Hare, "COVID-19."

The change in genre from caricature to dystopia also signals a change in rhetorical strategy. The rhetorical strategy in chapters 2–3 focused on disgust and shame about profligate wife Judah, but chapters 4–6 seek to elicit pity for endangered daughter Zion. Daughter imagery is distinct from the marital metaphor. In Jeremiah 4–6, Jerusalem is now described as "daughter Zion" (בת ציון, *bt-ṣywn*, 4:31; 6:2, 23), and Jeremiah uses the idiom "the daughter of my people" (בת עמי, *bt ʿmy*, 4:11, 6.26).³¹ Corinne Carvalho notes that "while not all the references to daughter Zion are positive, she is not accused of sexual transgression."³² The daughter metaphor is also used about other nations, who are not depicted as God's wives (46:11; 48:18; 49:4; 50:42). I will argue that the marital metaphors of chapters 2–3 should not be read into chapters 4–13, which focuses on daughter Zion.³³

Jeremiah 4–6 depicts a horrifying dystopia of war and suffering for the land and its people, warning its first hearers of the trajectory of present evil, with the goal of inviting repentance. In this future vision, the earth (ארץ, *ʾrṣ*) has returned to being formless and void (תהו ובהו, *thw wbhw*), devoid of birds, animals, and people (4:23–28). God mourns for "the daughter of my people" (בת עמי, *bt ʿmy*) in the path of a desolating storm (4:11); and for "daughter Zion" (בת ציון, *bt-ṣywn*) who is still foolishly seeking alliances but is in anguish like a woman in labor, fainting before her killers (4:30–31).³⁴ The dystopia of chapters 4–6 is not God's angry response to Israel's unfaithfulness, but a warning of what will happen if they do not accept the safety measures he has put in place for their protection. The accusations in the preceding section about "my people" (עמי, *ʿmy*, 2:11, 13, 32) shift in chapter 4 to sympathy for the sufferings of "the daughter of my people" (בת עמי, *bt ʿmy*, 4:11; 6:26) and "daughter Zion" (בת ציון, *bt-ṣywn*, 4:31; 6:2, 23). The tears of God are prominent in the first half of the book (4:18; 8:18; 9:1; see also 8:19; 13:17; 14:17; 23:9).

The future dystopia continues in Jeremiah 13, using masculine and feminine images of honor and shame. The chapter opens with the masculine simile of a linen loincloth, which symbolizes Israel in intimate communion with God (13:1–11). Israel was to cling (דבק, *dbq*) to God as a loincloth clings to a man's loins (13:11), so that they might be a people, name (שׁם, *šm*), praise (תהלה, *thlh*), and glory (תפארת, *tpʾrt*).³⁵ However, if they refused,

31. Lallemann, *Jeremiah*, 95.
32. Carvalho, "Challenge," 109.
33. Contra Scholz, *Introducing*, 101; O'Connor, *Jeremiah*, 54, 107; Longman, *Jeremiah*, 54.
34. בת עמי (*bt ʿmy*) is literally "the daughter of my people," meaning "my people," see Lundbom, *Jeremiah 1–20*, 344. NRSV translates as "my poor people" in 4:11.
35. Lau, *Jeremiah*, 127 and Wright, *Jeremiah*, 156–66 link the honor and shame of

they would become useless (לא יצלח לכל, *lʾ yṣlḥ lkl*), like dirty, ruined (נשחת, *nšḥt*) underwear (13:7). In this masculine image, the prophet is left naked and dishonored.[36] The chapter continues with masculine plural language to warn of judgment, captivity, and pride, and God weeps bitterly, calling for pity for the ravaging of the land (13:12–19a).[37]

Using feminine language, Judah is seen as going into exile (גלה, *glh*, 13:19b). Using a play on words with גלה, which can mean exile or uncovering, Judah is shamed as her skirts are lifted up (גלה, *glh*, 13:22). This image parallels the shame in the masculine image of the rotten underwear of 13:1–11. The rhetorical purpose of this image is to warn Judah of the consequence of exile if they persist in their war against Nebuchadnezzar. Imaging Judah as feminine evokes the people's relationship with the LORD rather than their identity as aggressive male warriors, and may be intended to bring forth pity for the land and its people, thereby preventing an ill-considered dash into warfare.[38]

God and Intimate Partner Violence

Some scholars create a narrative of intimate partner violence by conflating the narrative of chapter 2–3 with chapters 4–13.[39] Renita Weems proposes a metaphor of a "battered wife" in these chapters.[40] Kathleen O'Connor writes of chapters 4–13, "Daughter Zion . . . is God's beloved wife . . . that sad family story continues here."[41] I have already argued that the rhetorical strategy of the marital imagery in the caricature of chapters 2–3 should be distinguished from the use of daughter imagery in the dystopia of chapters 4–13. In this section, I address the question of God, intimate partner violence, and weaponized rape.

Weems claims that that the marriage metaphor presumes an Old Testament world of "brutality, rape, and subjugation . . . The image of the

---

the loincloth and the lifting of Judah's skirt (13.22).

36. Carvalho, "Drunkenness," 612.

37. In Jeremiah 20.7, the prophet describes his struggle with God over his call using the language of enticement ("you have enticed me, and I was enticed," NRSV), or deceit ("you deceived me and I was deceived," NIV), פתיתני יהוה ואגת (*ptytny yhwh wʾgt*). The verb חזק (*ḥzq*), to overpower, is also used later in this verse. Some commentators have seen overtones of sexual seduction or forcing in the use of the words פתה (*pth*) and חזק (*ḥzq*), see Fretheim, *Jeremiah*, 290–92.

38. Reeder, *Gendering*, 88.

39. Scholz, *Introducing*, 101; O'Connor, *Jeremiah*, 54, 107; Longman, *Jeremiah*, 54.

40. Weems, *Battered*, 106.

41. O'Connor, *Jeremiah*, 49.

battered promiscuous wife . . . leaves unquestioned husbands' presumption that they have the authority to degrade and silence their wives."[42] Susanne Scholz writes, "The prophetic poem in Jeremiah 13 envisions God as relishing in the rape of woman Jerusalem, a rape that is perpetrated by the presumed Babylonian army and supported by the male God. It represents a climax of androcentric fury regarding women."[43]

The Old Testament neither commands, commends, nor models spousal abuse. Though, undoubtedly, some men degraded and hurt their wives in ancient times, as today, a review of the laws and narratives of the Old Testament shows that there are no instructions to physically strike wives and, surprisingly, no narratives of husbands hitting their wives. Similarly, rape is rejected as a vile outrage, a thing not done in Israel, in the three extended Old Testament rape narratives of Dinah (Gen 34:7), the Levite's concubine (Judg 20:6), and Tamar (2 Sam 13:12–13). Abraham and Isaac are both rebuked in horror for offering their wives to other men (Gen 12:18–20; 26:8–11). There is no command to rape women in war.[44] In fact, captive women must be given time to mourn, must be treated as a wife, and cannot be sold on (Deut 21:10–14). Intimate partner violence and weaponized rape are never affirmed in the Old Testament.

A detailed examination of the vocabulary of Jeremiah 13.22 and 26 suggests that they may refer to "public humiliation" rather than rape.[45] Jeremiah 13:22b literally reads, "your heels were violated" (נחמסו עקביך, *nḥmsw ʿqbyk*, 13:22).[46] Many scholars consider that the phrase denotes rape.[47] However, the terms "lifted up" (גלה, *glh*), "heel" (עקב, *ʿqb*), and חמס (*ḥms*, "violated," NRSV, or possibly "exposed," Allen) are not usually used in the Old Testament to denote rape.[48] Whether or not rape is signified in this verse, the purpose of using feminine metaphors in chapter 13 is to evoke fear, shame, and pity in male leaders, not to advocate weaponized rape. This text does not provide a basis for a claim that God would approve the rape of Judah by enemy forces.

42. Weems, *Battered*, 86. See also Carvalho, "Challenge," 112.

43. Scholz, *Introducing*, 101.

44. Contra practice invited in *Iliad* 2.415f, 22.66f, see Shay, *Achilles*, 104–5.

45. McKane, *Jeremiah*, 306, translates 13:22, "your modesty is violated," or "your nakedness is uncovered," and argues that this is "public humiliation . . . an allusion to rape in v. 22 is inappropriate." (311).

46. Lundbom, *Jeremiah 1–20*, 683.

47. Holladay, *Jeremiah 1*, 414; Clements, *Jeremiah*, 87; Lallemann, *Jeremiah*, 147; Longman, *Jeremiah*, 116.

48. חמס is translated as "exposed," by Allen, *Jeremiah*, 162, who, however, exegetes חמס as rape in this text (164). Keil, *Jeremiah*, 241 suggests a barefoot journey into exile.

Even more serious accusations are leveled at God concerning Jeremiah 13:26, where O'Connor says, "God rapes the beloved Daughter of Zion,"[49] and Scholz writes, "God is the sexual violator."[50] Jeremiah 13:26 explicitly focuses on shame: "I myself will lift up (חשׂף, *ḥśp*) your skirts over your face, and your shame will be seen" (13:26, NRSV). The first half of the verse is similar to v. 22, though a different Hebrew verb for uncovering is used, חשׂף (*ḥśp*) in place of גלה (*glh*). The verb חשׂף (*ḥśp*) is not used elsewhere in the Old Testament to signify rape. The second part "and your shame will be seen" indicates shame, without any suggestion of violence.[51] In similar images in other prophets where God lifts the skirts, the purpose is also shame, not rape (Isa 3:17; 47:2–3; Ezek 16:39–40; Nah 3:5–7).

God does not desire the wounding of Judah. In the dystopia of chapters 4–13, he warns that the fall of Jerusalem will be the consequence of their failure to trust him (see also 38:17). The war described in chapters 4–13 is not a pronouncement of God's punishment for Israel's unfaithfulness, but a warning of the terrible result if Israel continues to reject all the escape routes offered by God through repentance or surrender (17:25; 22:4; 38:17). We are reminded that God's self-limitation and his use of means can result in outcomes that are not pleasing to him (44.10).

I have proposed that chapters 4–13 use the genre of dystopia to present an irreal future, which can be avoided if Judah turns back to God. The rhetorical purpose is to evoke fear and pity for Jerusalem, the land, and families, turning the elite back from their foolish plans of rebellion. Shifts in genre, time, and metaphor undermine the contention of a continuous narrative. God does not abuse or honor kill Judah, or approve weaponized rape, but invites her back into relationship (3:12, 14, 22; 6:8, 16, 26; 13:15–17). In the next section, I argue that God's preferred future for Judah involves not violence and shame but safety and flourishing, presented through the genres of *utopia* and *heterotopia*.

Utopia (Chapters 30–33)

From the beginning of the book of Jeremiah, God's promises show that his ultimate agenda for Judah is not death and disgrace but return to the land (3:15; 12:14–17; 16:14–15).[52] The dark feminine images of chapters 2–13 are reversed in the future *utopia* of chapters 30–33, which will be a time of

---

49. O'Connor, *Jeremiah*, 107 (see also 54).
50. Scholz, *Introducing*, 101.
51. Fretheim, *Jeremiah*, 211; see also Keil, *Jeremiah*, 242.
52. Swinton, *Becoming*, 184 describes this perspective as "after after."

reconciliation, safety, and delight for all (31:31, 35–37; 32:40; 33:20).[53] Masculine and feminine imagery alternate in the poetry of these chapters, as Jacob (30:10–11) receives comfort alongside Zion, who will be healed (30:17). God tells "Virgin Israel" (בתולת ישראל, *btwlt yśrʾl*), "I have loved you with an everlasting love" (31:3) and proclaims, "Ephraim is my firstborn" (בכרי, *bkry*, 31:9). "Virgin Israel" will again plant vineyards (31:4–5), young women (בתולה, *btwlh*) will rejoice in dancing (31:14), Rachel's tears for her children will be ended (31:15–17) and Rachel's grandson, Ephraim, will receive mercy (31:18–20). The return includes the blind and the lame (masculine singular), pregnant women, and women in labor (31.8). The land will be restored, and the voices of bride and bridegroom will be heard again (33:11, 12). God's long term plan is reconciliation through the new covenant (31:31–37).

Heterotopia (Chapters 24, 29, 40)

The seventy years before the return are also to be a time of God's protection and rehabilitation. In an unexpected twist, God declares that those who surrender to Nebuchadnezzar will live (21:8–9). Jeremiah repeatedly calls on Israel to surrender to avoid siege, warfare, death, and starvation (21:8–9; 27:7–8; 38:2).

The exile in Babylon can be seen as a *heterotopia*, an alternate real location where women and men can thrive and be blessed (24:6; 29:5–7).[54] The whirlwind coming from the north (4:11–13) has its center in Babylon, and God invites his people into the safety of the eye of the storm until the Babylonians are defeated by the Persians (24:4–7). The exiles are to flourish under God's protection in Babylon (24:4–7), and eventually return to the land (31:8). Only those who refuse this shelter will be subjected to the sword, famine, and pestilence (24:8–10). These disasters are not God's will for his people, but he will allow these consequences if they do not repent or accept the shelter he has prepared for them in Babylon (38:2, 17; 44:23).[55]

The exile is portrayed as a time of rehabilitation as well as protection and judgment. In modern times, families and medical professionals join together to confront an alcoholic or drug addict and invite the person to attend a rehabilitation facility. In his memoir *On Writing*, the novelist Stephen King tells of his family's successful intervention in his alcoholism as "a kind

---

53. This reversal is found in Rudolph Smend (1899) cited in Shields, *Circumscribing*, 6; see also, O'Connor, "Two Visions," 58.

54. For heterotopia, see Foucault, "Of Other Spaces," 4.

55. See Fretheim, *Jeremiah*, 29–41.

of *This is Your Life* in hell."[56] He says, "the point of this intervention . . . was that I was dying in front of them . . . Tabby said I had my choice: I could get help at rehab or I could get the hell out of the house."[57] In the same way, God offers time in Babylon to Israel, but if they reject it, the war will sweep over them and they may suffer sword, famine, pestilence (24:10).

In the heterotopia in Babylon, masculine and feminine imagery is uniformly positive. God says of the whole community, "I will build them up and not tear them down" (24:6) and pictures the community building houses, planting gardens, marrying and bearing of sons and daughters in peace (29:6) until the time of return from exile in peace (29:10). The exile is a one-time, time-limited measure, but the eternal covenant will remain as long as the sun and moon endure (Jer 31:35–37).

Blessing is even offered to those who remained in the land after the fall of Jerusalem, including the poor, men, women, and children, and the king's daughters (40:7; 41:10). Gedaliah assures them that "it will go well with you" (40:9), and invites them to gather abundant wine, summer fruits, and oil, and to live in the towns abandoned by the exiles (40:10, 12).[58] Even in Egypt, there was a possibility of repentance (44:8), which both men and women rejected through their intransigence (44:15–19).

God's default attitude to women is not the negative caricature and dystopia of the early chapters, but the positive imagery of utopia and heterotopia. His preferred option for Judah is surrender and flourishing, not warfare and suffering.

Conclusion

The unattractive feminine metaphors in the early chapters of Jeremiah are not a critique of women, but part of a persuasive strategy including caricature (2–3) and dystopia (4–13), urging Judah to turn back to God in the extreme circumstances of the Babylonian invasion. God's vision for women is seen most clearly in the utopia of chapters 30–33, including the new covenant which he will never revoke. A surprising prelude to utopia is found in the heterotopia in Babylon (24, 29), and blessing may even be found in remaining in the fruitful land under Governor Gedaliah (40:10). The book of Jeremiah does not promise that human life will be free of horror or trauma, but that

---

56. King, *On Writing*, 107.

57. King, *On Writing*, 108.

58. The fertility of the land described in Chapter 40 is consistent with my argument that Jeremiah 4–13 is a future irreal dystopia, not a description of Israel after the fall of Jerusalem.

those who turn to God will find him to be trustworthy. God does not offer women the poisoned water of misogyny, intimate partner violence, or weaponized rape, and he is not an unreliable source of care. Our suffering is met by God's tears, and in every drought, his living water is offered to us.

Bibliography

Alderman, Naomi. *The Power*. New York: Viking, 2016.

Allen, Leslie C. *Jeremiah*. OTL. Louisville, KY: Westminster John Knox, 2008.

Bacon, Peggy. "Untitled Manuscript on Caricature." Bacon papers, George Arents Research library, Syracuse University, no date. Cited in "Peggy Bacon," *American Art* 6/4 (Autumn 1992) 17. https://www.journals.uchicago.edu/doi/pdfplus/10.1086/424166

Boda, Mark J. "From Dystopia to Myopia: Utopian (Re)visions in Haggai and Zechariah 1–8." In *Utopia and Dystopia in Prophetic Literature* edited by Ehud Ben Zvi, 210–48. Helsinki: Finnish Exegetical Society; Göttingen: Vandenhoeck & Ruprecht, 2006.

Brenner, Athalya. "Response to Mary E. Shields: About 'Jeremiah' as Reflected in Feminist Eyes." In *Jeremiah (Dis)placed: New Directions in Writing/Reading Jeremiah*, edited by A. R. Pete Diamond and Louis Stulman, 303–6. LHBOTS 529. New York: T&T Clark, 2011.

Brueggemann, Walter. *A Commentary on Jeremiah: Exile and Homecoming*. Grand Rapids, MI: Eerdmans, 1998.

Carroll, Robert P. *Jeremiah*. Old Testament Library. London: SCM, 1986.

Carvalho, Corrine L. "The Challenge of Violence and Gender under Colonization." In *The Hebrew Bible: Feminist and Intersectional Perspectives* edited by Gale E. Yee, 107–33. Minneapolis: Fortress, 2018.

———. "Drunkenness, Tattoos, and Dirty Underwear: Jeremiah as a Modern Masculine Metaphor," *CBQ* 80 (2018) 597–618.

Claassens, L. Juliana M. "Calling the Keeners: The Image of the Wailing Woman as Symbol of Survival in a Traumatized World." *JFSR* 26 (2010) 63–77.

Clements, R. E. *Jeremiah*. Interpretation. Atlanta, GA: John Knox, 1988.

Coleman, Claire G. *Terra Nullius: A Novel*. Easthampton, MA: Small Beer, 2017.

Davison, Peter. "George Orwell: 'Animal Farm: A Fairy Story' A Note on the Text." 2000. http://www.orwell.ru/library/novels/Animal_Farm/english/eint_pd

Ferguson, Neil M. et al., "Impact of Non-Pharmaceutical Interventions (NPIs) to Reduce COVID19 Mortality and Healthcare Demand." March 16, 2020. https://www.imperial.ac.uk/mrc-global-infectious-disease-analysis/news—wuhan-coronavirus/

Firth, Jill. "Is the God of the Book of Jeremiah Bad for Women?: Clarifying Genres, Metaphors, and Contexts." ETS Annual Meeting, San Diego, November 2019. https://www.wordmp3.com/details.aspx?id=35817

Foucault, Michel. "Of Other Spaces: Utopias and Heterotopias." ("Des Espaces Autres," March 1967). Translated from the French by Jay Miskowiec. *Architecture /Mouvement/ Continuité*, (1984) n.p. http://web.mit.edu/allanmc/www/foucault1.pdf.

Fretheim, Terence E. *Jeremiah*. SHBC. Macon: Smyth and Helwys, 2002.

———. "Violence and the God of the Old Testament." In *Encountering Violence in the Bible*, edited by Markus Zehnder and Hallvard Hagelia, 108–127. Sheffield: Sheffield Phoenix, 2013.

Genette, Gérard. *Palimpsests: Literature in the Second Degree*. Translated by Channa Newman and Claude Doubinsky. Lincoln: University of Nebraska Press, 1997.

Gwaltney, W. C. Jr. "The Biblical Book of Lamentations in the Context of Near Eastern Lament Literature." In *Scripture in Context II: More Essays on the Comparative Method*, edited by W. W. Hallo, J. C. Moyer and Leo G. Perdue, 191–211. Winona Lake: Eisenbrauns, 1983.

Hays, J. Daniel. *The Message of the Prophets: A Survey of the Prophetic and Apocalyptic Books of the Old Testament*. Grand Rapids, MI: Zondervan, 2010.

Holladay, William L. *Jeremiah 1: A Commentary on the Book of Jeremiah Chapters 1–25*. Philadelphia: Fortress, 1986.

Ivakhiv, Adrian. "Cinema of the Not-Yet: The Utopian Promise of Film as Heterotopia." *JSRNC* 5 (2011) 186–209.

Kalmanofsky, Amy. "The Monstrous Feminine in the Book of Jeremiah." In *Jeremiah (Dis)placed: New Directions in Writing/Reading Jeremiah*, edited by A. R. Pete Diamond and Louis Stulman, 190–208. LHBOTS 529. New York: T&T Clark, 2011.

Keil, C. F. *Jeremiah, Lamentations*. Translated by David Patrick and James Kennedy. Grand Rapids, MI: Eerdmans, 1950.

King, Stephen. *On Writing: A Memoir of the Craft*. London: Hodder, 2012.

Lallemann, Hetty. *Jeremiah and Lamentations*. TOTC 21. Downers Grove, IL: InterVarsity, 2013.

Lau, Binyamin. *Jeremiah: The Fate of a Prophet*. Maggid Studies in Tanakh. Translated by Sarah Daniel. Jerusalem: Maggid, 2013.

Longman, Tremper III. *Jeremiah, Lamentations*. NIBC. Peabody, MA: Hendrickson, 2008.

Lundbom, Jack R. *Jeremiah 1–20: A New Translation and Commentary*. The Anchor Bible. New York: Doubleday, 1999.

Martens, Elmer A. "Toward an End to Violence: Hearing Jeremiah." In *Wrestling with the Violence of God: Soundings in the Old Testament*, BBR Supplement 10, edited by M. Daniel Carroll R. and J. Blair Wilgus, 133–50. Winona Lake: Eisenbrauns, 2015.

McKane, William. *A Critical and Exegetical Commentary on Jeremiah*. ICC. Volume 1. Edinburgh: T&T Clark, 1986.

O'Connor, Kathleen M. *Jeremiah: Pain and Promise*. Minneapolis: Fortress, 2012.

———. "Jeremiah's Two Visions of the Future." In *Utopia and Dystopia in Prophetic Literature*, edited by Ehud Ben Zvi, 86–104. Helsinki: Finnish Exegetical Society; Göttingen: Vandenhoeck & Ruprecht, 2006.

O'Flinn, Paul. "Rereading Nineteen Eighty-Four in 1984." *International Socialism* 2:23 (1984) 76–98. https://www.marxists.org/history/etol/writers/oflinn/1984/xx/1984.html

Reeder, Caryn A. *Gendering War and Peace in the Gospel of Luke*. Cambridge: Cambridge University Press, 2018.

Scholz, Susanne. *Introducing the Women's Hebrew Bible: Feminism, Gender Justice, and the Study of the Old Testament*. 2nd edition. London: Bloomsbury, 2017.

Seibert, Eric. *The Violence of Scripture: Overcoming the Old Testament's Troubling Legacy.* Minneapolis: Fortress, 2012.

Shay, Jonathan. *Achilles in Vietnam: Combat Trauma and the Undoing of Character.* New York: Scribner, 1994.

Shields, Mary E. *Circumscribing the Prostitute: The Rhetoric of Intertextuality, Metaphor and Gender in Jeremiah 3:1—4:4.* London: T&T Clark, 2004.

Swinton, John. *Becoming Friends of Time: Disability, Timefullness, and Gentle Discipleship.* Studies in Religion, Theology, and Disability. Waco: Baylor University Press, 2016.

Thomas, Carol. "Sexual Assault: Issues for Aboriginal Women." In *Without Consent: Confronting Adult Sexual Violence, Proceedings of a Conference held in October 27–29, 1992, Report No. 20*, edited by P. Easteal. Canberra: Australian Institute of Criminology, 1993.

van Elsland, Dr. Sabine L., and Ryan O'Hare. "COVID-19: Imperial Researchers Model Likely Impact of Public Health Measures." March 17, 2020. https://www.imperial.ac.uk/news/196234/covid19-imperial-researchers-model-likely-impact/

Weems, Renita J. *Battered Love: Marriage, Sex, and Violence in the Hebrew Prophets.* Minneapolis: Fortress, 1995.

West, Gerald O. "Between Text and Trauma: Reading Job with People Living with HIV." In *Bible through the Lens of Trauma*, edited by Elizabeth Boase and Christopher G. Frechette, 209–230. Atlanta: SBL, 2016.

Winton, Tim. "The Turning," in Tim Winton, *The Turning*, 133–62. London: Picador, 2004.

Wright, Christopher J. H. *The Message of Jeremiah.* BST. Downers Grove, IL: InterVarsity, 2014.

Part III

New Testament Explorations

10

Grounded in His Lordship

Mary, Martha, and Me

Theresa Yu Lau

Introduction

When I received the invite to contribute to a book called "Grounded," my immediate desire was to call my chapter: "Why Did God Create the Mosquito?" What has this got to do with "Grounded"? Well, I was born in Malaysia, Sarawak, a place surrounded by tropical jungle, filled with mosquitos. Since childhood, catching, chasing, fighting, analyzing, and dissecting mosquitos has been part of my everyday life. I can never understand why God had to create such an "evil" thing—a being which, after much study, I must still conclude, brings only harm and diseases rather than common good.

However, I feel rather grounded when I ponder this question for which I have no answer. It reminds me to trust my loving God and acknowledge the endless wonder and mystery of his beautiful creation. I have been in theological education since 1993, being a student and then lecturer of the Bible. I have spent more than half of my life figuring God out. The temptation I face almost every day is to box God into a logical system, and sometimes, not just to box God, but also to boss God around like Martha.

And as I age, I find myself growing more gracious towards questions that I cannot answer. There are hundreds and thousands of them, but why

God had to create the mosquito is one most dear to me and continues to work the magic of putting me on the ground. I have no good answer, so all I can do is to trust. Trust in the goodness and perfect love of my Creator. So, after a more intelligent evaluation, I have changed my title to "Grounded in His Lordship: Mary, Martha, and Me."

After submitting the abstract, I went away forgetting the whole thing till I received an email from Ridley with the promotion website. To my shock and embarrassment, I found my revised title so incredibly egocentric and bold. How embarrassing; I am talking about ME! Within a short while, I was prompted to make peace with myself. What can I do? What more can I do? The title and abstract have been publicized. I felt it must be divine provision to make me admit in public that I am truly no different from my lovely fellow Chinese people, very egocentric and oblivious to rules, in this case the rule that "academics should not talk about themselves"—or at least they should not be so obvious about it, and they should *never* enlarge the M-word and put it on the title.

Of course, egocentricity is not just the problem of being Chinese, it is the problem of being human. Being human is already complicated enough; being Chinese is even more complicated. Being Chinese from Mainland China is vastly different from being diaspora Chinese. Then again, we diaspora Chinese can be very different among ourselves. There are numerous groups of diaspora Chinese: Hong Kong Chinese, Taiwan Chinese, Singapore-Malaysian Chinese, and so on. Then, the Chinese in Australia can be further divided into subgroups: Australian Chinese from Mainland, Australian Born Chinese (what we call ABC), and Australian Diaspora Chinese (from Hong Kong, Taiwan, Singapore, Malaysia, etc.). Though we have good similarities—for example, we are all residents in Australia, and we can all trace our root to China—the slight differences in our middle countries (Hong Kong, Malaysia, Taiwan) can often contribute to great divisions and differences in values and perspectives. It is almost like the diversity among the Jews in Second Temple Judaism. A diversity caused by each group's distinct reaction to Hellenization at different periods of times. Australian Chinese people are similarly very diverse, mainly because of each group's reaction to Westernization at different periods in time and in different locations.

Being Chinese in Australia is unifying, yet it is such a diverse experience at the same time that I am confident only in speaking for myself, not even for my children who are also Australian Chinese (who are very different from me, though raised by me). Once I start describing Chinese people in a general sense, I will soon find another group of Chinese people who do not fit my descriptions.

This is my dilemma here, hence the title Mary, Martha, and *me*. I have never felt confident speaking for the Chinese: a vastly diverse group. Most of the things I can say are only about Chinese people like me: Malaysian Australian Chinese (a very traditional and yet Westernized Chinese person who grew up in a post-British colony and was educated in another British Commonwealth country). Having said that, due to our common stubborn Chinese root, there is still something that I can generalize, which I will try to do, with great caution.

Mary, Martha, and Me

I chose to look at Luke 10:38–42 because I found this passage very close to my experience as an Australian Chinese woman, pastor, academic, and disciple of Jesus.

This passage is intriguing to me, especially where I hear Jesus say in Luke 10:42, "There is need of only one thing. Mary has chosen the better part, which will not be taken away from her." Mary and Martha both possesses great love for Jesus and strengths in character; however, if among all their good qualities Jesus singled out one special virtue, I would certainly like to find out what it is.[1] My multicultural backgrounds constantly bombard me with competing values. There are multiple ways of loving Jesus, multiple models, multiple virtues. If, according to Jesus, "there is need of only one thing," I am enticed. I feel a great desire to know it so that I can pursue this "one thing" more than any others on offer.

Luke described Mary sitting at the Lord's feet. She "listened to what he was saying" (10:39). Is this the "only one necessary thing" that Jesus is referring to? What intrigues me further is the fact that Mary's behavior looks rather egocentric, as has been hinted in Martha's complaining words. Mary seems to be oblivious to the fact that sitting at the feet of a Rabbi, among a crowd of Jewish men, is a definite "no-no" for a Jewish woman. Mary is being a rule breaker and game changer. As Darrell Bock and others have pointed out, "the picture of a woman in the disciple's position, at the feet of Jesus, would be startling in a culture where women did not receive formal teaching from a rabbi."[2]

---

1. It is necessary to note here that what Jesus said precisely is not exactly clear. Manuscripts differ on verse 42. I. Howard Marshall notes no fewer than six variant forms of the text. But, the main differences lie in the phrase, "One thing is needful," or "few things are needful," or "few things are needful or only one." According to Marshall, "the fact that Luke probably understood the saying in a spiritual sense, speaks strongly in favor of 'one' being original." Marshall, *The Gospel of Luke*, 452–54.

2. Neyrey, *Social World of Luke-Acts*, 62. See also Bock, *Luke*, 1037; Fitzmyer, *Gospel*

Let me quote N. T. Wright here:

> The real problem between Martha and Mary wasn't the workload that Martha had in the kitchen. That, no doubt, was real enough, but it wasn't the main thing that was upsetting Martha . . . No: the real problem was that *Mary was behaving as if she were a man*. In that culture, as in many parts of the world to this day, houses were divided in male "space" and female "space," and male and female roles were strictly demarcated as well. Mary had crossed an invisible but very important boundary within the house, and another equally important boundary within the social world . . .
>
> For a woman to settle down comfortably among the men was bordering on the scandalous. Who did she think she was? Only a shameless[3] woman would behave in such a way. She should go back into the women's quarters where she belonged. This wasn't principally a matter of superiority and inferiority, though no doubt it was often perceived and articulated like that. It was a matter of what was thought of as the appropriate division between the two halves of humanity.[4]
>
> In the same way, to sit at the feet of a teacher was a decidedly male role . . . To sit at someone's feet meant, quite simply, to be their student. And to sit at the feet of a rabbi was what you did *if you wanted to be a rabbi yourself*. There is no thought here of learning for learning's sake.[5] Mary has quietly taken her place as a would-be teacher and preacher of the kingdom of God.[6]

I find Wright's descriptions of the social framework rather familiar. He could well be describing a Chinese context. Growing up in Malaysia in the 70s and 80s, I often heard my mother recalling her desire to enter secondary school but being prohibited by my grandfather on the grounds that she is a woman. She cried for three days and accepted her fate.

The shame and honor of women's space and propriety also resonate with my experience of being a Chinese woman. Chinese has a famous saying for womanly propriety: the so called 「三从四德」 "threefold obedience

---

According to Luke, 892; Craddock, *Luke*, 152; Marshall, *Gospel of Luke*, 452.

3. I cannot find any language closer to heart than this one. Being "shameless," or being called "shameless," often inhibits our behavior. This is a Chinese woman's constant worry and inhibition.

4. Wright, *Luke for Everyone*, 130–31.

5. A close parallel to a popular Chinese value, whereby learning is seldom perceived as an end in itself; rather, learning is a means to something else.

6. Wright, *Luke for Everyone*, 131.

and the four virtues." In ancient China a respectable woman is expected to display three forms of obedience—to obey her father before marriage, her husband during married life, and her sons in widowhood—as well as four virtues –fidelity, speech, physical appearance, and work. In Nu Jie's work of Chinese Classical literature, *Admonitions for Women*, the work virtue is further defined thus: "A women should concentrate on weaving, preparing food and welcoming guests."[7]

Though not followed per se now, women's propriety displayed in these virtues and in obedience to men in general is still very much an unspoken expectation among various Chinese communities or individuals in Australia.[8] Interestingly, as N. T. Wright has pointed out correctly, the story of Mary and Martha "concerns what was thought of as the appropriate division between the two halves of humanity." This division within sexes can still be observed physically in some groups of Christians from China, and thus in associated groups of Chinese Christian community in diaspora,[9] though not perceivable in Australia due to our migration context. Education among women, though highly valued now, is not automatically perceived as a virtue in some more traditional communities, especially if the women's ability supersedes their husband's.[10] Instead, Chinese people have another popular saying: 女子无才便是德, "A woman without ability is her virtue." Some explain this to mean that a woman does not need a skill; she only needs to submit to her husband.[11]

---

7. See Knapp, "Sancong Side 三从四德," 524–25.

8. This is more so among diaspora Chinese. Mainland Chinese, having gone through the cultural revolution, often exhibit more liberated attitudes. However, it is also interesting to observe how various individuals from this latter group, after becoming Christians, fixate on and call for strict adherence to the few verses in the Pauline epistles regarding a wife's submission to her husband, as if they have found a long lost root to go back to, perhaps showing a stubborn regrowth of an otherwise repressed cultural memory.

9. For example, men and women sit on different sides of the church pews among Wenzhou people in Italy—observable not only in their adult congregations, but also in youth services. It reveals how deeply rooted this division between the sexes is in some Chinese communities.

10. Especially if it does not benefit the family or community. This does not mean women's education is discouraged altogether; it shows itself in the general discouragement of a woman's pursuing an education or a career responsibility higher than that attained by her husband.

11. This saying originated from a philosophical work called 安得長者言 (*An De Zhang Zhe Yan*) from the Ming Dynasty (1368—1644). The ideology is based on a similar root found in Nu Jie's *Admonitions on Women*, which stresses "the duty of women to realize the inferiority of their position and to serve their husbands" and "to concentrate on correct behavior both at home and abroad so as to retain her husband's respect." See Loewe, "Nu Jie," 463.

Even though many people claim that the original meanings of these two traditional sayings regarding womanly virtues are not as literal or demeaning to woman as they sound, many Chinese people continue to understand them as such.[12] Even with modern education and the popular concept of equality, these ideas, rather than disappearing, have become dominant undercurrents, moving and working in the background, creating confusion and difficulties for the community's progression. Added to this is the Chinese honoring of work and hospitality.[13] In light of these, Mary's idle and self-centered posture is rather disturbing. In front of many guests, presumably mostly men, a woman's honor will be to serve diligently, not to seat herself idly among men, especially when her sister is in need of her.

Given the baggage of such a thought and virtue system, a natural Chinese reading of the text tends toward finding Martha virtuous, while Mary's behavior among guests brings shame to the family. So, Jesus' praise of Mary instead of Martha shocks our system of thought and surprises our sense of honor. The story highlights the surprising and challenging nature of the gospel that Jesus brought.

Even though there is more I could say as a reader-response to the passage, I want to turn my attention to another more important matter, which I believe scholars have generally ignored when they read this passage: the theme of the Lordship of Jesus. While it is understandable that this pericope has been used to argue for various feminist concerns, it is not clear that Luke's main point is about female status per se.[14]

The Lordship of Jesus

In the story of Mary and Martha, Jesus' Lordship is emphasized. In this passage, Luke presents Jesus as "Lord" (*kurios*) three times: twice by the narrator (vv. 39, 41), and by Martha (v. 40). The context shows us that the narrator usually refers to Jesus by name, not by title (for example, see 10:29, 30,

---

12. On occasion, in some independent Chinese churches or organizations, I have encountered objections to ordaining women to a pastoring ministry (or allowing women any leadership role) that are based on such simplistic traditional values. Yet in some denominations of Chinese churches, ordination of women does not pose an issue at all, due to the fact that many early missionaries to China were women. I grew up in the Methodist Church in Malaysia, where women's ordination was never an issue. Note also the ordination of the first Anglican woman priest in the Diocese of Hong Kong and Macau. Chiu and Wong, *Christian Women in Chinese Society*, 6.

13. Which was the same for Luke's original audience. See Borgman, *Way According to Luke*, 102–3.

14. Byrne, *Hospitality of God*, 102–3.

37; 11:1, 37). But in this passage, the narrator diverts from his usual habit and calls Jesus Lord.[15] The concentrated appearance of the title Lord in this pericope is an intentional and playful design by Luke to convey important theology and reveal subtle attitudes in discipleship.[16]

Though Martha is verbally and theologically correct in calling Jesus Lord, her following words, "do you not care that my sister has left me to do all the work by myself? Tell her then to help me," reveal that her heart does not really perceive Jesus as Lord here. Luke skillfully shows that Martha, though addressing Jesus as "Lord," has subtly taken an attitude of a boss in her talk with Jesus. In her exasperated question and her imperative tone, we hear her commanding Jesus to do things for her. As a hostess of the house, she is bossing Jesus around! This posture is in direct contrast to Mary. Mary does not say a single word, yet her posture is silently declaring Jesus as Lord. I don't think it is too much to claim that the fourth and climactic reminder of Jesus as Lord is visible in the unspoken gesture of Mary.[17]

The supreme Lordship of Christ, as revealed through the narrative's artistic lens, captures the irony of human obedience. Martha, the perfect hostess, who has, according to Lukan narrative design, obeyed Jesus' command in the previous periscope of the good Samaritan "to do likewise" (v. 37)—that is, to be a good neighbor for the needy by providing "traveling mercy" to Jesus and his disciples who are on the road—is now receiving a loving reprimand. Why?

Not because she has acted wrongly, but because of her wrong attitude! Verse 40 highlights her attitude; it is in sharp contrast with Mary's. Both of them came to Jesus. But Martha came in order to boss Jesus around. She wants Jesus to listen to her—the Greek verb here is in imperative: "Tell her to come and help me!" In contrast, Mary came to Jesus in order to listen to Jesus, to learn from Jesus. Martha came to Jesus with a preconceived idea of

---

15. See Lee, *Luke's Stories of Jesus*, 230. The Chinese Bible, in particular, the Chinese Union Version (a popular version which can be compared to KJV in the English world), has ignored the obvious change in the title of Jesus and translated *kurios* as "Jesus" rather than "Lord" in this pericope—an indication, perhaps, of the oddity in the title change for general readers and the translator's need to keep consistency for better flowing narration. A new translation, Revised Chinese Union Version, with or without a deeper understanding of its theological significance, has recently changed it back to "Lord."

16. Ben Witherington observed that most instances of the title "Lord" in this Gospel are the result of Luke's editorial work. Witherington, "Lord," 489.

17. The majority of scholars see this as the posture of a disciple. "People normally sat on chairs or, at banquets, reclined on couches; but disciples sat at the feet of their teachers." Keener, *IVP Bible Background Commentary*, 218. However, postures of discipleship and worship are intimately linked.

the proper order of this world, revealed through her not-so-subtle questioning of Jesus' and Mary's behavior. One can easily pick up her sense of correct propriety: "Lord, do you not care that my sister has left me to do all the work by myself? Tell her then to help me." The Lord himself is being rebuked here. This attitude is similar to the lawyer's in the previous pericope (v. 29): "But wanting to justify himself, he asked Jesus, 'And who is my neighbor?'"[18]

Disagreeing with Fitzmyer, and others who believe that this story has no connection to the previous episode, I believe the two pericopes are interconnected[19] and are so linked by Luke to pave the ground for the climactic teaching of the Lord's prayer that follows. That is, the three pericopes (the parable of the good Samaritan, the story of Mary and Martha, and the Lord's teaching on prayer) need to be read side by side in order for us to understand the emphasis and meaning of the Lordship of Jesus. Reading together, the stories throw light upon one another and provide answers to questions that would otherwise remain open in the stand-alone episode, enriching and at the same time limiting, guarding against a plethora of imaginative assumptions.

Even though the use of *kurios* is not unusual in Luke as a whole,[20] its concentrated appearance here draws attention. It is Lukan artistic design to contrast the attitudes of Martha and Mary, in order to foreshadow the right attitude to prayer in the following chapter. Martha, though professing Jesus as Lord, is parallel to the lawyer, whom the story assumes to obey all the commandments, yet who did not come to the Lord with an open heart and teachable attitude. Rather, both the lawyer and Martha came with preconceived ideas of right and wrong, and thus a self-justifying attitude. In contrast, Mary came to the Lord with an open and humble heart and thus a learner's attitude.[21]

Confronting these two differing attitudes of the heart, Jesus declares, "there is need of only one thing. Mary has chosen the better part, which will not be taken away from her" (v. 42). What is this one thing that is necessary? Various interpretations had been put forward to delineate its meaning. The

---

18. Paul Borgman also compared Martha and the lawyer, in particular their preoccupation and anxious "me-talk." Borgman, *Way According to Luke*, 104.

19. Craig Evans also sees the connection between the two episodes: "The point of this episode is simple and relates in some ways to the parable that precedes it: It is more important to hear and obey the word of Jesus than to be busy with other matters, even though they may be commendable of themselves." Evans, *Luke*, 50.

20. Bock, "Gospel of Luke," 503–4.

21. This verb "sit beside" (*parakathezomai*) only occurs here in the NT, though Luke often uses "sit" (*kathezomai*) in general to describe a learner's posture (see Luke 2:46; Acts 20:9) and "sitting at one's feet" as a vivid sign of a disciple (see Luke 8:35; Acts 22:3). Hutson, "Martha's Choice," 140.

answers range from contemplative life (vs. active life),[22] devotion to Jesus (vs. devotion to service),[23] words of the Lord (vs. food that perishes),[24] Christianity (vs. Judaism) or justification by faith (vs. justification by works),[25] to one simple meal (vs. one elaborate meal). In the journey of interpretation, one may encounter a similar reprimand of the Lord: "You are worried and upset about many things." We are worried about censuring Martha too harshly, commending Mary too profusely,[26] or over-reading the context. Seemingly upset by the enigma within the passage, we try to save Martha from being minimized by the polarization of roles, to save Jesus from being unfair towards Martha, to save Mary from being unkind to her sister, to save Luke from being too androcentric in silencing Mary and domesticating Martha, and so on.[27] As a quote from Christopher Hutson illustrates:

> The usual reading of Mary and Martha dismisses Martha's service as unnecessary, even frivolous. Even those who are sympathetic to women's voices in Scripture seem unable to read the story any other way. Witherington, for example, asserts that "such things as even one's own family . . . must be seen as of lesser importance, indeed in an entirely separate and subordinate category, to the responsibility of hearing God's word and being Jesus' disciple."[28] Some feminists simply throw up their hands at Luke's hopelessly androcentric viewpoint. For example, Schottroff chafes at the pressure on Martha to conform to Mary's example, and she is embarrassed by Luke's portrayal of Jesus as "out of touch with kitchen work," who "makes the conflict between looking after people and being about the word Martha's problem, no matter how gently he does so." All these

---

22. Merton, *Entering the Silence*, 347. It must be noted that after arguing for the superiority of contemplation over activity, Merton also qualified that both may not stand in opposition "when they are properly ordered."

23 Byrne, *Hospitality of God*, 103.

24. Craig Evans first linked this passage with Deut 8:1–3 and suggested that Mary is pictured by Luke as showing the understanding that "one does not live by bread alone, but by everything that proceeds out of the mouth of the Lord" (Deut 8:3b) but Martha was pictured as focusing with the food that perishes (Deut 8:3a). Evans, "The Central Section," 43. See also Wall, "Martha and Mary," 19–35.

25. Frederick Louis Godet noted that "The Tübingen school has discovered depths in this narrative unknown till it appeared. In the person of Martha, Luke seeks to stigmatize Judaizing Christianity, that of legal works; in the person of Mary he has exalted the Christianity of Paul, that of justification without works and by faith alone." Godet, *Commentary on Luke*, paragraph 1353.

26. Using Craddock's expression here. Craddock, *Luke*, 152.

27. Hutson, "Martha's Choice," 144. Fiorenza, "Theological Criteria," 4–5.

28. Witherington, *Women and the Genesis of Christianity*

> interpreters read Luke as saying that the only legitimate choice is Mary's. Is it possible to read the text in such a way that it affirms Mary without castigating Martha?[29]

Hutson's lines of argument represent the typical route adopted by many modern interpreters. We are not satisfied by a simplistic perspective. I am not rejecting scrupulous academic endeavors or the importance of detailed exegesis towards finding right meanings and proper practice; I too am most curious about finding what this one necessary thing means so I can locate myself and my endeavors towards this solid ground. What I want to convey is that even though the academic pursuit has its sophisticated potentials and elaborate contributions to problem solving, it can sometimes distract and contribute to unnecessary worries and upset. One thing we can be sure about: academic pursuit is not "the one thing that is necessary" to a better relationship with the Lord. One must take this road with caution.

The fact that this story remains enigmatic and can be interpreted from various perspectives tells us something about human academic pursuit. Like many sacred and secular pursuits, it is loaded with preconceived ideas and self-justification (like my reader-response). It has its own potential and danger. However, as the episode has so artistically portrayed, only one preconceived idea is necessary. It is the Lordship of Christ.

Starting from the beginning of the Gospel, Luke has taken special care to highlight Jesus' ability to reveal human heart conditions. In chapter 2, Simeon's prediction anticipates Jesus' vocation: "this child is destined for the falling and the rising of many in Israel, and to be a sign that will be opposed. So that the inner thoughts of many will be revealed" (Luke 2:34–35). Many have pointed to the importance of this verse in the narrative, believing that Luke has the intention of using these verses as a map to show readers how he will write about Jesus.[30] John A. Darr even states:

> In the Lukan story the determinative factor in whether a character recognizes and/or responds correctly [to Jesus] is the status, or quality, of that character's "heart." . . . Characters who have hearts that are not fully right fail to grasp the message . . . The ability to perceive correctly, which is a prior necessity for correct response, is thus tied directly to one's value system and inner orientation.[31]

---

29. Hutson, "Martha's Choice," 148.
30. Dinkler, "'Thoughts of Many Hearts,'" 373–99.
31. Darr, *On Character Building*, 58.

This special interest in revealing human heart attitudes can be seen also in the pericopes of the good Samaritan and Mary and Martha. Hence, "the only one thing that is necessary" (10:42) is the correct attitude towards Jesus, that is, recognizing him as Lord. Mary has chosen the better part by honoring Jesus as Lord. And this Jesus will not be taken away from her. Martha appears to have served Jesus, and honored Jesus with her hospitality, but her words betray who is the real lord here. She is self-justifying; she is still her own boss, even a boss over Jesus.

Martha's obedience to the Lord's command to "go and do likewise," and her lack of submission to the supreme Lordship of Christ, reflects the conflicting nature of human obedience and the blindness of cultural convention. She worries so much about women's boundaries and propriety, if N. T. Wright's interpretation is correct. In contrast, Mary's motionless yet highly revolutionary gesture is being commended by the Lord as a wise choice. And this attitude that truly honors Jesus as Lord will be further expounded in the next episodes in the Lord's prayer: "Hallowed be your name. Your kingdom come."

As an Australian Chinese woman, I do find myself like Martha very often. I worry a lot about Chinese social rules, Chinese women's virtues, honor and shame, Australian social rules—and, when I became an academic, scholarly rules. Operating in multicultural contexts, the rules can be confusing and conflicting at times. However, it is comforting to hear Jesus say, "only one thing is necessary," that is, the right attitude towards Jesus, an attitude that is later expounded in the Lord's prayer.

Whether we follow Australian or Chinese conventions, whether we serve like Martha or Mary, whatever meaning they represent, we must not lose our perspective on the centrality of the Lordship of Christ. Grounded in the Lordship of Christ, we are given freedom to explore and express our love for him in various cultures and contexts. Grounded in the Lordship of Christ, we are given freedom to be ourselves, reflecting his image and the beauty of his created order. As Hutson has said:

> We all want to love God by attending to the word, and we all want to love our neighbors by attending to physical needs. But not all have the same gifts or the same opportunities. No one is a perfectly balanced Super Disciple, nor should we criticize one another for not doing everything equally well all the time. We should, rather, support one another in developing whatever gifts and using whatever opportunities each one has been given. If we unstop our ears to hear Martha's complaint, we may find

that she reflects some legitimate pastoral concerns that we need to consider as we work through gender issues.[32]

Bibliography

Bock, Darrell L. *Luke*. Baker Exegetical Commentary on the New Testament 3. Grand Rapids, MI: Baker Books, 1996.

———. "The Gospel of Luke." In *Dictionary of Jesus and the Gospels*, 495–510. Leicester: InterVarsity, 1992.

Borgman, Paul. *The Way According to Luke: Hearing the Whole Story of Luke-Acts*. Grand Rapids, MI: Eerdmans, 2006.

Byrne, Brendan. *The Hospitality of God: A Reading of Luke's Gospel*. Strathfield: St. Paul's, 2015.

Chiu, Patricia, and Wai-Ching Angela Wong. *Christian Women in Chinese Society: The Anglican Story*. Hong Kong: Hong Kong University Press, 2018.

Craddock, Fred B. *Luke*. Interpretation, a Bible Commentary for Teaching and Preaching. Louisville, KY: John Knox, 1990.

Darr, John A. *On Character Building: The Reader and the Rhetoric of Characterization in Luke-Acts*. 1st edition. Literary Currents in Biblical Interpretation. Louisville, KY: Westminster John Knox, 1992.

Dinkler, Michal Beth. "'The Thoughts of Many Hearts Shall Be Revealed': Listening in on Lukan Interior Monologues," *JBL* 133.2 (2015) 373–99.

Evans, Craig A. *Luke*. Grand Rapids, MI: Baker, 2011.

Evans, Christopher F. "The Central Section of St. Luke's Gospel," In *Studies in the Gospels: Essays in Memory of R. H. Lighfoot*, edited by D. E. Nineham, 37–53. Oxford: Basil Blackwell, 1955.

Fiorenza, Elisabeth Schüssler. "Theological Criteria and Historical Reconstruction: Martha and Mary: Luke 10:38–42." *Centre for Hermeneutical Study in Hellenistic and Modern Culture Protocol of the Colloquy* 53 (1987) 1–12.

Fitzmyer, Joseph A., ed. *The Gospel According to Luke: Introduction, Translation, and Notes*. 1st edition. The Anchor Bible, v. 28–28A. Garden City, N.Y: Doubleday, 1981.

Godet, Frederick Louis. *Commentary on Luke*. Translated by E. W. Shalders. Accordance electronic ed, paragraph 1353. Altamonte Springs: OakTree Software, 2006. https://accordance.bible/link/read/Godet_Commentary#1353

Green, Joel B., Scot McKnight, and I. Howard Marshall, eds. *Dictionary of Jesus and the Gospels*. Downers Grove, IL: InterVarsity, 1992.

Hutson, Christopher R. "Martha's Choice: A Pastorally Sensitive Reading of Luke 10:38–42." *Restoration Quarterly* 45.3 (2003) 139–50.

Keener, Craig S. *The IVP Bible Background Commentary: New Testament*. Downers Grove, IL: InterVarsity, 1993.

Knapp, Keith. "Sancong Side 三从四德 (Threefold Obedience and Four Virtues)." In *Encyclopedia of Confucianism,* edited by Yao Xinzhong, 524–5. Oxon: Routledge, 2015.

Lee, David. *Luke's Stories of Jesus*. England: Sheffield Academic, 1999.

---

32. Hutson, "Martha's Choice," 149.

Loewe, Michael. "Nu Jie." In *Encyclopedia of Confucianism*, 463. Oxon: Routledge, 2015.

Marshall, I. Howard. *The Gospel of Luke: A Commentary on the Greek Text*. The New International Greek Testament Commentary. Exeter: Paternoster, 1978.

Merton, Thomas. *Entering the Silence: Becoming a Monk and Writer, The Journals of Thomas Merton, II (1941–52)*. Edited by J. Montaldo. San Francisco: Harper, 1996.

Neyrey, Jerome H. *The Social World of Luke-Acts: Models for Interpretation*. Peabody, MA: Hendrickson, 2008.

Wall, R. W. "Martha and Mary (Luke 10:38–42) in the Context of a Christian Deuteronomy." *JSNT* 35 (1989) 19–35.

Witherington, Ben. "Lord." In *Dictionary of Jesus and the Gospels*, edited by Joel B. Green, Scot McKnight, and I. Howard Marshall, 489. Downers Grove, IL: InterVarsity, 1992.

Wright, N. T. *Luke for Everyone*, 2nd edition. Louisville, KY: Westminster John Knox, 2004.

11

Sensory Experience and the Gospel of John

Louise A. Gosbell

My twelve-year-old daughter lives with clinically diagnosed anxiety, triggered by a range of learning difficulties and health issues that cause her continual worry about her safety and her ability to communicate effectively with others. At times, her anxiety is such that she experiences panic attacks or meltdowns where she is completely overwrought with emotion. One technique that has worked well for her in moments of panic is a grounding technique rooted in sensory experience. The task requires her to observe closely her surroundings by identifying five things she can see, four things she can touch, three things she can hear, two things she can smell, and one thing she can taste. Through focusing on the activities of her senses, she is able to shift her focus from the cause of her worries and instead ground herself within her body and her environment in that moment. This tactile and sensorial experience helps my daughter align what is happening in her mind with the realities of her corporeal body, revealing the direct correlation between the state of her mind and body.

As the means through which we understand and come to know the world, as well as the means through which we can respond to it, the senses are central to our experience of living as embodied creatures in God's creation. Yet they are often overlooked in our expression of faith and our engagement with the Scriptures. What insights can we gain from the life, ministry, and teaching of Jesus that might inform our understanding of the role and function of the senses for believers today?

Setting the Scene

That the Gospel of John differs from the Synoptic Gospels in style, content, and vocabulary is well-known to readers of the fourth Gospel.[1] Already by the fourth-century CE, these differences were a matter of discussion for the early church fathers, some of whom wrote to defend the inclusion of John in the New Testament canon. In his fourth-century work *Ecclesiastical History*, Eusebius quotes Clement of Alexandria and his explanation for these differences. Clement claimed that the key point of departure was that the Synoptic Gospels were focused on *somatikon*, that is, on issues that relate to bodily or physical matter, while the Gospel of John is interested in *pneumatikon*, that is, spiritual matter. In this respect, Eusebius states: "Last of all, aware that the bodily (or physical) facts had been recorded in the Gospels, encouraged by his pupils and irresistibly moved by the Spirit, John wrote a spiritual gospel."[2] It is not an understatement to say that this branding of John as the "spiritual gospel" has loomed large over Johannine scholarship.

For this reason, investigations into embodied and sensory language in the Gospel of John are limited in number. When commentators have given attention to embodied and sensory language in the fourth Gospel, it has often been with a view to highlighting the inferiority of physical and bodily experience in leading people to a true faith in Jesus. The dualistic approach to human experience—that is, separating humanity into the bifurcate categories of body and mind (spirit)—has dominated Western philosophical thought from the time of the pre-Socratic Greek philosophers of the fifth century BCE. Indeed, the Gospel of John, with its native dualistic language (light/dark, life/death, spirit/flesh), is often called upon to support such a dichotomous view of human experience. For many commentators of the fourth Gospel, it does not merely present a dualistic approach to human experience but also promotes the experiences of the spirit as the only genuine and trustworthy ones. Experiences of the flesh (*sarx*) are semantically

---

1. I first began research for this paper in 2017 with funding from a grant co-awarded by the Ancient Cultures Research Centre and the Cognitive Sciences department at Macquarie University in Sydney. I continued research for this chapter during a research stay at the Bergische Universität in Wuppertal, Germany, December 2017 to January 2018, funded by the DAAD (German Academic Exchange). Many thanks to Dr. Wolfgang Grünstäudl and Prof. Tobias Nicklas for their feedback on the initial draft of this paper given at presentations in Wuppertal and Regensburg in January 2018.

2. Eusebius, *Hist. eccl.* 6.14.5–7.

aligned with the other negative corollaries of John's dualistic language: experiences of the flesh (*sarx*) are thus paired with darkness and death. In this way, discussions about flesh (*sarx*) become entangled with discussions regarding the body (*soma*) despite the two words being used quite distinctly in the fourth Gospel. As a result of the conflation of the ideas of flesh (*sarx*) and body (*soma*), many scholars interpret all bodily and sensory experiences in the Gospel as wholly negative.

And yet, the fourth Gospel is filled with bodily and sensory language far more than the Synoptic Gospels. This chapter aims to provide a brief introduction to sensory language in the Gospel of John. Before addressing the senses in John, I will first consider the recent growth in scholarship in sensory history and the important insights that can be gained by addressing the senses in historical sources. Following this, I will give a brief overview of the senses in John and offer some possible suggestions for future research in this area.

Sensory History

The last ten years have seen exponential growth in scholarship on the senses in a range of historical periods. This field of inquiry, which has become known as sensory history, investigates the way that people groups count, value, and interpret the senses in different ways at different points in history. For example, not all cultural groups consider the number of the senses to total five: some groups consider the number to be less while others more than five.[3] While many cultures prioritize sight over all the other senses,[4] this is not universal, with some cultures valuing smell over other sensory abilities.[5] As sensory historian Mark Smith has noted, sensory history "stresses the role of the senses . . . in shaping people's experience of the past."[6] The premise behind Smith's statement, and one of the fundamental

---

3. For example, Jack Goody suggests that "there is little evidence that the recognition of senses as a category, in particular of a group of five senses, is a widespread conceptualization outside Europe and Asia." *Anthropology of the Senses*, 18.

4. A 2019 social science publication records the results of an online survey attempting to measure whether sight is considered to be the most valued sense by the general public. The results found that this was the case (Enoch et al., "Evaluating Whether Sight is the Most Valued Sense," n.p.).

5. The Ongee people of the Andaman Islands (between India and Myanmar) order their world by smell in this way. The calendar of the Onge people is constructed on the basis of the odors of flowers that come into bloom at different times of the year. Each season is named after a particular odor, and possesses its own distinctive "aroma-force." Classen, *Worlds of Sense*, 1.

6. Smith, "Producing Sense," 842.

motivators for the entire field of sensory history, is the belief that the senses are more than simple passive receptors or data processors. Different cultures use and interpret the function and purpose of the senses in ways that sometimes parallel, but are sometimes divergent from, modern Western concepts of the senses. For this reason, when we read references to sensory experiences in ancient texts, we cannot assume that ancient audiences attributed the same purpose and value to those sensory experiences as we might as scientifically-informed, twenty-first-century readers. We are thus compelled to investigate references to the senses in ancient documents in more intentional and nuanced ways.

As sensory history has developed in tandem with other areas of sensory inquiry—such as that of cultural anthropological investigations of the senses—what has become more apparent is the idea, as Constance Classen has argued, that "sensory perception is a cultural, as well as a physical act. That is, sight, hearing, touch, taste, and smell are not only means of apprehending physical phenomena, but are also avenues for the transmission of cultural values."[7] The experience of perception, as well as the values attributed to that perception, are shaped and conditioned by culture. For this reason, Mark Smith suggests that "the senses are not universal, not trans-historical, and can only be understood in their specific social and historical contexts."[8]

If it is the case that the senses are significant "avenues for the transmission of cultural values,"[9] then investigation into the language of the senses and sensory experience in the biblical texts could be greatly beneficial to our understanding of the cultural worlds presented therein. The fact that the biblical texts are replete with sensory language compels us to investigate further the value and function attributed to the senses and sensory experiences within these texts.

Approaching the Senses in the Gospel of John

Before providing an overview of the use of sensory language in the Gospel of John, it first worth recognizing that we are approaching the Gospel of John with a vastly different sensory framework from that of the original audiences. While our understanding of the senses is one mediated through modern science and medicine, the original audiences of John's Gospel were informed

---

7. Classen, "Foundations," 401.
8. Smith, *Sensory History*, 3.
9. Classen, "Foundations," 401.

by their own cultural and social understanding of the senses, which included ideas that are entirely foreign to most Western audiences. One such example is that of the extramission theory of vision, promoted by the pre-Socratic philosophers, which was highly influential in the ancient world.[10] The extramission theory proposed that vision takes place because fiery rays emanate from the eyes, traveling to the object that was seen. Vision, then, for many in the ancient world, was not merely a form of sensory input but also output. The extramission theory is what lies behind the common belief in the "Evil Eye" in the ancient world, whereby a person, motivated by greed or jealousy, might send out power from their eyes onto another person in order to curse them with injury or illness.[11] The idea of sight as a form of sensory *output* is not one likely to occur to most modern readers of the text, and yet, such a concept is helpful in understanding Jesus' references to the eyes as a lamp, which appear in Matthew's Gospel.[12]

In addition to our different understanding of the role and function of the senses, modern readers also experience the stories of Jesus in John in a vastly different way to the original audiences by virtue of the fact we are *readers* rather than *hearers* of these accounts. The stories of Jesus recalled in John were circulated orally for sixty years before being committed to text.[13] As readers of text rather than hearers of oral accounts, we miss the sensory experience that would have been part of the original storytelling of the Jesus narratives. Richard Horsley, for example, reminds us that the Gospels were not just told but performed.[14] In a culture of high illiteracy rates, the performance aspect of oral communication was significant, with storytellers skilled in using oratory techniques designed to heighten the impact of their stories.[15] Such storytelling would have incorporated features like changes in pitch, volume, and tone, and the use of body language and facial expression. All of these aspects are absent for us as audiences who primarily engage with the Gospel as a written text.[16] These examples remind us that when we are

---

10. Squire, "Introductory," 16.

11. The belief was so commonplace in antiquity that many people purchased figurines or amulets, which were worn or hung in houses, to serve as apotropaia in order to ward off the possibility of becoming a victim of the "Evil Eye" (Gosbell, *The Poor*, 106–7). Note also the reference to the "Evil Eye" in Matthew's Gospel in the Sermon on the Mount (Matt 6:22–23); see Bridges, "The Evil Eye in the Sermon on the Mount," 69–79.

12. Matt 6:22–23.

13. This assumes a dating of John to the 90s CE (e.g., Keener, *Gospel of John*, 140).

14. Horsley, *Jesus in Context*, 14.

15. Stevens, "Sensory Media," 209–26.

16. Rhoads, "Biblical Performance," 157–63.

approaching references to the senses and sensory experience in the Gospel of John, our interpretations are mediated through our own social and cultural experiences and knowledge of the senses.

Prior to the publication of a number of texts on the senses in John in the last decade, dedicated research on this topic was rare.[17] When sensory experience is addressed by scholars of the fourth Gospel, many writers are skeptical about the reliability of the senses and their ability to lead a person into a genuine faith, especially in respect to those who see miracles. John Calvin's insistence on the priority of the Word of God in John's Gospel led him to suggest that genuine faith "does not depend at all on the sense and reason of the flesh."[18] For Calvin, the unreliability of sensory experience, especially that which is seen, meant that the function of the miracles in John's Gospel was not to lead the unfaithful to faith, but rather, they were "intended for the confirmation and progress of faith."[19] This is likewise the view of Craig Koester, who argues that "genuine faith, according to the fourth Gospel, is engendered through hearing" rather than seeing.[20]

In the last decade, there has been a greater interest in the senses in John's Gospel, with a number of articles and monographs published on the topic. In 2010, Australian scholar Dorothy Lee published an article in the *Journal of Biblical Literature* called "The Gospel of John and the Five Senses." In 2017, German publisher Mohr Siebeck published two volumes on the senses in the Gospel of John. The first, written by German scholar Rainer Hirsch-Luipold, is entitled *Gott Wahrnehmen: Die sinne im Johannesevangelium* (translation: *Perceiving God: The Senses in the Gospel of John*). The second volume, by Chinese scholar Sunny Wang, is focused on the link between sensory experience and testifying in the fourth Gospel and is entitled *Sense Perception and Testimony in the Gospel According to John*.[21]

This increase in scholarship on the senses in the Gospel of John has been part of a growth in interest in the senses across both the Hebrew Bible and the New Testament,[22] all of which assists in our growing understanding of the sensory worlds of the biblical texts.

---

17. One exception is Ernst von Dobschütz, "Die Fünf Sinne im Neuen Testament," from 1929.

18. Calvin, *Gospel*, 2:211.

19. Calvin, CO 47:42.

20. Koester, "Hearing," 348.

21. Note also the work of Kurek-Chomycz, "The Fragrance of Her Perfume: The Significance of Sense Imagery in John's Account of the Anointing in Bethany," 334–54.

22. Kurek-Chomycz, "The Sweet Scent of the Gospel in the Didache and in Second Corinthians," 323–44; Harvey, *Scenting Salvation*; Lawrence, "The Sense-Scape of Mark," 387–97; Thurkill, *Sacred Scents in Early Christianity and Islam*.

An Overview of the Senses in the Gospel of John

As Wang has rightly noted, the Johannine Gospel is filled with sensory language[23] and presents a highly complex sensory world. Right from its opening chapter, with the "tactile emergence"[24] of the *Logos* who became "flesh and made his dwelling among us" (John 1:14),[25] the fourth Gospel is filled with sensory and embodied language. From Jesus' first appearance to John the Baptist (1:35), the language of embodiment and sensory experience is vital to the Johannine presentation of Jesus. The importance of this sensory language, as Lee has observed, is its connection to "John's central theological motif, the incarnation."[26] The prologue of John expresses that a significant shift has taken place with the incarnation, that is, that the once invisible God has been made visible and could now be, to paraphrase Hirsch-Luipold, "perceived with all our senses."[27]

In the prologue, the divinity of the *Logos* is given in sensory language, especially vision-related language. The *Logos* is described as being "the light of all mankind" (1:4) who took on human flesh. In response to seeing the *Logos*, the writer of the fourth Gospel reflects that "we have seen his glory" (1:14). The writer's declaration about the divinity of the *Logos* becomes apparent: "No one has ever seen God, but the only begotten son has made God known" (1:18). It is through the *Logos* that God can now be perceived with the senses in a tangible way. It is the *Logos*, enfleshed in human form, who exegetes God—makes him known—to the world (1:18). This is made explicit in chapter 14 as the disciples ask Jesus to "show us the Father," and Jesus responds by saying, "Anyone who has seen me has seen the Father" (14:8–9).

Throughout John, the relationship between the Father and Jesus is also described repeatedly in sensory terms. Jesus acts because he hears the Father (11:41) and can only do what he sees the Father doing (5:19; 8:38). While others are described as being unable to hear or see the Father (e.g., 5:37–8), Jesus' perception of the Father is uninterrupted. The Father's love for Jesus is demonstrated in that the Father "shows him (the son) all he does" (5:20). This love is also demonstrated in the tactile description of the

---

23. Wang, *Sense Perception*, 1.
24. Gosbell, "Embodied Worship," 251.
25. All biblical quotes in this chapter are from the NIV.
26. Lee, "Gospel of John," 115.
27. Hirsch-Luipold, "Religiöse," 139.

Father giving over control of all things to the son by "plac[ing] everything in his [Jesus'] hands" (3:35).

Jesus' interactions with the people he encounters in the Johannine Gospel are also described in sensory terms. In Jesus' interaction with the woman at the well, although her knowledge of Jesus is based solely upon his spoken words to her, the woman announces that "I can *see* that you are a prophet" (4:19).[28] Throughout the Gospel, others too come to "see" Jesus as a prophet having heard him speak, such as the crowds who on hearing Jesus' words declare, "Surely this man is the prophet" (7:40; see also 1:37). Although scholars such as Calvin and Koester argue for the supremacy of responding to Jesus' words over a response to Jesus' miracles, it is apparent in the Gospel that seeing Jesus and his signs is meant to lead people to respond to him positively, because Jesus states "the one who looks at me is seeing the one who sent me" (12:45; 14:9). Likewise, in chapter 15, failing to respond positively to Jesus after witnessing a sign is described as sin: "If I had not done among them the works no one else did, they would not be guilty of sin. As it is, they have seen, and yet they have hated both me and my Father" (15:24).

The Gospel of John features only a small number of narratives that overlap with the Synoptic Gospels; however, where this does occur, sensory language permeates the Johannine versions of events. In chapter 12, the Gospel features the story of Jesus' anointing in Bethany,[29] where John describes Mary taking a large amount of oil and anointing Jesus' feet and then wiping them with her hair. The additional detail John adds here is that "the house was filled with the fragrance of the perfume" (12:3). And while the story of the cleansing of the temple appears in all four canonical Gospels,[30] John's version is placed at the beginning rather than the end of Jesus' public ministry, setting the scene for Jesus' tactile and disruptive displacement of the status quo. In John's version, the description of Jesus' act is far more embodied: Jesus is described as making a whip of cords and driving out all the money-changers along with the sheep and oxen (2:13–22).

In chapter 20, in the discussion of the resurrection of Jesus, verbs relating to sight occur thirteen times. Unlike the Synoptists, who simply refer to Jesus as having risen from the dead, in John the veracity of the resurrection is confirmed in the words of the witnesses: Mary says "I have seen the Lord," while the disciples tell Thomas, "We have seen the Lord." This same sensory language is used to describe the future kingdom in John's Gospel. Rather than simply believing in or praying for the breaking in of the future

28. Emphasis mine.
29. John 12:1–8; Matt 26:6–13; Mark 14:3–9; Luke 7:36–50.
30. Matt 21:12–17; Mark 11:15–19; Luke 19:45–48.

kingdom, the Johannine Jesus uses the dualistic language of life and death. Jesus speaks of those who obey his words as those who "will never see death" (8:51). This is in contrast with those who reject the Son, "who will not see life" (3:36). John, as well as the Synoptists, all refer to participation in the future kingdom in terms of those who will not "taste death."[31]

In John's Gospel, the miracles are also described in sensory language, indeed, they are referred to as "signs" (*sēmeion*).[32] This appears to be a deliberate decision of the Johannine author to announce that the miracles were not performed by Jesus as an end in themselves but were signs to point to the identity of Jesus. This is made explicit in John 20:30–31:

> Jesus performed many other signs in the presence of his disciples, which are not recorded in this book. But these are written that you may believe that Jesus is the Messiah, the Son of God, and that by believing you may have life in his name.

But as with all the sensory imagery in the Gospel, the results are varied. While there are many who witness the miracles of Jesus in the Gospel, not all respond to Jesus by announcing their faith in him. The Jewish leaders in chapters 5 and 9, for example, witness the results of Jesus' healing of the men with long-term disabilities, yet this is not enough to convince them of Jesus' identity as the Messiah. The Gospel writer explicitly states that "although (Jesus) had performed so many signs in their presence, they did not believe in him" (12:37). The signs, therefore, are not definitive in their outcome.

In addition to the varied responses to their sensory experiences of Jesus, the Gospel also reveals a great complexity with respect to the senses by intertwining literal and figurative sensory language. One of the most significant examples of this is with respect to the healing of the man born blind. Following the man's healing, Jesus says to the Pharisees, "I came into this world for judgment so that those who do not see may see, and those who do see may become blind" (9:39). And in response to the question "Surely, we are not blind, are we?" from the Pharisees, Jesus states that "If you were blind, you would not have sin. But now that you say, 'we see,' your sin remains" (9:41). The interplay between physical and metaphorical sight here is thus complex. The Pharisees are clearly blind metaphorically because although their eyes are functioning perfectly, they are not using their eyes to see and understand the identity of Jesus. And thus, the extended healing narrative in chapter 9 presents a great irony. The passage begins with the disciples trying to determine whether the blind man's personal sin lead to his disability but Jesus redirects

---

31. E.g., Matt 16:28; Mark 9:1; Luke 9:27; John 8:52.

32. This same word, however, is used in a negative sense in the other Gospels about those who seek a sign as proof of Jesus' divinity (Matt 12:39).

the question to speak about it happening in order to bring glory to God. And yet, the passage ends with Jesus' declaration that it is the spiritual blindness of the Pharisees that stops them from seeing Jesus. Therefore, while Jesus apparently dismissed the link between sin and disability for the man born blind (9:3), ironically, in the case of the Pharisees, their blindness, which is figurative, is the direct result of their sin (9:41).

The Purpose of Sensory Language in the Gospel of John

What is apparent from these brief examples of the sensory language in the Gospel of John is that the language of the senses is important in the Johannine representation of Jesus. Jesus himself, and his relationship with the Father, his disciples, and those he encounters, are often given in strong sensory language. However, the language is by no means straightforward. Though it appears to be the expectation that a sensory experience of Jesus should lead people to belief in him and a recognition that he is God incarnate, this is not always the case. Although many people hear Jesus' words or see his miracles, not all these encounters result in a recognition of Jesus' deity. The issue of literal versus metaphorical sensory language used throughout the Gospel also adds to the complexity of the presentation of the senses in the fourth Gospel.

What is the purpose of the heightened sensory language in John's Gospel? One way to interpret the presence of the sensory language is to say it served to enhance the experiences of the original hearers of the text. Such language engages the senses and makes the stories more vivid and real thus aiding memory for the original audience as well as for audiences today. While this is certainly true, there is more to it.

While scholarship on the fourth Gospel has steered away from a focus on bodily or sensory matters, the Gospel writer depicts a highly sensory world as the context for Jesus' relationship with the Father and all those he encounters. Rather than simply dismissing sensory functions as part of the physical, temporary body belonging to the present evil age, sensory abilities are depicted in John as the vehicle through which humans are meant to know and experience God through the incarnate Christ. Whether this response is to seeing a miracle, touching the wounds on Jesus' resurrected body, or hearing his spoken words, those who come into contact with Jesus encounter him in a sensory way. Indeed, when it comes to the first epistle of John, it is this sensory experience of Jesus to which John appeals, that others may trust in his words:

> That which was from the beginning, which we have heard, which we have seen with our eyes, which we have looked at and our hands have touched—this we proclaim concerning the Word of life. The life appeared; we have seen it and testify to it, and we proclaim to you the eternal life, which was with the Father and has appeared to us. We proclaim to you what we have seen and heard, so that you also may have fellowship with us. And our fellowship is with the Father and with his Son, Jesus Christ (1 John 1:1–2).

John also frames responses to Jesus in sensory terms, but these sensory terms are linked with words of action: speaking and walking/following Jesus. In this respect, John frames encounters with Jesus not just as analytical or cognitive responses to Jesus but as embodied and active. For John, then, Jesus models these embodied responses through demonstrating them himself—Jesus does not just speak or teach, but he demonstrates the Gospel in acts like the footwashing (13:1–17) and the cleansing of the temple (2:13–25), and he allows others to demonstrate their faith through enacted and embodied responses, for example, at the anointing at Bethany (12:1–3).

At the heart of the Gospel is a presentation not merely about the facts of the resurrection of Jesus, but the fact that the resurrection was *seen* and experienced and responded to in a bodily way by the followers of Jesus. John presents the Christian faith as one of active and embodied responses to God through Jesus. Sensory experience, therefore, is not just part of the fallen, sinful human body; it is one of the means through which believers can know and respond to God.

Finally, the senses are meant to lead to an understanding of God in Christ. However, the use of the senses is not foolproof. There are many occasions throughout John's Gospel where people witness a miracle of Jesus for themselves but do not come to a knowledge of God or respond to him. While people use their senses in a literal way to see or hear of an event, they do not employ their senses in the way in which they come to know or understand God for themselves. The interplay, then, between the physical use of the senses versus a spiritual use of the senses is made apparent throughout John.

Future Investigations into the Senses in John

Although the recent publications on the senses in the Gospel of John have been helpful in beginning to address the deficit of study in this area, what is yet to be done is to bring Johannine studies of the senses into dialogue with the growing field of sensory history and sensory anthropology. The works of Lee, Hirsch-Luipold, and Wang all offer erudite insights into the sensory language of John's Gospels, yet each scholar makes assumptions about the number, function, and value of the senses in the Gospel of John without acknowledging that these elements vary between cultures and historical periods. In order to be able to assess the significance of the senses in John's Gospel with greater cultural and historical sensitivity, future investigations must explore the sense-scape[33] presented by the Gospel writer himself. Scholars must endeavor to assess the way in which the Johannine Gospel itself depicts the number, function, and value of senses rather than simply overlaying it with our twenty-first-century assumptions on these matters.

One recent work that has attempted to recreate the sensory world of the historical texts is Yael Avrahami's 2012 publication, *The Senses of Scripture: Sensory Perception in the Hebrew Bible*. While modern Western readers are conditioned by the Aristotelian pentasensory model of the senses—that is, that there are five senses comprised of sight, hearing, smell, taste, and touch—Avrahami argues that the sense-scape of the Hebrew Bible actually presents a septasensory model of the senses. To the traditional Western five senses, Avrahami proposes that the Hebrew Bible adds the senses of kinesthesia and speech.[34]

Avrahami's close analysis of the senses in the Hebrew Bible has important implications for New Testament scholarship also. Given that ancient writers proposed a range of different numbers and interpretations of sensory functions, it cannot be assumed that the writer of John's Gospel enumerated the senses, or attributed the same value to the senses, in the same way as modern readers.[35] In this respect, future scholarship on the senses in John would benefit greatly from employing many of the techniques modeled in Avrahami's work, paying close attention to the Gospel writer's depiction of the senses within their unique socio-cultural context.

In addition, while many scholars in the modern West work alone, in silence, while reading through written versions of the Gospel text, there

---

33. The term "sense-scape," coined by Louise Lawrence in relation to her work on the senses in the Gospel of Mark, attempts to broaden the language of "landscape" from something that is only viewed (seen) to include other forms of sensory depiction and experience. Lawrence, "Exploring the Sense-scape," 387–97.

34. Avrahami, *Senses of Scripture*, 55–56.

35. E.g., Plato lists sight, hearing and smell as senses, but instead of touch he lists perceptions of hot and cold and adds sensations of pleasure, discomfort, desire, and fear to the list of bodily senses (Plato, *Timaeus* 65b4–c1; cf. 64a2–5). Philo wanted to align the senses with the biblical number seven, the number of wholeness, and so added to the Aristotelian senses that of genital sensation as well as speech (Philo, *Legum Allegoriarum* 1.11).

is much to be learned from the growing field of biblical performance criticism and the consideration given to the way the Gospels would have sounded to their original audiences as they were performed.[36] A greater understanding of the sensory experiences of audiences who engaged with the Gospel texts could also help inform our understanding of how they may have interpreted references to the senses within those texts. Such analyses could provide us new conceptual frameworks through which to understand and interpret references to the senses throughout the Gospels and the New Testament as a whole.

As Hector Avalos has argued, the benefits of participating in sensory studies of the biblical texts are numerous and varied, affording us the opportunity to "gain a better appreciation of how biblical authors conceptualize and treat human embodiment."[37] Not only this, but if, as Classen has argued, the senses are a vehicle for the transmission of cultural values,[38] further investigation into the language of the senses and sensory experience in the biblical texts could be greatly beneficial to our understanding of the cultural worlds presented therein.

Conclusion

The fourth Gospel provides us with a rich sense-scape filled with aromas, tastes, and physical sensations. From the tasting of the wine at the wedding of Cana, to the stench of Lazarus's body, to the sight of the resurrected Lord, the Gospel of John highlights the importance of sensory experience in the presentation of Jesus as the visible representation of the invisible God come to breach the gap between fallen humanity and a holy God. Not only this, but in response to such a sensory and tactile act, those who encounter this incarnate God are called to have not just a cognitive response but one that causes them to speak and act of what it is they have seen and heard in order that "you may believe that Jesus in the Messiah, the Son of God, and that believing you may have life in his name" (20:31).

Bibliography

Avalos, Hector. "Introducing Sensory Criticism in Biblical Studies: Audiocentricity and Visiocentricity." In *This Abled Body: Rethinking Disabilities in Biblical Studies*,

36. E.g., Perry, "Biblical Performance Criticism: Survey and Prospects," 1–15; Rhoads, "Biblical Performance," 157–63.
37. Avalos, "Introducing," 59.
38. Classen, "Foundations," 401.

edited by Hector Avalos, Sarah J. Melcher, and Jeremy Schipper, 47–59. Semeia Studies 55. Atlanta: Society of Biblical Literature, 2007.

Avrahami, Yael. *The Senses of Scripture: Sensory Perception in the Hebrew Bible*. LHBOTS 545. London: Bloomsbury/T&T Clark, 2012.

Bridges, Carl B. "The Evil Eye in the Sermon on the Mount." *Stone-Campbell Journal* 4 (2001) 69–79.

Calvin, John. *The Gospel According to St. John 11–21 and the First Epistle to John*. Translated by T. H. L. Parker. Edinburgh: Oliver & Boyd, 1959.

Classen, Constance. "Foundations for an Anthropology of the Senses." *International Social Science Journal* 49.153 (1997) 401–12.

———. *Worlds of Sense: Exploring the Senses in History and Across Cultures*. London: Routledge, 1993.

Enoch, J., et al. "Evaluating Whether Sight is the Most Valued Sense." *JAMA Ophthalmology* October 2019. doi:10.1001/jamaophthalmol.2019.3537.

Goody, Jack. "The Anthropology of the Senses and Sensations." *La Ricerca Folklorica* 45 (2002) 17–28.

Gosbell, Louise. *"The Poor, the Crippled, the Blind, and the Lame": Physical and Sensory Disability in the Gospels of the New Testament*. WUNT II 469. Tübingen: Mohr Siebeck, 2017.

———. "Embodied Worship: Reflecting on the Inclusion of People with Disabilities in Church Communities." *Practical Theology* 12.3 (2019) 250–2.

Harvey, Susan Ashbrook. *Scenting Salvation: Ancient Christianity and the Olfactory Imagination*. Los Angeles: University of California Press, 2006.

Hirsch-Luipold, Rainer. "Die religiös-philosophische Literatur der frühen Kaiserzeit und das Neue Testament." In *Religiöse Philosophie und Philosophische Religion der Frühen Kaiserzeit*, edited by Rainer Hirsch-Luipold et al., 117–46. STAC 51. Tübingen: Mohr Siebeck, 2008.

———. *Gott Wahrnehmen: Die sinne im Johannesevangelium*. WUNT I 374. Tübingen: Mohr Siebeck, 2017.

Horsley, Richard. *Jesus in Context Power, People, and Performance*. Minneapolis: Fortress, 2008.

Keener, Craig S. *The Gospel of John: A Commentary*. 2 vols. Peabody, MA: Hendrickson, 2003.

Kemp, Joanna. "Movement, the Senses and Representations of the Roman World: Experiencing the Sebasteion in Aphrodisias." *Exchanges* 3.2 (2016) 157–84.

Koester, Craig. "Hearing, Seeing, and Believing in the Gospel of John." *Biblica* 70.3 (1989) 327–48.

Kurek-Chomycz, Dominika A. "The Sweet Scent of the Gospel in the Didache and in Second Corinthians: Some Comments on Two Recent Interpretations of the Stinoufi Prayer in the Coptic Did. 10.8." *Vigiliae Christianae* 63.4 (2009) 323–44.

———. "The Fragrance of Her Perfume: The Significance of Sense Imagery in John's Account of the Anointing in Bethany." *Novum Testamentum* 52.4 (2010) 334–54.

Lee, Dorothy. "The Gospel of John and the Five Senses." *Journal of Biblical Literature* 129.1 (2010) 115–27.

Milner, Matthew. *The Senses and the English Reformation*. Abingdon: Routledge, 2016.

Perry, Peter S. "Biblical Performance Criticism: Surveys and Prospects." *Religions* 10.2 (2019) 1–15.

Rhoads, David. "Biblical Performance Criticism: Performance as Research." *Oral Tradition* 25.1 (2010) 157–98.

Smith, Mark. "Producing Sense, Consuming Sense, Making Sense: Perils and Prospects for Sensory History." *Journal of Social History* 40.4 (2007) 841–58.

———. *Sensory History*. Oxford: Berg, 2007.

Squire, Michael. "Introductory Reflections: Making Sense of Ancient Sight." In *Sight and the Ancient Senses*, edited by Michael Squire, 1–35. The Senses in Antiquity. Abingdon: Routledge, 2016.

Stevens, Benjamin Eldon. "Sensory Media: Representation, Communication, and Performance in Ancient Literature." In *A Cultural History of the Senses in Antiquity*. Vol. 1: A Cultural History of the Senses, edited by Constance Classin, 209–16. London: Bloomsbury, 2016.

Thurkill, Mary F. *Sacred Scents in Early Christianity and Islam*. Lanham: Lexington Books, 2016.

Wang, Sunny Kuan-Hui. *Sense Perception and Testimony in the Gospel According to John*. WUNT II 435. Tübingen: Mohr Siebeck, 2017.

12

At Jacob's Well

*Re-grounding the
Samaritan Woman*

DEBORAH STORIE

JOHN'S STORY OF JESUS' encounter with a Samaritan woman has fascinated and inspired generations of Christians.[1] Until recently, dominant traditions of interpretation focused on the woman's dubious reputation, shady past, and presumed immorality, often disparaging her intellectual ability and sometimes associating her personal failings with the alleged idolatry of her people. Some interpreters struggled to accept that the encounter at Jacob's well happened as John narrates it. A few could not believe that a *woman's* testimony led *men* to faith. Others could not credit that a woman could have had five successive husbands. Unable to imagine such realities, they interpreted the story symbolically: the five husbands became the five gods of Samaria; the woman herself became a cipher for idolatry.

More recent interpretive traditions tend to valorize the woman. Missiologists claim her as the first apostle, evangelist or missionary. Feminists are delighted that John's discourse-heavy Gospel honors a woman with its longest one-on-one conversation with Jesus. A few insist that the text gives no indication that the woman's sexual history was in any way untoward. All

---

1. I refer to the Gospel writer as "John" without ascribing to any particular authorship theory. All biblical citations are NRSV.

these traditions focus primarily on the spiritual/religious dimensions of the story and overlook the economic, social, and cultural realities that may have constrained this woman's life.

In this chapter, I offer a "discipleship reading" of John 4:1–42. After briefly describing the contours of discipleship readings, I invite readers to accompany me as I retrace my own reading of John 4:1–42. This reading developed over a particular time period (1992–2019) and in particular places (Australia, Afghanistan, Nepal, India, and Africa). It is informed by particular experiences of the world and not by others. Disciples of Jesus located in different times and places and shaped by different life experiences will—and should—read this text differently.

A primarily narratological approach is consonant with discipleship reading interests and invited by the text itself. As we read, we attend to the expectations that the time, place, and manner of Jesus' encounter with the Samaritan woman evoke within scriptural tradition, the give and take of the dialogue, the layers of meaning conveyed through well and water imagery and some provocative nuances of the Greek text, and ambiguities, questions, and possibilities that the narrative leaves unresolved. I refer to the extensive secondary scholarship only as it enhances my own engagement with the text. Recognizing how profoundly power, privilege, and life experience, as well as time, geography, culture, and language, estrange us from the worlds of and behind the text, we step back from the narrative upon occasion to invite the experiences of contemporary women and men who navigate similarly precarious situations to ground and guide our reading. Finally, I consider the varieties of discipleship response that this text might motivate and generate in our time and place.

Reading as Disciples

As disciples of Jesus, we expect our readings to challenge, chasten, and change us. We pray that the Spirit will guide and discipline our readings and responses. Our dependence on the Spirit does not diminish our responsibility as reader-disciples. We long for the kingdom to come in all its fullness and are committed to live and to read to that end. This requires us to ground our readings and responses, analyzing and engaging the contexts in which we follow Jesus (our worlds in front of the text) as intentionally as we do the text itself.[2] Aware of our estrangement from the text, we seek to understand the historical context the text purports to portray (the world behind the

---

2. Note intersections with "intercultural hermeneutics" as described by Ukpong, "Inculturation and Hermeneutics"; "Biblical Interpretation in Africa," 59–60.

text) and watch the gap between our foundational cultural assumptions and those the text assumes. We read and respond with humility, recognizing that our commitment to respond in ways that "seem good to the Spirit and to us" (Acts 15:28) does not guarantee success.

A Discipleship Reading of John 4:1–42

Jesus left Judea when he learned that the Pharisees had heard that he was baptizing more disciples than John (4:1-2). We are not told why this prompted Jesus' departure. However, by this point in the Gospel we know that Jesus had attracted considerable attention in Jerusalem (2:13-23) and had reason not to "entrust himself" to people there (2:24); that "a Pharisee . . . a leader of the Jews . . . [had come] to Jesus by night" (3:1-21); and that John had not *yet* been imprisoned (3:24). Although the precise nature of the threat is not revealed, it seems likely that Jesus left Judea because it would have been dangerous to remain.

Nor are we told why it was necessary (ἔδει) for Jesus to pass through Samaria (4:3), the quickest and possibly safest route back to Galilee. Ἔδει could imply geographical or theological necessity or both.[3]

The "geographical and historical concreteness" of vv. 1–3 prompts us to recall the social and political realities of early first-century Judea, Galilee, and Samaria.[4] These names speak of terrain, territory, and terror: the human consequences of Roman/Herodian rule (tribute, militarization and subjugation, inequality, dispossession, slavery, and debt), intra-Jewish tensions and conflicts, and the history of Jewish/Samaritan relations.[5]

Jesus arrives at the city of Sychar in Samaria (v. 5), the precise geographical location of which is unknown.[6] We are in the territory that Jacob gave to his son Joseph (Gen 48:22; Josh 24:32), and "Jacob's well" is here (v. 6a). Although the Old Testament mentions neither Sychar nor a well provided by Jacob, the patriarchal imagery of these verses invites us to recall the common ancestry and traditions of the Samaritans and Jews. As the narrative unfolds, we discover that Mount Gerizim is nearby (vv. 20–21) and recall the blessings of the covenant (Deut 11:29; 27:12).

---

3. Only here does the narrator use the verb δέω for an explanatory purpose. Elsewhere in John, δέω indicates theological necessity in direct speech (3:7, 14, 30; 4:20, 24; 9:4; 10:16; 12:34) and is used in a narratorial reference to Scripture (20:9).

4. O'Day, *Preaching*, 34.

5. On Samaritan-Jewish relations, see Mukansengimana-Nyirimana and Draper, "Peacemaking," 300–302.

6. Sychar is frequently identified with the town of Askar a few kilometers from Shechem and within view of Mount Gerizim; Brown, *John I-XII*, 169.

Jesus is tired, absolutely worn out. The disciples go into the city to find food. Jesus stays alone, resting at the well, at Jacob's well. It is the sixth hour (vv. 6, 8).

But, look! A woman is approaching, one woman, alone. That's strange. Women collect water from wells outside their city or village in groups. It's safer that way. Besides, collecting water is a social occasion, an opportunity to chat with friends, a reprieve from your children—and your mothers-in-law! Why does this woman come to the well alone in the middle of the day? Is she a social outcast whom other women shun? Or does she want to connect with strangers?[7]

But, look! Another strange thing. Jesus sees the woman yet remains seated at the well. In Afghanistan, as in the Middle East and many other regions where women still collect water, courtesy requires men to withdraw from wells whenever women approach. This assures the women that they are safe and will not be molested. When, for whatever reason, men do not withdraw from a well, women hover at the edge of town, waiting for the men to move on. Women sometimes wait for hours and, if dusk falls, return home without water. Better to be thirsty for one night than to take such a risk.

On this occasion, Jesus sees the woman and does not withdraw.[8] The woman does not wait for the strange man to leave. She approaches anyway. Is she brave? Is she stupid? Or is something else going on? This is Jacob's well, after all.

Meetings at Wells in Scriptural Tradition

For scripturally literate readers, expectations rise whenever men meet women at wells. These expectations are heightened by the bridegroom imagery previously used of Jesus (3:29), and the patriarchal references used to describe the location and the well (4:5, 6). "The shocker," as F. Scott Spencer sees it, "is not so much Jesus speaking with a *woman* or even his speaking with a woman *in public* but rather his speaking with a woman in public *at a well!*"[9]

The story and backstory of Jacob's encounter at a well are related in Genesis 28–29. Jacob tricked his brother Esau and, on his mother's advice,

---

7. Bligh, "Jesus," 335–36, asks whether the woman harbored matrimonial designs on Jesus.

8. Madame Cecilia, *St. John*, 95, wonders whether Jesus stopped at the well at such an unusual hour in order to "speak with the poor woman alone."

9. Spencer, "Jesus, Women and Converation," 31. Emphasis original.

fled to his Uncle Laban. Reaching Laban's region, Jacob saw shepherds and sheep by a well. Did the shepherds know his uncle? They did. And look, Laban's daughter, Rachel, was approaching with his sheep. When Jacob saw Rachel and the sheep, he kissed Rachel and marriage negotiations were soon underway.

Jacob's father, Isaac, didn't woo his own bride (Gen 24:10–61). Abraham delegated that task to a servant. Where did the servant meet Rebecca? At a well.

A well-side encounter also played a pivotal role in Moses' marriage (Exod 2:15b–21). On the run after killing an Egyptian (Exod 2:11–15a), Moses sat down by a well in Midian. The seven daughters of Jethro came to water their flock, and shepherds attacked them. Moses fought off the shepherds and watered the flock. In due course, Moses married Zipporah, one of Jethro's daughters.

Robert Alter classifies these betrothal stories as type-scenes that share a series of common elements:[10] a young man traveling through a foreign land encounters a woman at a well; water is drawn; the woman departs to share news of the man's arrival; gifts may be given; the couple are betrothed. Two further common elements are less frequently discussed. Constellations of fertility motifs suffuse each of these scenes: the well, the woman, the drawing of water, the vessel with which water is drawn, and the presence of a man and a woman, not necessarily alone.[11] Within the wider narratives of Genesis and Exodus, each of these scenes signal a male character's "initiation into adult independence and autonomy" and a female character's "transfer from her father's custody to her husband's custody."[12]

Other biblical encounters at wells raise different expectations. First, consider the story of Hagar (Genesis 16 and 21). Hagar was Sarai's slave. Failing to conceive herself, Sarai told Abram to sleep with Hagar. When Hagar became pregnant, Sarai abused her so cruelly that Hagar ran away. The angel of the LORD found Hagar at a well in the wilderness, reassured and blessed her, and bade her return to her mistress. Sarai, now Sarah, finally became pregnant and Isaac was born. Sarah insisted that Isaac not share the inheritance with the slave woman's son and Abram, now Abraham, sent Hagar and Ishmael into the wilderness with a skin of water and some bread. The water gone, Hagar could not bear to watch the child die. Sitting some distance away, she lifted up her voice, and wept. The angel of God called to Hagar, reassuring and blessing her. God opened her eyes to

---

10. Alter, *Biblical Narrative*, 51–60.
11. Cahill, "Narrative Art," 46.
12. Fuchs, "Biblical Betrothal Type-Scenes," 12.

reveal a well and water. An angel of the LORD/God met Hagar, a desperate outcast woman, at a well—twice.

Second, consider Abraham and Abimelech's well-side negotiations (Gen 21:25–35). Abraham complained that Abimelech's shepherds had seized a well. Abraham gave Abimelech an unspecified number of sheep and oxen and the two men made a covenant. Abraham set apart a further seven ewe lambs for Abimelech on the undertaking that Abimelech acknowledge that "I (Abraham) have dug this well." Given the complicated back story and chronology of promises, harems, and children (Gen 18:1–15; 20:1–18; 21:1–4, 22–24), and the potent sexual symbolism of wells, digging wells, and ewe lambs, might this covenant have pertained to the paternity of Isaac as well as to the digging of an actual well?

In Israelite tradition, you never know what will happen at wells. Romance? Danger? An encounter with God? Covenants about provenance/paternity? Perhaps all four?

A Man, a Woman, and the Language of Water at Jacob's Well

Back at Jacob's well, Jesus sees the woman and remains seated. The woman (alone) approaches anyway. Jesus (also alone) says, "Give me a drink" (v. 7). Is Jesus simply asking for water, or might his question be taken to mean more than his words, when taken plainly, say?[13]

Kenneth Bailey explains that Jesus breaks a social taboo by speaking with the woman. "A man does not talk to a woman, particularly not in uninhabited places with no witnesses. In village society, men do not even make eye contact with women in public."[14] Although Bailey overstates the extent and pervasiveness of gender segregation in contemporary and ancient Mediterranean worlds,[15] the disciples' consternation (v. 27) indicates that, in this case at least, Jesus does indeed transgress cultural expectations.

---

13. According to Kenner, *Background Commentary*, 272, "even asking water from a woman could be interpreted as flirting with her." Carmichael, "Marriage," 336, hears an intentional "double meaning" and "unmistakable" marital/sexual allusion in Jesus' request.

14. Bailey, *Middle Eastern Eyes*, 202.

15. The Gospels depict Jesus and other men interacting with women in a range of contexts. Female ethnographers, anthropologists, and historians point out that cultural codes apply differently across social strata, often affording peasant women more freedom of movement and association than their elite sisters. See, for example, Hallett, "Women's Lives"; Kraemer, "Women's Lives"; D'Angelo, "(Re)Presentations"; LaHurd, "Arab Christian Women." For a more detailed critique of Bailey's stance, see Storie, "Review."

As for the woman, she neither ignores Jesus nor gives him a drink. She answers—and provocatively (v. 9). Although the English translations don't pick this up, her language is unnecessarily gendered, stressing their sexual rather than racial/religious differences. Translated literally, the woman says: "How is it that you, a male Jew (Ἰουδαῖος), ask a drink of me, a woman, a female Samaritan (γυναικὸς Σαμαρείτιδος)?" Similarly, when the disciples return, they are shocked that Jesus is speaking with a woman and say nothing about her being a Samaritan woman (v. 27). The explanatory aside, "Jews do not share things in common with Samaritans" (v. 9b), reminds us that gender is not the only difference in play.[16]

The sexual tone her gendered language lends to the woman's question is not accidental. It conveys an implicit question. That's not surprising. *This woman went to the well alone in the middle of the day and didn't wait for the stranger to leave.*

The surprise is in how Jesus responds. "If you knew the gift of God, and who it is that is saying to you, 'Give me a drink,' you would have asked him, and he would have given you living water . . . Those who drink of the water that I will give them will never be thirsty. The water that I will give will become in them a spring of water gushing up to eternal life" (vv. 10, 14). Gift of God. Living water. A spring of water gushing up to eternal life. This language could refer literally to water and springs—or could mean something quite different.

Later in the Gospel (7:38–39), John explains "the rivers of living water that flow out of the believer's heart" in terms of the Holy Spirit. While this enriches our appreciation of the currents of water symbolism flowing through John's Gospel, we would be unwise to read that meaning back into a dialogue that took place decades before the Gospel was written.

The Old Testament uses the imagery of water, wells, and springs for two strikingly different purposes. Space permits only a few of many examples.

> My people have committed two evils: they have forsaken me, the fountain of living water, and dug out cisterns for themselves, cracked cisterns that can hold no water (Jer 2:13).
>
> O hope of Israel! O Lord! All who forsake you shall be put to shame; those who turn away from you shall be recorded in the underworld, for they have forsaken the fountain of living water, the Lord (Jer 17:13).

---

16. Verse 9b sits uneasily within the immediate narrative context in which the (Jewish) disciples are at that very moment "dealing with" Samaritans in order to purchase food. Most English versions attribute v. 9b to the narrator. The CEV and NLV attribute it to the woman.

Here, the fountain/spring of living water symbolizes God, Giver of All Life. But the Old Testament also uses water and well imagery to radically different effect. Song 4:15 describes the bride as a "well of living water." Proverbs 5:15–18 reads:

> Drink water from your own cistern,
>
> flowing water from your own well.
>
> Should your springs be scattered abroad,
>
> streams of water in the streets?
>
> Let them be for yourself alone,
>
> and not for sharing with strangers.
>
> Let your fountain be blessed,
>
> and rejoice in the wife of your youth.

I think we know what this means. What *is* going on at that well?

How Do Women Connect with Strangers in Gender-Segregated Societies?

Having recognized the sexual connotations of this exchange,[17] we step out of the story to consider strategies women in one contemporary gender-segregated context use to connect with strangers. This is not to suggest that vulnerable women in first century Palestine used identical strategies, only to broaden our understanding of how such interactions might occur.

A development agency in Afghanistan worked with vulnerable woman and children to prevent trafficking and other abuse. They were unable to identify any Afghan women who had chosen to engage in sex work.[18] Some women were forced into prostitution by creditors or their mothers-in-law. Others, desperate to feed and educate their children, were forced into it by poverty. In a context where women are stoned for adultery, how do female sex workers contact potential clients? How do they survive?

This drawing illustrates a common strategy:[19]

---

17. On the sexual imagery implicit in John 4:1–42, see Eslinger, "Wooing"; Lincoln, *The Gospel*, 173–76; Carmichael, "Marriage." Carmichael, "Marriage," 335, notes commentators' "remarkable reluctance" to investigate water imagery with sexual symbolism in the Old Testament or gender dynamics in John 4:1–42. Although we cannot explore it here, the wordplay between πηγή (spring, well) in vv.6, 14 and φρέαρ (well, cistern) in vv.11, 12 and LXX intertexts is quite suggestive.

18. Bazger and Young, "Survey."

19. Sketch by the author. Also see Bazger and Young, "Survey," 9.

Many Afghan women veil when venturing out in public. This is partially for protection. It also safeguards their honor. On close examination, the drawing reveals a subtle asymmetry between the woman's right and left hands. When a woman suspects a man is interested, she adjusts her veil to reveal the fingers of her left hand—carefully manicured with brightly painted nails. Most men don't notice. If an honest man happens to glimpse her fingers, he averts his eyes so as not to shame her. Potential clients recognize the signal and subtly show their interest. The woman walks away. They follow at a discreet distance. If a hostile man recognizes the signal, the woman swiftly retracts her manicured hand and reveals her right hand—rough and dirty with cracked broken nails—leaving the man wondering whether he saw something or only imagined it.

Back at Jacob's well, the woman walks a tightrope between life and death as she does most days. She veils her dangerous invitation with a semblance of innocence, ostensibly speaking about one thing while meaning another.[20] She conveys her message in a way that lets her deny it should the stranger grasp her meaning and not welcome it. Testing the waters a little more deeply with each response, she uses metaphors that permit her to claim to have spoken literally about water even when confident to risk an invitation: "Lord, give me this water, so that I may never be thirsty or have to keep coming here to draw water" (v. 15).[21]

Jesus response, "Go call your husband and come back" (v. 16), is not what she expects.[22] It brings the implicit sexuality of their conversation to the surface, showing that he is well aware of the sexual overtones of the conversation—and that he will not pursue them.

The woman answers equally plainly: "I have no husband" (v. 17). Some interpreters consider her reply "a prevarication," an attempt to change the topic to "hide her sin" and "avoid further embarrassment."[23] Is that really what the Gospel writer would have us infer? There is no mention of sin, judgement, repentance, or forgiveness. "Jesus does not judge this woman; any moral judgements are imported into the text by its interpreters."[24]

A Question of Multiple Marriages

Jesus replies, "You are right in saying, 'I have no husband'; for you have had five husbands, and the one you now is not your husband. What you have said is true!" (vv. 17–18).

Was it possible for a woman to marry five times? Many biblical scholars suppose not.[25] Yet, when we listen to the stories of the poor, we discover

---

20. Scott, *Hidden Transcripts*, describes the many strategies vulnerable people use to communicate in situations in which frank communication is foolish and careless words or unguarded gestures risk dire consequences.

21. Many interpreters take v. 15 as evidence of the woman's inability to distinguish between literal and figurative speech. Morris, *The Gospel*, 233, for example, writes. "If the woman has any inkling of the meaning Jesus is giving the living water she chooses not to display it . . . She understands the words with a crass literalism."

22. Most commentators see little connection between v. 16 and the preceding dialogue. Morris, *The Gospel*, 234, for example, suggests that Jesus changes the topic abruptly to bring "the woman's sin into the open" and "prepare her for the repentance that must precede salvation."

23. Citations from Morris, *The Gospel*, 236.

24. O'Day, "Gospel of John," 567. *Contra* Kim, "Korean Feminist Reading"; Lim, "Anit-Colonial Mimicry"; Dube, "Decolonization."

25. Schneiders, *Revelatory Text*, 195, for example, considers this marital history "totally implausible" for "a woman of that religious culture."

that it is quite possible for a woman to have had five husbands through no fault of her own.

Students at Gurukul Lutheran Theological College, India, performed an adaption of John 4 on International Woman's Day, 2004. As Monica Jyotsna Melanchton remembers it, a Dalit woman meets Jesus by a well and introduces him to a day in her life before sharing "her story of how she ended up having five husbands."

> Her first husband divorced her on account of her bringing an insufficient dowry. Another came forward to marry her but divorced her since she was unable to bear a male child. The third man who married her was an alcoholic who beat her black and blue every night, and she ran away unable to tolerate the violence. The fourth man was much older than she was and was poor and sickly. He died. The fifth husband divorced her for a younger woman . . . Jesus, hearing the story, makes no moral judgment or condemnation . . . The woman's plight is simply acknowledged as a fact of life that in no way denigrates her.[26]

It is equally possible for a man to have had five wives through no fault of his own. I met Jid Pahanna Ranna in Butwal, Nepal, while evaluating a development project designed to help children whose parents have leprosy stay in school.[27] I asked Jid to share his story. Night fell as we sat outside his hut. Jid's first wife left when she noticed a white spot on his leg and suspected leprosy. His second wife died in childbirth. His third wife left when he could no longer work in the fields. And so it went on. His son's mother was wife fourteen. She arrived in the leper colony not knowing who she was or where she'd come from. The colony elders suggested she marry Jid. After several happy years together, her sickness suddenly returned and one night she simply disappeared. Jid searched for months before accepting that she was gone. He tells their son, "God gave your mother to us. She gave me you. Then God took her away again. Your mother is a good woman. Wherever she is, she is with God."

Returning to John 4:1–42, the text does not reveal the specific circumstances of the Samaritan woman's marital history or present domestic arrangements. Even so, what we know about the worlds behind the text, together with biblical traditions that vindicate sexually compromised women (Hagar, Tamar, Ruth) and the testimonies of contemporary people

---

26. Melanchthon, "Samaritan Woman," 46.

27. A project of Partnership for New Life, a Christian agency formed by local Nepali churches. This project was partially funded by TEAR Australia, under whose auspices I visited the project.

in somewhat similar circumstances, indicate that external economic and social factors beyond the woman's control probably compelled her to marry repeatedly, enter a non-marital arrangement, and solicit strangers at wells. There is no warrant for the "exegetical extravaganzas," allegorical or misogynist, of interpreters who erase the woman's suffering or attribute it to her sinfulness, wantonness, and lust.[28]

So, What Is Going On At Jacob's Well?

Jesus meets the woman on her ground, in her timing, using her language. Starting where she is, he makes a connection. He does not shame or belittle her when he abruptly changes the conversation's direction (v. 16). He acknowledges the facts of her life and does not blame her for them. Equally quick on her feet, she does not change the topic or prevaricate. She simply picks up the spiritual-God-thread that was implicit in their preceding conversation all along. From this point on, both she and Jesus speak plainly without resorting to double-speak or metaphors. They connect. It is not the connection the woman had in mind when she came to the well alone at the sixth hour. It is infinitely truer and deeper than that.

When Jesus' disciples return, they are astonished to find him speaking with a woman. They are too afraid to ask, "What do you want?" or, "Why are you speaking with her?" (v. 27). It looks bad.[29] When Jesus says that he's already eaten (v. 32), it seems to confirm their fears. If the woman has fed him, what else might she have done? What else might *they* have done?[30]

The woman returns to the city and tells the people (ἄνθρωποι), women and men, "Come and see a man [ἄνθρωπος] who told me everything I have ever done! He cannot be the Messiah, can he?" (v. 29). She, not the disciples, spreads the news about Jesus. Her past and present circumstances do not disqualify her from God's mission on earth.

Going to Jesus, the people ask him to stay with them (vv. 30, 40). Many Samaritans believe because of the woman's testimony (v. 39). Many more believe because of Jesus' word (v. 41). They tell the woman, "It is no longer because of what you said that we believe, for we have heard for

---

28. D'Angelo, "(Re)Presentations," 134. Similarly, O'Day, *Revelation*, 67; Schottroff, *Revelatory Text*, 186, 194.

29. Moloney, *John*, 134: "Sexual innuendo is not far from the surface in the disciples' unspoken questions."

30. Moloney, *John*, 138, suggests that this exchange revitalizes the disciples' earlier doubts. Kelly and Moloney, *Experiencing God*, 106, see the disciples "forced back to their scandalized amazement of the situation: 'Has anyone brought him food?' (4.33). What has been going on between him and the woman who has just left?"

ourselves, and we know that this is truly the Savior [σωτήρ] of the world [κόσμος]" (v.42).

The title "the Savior of the world" has "striking imperial connotations."[31] The emphatic "truly" contrasts Jesus, the one true Savior of the World, with Roman Caesars and other idolatrous pretenders. We hear Jesus' words, "I am [Ἐγώ εἰμι]" (v. 26), as if spoken directly to us, and ask with Hagar, "Have we seen God and lived?"

So, what was going on at Jacob's well? The Savior of the world met a desperate outcast woman and offered her living water. Unlike Nicodemus, she understood. She understood, but did she believe? If she believed, did her life change?

The people of the city confessed that Jesus was truly the Savior of the world, but did they reorient their lives in that light? Did they become Jesus' disciples and live toward his kingdom, creating a community whose economic life enabled all its members to live with dignity? We are not told and do not know.

Yet, as we participate in the story, the questions of the woman's ongoing relationship with Jesus, and of the people's discipleship, challenge us to respond. Will we-with-the-Samaritan-woman confess Jesus as the Savior of the world? How will the Spirit call us-with-the-people-of-the-city to live out our discipleship? Will we respond?

Towards a Grounded Discipleship Response

We do not live in first century Samaria and rarely draw water from wells. Our survival, at least for most of us, does not depend on soliciting strangers. We follow Jesus—we can *only* follow Jesus—where we are, here and now, in this place and at this time, in all the messiness of our lives, wherever and however we are located in an increasingly globalized world scarred by (modern manifestations of) tribute, militarization and subjugation, inequality, dispossession, slavery, and debt.

How we read and respond to John 4:1–42 as disciples of Jesus will depend, at least in part, on how we and our communities are located within global structures of power and privilege and on our unique combinations of skills and capabilities, limitations and possibilities, and actual and potential networks of influence. It also depends on our pasts.

We have all done things of which we are not proud. Some of us— whether through coercion, desperation, naivety, apathy, or momentary

---

31. Koester, "Savior," 666. Similarly, Carter, *John and Empire*, 188–91.

weakness—may have engaged in transactional sex.[32] For us, Jesus' encounter at Jacob's well brings reassurance, affirmation and hope. We are not condemned. Jesus invites us to serve him, respects us, and offers us living water. He enjoys our company, takes our questions seriously, and trusts us to go and share our questions and our excitement. John's story of the Samaritan woman gives us, together with other marginalized people, a biblical warrant to recover dignity and agency, transgress culturally and socially constructed boundaries, and participate fully in proclaiming and living out the Gospel.[33] However painful our histories, however inadequate our present circumstances, we have a place in God's story.

For those of us with less compromised pasts, this story both reassures and confronts. There is no denying that John 4:1–42 has too often been interpreted and expounded in ways that further disenfranchise marginalized women and other oppressed groups. This fraught history of interpretation challenges us to interpret the text responsibly with regard to its human and ecological consequences. It demonstrates the need to interrogate our own readings, however well-intentioned. Might, for example, attempts to defend the Samaritan woman's reputation inadvertently prevent those currently involved in sex work from finding their place in this text? Might interpretations that conflate the Samaritan woman's marital history, ambiguous domestic arrangements, and soliciting with (her) personal depravity and sin, condemn other women contending with extremely difficult life circumstances while enabling affluent interpreters to avoid recognizing our complicity in social and economic arrangements that deny such women other viable options?

Pope Francis calls our current global arrangements "an economy that kills."[34] It is also an economy that enslaves and prostitutes women and chil-

---

32. The Burnet Institute, "Approach," explains: "[T]here is a spectrum of transactional sex. Women exchange sex for money, favours or goods for a range of reasons. . . . A woman who has three or four regular sex partners who support her by paying her rent or children's school fees may not view herself as a sex worker. The exchange of sex for money or material goods such as clothing or gifts may be part of many relationships which neither partner views as sex work . . . [While acknowledging that] there are women who enjoy sex work and have been in a position to choose that occupation freely . . . the majority of women who participate in sex work have been compelled through financial need, have very limited choices in life, or may have been forced through violence or threat to do so."

33. For examples of how this works, see: Burgonio-Watson, "Racial Ethnic Women"; Mukansengimana-Nyirimana and Draper, "Peacemaking"; Nelavala, "A Dalit Feminist Reading."

34. Tornielli and Galeazzi, *This Economy Kills*, vii.

dren on a massive scale.[35] The number of prostituted persons is increasing rapidly due, in large part, to the internationalization and deregulation of markets and the impact of mutually reinforcing crises besetting our world: deepening inequality, entrenched human deprivation, increasing violence, and widespread environmental degradation.[36] As markets channel more and more of the world's resources to provide products and services for those who can buy them, vulnerable communities are dispossessed and driven into debt, creating conditions conducive to coercion, forced labor, trafficking, and sex work.

Reading the Gospels, we notice that Jesus welcomes and respects people whom others despise. He does not tell them they are sinners nor call them to repent. He reserves his harsh words for people of power and influence, people who rarely identify as sinners. It is not for us to judge the characters and actions of those whose personal circumstances are much more difficult than our own. Yes, there is sin involved, but might it be the sin embodied in unjust structures and processes that should concern us here, the sin that serves some while holding others captive, the sin in which we are all complicit?[37] With Judah, we say "She is more in the right than I" (Gen 38:26). We hear Jesus' words to another woman as if spoken directly to us: "Neither do I condemn you. Go and sin no more" (John 8:11).

Bibliography

Alter, Robert. *The Art of Biblical Narrative*. London: Allen and Unwin, 1981.
Bailey, Kenneth E. *Jesus through Middle Eastern Eyes: Cultural Studies in the Gospels*. London: SPCK, 2008.
Bazger, Farid, and Andrew T. Young. "Survey of Groups at High Risk of Contracting Sexually Transmitted Infections and HIV/AIDS in Kabul." Kabul: ORA, 2005.
Bligh, John. "Jesus in Samaria." *Heythrop Journal* 3 (1962) 329–46.
Brown, Raymond E. *The Gospel According to John (I–XII)*. NY: Doubleday, 1966.
Burgonio-Watson, Thelma B. "Sexism and Racial Ethnic Women in the Church: A Reflection on the Samaritan Women." *Church and Society* (2005) 89–93.
Burnet Institute. "The Burnet Institute's Approach to Working with Women in Sex Work." Melbourne: Burnet Institute, 2006.
Cahill, P. Joseph. "Narrative Art in John IV." *Religious Studies Bulletin* 2 (1982) 41–47.

35. For recent estimates, see ILO, *Modern Slavery*; Foundation Scelles, *Sexual Exploitation*; Quadara, "Sex Workers"; Renshaw et al.; Parliamentary Joint Committee, "Inquiry," 20–22. On how slavery and sexual servitude function within global and Australian economies, see Romero, *Maid*; Kara, *Modern Slavery*; Jeffreys, *Industrial Vagina*; UNODC, *Trafficking*.

36. UNDP, *Human Development Report*, 1–21.

37. On the historical, political, and institutional nature of sin, see Nthla, "A Black View."

Carmichael, Calum M. "Marriage and the Samaritan Woman." *New Testament Studies* 26 (1980) 332–46.

Carter, Warren. *John and Empire: Initial Explorations.* New York: T&T Clark, 2008.

D'Angelo, Mary Rose. "(Re)Presentations of Women in the Gospels: John and Mark." In *Women and Christian Origins,* edited by Ross Shepard Kraemer and Mary Rose D'Angelo, 129–49. New York: Oxford University Press, 1999.

Dube, Musa W. "Reading for Decolonization (John 4:1–42)." *Semeia* 75 (1996) 37–59.

Eslinger, Lyle. "The Wooing of the Woman at the Well: Jesus, the Reader and Reader-Response Criticism." *Journal of Literature and Theology* 1 (1987) 167–83.

Foundation Scelles. *Sexual Exploitation: New Challenges, New Answers.* Paris: Foundation Scelles, 2019.

Fuchs, Esther. "Structure and Patriarchal Functions in Biblical Betrothal Type-Scenes: Some Preliminary Notes." *Journal of Feminist Studies in Religion* 3 (1987) 7–13.

Hallett, Judith P. "Women's Lives in the Ancient Mediterranean." In *Women and Christian Origins,* edited by Ross Shepard Kraemer and Mary Rose D'Angelo, 13–34. New York: Oxford University Press, 1999.

ILO. *Global Estimates of Modern Slavery: Forced Labour and Forced Marriage.* Geneva: International Labour Organisation and Walk Free Foundation, 2017.

Jeffreys, Sheila. *The Industrial Vagina: Political Economy of the Global Sex Trade.* London: Routledge, 2009.

Kara, Siddharth. *Modern Slavery: A Global Perspective.* New York: Columbia University Press, 2017.

Kelly, Anthony, and Francis J Moloney. *Experiencing God in the Gospel of John.* New York: Paulist, 2003.

Kenner, Craig S. *The IVP Bible Background Commentary: New Testament.* Downers Grove, IL: IVP Academic, 2014.

Kim, Jean K. "A Korean Feminist Reading of John 4:1–42." *Semeia* 78 (1997) 109–19.

Koester, Craig R. "'The Savior of the World' (John 4:42)." *Journal of Biblical Literature* 109 (1990) 665–80.

Kraemer, Ross S. "Jewish Women and Christian Origins: Some Caveats." In *Women and Christian Origins,* edited by Ross Shepard Kraemer and Mary Rose D'Angelo, 35–49. New York: Oxford University Press, 1999.

LaHurd, Carol Schersten. "Reviewing Luke 15 with Arab Christian Women." In *A Feminist Companion to Luke,* edited by Amy-Jill Levine and Marianne Blickenstaff, 246–68. London: Sheffield Academic, 2002.

Lim, Sung Uk. "Speak My Name: Anti-Colonial Mimicry and the Samaritan Woman in John 4:1–42." *Union Seminary Quarterly Review* 62 (2010) 35–51.

Lincoln, Andrew T. *The Gospel According to St. John.* Peabody: Hendrickson/Continuum, 2005.

Madame Cecilia. *The Gospel According to St. John with Introduction and Annotations.* London: Burns Oates & Washbourne, 1923.

Melanchthon, Monica Jyotsna. "Akkamahadevi and the Samaritan Woman: Paradigms of Resistance and Spirituality." In *Border Crossings: Cross-Cultural Hermeneutics,* edited by Devadasan Nithya Premnath, 35–54. Maryknoll, NY: Orbis, 2007.

Moloney, Francis J. *The Gospel of John.* Collegeville: Liturgical, 1998.

Morris, Leon. *The Gospel According to John.* Grand Rapids, MI: Eerdmans, 1995.

Mukansengimana-Nyirimana, Rose, and Jonathan A. Draper. "The Peacemaking Role of the Samaritan Woman in John 4:1–42: A Mirror and a Challenge to Rwandan Women." *Neotestamentica* 46 (2012) 299–318.

Nelavala, Surekha. "Jesus Asks the Samaritan Woman for a Drink: A Dalit Feminist Reading of John 4." *Lectio difficilior* 1 (2007). http://www.lectio.unibe.ch/

Nthla, Moss. "A Black View of White Christianity." *Working Together* 3 (1999) 1–5.

O'Day, Gail R. "The Gospel of John: Introduction, Commentary and Reflections." In Vol. IX of *New Interpreter's Bible: A Commentary in Twelve Volumes*, edited by Leander E. Keck, 491–865. Nashville: Abingdon, 1995.

———. *Revelation in the Fourth Gospel: Narrative Mode and Theological Claim.* Philadelphia: Fortress, 1986.

———. *The Word Disclosed: Preaching the Gospel of John.* St. Louis: Chalice, 2002.

Parliamentary Joint Committee of the Australian Crime Commission. "Inquiry into the Trafficking of Women for Sexual Servitude in Australia." Canberra: Parliament of Australia, 2004.

Quadara, Antonia. "Sex Workers and Sexual Assault in Australia: Prevalence, Risk and Safety." Melbourne: Australian Institute of Family Studies, 2007. https://aifs.gov.au/publications/sex-workers-and-sexual-assault-australia/sex-work-australia

Renshaw, L., et al. "Migrant Sex Workers in Australia." Australian Institute of Criminology, 2015. https://aic.gov.au/publications/rpp/rpp131

Romero, Mary. *Maid in the USA.* New York: Routledge, 2002.

Schneiders, Sandra. *The Revelatory Text: Interpreting the New Testament as Sacred Scripture.* San Francisco: HarperCollins, 1991.

Schottroff, Luise. "The Samaritan Woman and the Notion of Sexuality in the Fourth Gospel." In *What Is John?* edited by Fernando Segovia, 157–81. Atlanta: Scholars, 1998.

Scott, James C. *Domination and the Arts of Resistance: Hidden Transcripts.* New Haven: Yale University Press, 1990.

Spencer, F. Scott. "'You Just *Don't* Understand' (or Do You?) Jesus, Women and Conversation in the Fourth Gospel." In *A Feminist Companion to John*, edited by Amy-Jill Levine and Marianne Blickenstaff, 15–47. London: Sheffield Academic, 2003.

Storie, Deborah. Review of *Jesus through Middle Eastern Eyes: Cultural Studies in the Gospels*, by Kenneth E. Bailey. *Pacifica* 22 (2009) 96–109.

Tornielli, Andrea, and Giacomo Galeazzi. *This Economy Kills: Pope Francis on Capitalism and Social Justice.* Collegeville: Liturgical, 2015.

Ukpong, Justin S. "Rereading the Bible with African Eyes: Inculturation and Hermeneutics." *Journal of Theology for Southern Africa* 91 (1995) 3–14.

———. "Developments in Biblical Interpretation in Africa: Historical and Hermeneutical Directions." In *Voices from the Margins: Interpreting the Bible in the Third World*, edited by R. S. Sugirtharajah, 49–63. Maryknoll, NY: Orbis, 2006.

UNDP. *Human Development Report: Human Development for Everyone.* New York: United Nations Development Program, 2016.

UNODC. *Trafficking in Persons: Global Patterns.* Vienna: United Nations Office of Drugs and Crime, 2006.

Part IV

Applied Theology

13

"Wisdom Cries Out"

Towards a Feminist Pentecostal Theology of (Dis)ability

Tanya Riches

This chapter considers the witness of the people of God at worship, in light of eschatological realities. It seeks to re-embed the "divine voice" of God into embodied Pentecostal liturgies. More particularly, it appropriates feminist Pentecostal pneumatology and draws it together with disability studies to identify and evaluate different theologies of the body within the Pentecostal worship service.[1] This task is undertaken in pursuit of a "theology of consensus." Adopting an appreciative reading of the diversity of Pentecostal practice decenters the normative white, able-bodied pastoral model of leadership often promoted in the Australian Pentecostal Christian tradition, but does not silence it, instead opening it up to the movement's other wisdoms. In this way I seek to "vocalize" uncommon wisdoms by centering bodies who may previously have been dismissed on church platforms and in theological circles.

The "pentecostalization" of the evangelical church is a phrase that signifies a global move towards Christian expressions relevant in a market

---

1. The term (dis)ability is here used to recognize disability as differently abled people. However, "Dis/Ability" is preferred by Yong, "Many Tongues," 167.

economy (rather than more formal or structural arrangements with the state).[2] It is therefore unsurprising that Australian Pentecostals are criticized by both theologians and the press for embracing secular consumerism and individualism. In particular, Australian Pentecostal women have been critiqued for being noticeably fashionable, for enjoying sex, and for promoting the virtues of popular personalities such as Princess Diana.[3]

This contemporary picture contrasts with the history of the Pentecostal movement, which has been overviewed in great depth.[4] At their origin, the Pentecostals were known for emphasizing ecstatic, embodied religious experience. Drawing upon the biblical event of Pentecost, in which the believers were filled with the Spirit and spoke other languages, they promoted a direct or unmediated bodily experience of God. Today, Pentecostal worshippers continue to practice these spiritualities, including extemporaneous glossolalic prayer (or "speaking in tongues") and attentiveness to hearing the voice of God.

I argue that the Pentecostal leadership emphasis today upon brand, image, and performance needs to be placed in the wider context of its tradition, both biblically and historically. Adopting a practical theology approach, I here contrast two types of Pentecostal spirituality evident in the Australian Pentecostal church, assessing both to review how the body can be the site of the Spirit speaking, or, in fact "crying out."

Method

Pentecostal/charismatic theology provides the location for my own faith and teaching and is central to this chapter's method.[5] That is, a pneumatological focus with an eschatological lens is adopted here. But rather than investigating the Pentecostal church's preached ideals, I assess its practice, in particular, two spiritualities observable in the worship space, which are contemplated as the site of the Spirit speaking. To take this view, we must first acknowledge the body as a site of our theologizing or questioning, and

---

2. Coleman, *Globalisation*, 15.

3. Maddox, "Warrior Princess Daughters," 18.

4. Traditionally, the movement's history was traced back to Asuza Street in Los Angeles and the congregation led by black preacher William Seymour. See, e.g., Anderson, *Introduction to Pentecostalism*, 41. However in recent times this "made in America" narrative has been questioned by leading historians. See Hutchinson, "The Problem with Waves," 34.

5. "Pentecostal/charismatic" encompasses Coakley and Hollingsworth's approaches. However, I use the more specific term "Pentecostal."

then we must attend to ways the Spirit cries out (via individual bodies and the church corporate).

Methodologically, this is a review of lived religious practice with theological intent,[6] or an anthropological exercise in pursuit of good pastoral practice. This discussion is grounded in the real, rather than the fantastical, church. Famously Meredith McGuire encourages reviewing actual practices rather than ideals. She states, "We must grapple with the complexities, apparent inconsistencies, heterogeneity, and untidiness of the range of religious practices that people in any given culture and period find meaningful and useful."[7]

This allows various Christianities to be distinguished and also affords the possibility of improving pastoral practice by recognizing where theological ideals become tangible. Correspondingly, Mark Cartledge models practical theology based on ethnography or participant-observation, viewing the church's worship performance through a theoretical lens. My own participant observation of (and some formal leadership within) Australian Pentecostal churches undergirds this review of practices through the lens of feminist Pentecostal pneumatology and disability studies.[8]

Often in more conservatively aligned denominations, Scripture is interpreted to contain injunctions for women to remain quiet and submissive, as well as prohibitions on pulpit teaching drawn from New Testament passages (e.g., 1 Tim 2:5–19). That debate is not the focus of this paper; Pentecostal women have always preached. Instead, this chapter is based on an entirely different premise. In the wisdom literature, the feminine Sophia cries out in the public square or marketplace (e.g., Prov 1:20). This provides a basis for searching out godly wisdom that emanates from unauthorized voices who yet bring a wisdom (or leadership) relevant for witness and which can "speak" in the commons. It assumes that all bodies may "cry out" in wise ways. The Scripture invites us to heed Wisdom's cries (e.g., Prov 7:4). This is what I have here termed a feminist Pentecostal theology of (dis)ability.

The theoretical center for this discussion is generated by drawing on selected literature from the relevant discourses; Pentecostal theology, feminist theology, and disability studies. Then, the critiques of the Pentecostal church are revisited, but particularly the pressure on women's

---

6. McGuire, *Lived Religion*, 14.
7. McGuire, *Lived Religion*, 14.
8. Cartledge, *Practical Theology* emphasizes the Pentecostal preaching tradition. Rather than describing Pentecostal liturgy, here I summarize it into two symbolic spaces—one of "flourishing" leaders on the platform, and another of the diverse congregation. While there will always be exceptions to the rule, this demarcation is predominant in most (if not all) Pentecostal churches.

bodies to display desirability, or to perform youthfulness and vigor. This is intentionally viewed appreciatively, as Pentecostal leaders communicate in a world increasingly dominated by new media and with visually appealing "social influencers." This practice is explored here as a theological *telos* or a "short-term goal" and reviewed for its potential to witness to Christ's message of human flourishing in context. Following this, the lens of eschatology helps identify a "longer-term good," or, the Christian's ultimate end. This allows us to see aging and disabled bodies as *also* witnessing to Christ at work in the congregation, and to acknowledge the wisdom of those who may *not* be deemed "leaders" in the church.

This framework is offered in hope of both making sense of current church practice and setting precedence for the notion of *bodies made fully alive* but also the important Christian witness of *the resurrection of the dead*.[9]

Literature: Body, Performance and "Using" Sarah Coakley's Feminist Theology

As mentioned, Pentecostalism is known to emphasize embodiment.[10] Pentecostal worship facilitates an experience of the Spirit termed "an encounter."[11] This direct, or unmediated, experience of God brings liberation to the oppressed body and empowers the church for its witness. Thus, for Pentecostals, the worship event is of crucial importance. Gatherings serve as the site of the community's theologizing. Within them, the Pentecostal body is "entrained" to sense the presence of God in increasing ways.[12] As J. K. A. Smith explains,

> A Pentecostal social imaginary takes practice; it is practice. In other words, a Pentecostal worldview is first embedded in a constellation of spiritual practices that carry within them an implicit understanding. Pentecostal worship performs the faith.[13]

---

9. The phrase "fully alive" is attributed to Irenaeus, Bishop of Lyons, late in the second century.

10. Wilkinson, and Althouse, "Social Theory, Religion," 18. The authors note this does not suggest absent rational or theological reflection, and advocate that all religions be examined as embodied.

11. Johns, *Pentecostal Formation*, 36.

12. Myrick, "Relational Power," 5.

13. Smith, *Thinking in Tongues*, 31.

The driver for change in the Pentecostal community is practice rather than doctrinal statements or scholarly literature. Often, Pentecostals argue that prioritizing the body over the written text (i.e., oral theology) is a return to the premodern or early church.[14]

Andrea Hollingsworth, in "Spirit and Voice: Toward a Feminist Pentecostal Pneumatology," draws on Sarah Coakley's work to produce a "feminist Pentecostal pneumatology."[15] There is an interesting juxtaposition between these authors—a relatively unknown Pentecostal American PhD, and an acclaimed charismatic Anglican professor with a prestigious Oxford chair. Importantly, Hollingsworth notes that Coakley's pneumatology prevents side-lining of the Spirit as feminine. Instead, her work encourages contemplation in the Spirit (drawing upon the mystical traditions). While the theological guild often prefers rational thought over emotion, Coakley instead proposes a charismatic ecstatic "power-in-vulnerability." From this, Hollingsworth posits Spirit as the "divine voice" in worship which generates an "emboldening" or "courage" for Christian leadership in the home and public square. She claims this occurs as a "holy conversation" that amplifies the lowly and reduces the powerful:

> In dialectical vocal exchanges between listener and listened-to, the Spirit manifests as the creator voice that brings forth a new and shared understanding through human language. The divine voice is not simply "heard" in the voices of those who are being brought-to speech, but also in the hospitable, evocative, listening presences of the ones who are challenging themselves to truly listen.[16]

She contours precedence for this in the Hebrew passages where divine breath creates the world and animates the prophets. The Spirit's voice in the Gospels announces Jesus, and at Pentecost spirited vocalizations fill the room. Paul's ministry is concerned with voice and its use in the early church.[17] Voice was also significant for historical figures such as Hildegard of Bingen.

There are some issues with Hollingsworth's proposition. For example, Coakley promotes *contemplation* rather than *experience* as the beginning of theology and does not promote the mastery of prayer as a spiritual practice but instead its opposite, "unmastery."[18] This is potentially quite unlike the

14. Cox, *Fire from Heaven*, 178.
15. Hollingsworth, "Spirit and Voice," 205.
16. Hollingsworth, "Spirit and Voice," 207.
17. Hollingsworth, "Spirit and Voice," 206.
18. Coakley, *God, Sexuality, and the Self*, 84–85 states, "the silence of contemplation is of a particular, sui generis, form: it is not the silence of being silenced. Rather, it is

God experience in Pentecostal ecstasies, which may overwrite more nuanced charismatic ones. Still, Hollingsworth states,

> the embodiedness of Pentecostal Spirit ecstasy (not only in vocalization, but in other rituals such as dance and hand-clapping) holds potential to challenge entrenched mind/body, spirit/matter dualisms that plague much of Christian pneumatology.

She therefore advocates examining these spiritualities (including but not only glossolalia) more fully. Yet, even so, she notes the worshipping community's shortfalls:

> Large-scale Pentecostal movements throughout the Two-Thirds World regularly advance (via mass media) a glitzy form of globalized and westernized religion—a religion led by enthusiastic, enigmatic leaders who too frequently tell the poor that what the Holy Spirit wants most is their money.[19]

Such challenges for Pentecostalism run throughout the literature.[20] Consequently, it is vital that the movement's spiritualities be assessed in liturgical context, or, in other words, where these theologies are generated.

Though Pentecostalism emphasizes localized worship, a shared global worship performance has developed over the last century.[21] This can be considered the movement's liturgy. Daniel Albrecht suggests it is possible to break Pentecostal services into smaller "microrites,"[22] which he defines as "sanctioned practices, behaviors, [and] gestures."[23] But he links these parts of the service with seven "embodied attitudes" used by Pentecostal leaders to guide the congregation through each worship ritual and ensure its successful outcome.[24] These are described by Wade and Hynes as affective or emotional stances.[25]

---

the voluntary silence of attention, transformation, mysterious interconnection, and (in violent, abusive, or oppressive contexts) rightful and divinely empowered resistance: it is a special 'power-in-vulnerability,' as I have elsewhere called it."

19. Hollingsworth, "Spirit and Voice," 195.

20. McClymond, "Embodying the Spirit," 266; Jennings, "Great Risk for the Kingdom," 237.

21. Coleman, *Globalisation of Charismatic Christianity*, 2.

22. Albrecht, *Rites in the Spirit*, 25.

23. Albrecht, *Rites in the Spirit*, 25.

24. Albrecht, *Rites in the Spirit*, 179, states, "Clearly the Pentecostal ritual field is not accident. It is both a conscious and intuitive effort to construct a sphere in which together a congregation most likely will encounter God."

25. Wade and Hynes, "Worshipping Bodies," 173.

Amplification of the leader's voice is a common feature of the Pentecostal service. Therefore, sociologists argue, only a small number of people exercise agency, while a large number do not.[26] Any scholar of Pentecostalism is forced to pay attention to these dynamics. While the intention of those on the platform is to serve the congregation and facilitate their bodily encounter of God, unfortunately an increasing corpus of written work outlines the experience of those who feel disempowered rather than empowered by the global liturgy of the Pentecostal church.[27] This includes the disabled, who are often not visible on the platform.[28] It is claimed that, particularly in the megachurch, various groups are (to different extents) silenced by the strong Pentecostal liturgical form.

It is not Hollingsworth's intention to gloss over these complexities. However, I believe that reviewing the entire worship ritual provides *more* opportunity to extend her claims, not less. Today's Christian emphasis upon brand, image, and performance cannot be denied. But I suggest the practices of modern Pentecostalism be re-examined in context, to provide a more generous (and also subversive) reading of the Pentecostal congregation. In a structured form that prioritizes Spirit-led prophetic prayer, the Pentecostal leader and congregation practice becoming attuned or attentive to hearing the voice of God. The Spirit cries out through the diverse bodies gathered, who contribute these charisms or wisdom gifts back to the community.

Grounding in Embodied Realities

This project builds upon the premise that reviewing Pentecostal practice is the best way to (re)generate an embodied understanding of the Spirit who speaks. This embeds the Spirit as divine voice within the body, in the corporate sense of Christ's body, with special attention to the liturgy of the Pentecostal church. Despite all our technologies to date, it is impossible for a person to exist outside of their body.[29] To be embodied is therefore central

---

26. Coleman, *Globalisation of Charismatic Christianity*, 51; Lewis, *Christianity Reborn*, 58.

27. Therefore in this way the Pentecostal worship service can simultaneously be described as a site in which people experience God and do not experience God.

28. Clifton, "The Dark Side," 215, states, "NCLS research thus confirms that Pentecostal congregations have substantially lower percentages of people with a disability; or, said another way, Pentecostal constituents have much less contact with people who have a disability . . . while these statistics need to be treated with some caution, they do confirm the testimonies and intuition informing this paper, implying that people with disabilities do not feel comfortable attending Pentecostal churches."

29. The incarnation is a feature of Christian theology. Therefore, re-embedding

to what it means to be human. There is little doubt that our individual bodily characteristics, including gender/sex and ethnicity, impact our thoughts about God. Nevertheless, we do not craft an identity from all of our physical features (famously, Amartya Sen used the example of an unlikely association of size eight shoe wearers).[30] Where physical characteristics do inscribe upon our identity, however, it is meaningful, and so, to ignore the body is misguided. Accordingly, I will now bring Hollingsworth's feminist Pentecostal pneumatology into conversation with critical disability studies.

Definitions of "disability" are highly contested, but usually incorporate both a physical impairment of the body and a resulting economic and social disablement.[31] The experience of disability is common internationally. The World Bank estimates that one billion people (or 15 percent of the world's population) experience some form of disability. Of this number, between 110 million and 190 million people experience *significant* disabilities.[32] As countries develop and aging increases, disability is becoming increasingly frequent. Therefore, rates are often higher in Western nations; in Australia, 35.9 percent residents report a disability.[33] Therefore, disability is an important lens to view the world.

Disability studies (and theology) uses different models to explain the experience of disability in context.[34] For example, the *moral model* places moral categories of "good" or "bad" over disability.[35] In contrast, the *medical model* sees disability primarily as a disease that must be cured. The *social model* holds disability to be a product of society. The World Health Organization promotes the *"bio-psycho-social model,"* which recognizes both an individual's biological and psychological impairments and also their limitations within society.[36] Newer approaches to disability theology recommend attending to how these models interact.[37] Indeed, these models often coexist in Pentecostal practice.

Our human experience influences the theological questions we ask (and answers we accept) and is therefore important to the church's teaching and witness. Inevitably, those who undertake theology with a disabled

---

voice into the body is a thoroughly Christian project.

30. Sen, *Identity and Violence*, 26.
31. McKinney Fox, *Disability*, 1.
32. https://www.worldbank.org/en/topic/disability
33. https://www.and.org.au/pages/disability-statistics.html
34. Creamer, "Disability Theology," 340.
35. Creamer, "Disability Theology," 340.
36. WHO, "World Report," 29.
37. McKinney Fox, *Disability*, 11.

body are influenced by their location.[38] However, most theology to date is done from the location of a normative "able" body, whether this is made explicit or not.[39] A similar disconnect was famously addressed by South American liberation theologians (e.g., Gustavo Gutiérrez and Virgilo Elizondo) when the questions of the poor were largely excluded from seminaries.[40] Nowadays, women's issues are explored via the feminist and (more intersectional) "womanist" theological movements.[41] People of color have adopted Black, Mestizo, Hispanic, and indigenous theologies (among others). Even still, these are sometimes considered a variant on the norm and superfluous to the central task of theology.

Pentecostal theology, however, promotes a diversity of voices raised at Pentecost; this is its natural starting point. Importantly, Amos Yong argues that this generates a universal theology, which can be considered to be the areas of *consensus* between all these voices (or "consensual theology"). He suggests this as the hermeneutic by which Pentecostal theology is done.[42] If theology starts with the assumption that the church is comprised of *many* types of bodies then we will seek theology that works for them all.[43] In other words, as *all* the bodies speak out, the Spirit works to assist the listener to discern God's message for the gathered community and for those yet to come.

The Desirable Pentecostal Body: Smiley, Good-Looking Preachers

Undoubtedly, Pentecostal churches have adopted mass media to broadcast their message into the global marketplace, with the intent of transforming recipients.[44] The Australian Pentecostal church has had an extraordinarily fast transformation from the margins of society to its center. Perhaps this explains its emphasis on "leadership."[45] By promoting contextualization (or "relevance"), church leaders often shun more ascetic forms of the body in

---

38. Eiesland, "Encountering," 4.

39. This theological "norm" is an able-bodied, white, Western, middle-class, heterosexual male. See Saiving, "The Human Situation," 100.

40. Gutierrez, *Power of the Poor*, ix.

41. Peters and Kao, *Encountering the Sacred*, Loc 178.

42. Yong, "The Hermeneutical Trialectic," 22–39.

43. There is some complexity to this picture; however, space does not permit further examination.

44. Myers, "Progressive Pentecostalism," 115–20.

45. Clifton, *Pentecostal Churches*, 133.

favor of an image of the young, fashionable, thriving Christian leader. This serves to make Christianity appealing or desirable. Critics have responded harshly to this Pentecostal focus upon the body beautiful, claiming that it fails to offer an alternative to wider society. Celebrity, scholars argue, centers the powerful, the beautiful, and those who conform to the neoliberal values of consumption.[46] On social media sites such as Instagram, the line between celebrities' private and public lives are often blurred, with bodies co-opted for the sale of products. The Christian message, they claim, is convoluted by this emphasis upon the temporal.

The critique sharpens in relation to women's ministries and leaders in Australia's Pentecostal churches. In a previously published chapter in my coedited volume *The Hillsong Movement Examined*,[47] I noted that scholars reject Hillsong Church's women's ministries, claiming they promote traditional gender roles; this reduces women's contribution to a two-dimensional image labeled "princess theology."[48] The research tends to overlook ways in which women in the congregation are empowered in these ministries (via "secular" development measurements). In addition, Hillsong Global Senior Co-Pastor Bobbie Houston argues that the Sisterhood movement furnishes a social good.[49] Her intention is to "create pathways that lead people toward purpose, fulfilment, happiness, and ultimately freedom."[50] Thus, while scholars depreciate these religious forms, the prevailing logic of these forms is largely about women leading a flourishing life. Here, Hollingsworth notes similar findings in Latin America.[51]

Rather than drawing scholarly attention away from Pentecostal stage craft, historian Leah Payne instead employs feminist studies to demonstrate how Pentecostal women preachers use the platform in order to further their aims. For example, the female preacher's voice opened space for her public ministry at the turn of the century.[52] Performing a desirable faith often enabled women's participation in church leadership and public life. For example, Aimee Semple McPherson adopted Hollywood fashion and dramatized imaginary conversations that refuted any opposition to her

---

46. Maddox, "Prosper, Consume," 108–15; Maddox, "Goofy Parking Lot," 146–58.

47. Riches, "Feminine Key," 85–106.

48. Grey, "Princess Theology," 75; Maddox, "Warrior Princess Daughters," 9–26; Miller, "Women in Australian Pentecostalism," 64.

49. Payne, *Gender and Pentecostal Revivalism*, 91.

50. Payne, *Gender and Pentecostal Revivalism*, 198.

51. Hollingsworth, "Spirit and Voice," 207.

52. Hollingsworth, "Spirit and Voice," 31.

leadership.[53] Comparably, Maria Woodworth-Etter embodied holiness via simple, modest attire.[54] Both women not only adopted bodily techniques but also revised church architecture to "create spaces that displayed their power as ministers and their status as 'womanly women.'"[55]

Reviewing such differentiations in a positive light, with attention to their *telos* or end, we can read Pentecostal leaders as concerned with the Christian vision for human flourishing. With this pursuit, the Pentecostal platform promotes *the desirable body* in the hopes that it encourages newcomers to see Jesus via examples of those living fully alive. In general, Pentecostals seek to minimize tensions between those leading the rituals and the participants.[56] Still, there can be a strong demarcation in regard to the bodies presented on the platform and those in the seats. Therefore, in the next section an alternative embodied Pentecostal witness will be presented.

The "Undesirable" Pentecostal Body: Disability, Healing, and Death

Developing this logic, there are complexities for Pentecostal theology; one of those is the real limitations of the body. As the human body grows and develops, it *also* declines and, ultimately, dies. Accordingly, Victoria Rue states, "we need a body-affirming theology, perhaps one based on the cycles of nature, the cycle of life and death, including the experience of our dissolving form."[57]

What if, while seeking human flourishing, our prayer does not result in healing, and the person's body remains impaired?[58] What happens when sickness leads to the inevitable outcome of death? Through the lens of disability, the theologian may ask, what are we to do with *undesirable bodies*? Such tensions become profound for any pastor faced with the stark reality of aging, suffering, and disability, even while promoting an image of success and human flourishing. As Western medicine improves and prolongs

---

53. Hollingsworth, "Spirit and Voice," 64.
54. Hollingsworth, "Spirit and Voice," 68.
55. Payne, *Gender and Pentecostal Revivalism*, 75, 81.
56. Moore, "Appreciating Worship," 79–90.
57. Rue, *Encountering the Sacred*, Loc 2394.
58. For my friends with disability, this exercise is not intended to imply that disabled bodies cannot be flourishing bodies. In fact, its goal is the opposite, to outline how they can be flourishing bodies, and how they testify in liturgical space. See Clifton et al., "Quadriplegia," 20.

our life with little attention to wellbeing, how do we live "Christianly" while struggling within our bodies?

Before working in disability studies, rarely had I heard reference from the pulpit of a person who was not "overcoming" illness or disability. Pentecostals overall tend to display a general discomfort with bodies that resist healing, and continue to petition God for this outcome.[59] Although there are a number of significant Christians with impaired bodies whose voices do speak (e.g., North American Joni Erickson Tada and Australian theologian Shane Clifton), the Pentecostal pulpit promotes the healing of the body as a distinctive doctrinal emphasis.[60] As others have shown, early Pentecostal doctrinal emphasis tended to associate sickness and impairment with sin and promoted physical health above wholeness.[61] Yet, as Clifton notes, "supernatural healing itself is rare—is miraculous—and injury, suffering, and disability are a part of life."[62] So, he asks, "what is the significance of those stories that normally go untold; those that tell of the absence of healing and the hurt that sometimes results from prayer?"[63] He laments, "those with permanent sickness, injury, and disability are given no opportunity to testify about their experience." The silence around bodies that do not conform to the typical image of flourishing is significant. Thus he considers "giving voice to their silence" vital.

Rather than viewing suffering or illness as antithetical to the Christian message, disability theologians consider the witness that this disability provides. Famously, Nancy Eiesland proposed that we recognize "the Disabled God" within the biblical text.[64] She claims that Jesus' invitation to touch his scars pushes cultural taboos. Of this Creamer states,

> The image of the Disabled God rejects the notion that disability is in any way a consequence of individual sin (Jesus did not sin and yet became disabled) and protests the exclusion of people with disabilities from worship or leadership (Jesus' scars did not make him ineligible for continued leadership).[65]

59. Clifton, "The Dark Side," 206.

60. Many Pentecostal scholars emphasize healing rituals, including the laying on of hands, which Clifton notes in his paper can result in healing but also can reject people with disabilities even in the pursuit of this healing.

61. Within his MTh dissertation, Luke Thompson links this view to influential Pentecostal founding figure William Seymour, who was physically impaired. In "Bringing Healing," 11, 13, 15.

62. Thompson, "Bringing Healing," 213.

63. Thompson, "Bringing Healing," 206.

64. Eiesland, "Encountering," 1.

65. Creamer, "Disability Theology," 342.

The point of this metaphor or image is to move Christians beyond sympathy or pity towards constructive engagement with injured, broken, and dying bodies.

It should be emphasized that this proposal is not a rejection of the traditional Pentecostal emphasis on leadership or divine healing[66] but instead constitutes a plea to the church to steward the gift or "charism" of healing in tension with the larger Christian narrative. While the Pentecostal church has often focused on an intermediate *telos* or goal of healing in order to achieve the desirable state of human flourishing, this is not the Christian's ultimate end. The Westminster catechism famously states, "Man's chief end is to glorify God and to enjoy him forever." Following Hollingsworth's proposal, the Spirit does indeed speak in the Pentecostal church—but not only through the bodies of those with the microphone. In worship, the *ordinary* Pentecostal body is "caught up" in glory. Acknowledging the people of God in their diversity means to acknowledge their inevitable disabilities and impairments of function, particularly as bodies age. Christians need no authorization from the surrounding society, which often empowers the abled over the disabled body. Those filled with the Spirit "cry out" with glossolalic utterances, similar to the Proverbs woman crying in the marketplace. The beauty of this picture is the fully embodied cry of the congregation in worship of Jesus. This points to the end of history, or eschaton, where healing pales in comparison to the Christian's ultimate goal of resurrection with Christ.

Conclusions: Finding a Way Forward

Tensions arise when the church promotes an image of flourishing or "successful" human expression at the expense of a dying or "failing" one. What do we do with these differing experiences? Are they actually competing? Here I suggest that recognition of diverse bodily states is complementary.

The biblical account of Acts 2 provides the guiding narrative of Pentecostalism. Within this story two types of vocalizations can be observed. The first is glossolalia, the inaugural sign of the church. During this event the people speak out and the Spirit is heard among them. This can be interpreted as the Spirit "giving voice" to all, even those with seemingly undesirable bodies. The second is the interpretation of this sign by the "leader" Peter, who stood and addressed the crowd to announce tongues

---

66. Thompson states, "As a result of the Pentecostal view of Scripture, healing has always occupied a central place within Pentecostal theology and praxis. Some scholars even assert that a historical examination of Pentecostalism reveals that healing has been more central than glossolalia (or xenolalia)." In "Bringing Healing," 1.

as the Spirit's promised or embodied presence (Acts 2:14–21). By drawing on feminist authors who highlight speech acts as sites of resistance,[67] it is therefore possible to argue for the space for *both* the voices of Pentecostal leaders and Pentecostal people to speak.

Here I sought to embed the divine voice, demonstrating the witness of all worshipping bodies, both desirable and undesirable. In this way, the experience of the Spirit is grounded in the church as the ecclesial body. Layers of Pentecostal witness are arguably lost when reading the church only via the authorized Pentecostal preacher speaking from the platform (which sociologists tend to do). A more subversive Pentecostal reading includes the vocalizations of the gathered peoples and the testimony that arises because of (rather than in spite of) their diversity.[68] This opens more possibilities for reading the church's practices as a text viewed from the locations of the people represented within the congregation.

In summary, I argue that any focus on the immediate or miraculous present (or *telos*) should not cause Pentecostals to overlook the ultimate end (*eschaton*), lest we forget the larger arc of God's story. The witness of our body to Christ is *both* when it is alive *and* when it is impaired or dying. Therefore may we truly say along with Paul in Romans 14:8, "If we live, we live for the Lord; and if we die, we die for the Lord. So, whether we live or die, we belong to the Lord."[69]

Bibliography

Anderson, Allan. *An Introduction to Pentecostalism: Global Charismatic Christianity.* Cambridge: Cambridge University Press. 2004.

Albrecht, Daniel. *Rites in the Spirit: A Ritual Approach to Pentecostal/Charismatic Spirituality.* Sheffield: Sheffield Academic, 1999.

Cartledge, Mark. *Practical Theology, Charismatic and Empirical Perspectives.* Eugene, OR: Wipf & Stock, 2012.

Clifton, Shane. *Pentecostal Churches in Transition: Analysing the Developing Ecclesiology of the Assemblies of God in Australia.* Leiden: Brill, 2009.

———. "The Dark Side of Prayer for Healing: Toward a Theology of Well-Being." *Pneuma* 36 (2014) 204–25.

Clifton, Shane et al., "Quadriplegia, Virtue Theory, and Flourishing: A Qualitative Study Drawing on Self-Narratives." *Disability & Society* 33.1 (2018) 20–38.

Coakley, Sarah. *God, Sexuality, and the Self.* Cambridge: Cambridge University Press, 2013.

---

67. Ortega, "Speaking in Resistant Tongues," 313–18.
68. See Yong, "Many Tongues," 167–88.
69. New International Version.

Coleman, Simon. *The Globalisation of Charismatic Christianity*. Cambridge: Cambridge University Press, 2000.

Cox, Harvey. *Fire from Heaven: The Rise of Pentecostal Spirituality and the Reshaping of Religion in the 21st Century*. New York: Avalon, 2013.

Creamer, Deborah Beth. "Disability Theology." *Religion Compass* 6.7 (2012) 339–46.

Eiesland, Nancy. "Encountering the Disabled God." *The Other Side* 38.5 (2002) 1–6.

Grey, Jacqui. "'Princess Theology' and the Promotion of Women within Pentecostalism." In *Public Theology and the Challenge of Feminism*, edited by Stephen Burn and Anita Monro, 75–85. Oxford: Routledge, 2015.

Gutierrez, Gustavo. *The Power of the Poor in History*. Eugene, OR: Wipf & Stock, 2004.

Hollingsworth, Andrea. "Spirit and Voice: Toward a Feminist Pentecostal Pneumatology." *Pneuma* 29.2 (2007) 189–213.

Hutchinson, Mark. "'The Problem with 'Waves': Mapping Charismatic Potential in Italian Protestantism 1890–1929." *Pneuma* 39 (2017): 34–54.

Jennings, Mark. "Great Risk for the Kingdom: Pentecostal-Charismatic Growth Churches, Pastorpreneurs, and Neoliberalism." In *Multiculturalism and the Convergence of Faith and Practical Wisdom in Modern Society*, 236–48: Pennsylvania: IGI Global, 2017.

Johns, Cheryl Bridges. *Pentecostal Formation: A Pedagogy among the Oppressed*. Eugene, OR: Wipf & Stock, 1998.

Lewis, Donald M. *Christianity Reborn: The Global Expansion of Evangelicalism in the Twentieth Century*. Grand Rapids, MI: Eerdmans, 2004.

Maddox, Marion. "'In the Goofy Parking Lot': Growth Churches as a Novel Religious Form for Late Capitalism." *Social Compass* 59.2 (2012) 146–58.

———. "Prosper, Consume and Be Saved." *Critical Research on Religion* 1.108 (2013) 108–15.

———. "'Rise up Warrior Princess Daughters': Is Evangelical Women's Submission a Mere Fairy Tale?" *Journal of Feminist Studies in Religion* 29.1 (2013) 9–26.

McClymond, M. J. *Embodying the Spirit: New Perspectives on North American Revivalism*. Baltimore, MD: Johns Hopkins University Press, 2004.

McGuire, Meredith. B. *Lived Religion: Faith and Practice in Everyday Life*. New York: Oxford University Press, 2008.

McKinney Fox, Bethany. *Disability and the Way of Jesus: Holistic Healing in the Gospels and the Church*. Downers Grove, IL: InterVarsity, 2019.

Miller, Elizabeth. "Women in Australian Pentecostalism: Leadership, Submission, and Feminism in Hillsong Church." *Australian Religion Studies Review* 29.1 (2016) 52–76.

Moore, Gerard. "Appreciating Worship in All Its Variety." *Australian Journal of Liturgy* 10.3 (2006) 79–90.

Myers, Bryant L. "Progressive Pentecostalism, Development and Christian Development NGOs: A Challenge and an Opportunity." *International Bulletin of Missionary Research* 39.3 (2015) 115–20.

Myrick, Nathan. "Relational Power, Music, and Identity: The Emotional Efficacy of Congregational Song." *Yale Journal of Music & Religion* 3.1 (2017) 77–92.

Ortega, Mariana. "Speaking in Resistant Tongues: Latina Feminism, Embodied Knowledge, and Transformation." *Hypatia* 31.2 (2016) 313–18.

Payne, Leah. *Gender and Pentecostal Revivalism: Making a Female Ministry in the Early Twentieth Century*. New York: Palgrave Macmillan, 2015.

Peters, Rebecca Todd, and Grace Yia-Hei Kao. *Encountering the Sacred: Feminist Reflections on Women's Lives*. London: Bloomsbury, 2018

Riches, Tanya. "Hillsong in a Feminine Key." In *The Hillsong Movement Examined: You Call Me out upon the Waters*, edited by Tanya Riches and Tom Wagner. New York: Palgrave McMillan, 2017.

Rue, Victoria. in *Encountering the Sacred: Feminist Reflections on Women's Lives*. Edited by Rebecca Todd Peters and Grace Yia-Hei Kao. London: Bloomsbury, 2018.

Saiving, Valerie. "The Human Situation: A Feminine View." *Journal of Religion* 40.2 (1960) 100–112.

Sen, Amartya. *Identity and Violence: The Illusion of Destiny*. London: Penguin, 2007.

Smith, J. K. A. *Thinking in Tongues: Pentecostal Contributions to Christian Philosophy*. Grand Rapids, MI: Eerdmans, 2010.

Thompson, Luke S. C. A. "Bringing Healing, Health and Wholeness to a Broken Church: A Biblical Critique of Pentecostal Healing Praxis." MTh Diss., King's College, University of Aberdeen, 2015.

Wade, Matthew, and Maria Hynes. "Worshipping Bodies: Affective Labour in the Hillsong Church." *Geographical Research* 51.2 (2013) 173–79.

Wilkinson, Michael, and Peter Althouse. "Social Theory, Religion and the Body." In *Annual Review of the Sociology of Religion*, edited by Michael Wilkinson, 1. Leiden: Brill, 2017.

World Health Organization (WHO). World Report on Disability. New York: United Nations. 2011.

Yong, Amos. "The Hermeneutical Trialectic: Notes toward a Consensual Hermeneutic and Theological Method." *The Heythrop Journal* 45.1 (2004) 22–39.

———. "Many Tongues, Many Senses: Pentecost, the Body Politic, and the Redemption of Dis/Ability." *Pneuma* 31 (2009) 167–88.

14

Grounding our Discussion of Abortion

Denise Cooper-Clarke

Reflection on the morality of abortion needs to be grounded both in Scripture and in the concrete realities of life for women and children, including the unique bodily relationship between a mother and her unborn child.

Yet much evangelical discourse about abortion is much more narrowly grounded, centering on three claims. First, that the starting point and decisive factor is the determination of the moral status of the fetus: "The one most important question has frequently been identified as the question of the status of the fetus. On the answer to that question all the law and the prophets with respect to abortion are sometimes presumed to hang."[1] Second, that for Christians there is only one possible view of this, because the Scriptures clearly teach that the human fetus has the same moral status as a born human being from the moment of conception (understood as fertilization). And third, that this is the traditional view of the church, from its beginning.

I begin with an examination of the latter two claims. Against these claims, I will argue that the Scriptures are silent on abortion and ambiguous in relation to the moral status of the fetus, and that there is no single view in the tradition on the moral status of the early fetus. Then I return to the first claim, that the moral status of the fetus is the one most important question. I examine an alternative starting point and decisive factor,

---

1. Lammers and Verhey, "Abortion," 583.

namely the welfare of women, and I then propose a way of pursuing the welfare of both mother and fetus, grounded in the scriptural account of the fallen relationship between men and women.

Scripture

The Scriptures are silent on abortion and ambiguous in relation to the moral status of the fetus.

Does the proscription of murder, based on humankind being made on the image of God, apply to the unborn? Many evangelicals, especially in the U.S., believe that is does. John Piper, for example, who is strongly anti-abortion, says that abortion is a "God issue."[2] The President of the National Association of Evangelicals in the U.S. writes that "As evangelical Christians who take the Bible seriously and believe in the sanctity of all human life created in the image of God, abortion is about life more than about politics . . . We are pro-life because of God and life . . ."[3] Yet the Scriptures do not mention induced abortion at all, and make no clear statement about the moral status of the fetus or when life begins. Paul Jewett writes, "Scripture offers no direct teaching on the question of the participation of the fetus in the divine image."[4] Even some strongly pro-life advocates acknowledge this: "Although the Bible does not directly state that personhood begins with conception (in the technical sense), such a conclusion is warranted by an appeal to common sense and continuity."[5]

The silence of both Old and New Testaments in this area is puzzling, given that abortion was widespread—though often ineffective and dangerous for the mother—in the ancient pagan world. Michael Gorman argues that there was a consensus in the Jewish community that made abortion unthinkable and that the silence of the New Testament reflects the same assumption.[6] But it can also be argued that the Scriptures are silent on the issue because they do not take a definite view.

Despite this silence on abortion, it is frequently claimed that the Bible teaches the personhood of the unborn. Two texts are often cited: Exodus 21:22–25 and Psalm 139:13–16.

Exodus 21:22–25 is a difficult passage, as the difference between translations attests:

2. Taylor, "Abortion is About God," 337.
3. Anderson, "Too Many Abortions."
4. Jewett, "Relation of the Soul," 7.
5. Sullivan, "The Conception View," 17.
6. Gorman, "New Testament Silent?" 28.

> When people who are fighting injure a pregnant woman so that there is a miscarriage, and yet no further harm follows, the one responsible shall be fined what the woman's husband demands, paying as much as the judges determine. If any harm follows, then you shall give life for life, eye for eye, tooth for tooth, hand for hand, foot for foot, burn for burn, wound for wound, stripe for stripe (NRSV).

> If people are fighting and hit a pregnant woman and she gives birth prematurely but there is no serious injury, the offender must be fined whatever the woman's husband demands and the court allows. But if there is serious injury, you are to take life for life, eye for eye, tooth for tooth, hand for hand, foot for foot, burn for burn, wound for wound, bruise for bruise (NIV).

There are two ways in which this passage has been interpreted. The first (reflected in the NRSV) is that it refers to a miscarriage, with the death of the unborn child, and that the "further harm" refers to the mother. In this view, *lex talionis* (the law of retaliation) only applies if the mother is killed or injured, suggesting that the unborn child does not have the same moral status as her mother. In the second, minority interpretation, this passage refers to a premature birth (as in the NIV), and whether *lex talionis* applies depends on whether either the child or the mother dies. "The majority view, both in ancient times among rabbinical interpreters and modern exegetes, is that the death of the child is assumed throughout the case."[7] In ancient times, traumatic premature birth would almost always result in the death of the fetus. Human viability, defined as the gestational age at which the chance of survival for a baby if delivered is 50 percent, is 23–24 weeks in developed countries with neonatal intensive care facilities, but closer to 34 weeks in low and middle income countries without such facilities (and also presumably in ancient times).[8] Comparison with other ANE codes reveals similar laws about accidental miscarriage, all of which assume the death of the child.[9]

Nevertheless, the minority interpretation that the survival of the fetus is critical has existed since at least the time of Philo of Alexandria and continues to be used today to argue that the life of the fetus has the same value as that of her mother.[10] So no definite conclusion about induced abortion can be drawn from this passage. Since accidental death of the unborn is punished

---

7. Sprinkle, "Exodus 21:22–25," 235.
8. Glass et al., "Outcomes," 1338–40.
9. Sprinkle, "Exodus 21: 22–25," 250.
10. Sprinkle, "Exodus 21: 22–25," 235–36.

(by a fine), it is certainly possible that deliberately inducing his or her death would be regarded more seriously, even as murder. Yet the possibility that the death of the fetus was regarded as of lesser moral significance cannot be ruled out, and indeed seems the more likely interpretation.

Now to the text most frequently cited by anti-abortionists, Psalm 139:13–16:

> For it was you who formed my inward parts;
>> you knit me together in my mother's womb.
>
> I praise you, for I am fearfully and wonderfully made.
>> Wonderful are your works;
>
> that I know very well.
>
> My frame was not hidden from you,
>
> when I was being made in secret,
>> intricately woven in the depths of the earth.
>
> Your eyes beheld my unformed substance.
>
> In your book were written
>> all the days that were formed for me,
>> when none of them as yet existed.

The use of Psalm 139 is a recent phenomenon in the abortion debate. It "arrived in the antiabortion discourse in the late 1970s, along with conservative Protestants."[11] The slogan "Fearfully and Wonderfully Made" began to appear on posters, and the Southern Baptist Convention called its funding program for pregnancy ultrasounds "The Psalm 139 Project."[12]

Yet Psalm 139 is poetry, not biology, let alone law. It indicates the continuity between born and unborn life, but does not say when this life begins, let alone that it begins at fertilization. The psalm may in fact "prove too much," as it says that God knows us not only in the womb, but even before we exist at all (v. 16).

Jewish rabbi and bioethicist Elliot Dorff urges caution in using Psalm 139 in argument about abortion, pointing out that it has never been part of rabbinical discussion of the issue. He claims that ancient jurists would have regarded the legalistic use of psalms as a "category mistake," since they regarded psalms as emotional, metaphorical speech.[13]

---

11. Van Biema, "One Psalm," para. 15.
12. Van Biema, "One Psalm," para. 21.
13. Cited in Van Biema, "One Psalm," para. 29.

Further, this psalm has also been used by pro-abortionists, who see the language of being "knit together," "woven," and "unformed" as pointing to a process in the womb whereby a fetus becomes a person, just as a pupa in a cocoon is not a butterfly but is in the process of becoming one.[14] So this psalm will not provide us with a definite answer as to the moral status of the fetus.

Christian Tradition

There is no consistent teaching in the tradition on abortion, nor a single view on the moral status of the early fetus.

There is disagreement as to whether Jewish tradition opposed induced abortion. Gorman claims that one can deduce a clear anti-abortion ethos from extra-canonical Jewish documents contemporaneous with the New Testament.[15] Paul Simmons, however, sees this witness as "nonnormative," and regards later rabbinic Judaism, which did not prohibit abortion, as normative.[16]

There is also disagreement about whether early church documents that strongly oppose abortion, such as the *Didache* and *Pseudo Barnabas*, were normative for Christians,[17] and about whether the early Christian attitude to abortion was continuous or discontinuous with the Jewish attitude of the pre-Christian and early Christian era.[18] Further, we do not know to what extent negative attitudes to abortion arose from concern for the pregnant woman rather than or in addition to concern for the life of the unborn, given the high maternal mortality rate of the procedure in ancient times. Daniel Maguire claims that "There is no 'clear and constant' teaching on abortion, and Catholic moral theology and Christian ethics generally have been pro-moral choice ever since we started looking at the circumstances of abortion."[19]

According to Lindsay Disney and Larry Poston, "much of the disagreement about abortion and the moral status of the early foetus was based on a distinction between the beginning of biological life and 'ensoulment' and

---

14. Verhey, *Strange World*, 204.
15. Gorman, "Scripture, History and Authority," 85.
16. Gorman, "Scripture, History and Authority," 85.
17. Gorman, "Scripture, History and Authority," 90.
18. Maguire and Burtchaell, "Catholic Legacy," 588.
19. Maguire and Burtchaell, "Catholic Legacy," 588.

differing views of when 'ensoulment' occurs."[20] There are two main views: Traducianism and Creationism.

Traducianism maintains that when the egg and sperm unite, "the combination forms a new 'soul' automatically and immediately."[21] This was the view of Tertullian, Clement of Alexandria, Gregory of Nyssa, and Maximus the Confessor.

Creationism maintains that "the 'soul' is created and introduced into a fetus by God at a point of his choosing, either at the time of a fetus's first breath, as was the case with Adam in Genesis 2:7, or when God in his sovereignty knows that a fetus is not going to be spontaneously (meaning 'naturally') or intentionally aborted."[22] In this view, based on Aristotelian philosophy, there is a marked distinction between the body, from the earth, and the soul, from God. Aristotle held that ensoulment occurred at forty days for male fetuses and ninety days for female. Augustine adopted this view and considered that, while "formed" fetuses will participate in the resurrection of the dead, "with regard to undeveloped foetuses, who would not more readily think that they perish, like seeds that did not germinate?"[23] So also Aquinas, and this view was the norm in the Christian West from the early fifth century to the late nineteenth. Hence, abortion was allowed prior to forty days. Between the fifteenth and nineteenth centuries, Catholic ethicists justified early (and sometimes later) abortion on the grounds of risk to the mother's health or even reputation.[24] The "forty-day rule" was not finally repealed until 1869, when all abortion was prohibited by the Catholic church.[25]

In relation to evangelicals, it may be surprising to hear that "there was a time in the not too distant past when the majority of Protestant Christians, including those who called themselves evangelical, did not consider the point at which the fertilized ovum or developing embryo or fetus becomes a human being to be clearly defined, indisputable, and settled for all time."[26] There were sharp disagreements, but differing views were respected, with no one view being regarded as a litmus test of a true Christian. Many evangelicals welcomed *Roe v. Wade* (1973) because it addressed the problem of unsafe illegal abortions. A one-time President of the Southern Baptist Convention

20. Disney and Poston, "Ensoulment," 274
21. Disney and Poston, "Ensoulment," 275.
22. Disney and Poston, "Ensoulment," 277.
23 Augustine, *Enchiridion*, Chapter XXIII, para. 85.
24. Maguire and Burtchaell, 590.
25. Disney and Poston, "Ensoulment," 278.
26. Scanzoni, "When Evangelicals were Open," para. 6.

told *Christianity Today*: "I have always felt that it was only after a child was born and had a life separate from its mother that it became an individual person, and it has always, therefore, seemed to me that what is best for the mother and for the future should be allowed."[27] Dallas Theological Seminary professor Bruce Waltke wrote in a 1968 article that "God does not regard the fetus as a soul, no matter how far gestation has progressed."[28]

In August 1968, a *Protestant Symposium on the Control of Human Reproduction* produced the written consensus of twenty-five evangelical scholars (from theology, medicine, law, and sociology; all shared an acceptance of the Bible as final authority on moral issues, and all were men). It affirmed that "where specific answers are lacking (in the Bible) Christians acting under the authority of Scripture may differ from one another in the conclusions they reach because different weight may be given to different principles"; that "as to whether or not the performance of an induced abortion is always sinful we are not agreed, but about the necessity and permissibility for it under certain circumstances we are in accord"; and that "the Christian physician will advise induced abortion only to safeguard greater values sanctioned by Scripture. These values include individual health, family welfare and social responsibility."[29]

Two years before *Roe v. Wade*, the Southern Baptist Convention adopted a resolution calling on Southern Baptists "to work for legislation that will allow the possibility of abortion under such conditions as rape, incest, clear evidence of severe fetal deformity and carefully ascertained evidence of the likelihood of damage to the emotional, mental and physical health of the mother."[30] This may be compared with the first resolution passed at the June 2019 gathering of Southern Baptists in Alabama, titled "On Celebrating the Advancement of Pro-Life Legislation in State Legislatures," which urged the U.S. Supreme Court to overturn *Roe v. Wade*.[31]

In summary, there have been diverse views throughout church history, even until quite recently, on the morality of abortion and the moral status of the fetus. None, however, have maintained that the fetus is of no moral significance or that abortion is permissible for any but a grave moral reason.

---

27. "Abortion Decision," 48.
28. Waltke, "Old Testament and Birth Control," 3.
29. Christian Medical Society, "Protestant Symposium," 46–47.
30. Scanzoni, "When Evangelicals were Open," para. 10.
31. Burgess, "Southern Baptists," para. 7.

The Interests of Women

At times, strange as it may seem, women are invisible in Christian discussion of abortion. It is as if the fetus exists in isolation from a woman's body (as an embryo sometimes exists in a laboratory after *in vitro* fertilization). Christian feminist Beverly Harrison claims that "from the patristic period onward, the selective perceptions operative in the historical judgments of Christian teaching in abortion are skewed, because women's wellbeing is not perceived as a central moral issue and women's experience and reality are not understood as relevant to a moral analysis of abortion."[32] Similarly, Margaret Farley points to the neglect by "strong" antiabortionists of "the needs and claims of women, of pregnant mothers."[33]

For pro-choice feminists, on the other hand, the fetus often seems to be invisible. The starting point and decisive factor for them in considering abortion is the welfare of women, and the belief that "abortion rights are prerequisites for women's full development and social equality."[34] So Australian feminist Anne Summers claims that "you cannot support women's rights without supporting abortion." According to Summers, "feminism boils down to one fundamental principle and that is women's ability to be independent," and "there are two fundamental preconditions to such independence: ability to support oneself financially and the right to control one's fertility . . . To guarantee the second, women need safe and effective contraception and the back-up of safe and affordable abortion."[35]

Pro-abortion feminists hold various positions in relation to the moral status of the fetus. For some it seems irrelevant, as the woman's choice will always trump any moral claim to life the fetus might have. Yet most feel the need to justify the killing of a human individual, albeit very young, whose biological life at least begins at fertilization. Farley describes the "'bad faith' in a pro-abortion position which, in contradiction to persistent empirical evidence, rests its argument wholly on the claim that the fetus is simply a part of the pregnant woman, a piece of tissue no more unique than an appendix."[36] Some adopt the argument of bioethicists such as Peter Singer that the human fetus (and young infant) is not entitled to the same protection as a "person," defined by John Locke as having rationality

---

32. Harrison, *Our Right to Choose*, 155.
33. Farley, "Liberation," 635.
34. Callahan, "Pro-Life Feminism," 623.
35. Summers, "No Such Thing," para. 9.
36. Farley, "Liberation," 635.

and self-awareness.[37] Some adopt the position that the value of a fetus is contingent on the mother bestowing value on him or her—a process of "humanization" that can only be granted by the woman in whose body the fetus lives.[38] Others argue for a particular point in gestation when the fetus attains moral status and so the right to protection. Beverly Harrison, for example, names viability as that point.[39]

Another pro-abortion position is that even if the fetus has the same moral status as a "person," the mother still has a right to refuse to sustain its life. Judith Jarvis Thompson put this argument in 1971, using the analogy of someone finding themselves connected (without having consented) to the life support system of a famous violinist and being told they needed to remain connected for nine months or the violinist would die. Thomson claimed they would have no obligation to remain connected.[40] Hence, she concludes, a woman has no obligation to continue to sustain the life of her unborn child. This argument has a number of flaws, including the failure to acknowledge the greater moral obligations owed by parents to their children than to strangers. However it does have two interesting implications.

First, in relation to Thomson's claim that there is no obligation to continue the pregnancy if a woman has not consented to it, it can be argued that consent to sexual intercourse is implicit consent to pregnancy, since pregnancy is a known consequence of sexual intercourse, even when contraceptive measures are used. But in the situation of rape, Thomson's analogy is more plausible.

Second, Thomson's argument is an argument for terminating a pregnancy, not for killing the fetus. It can therefore only be a possible argument for early, not late term, abortion. After viability (between twenty-two and twenty-four weeks), pregnancy can be terminated by inducing labor, allowing the fetus a chance of survival. Late term abortions (specified as after 20 weeks) therefore involve a lethal injection of potassium chloride into the fetal heart before labor is induced, to ensure delivery of a dead infant. Such a procedure is unnecessary for the purpose of preserving the mother's life or health; all that is required is that the baby be delivered. Indeed, in such cases, attempts are usually made to prolong the pregnancy as long as is safe for the mother, in order to give the baby the best chance of survival. When the fetus is killed before delivery, it is clear that the aim is not just termination of the pregnancy, but the death of the fetus. The most

---

37. Singer, *Rethinking*, 162.
38. Callahan, "Pro-Life Feminism," 625.
39. Harrison, "Feminist-Liberation View," 621–22.
40. Thomson, "Defense," 48.

common reason for such a procedure is fetal abnormality, usually severe abnormality. These seem to be cases of antenatal euthanasia, and could not be justified by Thomson's argument.[41]

If we must choose between either the welfare of the fetus or the welfare of women as the decisive factor in the abortion debate, we are at an impasse. As Farley says, on the one hand some experience a "compelling obligation to alleviate situations which are oppressive and harmful to women. On the other hand, some persons experience an equally compelling obligation to protect the lives of human foetuses . . . The goal of one cannot be had if the goal of the other is to be achieved."[42]

But, apart from the rare cases where pregnancy is a serious threat to a woman's life or physical health, is it necessarily the case that both goals cannot be achieved?

Pursuing the Welfare of Both Fetuses and Women

Both strong anti- and pro-abortion positions are individualistic in that they treat women and their unborn children as separate entities and potential antagonists. They either see the woman as a threat to the fetus, or the fetus as a threat to the woman. But the reality of pregnancy is an intimate relationship of the two that might be described as "inherently 'two-in-one.'"[43] Pregnancy is a unique state for both mother and fetus.

The early feminists defended the rights of both women and unborn children and deplored abortion.[44] Indeed, both feminism and the pro-life position have the same basis. The claim to equality for women is based on their humanity. Logically, this should also apply to our understanding of the unborn as equally human. "Debates conducted about the personhood of the fetus were once conducted about feminine personhood . . . In all patriarchal unjust systems, lesser orders of human life are granted rights only when wanted, chosen, or invested with value by the powerful."[45]

In Australia, it is estimated that about half of pregnancies are unplanned, and half of these end in abortion. Worldwide, there are between forty and fifty million abortions a year, nearly half of which are performed unsafely (inadequately skilled operators, harmful techniques and/or unsanitary conditions), resulting in an estimated fifty thousand maternal deaths.

---

41. Alward, "Thomson, the Right to Life," 101.
42. Farley, "Liberation," 634.
43. Rebecca Todd Peters, cited in Frykholm, "Two Ways," para. 9.
44. Foster, "Pro-Life Roots," para. 2.
45. Callahan, "Pro-Life Feminism," 626.

The maternal abortion-related death rate is much higher in countries with restrictive abortion laws than in those with less restrictive laws (thirty-four deaths per hundred thousand births compared to one or fewer per hundred thousand births) because of the much higher rate of unsafe abortions.[46] Abortion rates are not significantly different in countries where abortion is highly restricted (banned altogether or only allowed to save the woman's life) and where it is broadly legal: thirty-seven per thousand women in the former and thirty-four per thousand in the latter.[47]

It thus seems clear that if our goal is the welfare of both women and fetuses, campaigning for restrictive abortion laws will not achieve this. Restrictive abortion laws do not save fetal lives and are associated with maternal deaths and injury. On the other hand, some feminists now recognize that unrestricted access to abortion does "not bring women reproductive freedom, social equality, sexual fulfilment, or full personal development."[48] Abortions often serve the interests of men rather than women. If a woman claims the sole right to decide on abortion, why should anyone else share parental or social responsibility? Ready abortion "legitimizes male irresponsibility."[49] Abortion also often serves as a "quick fix" alternative to addressing the real needs of pregnant women, including safety in their home, financial security, health care, child care, and flexible employment: "Abortion has masked—rather than solved—the problems women face. Abortion is a failed experiment on women."[50]

The non-sectarian group *Feminists for Life*, whose slogan is "Women deserve better than abortion," was formed in 1972. Pro-life feminists affirm the right of women to full social equality, but argue that it is certainly possible, indeed necessary, to pursue the welfare of both women and their children. They claim that "women can never achieve the fulfilment of feminist goals in a society permissive toward abortion."[51]

Grounding the Pursuit of the Welfare of Both Women and Fetuses

As a result of the entry of sin into the world, three sets of relationships are affected: the relationship between men and women, humanity's

46. Gibson, "Editorial," 15.
47. Guttmacher Institute, "Induced Abortion," para. 19.
48. Callahan, "Pro-Life Feminism," 628.
49. Callahan, "Pro-Life Feminism," 629.
50. Foster, "Pro-Life Roots," para. 28.
51. Callahan, "Pro-Life Feminism," 623.

relationship with the earth, and humanity's relationship with God. Referring to the first of these, Genesis 3:16 is usually translated something like, "To the woman he said, 'I will greatly increase your pangs in childbearing; in pain you shall bring forth children, yet your desire shall be for your husband, and he shall rule over you.'"[52]

But a recent paper by Curley and Peterson points out that the word translated "pangs" (sometimes "pain") is the same word translated "toil" in Genesis 3:17, which, they argue from its usage elsewhere in the Old Testament, includes both physical and emotional toil and in this context "can just as legitimately, and more rightly, be translated as emotional sorrow or grief."[53] They also argue that the word translated "childbearing" is more accurately translated either "conception" or "pregnancy" and they favor "conception" in this verse. Therefore Genesis 3:16a would read "I will greatly multiply your sorrowful conceptions; in pain you will bring forth children." Curley and Peterson argue that the primary reference of "sorrowful conceptions" is to infertility. However, they concede that "all the issues related to conception are in play by the phrase 'sorrowful conceptions,' not just barrenness . . . This could include miscarriages, impotence and the unwillingness of men to impregnate their wives."[54]

If "sorrowful conceptions" is the correct reading, might this not also encompass conception/pregnancy that is unwelcome to the woman? In ancient Israel, children were regarded as a blessing and infertility a curse, yet not all women then would have welcomed every pregnancy, just as, for many reasons, not all pregnancies are welcome today. Their reasons, then and now, include the risks of pregnancy and childbirth and the toll multiple pregnancies take on women's health. These realities—together with fetal abnormalities, which are also given as reasons for abortion—are evidence of the general fallenness of creation. But the reasons a pregnancy is unwelcome and abortion considered also relate in many cases to the particular result of the fall stated in Genesis 3:16b: the "rule" of the man over the woman. The "general disordering" of women's reproduction[55] is connected to the disordering of relationships between men and women. Whether one adopts the view that the subordination of women to men is built into the creation order and now distorted by sin, or that it is only introduced as a result of the entry of sin, it is clear that this fallen "rule" of

---

52. NRSV.
53. Curley and Peterson, "Eve's Curse," 160.
54. Curley and Peterson, "Eve's Curse," 162.
55. Tamie Davis, email message to Denise Cooper-Clarke, June 15, 2019.

men over women is a negative consequence for women. It is a harsh and oppressive rule that entrenches male privilege.

Implications for Social Policy

Women are responsible for their moral choices in relation to abortion, but those choices occur in a broader cultural context characterized by male privilege.

If neither restrictive nor permissive abortion laws promote the welfare of both women and fetuses, we need an alternative approach to reducing abortion rates that recognizes the connection between the welfare of women and the welfare of their unborn children—an approach that challenges male privilege. This is not to say that Christians should not advocate for regulation of abortion through a legal framework. The law serves an educative function. There ought to be clear criteria for abortion, and stricter criteria after viability. There ought also to be mandatory independent counseling of women seeking abortion, strong protections for conscientious objectors in the health professions, and accurate recording of abortion statistics. In the broader social context, Christians may challenge the negative attitude to disability that underlies the abortion of fetuses with relatively minor abnormalities such as Down Syndrome or cleft lip and palate. The presence in our midst of such children whose parents chose to continue with a pregnancy, often despite medical advice, is a powerful witness.

The pro-abortionist position is based, according to Sidney Callahan, on "elitist acceptance of male models of sex."[56] In seeking to "move society from its male-dominated course," she advocates a feminized sexuality where "sex acts are embedded within deep emotional bonds and secure long term commitments"[57] in contrast to the male-oriented model that endorses casual sexual encounters with a variety of partners. When adopted by women, this male model of sexuality requires abortion so that a woman's body can be more like a man's. Callahan concludes that another "round of feminist consciousness is needed" in which, instead of "humbly buying entrée by conforming to male lifestyles, women will demand that society accommodate itself to them."[58]

---

56. Callahan, "Pro-Life Feminism," 629.
57. Callahan, "Pro-Life Feminism," 630.
58. Callahan, "Pro-Life Feminism," 632.

Daniel Maguire writes, "The most intelligent way to be anti-abortion is to look to the cause of unwanted pregnancies . . . I would list sexism as the first cause of unwanted pregnancies."[59]

Male privilege contributes to unwelcome pregnancies in diverse ways, including the extreme example of rape, prostitution, sex slavery, the coercion of women to have sex in casual relationships, family violence,[60] the particular obstacles faced in the workforce by women with children, and the cultural expectation that women assume most of the responsibility of raising children.

Conclusion

The argument against abortion based solely on the moral status of the fetus, while not unreasonable, not only abstracts women from their unborn children, but rests on shaky exegetical ground. It has also been generally unpersuasive in the public discourse. Rather than ground efforts to reduce abortion rates in such an interminable argument, we should ground them in a biblical understanding of the connection between abortion and male hegemony. The welfare of both women and their unborn children can be pursued by addressing the societal structures and attitudes that entrench male privilege.

Bibliography

"Abortion Decision: A Death Blow?" *Christianity Today* 17.10 (1973) 48.

Alward, P. "Thomson, the Right to Life and Partial Birth Abortion or Two MULES for Sister Sarah." *Journal of Medical Ethics* 28 (2002) 99–101.

Anderson, Leith. "Too Many Abortions among Evangelicals." February 5 (2012). https://www.nae.net/too-many-abortions-among-evangelicals.

Aston, Gillian, and Susan Bewley. "Review: Abortion and Domestic Violence." *The Obstetrician and Gynaecologist* 11 (2009) 163–68.

Augustine. "Enchiridion: On Faith, Hope, and Love." (1955). tertullian.org/fathers/augustine_enchiridion_ 02_trans.htm

Burgess, Katherine. "Abortion, Gay Christians and Critical Race Theory: The Statements Southern Baptists Made at Their Annual Meeting." *Memphis Commercial Appeal*. June 13, 2019. https://www.commercialappeal.com/story/news/2019/06/13/southern-baptist-convention-resolutions-sbc-annual-meeting/1440135001/.

---

59. Maguire and Burtchaell, "Catholic Legacy," 591.

60. According to Aston and Bewley, "Abortion and Domestic Violence," 165, "A survey of 1127 women undergoing a second or subsequent abortion found that they were more likely to have experienced physical abuse by a male partner, sexual abuse, or coercion."

Callahan, Sidney. "Abortion and the Sexual Agenda: A Case for Pro-Life Feminism." In *On Moral Medicine*, edited by Stephen E. Lammers and Allen Verhey, 623–32. Grand Rapids, MI: Eerdmans, 1998.

Christian Medical Society. "A Protestant Affirmation on the Control of Human Reproduction." *Journal of the American Scientific Affiliation*, 22 (1970) 46–47.

Curley, Christine, and Brian Peterson. "Eve's Curse Revisited: An Increase of Sorrowful Conceptions." *Bulletin for Biblical Research* 26.2 (2016) 157–72.

Disney, Lindsey, and Larry Poston. "The Breath of Life: Christian Perspectives on Conception and Ensoulment." *Anglican Theological Review* 92.2 (2010) 83–96.

Farley, Margaret. "Liberation, Abortion and Responsibility." In *On Moral Medicine*, edited by Stephen E. Lammers and Allen Verhey, 633–38. Grand Rapids, MI: Eerdmans, 1998.

Foster, Serrin M. "The Feminist Case against Abortion: Recovering the Pro-Life Roots of the Women's Movement." *America* 212.2 (2015) 14–18. https://www.americamagazine.org/faith/2015/01/07/feminist-case-against-abortion-pro-life-roots-womens-movement.

Frykholm, Amy. "Two Ways of Being Christian and Pro-Choice: Is Abortion Only the Lesser of Two Evils, or Can It Be a Moral Good?" *The Christian Century*. October 8, 2018. https://www.christiancentury.org/review/books/two-ways-being-christian-and-pro-choice.

Gibson, Gillian. "Editorial." *O&G Magazine* 20.2 (2018) 15.

Glass, Hannah, et al. "Outcomes for Extremely Premature Infants." *Anesthesia & Analgesia* 120.6 (2015) 1337–51.

Gorman, Michael J. "Scripture, History and Authority in a Christian View of Abortion: A Response to Paul Simmons." *Christian Bioethics* 2.1 (1996) 83–96.

———. "Why Is the New Testament Silent About Abortion?". *Christianity Today* 37.1 (1993) 27–29.

Guttmacher Institute. "Induced Abortion Worldwide." Guttmacher Institute blog. March 2018. https://www.guttmacher.org/fact-sheet/induced-abortion-worldwide.

Harrison, Beverly W. "A Feminist-Liberation View of Abortion." In *On Moral Medicine*, edited by Stephen E. Lammers and Allen Verhey, 617–22. Grand Rapids, MI: Eerdmans, 1998.

———. *Our Right to Choose: Toward a New Ethic of Abortion*. Boston: Beacon, 1983.

Jewett, Paul. "The Relation of the Soul to the Fetus." *Christianity Today* 13 no. 3 (1968) 6–9.

Lammers, Stephen E., and Allen Verhey. "Abortion." In *On Moral Medicine*, edited by Stephen E. Lammers and Allen Verhey, 583–85. Grand Rapids, MI: Eerdmans, 1998.

Maguire, Daniel C., and James T. Burtchaell. "The Catholic Legacy and Abortion: A Debate." In *On Moral Medicine*, edited by Stephen E. Lammers and Allen Verhey, 586–99. Grand Rapids, MI: Eerdmans, 1998.

Scanzoni, Letha Dawson. "When Evangelicals Were Open to Differing Views on Abortion." *Christian Feminism Today*. 2012. http://eewc.com/evangelicals-open-differing-views-abortion.

Singer, Peter. *Rethinking Life and Death*. Melbourne: Text, 1994.

Sprinkle, Joe M. "The Interpretation of Exodus 21:22–25 (*Lex Talionis*) and Abortion." *Westminster Theological Journal* 55 (1993) 233–53.

Sullivan, Dennis M. "The Conception View of Personhood: A Review." *Ethics and Medicine*, 19 (2003) 11–33.

Summers, Anne. "There Is No Such Thing as a Pro-Life Feminist." *The Sydney Morning Herald*. January 22, 2012. https://www.smh.com.au/politics/federal/there-is-no-such-thing-as-a-pro-life-feminist-20120121-1qbao.html.

Taylor, Justin. "'Abortion Is About God': Piper's Passionate, Prophetic Pro-Life Preaching." In *For the Fame of God's Name*, edited by Sam Storms and Justin Taylor. Wheaton, IL: Crossway, 2010.

Thomson, Judith Jarvis. "A Defense of Abortion." *Philosophy and Public Affairs* 1.1 (1971) 47–66.

Van Biema, David. "One Psalm, Two Causes, Two Meanings." *The Christian Century*. April 2, 2012. https://www.christiancentury.org/article/2012-04/one-psalm-two-causes-two-meanings.

Verhey, Allen. *Reading the Bible in the Strange World of Medicine*. Grand Rapids, MI: Eerdmans, 2003.

Waltke, Bruce. "The Old Testament and Birth Control." *Christianity Today* 13.3 (1968) 3–6.

15

Christianity in Contemporary Australian Media

"Get Your Rosaries Off My Ovaries."

Enqi Weng

An Emerging Field

At the 2016 International Communication Association pre-conference workshop on media and religion in Seattle, Washington, Emeritus Professor Ellul Katz, a sociologist and communications specialist, made a memorable statement: while the Jews guarded God's message of peace close to their hearts, it was the Christians who broadcast the good news far and wide.

Scholars of religion and media have recently acknowledged that there is a close relationship between the disciplines that requires closer examination. Scholarship in this intersecting field has often attributed its birth to the development of the printing press. Mass printing and dissemination of the Bible to the common people made the message of God much more accessible. Translation works further contributed to the transmission of the gospel message to all peoples of many languages. This intimate connection between religion (and for the purpose of this chapter, Christianity) and media is arguably God's initiative, through which the apostles and churches have continued to broadcast the gospel up to the present time.

Popular understanding of "religion" is applied here to refer to a system of organized beliefs and practices, and ideas and concepts associated with it. While the term "media" is more frequently used in limited ways of print, broadcast, and more recently digital media, it is used more broadly within media studies as any form of vehicle that transmits a message. Sacred forms are expressed and performed through media that include "written texts, ritual gestures, images and icons, architecture, music, incense, special garments, saintly relics and other objects of veneration, markings upon flesh, wagging tongues and other body parts."[1]

This chapter presents findings from my doctoral research that considers the extent of cultural interpretations of Christianity (comprising Protestantism and Catholicism) that are in circulation in contemporary Australian media. Atheist Catherine Deveny's response to former Australian Federal Health Minister and Catholic Tony Abbott to "get [his] rosaries off [her] ovaries"[2] in some sense encapsulates my findings. References to religion in media discourses—mostly Christian in the context of my research—frequently draw upon moralistic notions arguably bound up with European/British colonialist understandings. Narrowly informed institutional, gendered, and racialized perspectives repeatedly inform these discussions on religion, to the exclusion of other perspectives. The recurrence of certain topics, ideas, and concepts about religion further demonstrates their rootedness in the national imagination, informed by Australia's problematized colonial past.

Informed by these findings, the chapter raises questions for Christian leaders and authorities, to be discerning in their media engagements, depending on the message, platform, and audience. It also raises considerations for Christians in this digital age, where the material and spiritual, and the analog and digital selves, collide.

Media and Religion: Contemporary Debates

Especially since the 9/11 terror attacks in 2001, scholars from the fields of religious and media studies have agreed that there is a strong relationship between them that warrants greater sociological attention. Two key theories currently inform this intersecting field and its research: the theories of mediatization and mediation of religion. Points of contention between these approaches mainly involve the type of media and the extent of media influences on religious and social change.

1. Stolow, *Religion and/as Media*, 125.
2. Australian Broadcasting Corporation, "The Indonesian Non-Solution."

Mediatization of religion theory, led by Stig Hjarvard, suggests that contemporary media, which are enabled by digital technologies and becoming increasingly complex and networked, have superseded the role and function of institutional religion to become the center of social meaning-making.[3] Media systems and their processes have become the master crafter of messages, meanings, and symbols about religion, whether they are benign, meaningful, or destructive. Furthermore, the media are able to nullify the sacred meanings and powers of religions, as religious symbols and meanings become popularized, especially in entertainment media.[4]

Mediation theorists, on the other hand, propose that religions are cultural products and performances and, as such, their messages and practices are necessarily contextually situated and mediated.[5] Geertz's definition of culture is applied here as "an historically transmitted pattern of meanings embodied in symbols, a system of inherited conceptions expressed in symbolic forms by means of which men communicate, perpetuate, and develop their knowledge about and their attitudes toward life."[6] In the footsteps of Marshall McLuhan's "the medium is the message,"[7] the transmitted message will always take on some aspect of the vehicle through which it is carried—with the medium's emphasis and particularity. This means that any religious beliefs and practices, including Christianity, are not only informed by their theological bearings but also embody aspects of the culture where such beliefs and practices are expressed.

Horsfield highlights that the emphasis of Christian messages has changed significantly in times of media convergences—those times when one medium has superseded another in its popularity. In the shift of media culture from oral tradition to written texts, for example, Paul's use of writing letters to disseminate information "placed his particular reinterpretation of Jesus and the work Paul was doing into the wider currents of circulation of what was the elite medium of his time."[8] This practice not only encouraged increased circulation of his message, it also allowed his message to be reworked contextually upon delivery.

Contemporary public perceptions of Christianity reflect sustained mediation of discourses and narratives over a period of time. As such,

---

3. Hjarvard, *Mediatization of Culture*; *Mediatization of Religion*; *Mediatisation of Religion*.
4. Hjarvard, *Mediatisation Of Religion*, 128.
5. Clark, *Why Study Popular Culture?* 11.
6. Geertz, *Interpretation*, 89.
7. McLuhan, *Understanding Media*.
8. Horsfield, *From Jesus*, 36

there are diverse Christian expressions and practices dependent on their cultural contexts. For example, in Singapore the idea of spiritual kinship in God's family parallels Confucius's nuclear-familiar practices. Concurrently, Christianity is still viewed as a "white man's religion," a perception informed by collective memory of British colonialism in the region. Similarly, in the Australian context, Anglicanism typically has a keen focus on a rational-critical approach towards understanding the gospel message, influenced in part by the importing of Christianity into Australia not long after a post-Enlightenment period.[9] Pentecostals in Australia, in contrast, tend to be popularly judged as "happy clappers."

Religion gained special media prominence after the 9/11 attacks, and Australia was no exception. This visibility of religion jolted the Western world's normalized expectation that religions were fading in social, cultural, and political significance.[10] While news reporting about religions is not a new phenomenon, global attention on Islam post-9/11 was unprecedented. Religion was thrust into Australian politics soon after through the rise of a conservative strand of Christianity during the period of the Howard Government from 1996 to 2007.[11] In the same period, Christianity-inspired political groups such as the Australian Christian Lobby and the Family First Party began advocating for conservative pro-family values in policies.[12] This politicization of Christianity was underpinned by Howard's conflation of Australian values with the nation's "Judeo-Christian" heritage. Scholars argue that this Christian interpretation of Australian values is more similar to nineteenth-century English values, informed by the Ten Commandments.[13]

Religion and politics continue to take center stage in contemporary Australian media. Prime Minister Scott Morrison's Pentecostal Christian faith made news headlines in the lead-up to the 2019 Federal Election. His faith has also been questioned more recently in his handling of environmental concerns in light of the 2019 bushfires and his reliance on God's miracles in the face of the COVID-19 pandemic. Religion has been contested and embroiled in public discourse since the arrival of Christianity in Australia in 1788 and will very likely remain a significant, albeit contested, aspect of Australian public life.

9. Lake, *Bible*.
10. Casanova, *Public Religions*; Bruce, *God is Dead*.
11. Maddox, *God Under Howard*.
12. Barlow and Haxton, *Family First Party*.
13. Randell-Moon, '*Common values*'; Stratton, *Whiteness, Morality*.

Social and Religious Changes

With the arrival of British convicts and the establishment of a penal colony, a British interpretation of Christianity was established and continues to inform Australian religiosity. This introduction of institutional Christianity also contributed to fraught relationships between Aboriginal Australians and European/British settlers. As these settlers seized Aboriginal land through frontier missions, Christian missionaries—often with good intentions—were obliterating Aboriginal culture, identity, and spirituality through evangelistic efforts.[14] Establishing strong governance was prioritized over building neighborliness with Aboriginal Australians.[15] The relationship between Aboriginal Australians and the Anglo majority remains contentious to this day, evidenced by symbolic contestations over the celebration of Australia Day (or Invasion Day) and by calls for greater Aboriginal representation in Parliament through the Uluru Statement in 2017.

In those early days of European settlement, Christianity was frequently associated with moralism. The early settlers had divided viewpoints about religion since it was introduced as a tool to manage the moral standards of the large convict population, implemented by importing British clergy to hold government positions.[16] New towns with church buildings and clergy were viewed as morally respectable.[17] Scholars have generally agreed that the convict settlers (and subsequent European settlers) were mostly at best of mediocre religiosity.[18] Sectarian divisions and clashes between Protestants and Catholics that began in Europe were also imported into Australia. Some of these differences were expressed in matters such as education and welfare. Then, Protestant Christianity was pervasively considered as culturally and morally superior to Irish Catholicism. This public image of Christianity as a moralistic "do-gooder" religion has been deeply etched into the Australian memory, and continues to inform public discourse about religion in contemporary Australia.

With the dismantling of the White Australia Policy in the 1970s and the introduction of multiculturalism policies, Australia became more culturally and religiously diverse. Concurrently, affiliation to Christianity has been in consistent decline since the first Census of 1911. Down from 96 percent

---

14. Lake, *Bible*.
15. Thompson, *Religion in Australia*, 5–6; O'Farrell, *Catholic Church*, 34.
16. Bouma, *Australian Soul*, 39; Thompson, *Religion in Australia*, 5.
17. Frame, *Losing My Religion*, 46.
18. Bouma, *Australian Soul*, 39.

in 1911, only 52 percent of Australians claimed to be Christians in 2016.[19] Viewed through the Census question on religiosity, majority denominations such as Anglicanism and Catholicism have declined in numbers, while minority denominations such as Pentecostalism have experienced growth.[20] A significant proportion of Aboriginal Australians still identify as Christian, although this figure has declined from 69 percent in 2001 to 54 percent in 2016.[21] Buddhism and Islam were introduced as new religions in the 1991 Census.[22] The "no religion" group has also increased since the first Census. Making up only 0.4 percent in 1911, this group increased to 22.3 percent of the population in 2011 and to 30.1 percent just five years later.[23]

Christian responses to these social, cultural, and religious changes have been divergent. Most seem to welcome new immigration and cultural diversity and see these changes as ripe opportunities to share the gospel message. Some have lamented the decline of Christianity, viewing it as the erosion of Christendom and Judeo-Christian or Western values.[24] Others have problematically conflated Western culture and Christianity when invoking their so-called Christian identities in nationalistic, anti-migration, anti-Muslim hate speeches (e.g., Fraser Anning, Rise Up Australia).

Media representations of Christianity in this contemporary mediatized context have presented a form of challenge to public perceptions of religion. Hardy suggests that this disconnect between media representations of religions and lived religious experience is because of a lack of common language between journalists and religious communities.[25] Media discourses about religions also have a tendency to employ simplistic, repetitive tropes that hinder deeper understandings about religions.[26] Biased media representations have real social consequences: although a direct connection between media representation of a religious group and the perception it creates is a challenge to demonstrate, it can be shown that in 2014, 15 percent of respondents had "very negative" attitudes towards Muslims, a figure five times more than the percentage of negative attitudes towards Christians and Buddhists.[27] Similarly, surveys done after the recent Christchurch attacks on mosques found

19. Australian Bureau of Statistics, *Religion in Australia 2016*.
20. Riches, *Evolving Theological Emphasis*.
21. Australian Bureau of Statistics, *Religion in Australia 2016*.
22. Frame, *Losing My Religion*, 91.
23. Australian Bureau of Statistics, *Religion in Australia 2016*.
24. Chilton, *Evangelicals*.
25. Hardy, *Reporting on Evangelical*, 71.
26. Weng, *Through a National Lens*.
27. Markus and Dharmalingam, *Mapping Social Cohesion*.

that New Zealanders viewed evangelical Christians most negatively compared to other religions and Christian denominations.[28]

It is critical, however, to consider that the media are not a full reflection of social sentiments. A review of research that examined Australian attitudes towards religions still reported mixed findings. Recent research on Australian Generation Z and their attitudes towards religions found that 91 per cent of respondents said that "having people of many different faiths makes Australia a better place to live."[29] The Australian Community Survey shows that only 20 percent of respondents were strongly against the statement that "religion is good for Australian society."[30] On the other hand, when asked about the benefit of religion in society, 63 percent of Australians surveyed believe that "religion does more harm than good."[31] Hence, while it is pervasive in Australian Christian circles to view public discourse about religions as mostly anti-religious—and might I add, Christians are "most vocal" about this media phenomenon in the UK too[32]—I would like to suggest that Christianity retains a privileged, albeit increasingly contested, position within media and political discourse in Australia. Findings from my doctoral research will expand on this further.

Media Reflections and Distortions

The premise of my doctoral research was that "religion" is a highly problematic term in media discourses and is subject to multiple interpretations. This interpretation is also in a constant state of change. Religion is often used interchangeably to mean moralism, Christianity, cult, and superstitions, to name just a few definitions.

With an interest in examining when and how religion emerges as a topic of contemporary discussion, I selected the state-funded Australian Broadcasting Corporation's *Q&A* current affairs discussion program as a media subject. A total of 93 one-hour episodes, made up of two years of episodes (2009 and 2012) and special episodes selected on the basis of dates of religious and secular significance (from 2010 and 2013) comprised my data set. The special dates identified were Easter, Ramadan, the Federal Election, and ANZAC Day. A quantitative and qualitative approach employing content and discourse analyses was undertaken. A total of 3,282 references

28. Chapple, *New Survey*.
29. Singleton et al., *AGZ Study*.
30. Pepper and Powell, *Australian Community Survey*.
31. Ipsos, *Global Study*.
32. Day, *Conflict*.

to religion were coded. The themes of religion and atheism, religion and politics, and religious diversity became evident through tallying up these references into social patterns.

To examine "religion" data through its multiple interpretations, the term was methodologically expanded into three main principles: conventional religion, common religion, and the secular sacred.[33] This approach focused on a neo-Durkheimian consideration of the concept of the sacred, which identified the sacred as a set-apart, non-negotiable value present in religious and secular forms.[34]

Institutional religions such as Christianity, Buddhism, Hinduism, and Islam make up the first category; folk and superstitious beliefs and practices are considered as common religion. The secular sacred is made up of two main subcategories: the first is systems of beliefs that are non-religious in nature such as humanism, philosophy, and atheism. The second consists of references made to transcendence or other-worldliness that may adopt the use of religious vernacular but can also frequently refer to its non-negotiability.[35]

Findings show that the media continue to play a significant role in instigating and framing discussions about religion. However, limited concepts and issues related to religion were given most attention within these discussions and primarily involved selected religious perspectives. Although it is not necessarily the role and interest of the media to be fully representative of every societal demographic, it needs to be considered that the sustenance of narrow perspectives about religions can have real consequences. Horrific acts of terror like the Christchurch and Sri Lanka attacks certainly suggest negative possibilities in a context where the media are complexly interconnected with social worlds and practices.

Christianity continues to be a key influencer and shaper of Australian society and culture, evident from discussions about religion on Q&A. The religion remains a key cultural definer and an aspect of a normative cultural framework that other religions are benchmarked against. When other religions are challenged in these public discussions, Christianity is inevitably implicated. Easter was viewed as a day of religious significance and was primarily used as a key date to design discussions about religion. When comparing across the special dates chosen (from 2010 to 2013), Easter episodes had a significantly higher number of references (average of 114.3 references) when compared to the other special dates (Federal

---

33. Knott et al., *Media Portrayals*.
34. Knott, *Secular Sacred*; Lynch, *Sacred*; Anttonen, *Sacred*.
35. See Weng, *Media Perceptions*, 69–71; 117; 127 for some examples.

Elections was 21.3 references). Episodes designed for discussions about religion occurred around Easter of 2010, 2012, and 2013. The 2011 episode occurred a day after Easter Sunday that year, on ANZAC Day (25 April), and was constructed as an ANZAC Day episode.

Institutionalized, racialized, and gendered Catholic perspectives on Christian faith were observed to be over-represented in these episodes. There was frequently a lack of distinction made between Catholic and Protestant perspectives in this regard. Moreover, Catholic and atheist perspectives were influential in shaping discussions about religion, frequently positioned in adversarial ways throughout the period examined. In the afore-mentioned Easter episodes, Catholic representatives were former politician Tony Abbott, who has a public faith, Catholic Archbishop of Sydney Cardinal George Pell, and Catholic Archbishop of Brisbane Mark Coleridge. Atheist perspectives presented within these episodes included Richard Dawkins (2012) and comedian Josh Thomas (2013). In 2009, an episode was also constructed around religion through the attendance of the late Christopher Hitchens.[36] Father Frank Brennan was on the panel in that episode, representing Catholicism. Although there were some female and ethnic minority and religious minority perspectives presented in some of these episodes (2009 and 2013), these perspectives were constructed as "other" to the normative male Anglo Christian framework. Most of the questions were directed to the Anglo male panelists, whether Catholic or atheist. Although there were some Protestant Christian panelists during the period studied, they were dispersed across episodes that did not have a key religious focus. Some of these episodes included the participation of Peter Jensen, Anglican Archbishop of Sydney, Craig Gross, controversial American pastor, and John Dickson, former Director of the Centre for Public Christianity.

This narrow representation of Christianity primarily through Catholicism fails to account for the richness and diversity of religious expressions within the broad church, which are often informed by diversity in cultural backgrounds. This lack of attention to religious diversity also fails to account for other gendered and culturally-informed religious expressions that can contribute to the breadth and depth of the Christian faith.

An Anglo-Celtic interpretation of Christianity continues to strongly inform public discussions and perceptions about religion, while also maintaining heritage connections between Australia and Britain. It is significant that Dawkins and Hitchens, both of Anglo heritage, were able to garner substantial media attention in their appearances and participation on *Q&A* in these discussions. Their invitation to participate in an Australian discussion

---

36. Australian Broadcasting Corporation, "God, Sodomy."

demonstrates the continued permission given to British representatives in shaping Australian religiosity. Interestingly, Australian responses to these atheistic perspectives were mixed. Just as Bouma has discovered that Australians have a distaste for exuberant expressions of religiosity, the same aversion applied to antagonistic expressions of anti-religiosity. While there was evidence of support for Dawkins and Hitchens in the program, they were also questioned about their version of atheism.

References to cultural interpretations of Christianity were frequently applied in these public discussions, and they bore similarities to a historically-informed understanding of Christianity. Religion was frequently viewed through moralistic lenses, arguably characteristic of the English culture that entered Australia with Christianity in the colonial period.[37] Religion was often criticized for assuming moral superiority; similarly, panelists that represented institutional religious offices were often introduced as persons of moral authority in the program. The prevalent reliance on this moralistic discourse was evident from tweets that appeared in *Religion and Atheism* (2012), the episode with biologist Richard Dawkins and Cardinal George Pell. These tweets, which appeared on-screen during discussion, included "Religion should not make the person #qanda" by Tr1shM and "Children aren't born in sin, how can a baby be born and be a sinner? #qanda" by Caramelcat123. Such comments frequently emerge in media discourses that demonstrate an ongoing perception of and resistance to a moralistic understanding of religion. Moralism, a characteristic of the colonial invasion with its need to exert moral supremacy, has been persistently associated with Christianity in public discussion in Australia.

Engagements with Christian concepts, doctrines, and discourses were frequently limited and repetitive. This is perhaps indicative of the public's lack of religious literacy or the limited scope in which religion was a topic of public interest. Two main findings support this explanation; the first is that a significant portion of references to religion were mostly Christian in nature, and they were more generally religious than religion-specific. These references tended to be conceptual or refer to practices. They were often generalized in a way that could refer to any religion or Christian denomination without specificity such as "prayer," "hell," "religious," "church," and "holy." Such references emerged more significantly in numbers than religion-specific terms such as "Sunday mass" for Catholicism, and "Anglicanism" for Protestant Christianity. References to Christianity were mostly neutral, although more frequently negatively applied than positive. This is

---

37. Lake, *Bible*; Stratton, *Whiteness, Morality*, 29.

notable when compared with references to the secular sacred, which were most frequently positively applied.

The second finding that revealed the circulation of limited Christian ideas is that discussions about religion were also frequently confined to specific topics: creationism versus evolution, heaven, hell, and the existence of the soul after death. This repetition of Christian concepts could be seen from a comparison between two Easter *Q&A* episodes in 2012 and 2013. Then host of *Q&A*, Tony Jones, is involved in the question selection process. Questions related to the compatibility of science and religion and the belief in creationism were repeatedly selected, and sometimes redirected to panelists during discussion. For example, Jones asked Pell in 2012 if he "accepted[ed] that humans evolved from apes." The original question was a general one that asked for "the Roman Catholic Church's position on evolution and comment on whether the dichotomy between science and religion is, in fact, real." The following year in a religiously diverse panel, Jones reframed a question on the presence of a creator subsequent to Archbishop of Brisbane Mark Coleridge's response: "Okay. But were humans created—in your version of this were humans created by evolution? Did they spring from apes?" From these reframing and redirecting of questions, I suggest that there was an instinctive media perception about which topics are of interest to a general audience and that this perception guided Jones to lead the discussion in a particular trajectory. There were no further Easter episodes (2014 to 2019) dedicated to discussions about religion, perhaps confirming the limitations in religious knowledge and interest from a general audience, as viewed from a media editorial perspective.

Evidence of religious remixes was also prevalent in the data where the general public do express some form of religious literacy. Often, religious meanings, texts, symbols, and concepts were dissected, reconstructed and/or amalgamated with popular cultural references to derive new meanings. Religious remixing was popularly used in tweets within the program. In the episode with Pell and Dawkins,[38] Twitter user SilkCharm participated by drawing upon a familiar verse from John 1:1 to give it a playful recontextualization: "In the beginning was The Word. Then there were a whole lot more Words. Then there was #QandA. End of subject. :)." The late disability activist Stella J. Young also chimed in with this: "It's not possible for a wheelchair user to go heaven. Apparently there's only a stairway. #qanda." There was no way of telling if she was referring to Jacob's dream in the book of Genesis or Led Zeppelin's song "Stairway to Heaven." Religious references, mostly Christian ones, were frequently used. Such cultural expressions of

---

38. Australian Broadcasting Corporation, "Religion and Atheism."

Christianity are less politicized and visible, far more subtle, and provide insights into public religious literacy, interest, and the creative reworking of religious symbols, concepts, and meanings.

Although there were Christian leaders and authority figures who participated as audience members and panelists on the program, their ability to engage theologically with discussions about religion was limited by the program's media logic, the scope of the question, and Jones's facilitation of the discussion. Religious authority figures frequently faced the challenge of confronting and challenging cultural interpretations of religion in these media spaces. Similar to a broader breakdown in the trust of institutions and authorities, these religious figures frequently encountered opposition to their theological interpretations of social and cultural phenomena. Participants on the program tended to view these religious participants primarily from the perspective of their religious identity, even if they held secular positions. Father Frank Brennan and social commentator Waleed Aly (who is Muslim) were both asked specifically for their religious response on the issue of homosexuality and were called out by Hitchens when they presented responses that complexly integrated their religious and secular perspectives and obligations.

Furthermore, panelists of religious dispositions often attempted to legitimize their religious argument by first outlining their scientific understandings. Pell, Coleridge, and Brennan were observed to have done this. On why God allows natural disasters to occur, Brennan attempted to explain: "Natural disasters happen and an omnipotent God lets them happen, for those of us who believe in God. It's not about God saying that we won't let nature take its course. Those of us who do have a religious faith, we equally, I think, are committed to science but, like Christopher says, we all look for patterns."[39] These religious figures' provision of some scientific justifications can be construed as attempts to obtain credibility for their religious perspectives as they negotiated presenting their religious and secular perspectives on issues within what would appear to them to be religiously-hostile environments.

Media Expressions of Christianity and Considerations

Cultural interpretations of Christianity circulate strongly on *Q&A*, where participants draw upon rudimentary understandings of Christianity, frequently conflated with a discourse of moralism largely informed by Australia's

---

39. Australian Broadcasting Corporation, "God, Sodomy."

colonial history. Christianity is most often reduced to simplistic, repetitive, and abstract concepts such as heaven and hell, or it becomes politicized and applied in controversial topics such as the same-sex marriage debate. The quality, density, and variety of lived religious experiences are missing from, and appear somewhat irrelevant within, these discussions.[40]

During historical periods of media convergence and change, religious communities and the way they engaged with the dominant media forms have contributed to changes in attitudes and practices. When the Bible was mass produced and made available to the common people, there was anxiety over the loss of religious authority in the interpretation of Scripture, especially since this mass production coincided with increasing literacy. Challenges to religious authorities persist in this digital era where, within the same media spaces, boundaries between the private and public, the profane and sacred, gospel messages, religious hate speech, and fake news are blurred and blended. This challenge is similarly present for lay Christians; influencer culture has challenged Christians to embed and share the gospel in a variety of creative ways.[41]

The ubiquity of digital media has brought new considerations into this relationship between religion and media. Mobile digital technologies are increasingly seen as an extension of the human self and identity.[42] In other words, human life and existence are no longer bound materially but simultaneously co-exist in immaterial digitality. This shift in thinking raises questions on how our "analogue" bodies, bound by materiality, can co-exist in the unlimited time and space that digitality affords.[43] As digital media continue to be pervasive in everyday life, what sort of impact and influence does the gospel have in these domains? How can Christian beliefs and practices be translated into these digital spaces? How do these considerations of materiality and spirituality inform the way we engage with various social circles on digital media? Digital spaces present themselves as particularly challenging for deeper engagements, since they frequently afford little time and reflective space to deal with complex topics such as religion.

Perhaps framing our media engagements (or deliberate avoidance of them) in relation to our spiritual gifts is appropriate here. Media engagements with a religious or secular audience are exercises of discipline and discernment. Where one gifted in apologetics may feel compelled to engage with a wider audience through social media platforms to defend Christianity, not

40. Ammerman, *Sacred Stories*.
41. Ward, *Celebrity Worship*.
42. McLuhan, *Understanding Media*.
43. Hassan, *There Isn't an App*.

all of us are required to make a stand on social issues within these spaces. Engagements within these spaces do not necessarily add to, and certainly do not define, our Christian identity. Rules of engagement also differ based on the logic of the media platforms, their audiences, and contemporary cultural climate. These are just some factors to consider when engaging in media spaces of diverse religious and secular perspectives.

Historical Christianity, both confessionally and culturally in its import into Australia, continues to inform how we perceive, believe, and express the faith. Public discussions about religion frequently draw upon cultural Christian tropes and themes, and they strongly inform public understandings of religions, especially in an increasingly religiously illiterate public in secular Australia. There is evidence of these cultural expressions in Australian church life and meaning-making too, where Western-cultural practices are often viewed interchangeably with being Christian.

We should take this into account as we consider gospel sharing with people from different cultural backgrounds. Just as Paul was astute in tailoring his gospel message based on his audience and their cultural backgrounds—his approach to the Jews (who had prior knowledge of the Old Testament) differed significantly from his approach towards the Gentiles (who had other gods)—we might consider expanding our cultural understandings and repertoires. Culture continues to play a significant, albeit less visible role in how we view and apply our beliefs in our everyday; culture also often lurks in our blind spots. It is critical for us to look backwards—and to reflect upon our collective past and present so as to move forward.

Bibliography

ABC News. "George Pell Spends Night in Melbourne Assessment Prison after His Bail Is Revoked." *ABC News*, 2019.

Ammerman, Nancy Tatom. *Sacred Stories, Spiritual Tribes: Finding Religion in Everyday Life*. New York: Oxford University Press, 2013.

Anttonen, Veikko. "Sacred." In *Guide to the Study of Religion*, edited by B. Willi and R. T. McCutcheon, 271–82. London: Continuum, 2007.

Australian Broadcasting Corporation. "God, Sodomy and the Lash." *Q&A* television program, 60 mins, produced by Peter McEvoy. Sydney, 2009.

———. "The Indonesian Non-Solution." *Q&A* television program, 60 mins, produced by Peter McEvoy. Sydney, 2009.

———. "Religion and Atheism." *Q&A* television program, 60 mins, produced by Peter McEvoy. Sydney, 2012.

Australian Bureau of Statistics. *Religion in Australia, 2016*. 2017. http://www.abs.gov.au/ausstats/abs@.nsf/Lookup/by%20Subject/2071.0~2016~Main%20Features~Religion%20Article~80.

Barlow, Karen, and Nancy Haxton. "Family First Party Campaigns on Family Values." *ABC* news release, September 20, 2004.
Bouma, Gary. *Australian Soul: Religion and Spirituality in the 21st Century.* Melbourne: Cambridge University Press, 2006.
Bruce, Steve. *God is Dead: Secularization in the West.* Victoria: Blackwell, 2002.
Casanova, Jose. *Public Religions in the Modern World,* Chicago: University of Chicago Press, 1994.
Chapple, Simon. "New Survey Reveals Which Religions New Zealanders Trust Most—and Least—after Christchurch Shootings." *The Conversation,* August 7, 2019.
Chilton, Hugh. *Evangelicals and the End of Christendom: Religion, Australia and the Crises of the 1960s.* London: Routledge, 2019.
Clark, Lynn Schofield. "Why Study Popular Culture? Or, How to Build a Case for Your Thesis in a Religious Studies or Theology Department." In *Between Sacred and Profane: Researching Religion and Popular Culture,* edited by Gordon Lynch, 5–20. New York: I. B. Tauris, 2007.
Day, Abby. "The Conflict between Religion and Media Has Deep Roots." LSE blog *Religion and Global Society,* August 22, 2016. (accessed 8 September).
Frame, Tom. *Losing My Religion: Unbelief in Australia.* Sydney: University of New South Wales Press, 2009.
Geertz, Clifford. *The Interpretation of Cultures.* New York: Basic, 1973.
Hardy, Ann. "Reporting on Evangelical Christian Protest in the New Zealand Media: The Case for Training in Religious Journalism." *Australian Journalism Review* 29 (2007) 63.
Hassan, Robert. "There Isn't an App for That: Analogue and Digital Politics in the Age of Platform Capitalism." *Media Theory* 2 (2018) 1–15.
Hjarvard Stig. "The Mediatisation of Religion: Theorising Religion, Media and Social Change." *Culture and Religion: An Interdisciplinary Journal* 12 (2011) 119–35.
———. *The Mediatization of Culture and Society,* New York: Routledge, 2013.
———. "The Mediatization of Religion: A Theory of the Media as Agents of Religious Change." *Northern Lights* 6 (2008) 9–26.
Horsfield, Peter. *From Jesus to the Internet: A History of Christianity and Media.* West Sussex: Wiley-Blackwell, 2015.
Ipsos. "Global Study Shows that Six in Ten Britons—above the Global Average—Believe Religion Does More Harm Than Good." Ipsos blog, October 12, 2017.
Knott Kim. "The Secular Sacred: In Between or Both/And?" *Social Identities Between the Sacred and the Secular,* edited by Abby Day, Giselle Vincett and Christopher R. Cotter, 145–60. Oxon: Routledge, 2016.
Knott, Kim, Elizabeth Poole, and Taira Teemu. *Media Portrayals of Religion and the Secular Sacred.* Surrey: Ashgate, 2013.
Lake, Meredith. *The Bible in Australia: A Cultural History.* Sydney: NewSouth, 2018.
Lynch, Gordon. *The Sacred in the Modern World: A Cultural Sociological Approach.* New York: Oxford University Press, 2012.
Maddox, Marion. *God Under Howard: The Rise of The Religious Right in Australian Politics.* Crows Nest: Allen & Unwin, 2005.
Markus, Andrew, and Dharmalingam Arunachalam. "Mapping Social Cohesion." *The Scanlon Foundation Surveys* (2014) 1–54.
McLuhan, Marshall. *Understanding Media: The Extensions of Man.* Cambridge, MA: MIT, 1994.

O'Farrell, Patrick. *The Catholic Church and Community in Australia*. Melbourne: Thomas Nelson, 1977.

Pepper, Miriam, and Ruth Powell. *Australian Community Survey*. Sydney: NCLS Research, 2016.

Randell-Moon, Holly. "'Common Values': Whiteness, Christianity, Asylum Seekers and the Howard Government." *Australian Critical Race and Whiteness Studies e-Journal* 2 (2006) 1–14.

Riches, Tanya. "The Evolving Theological Emphasis of Hillsong Worship (1996–2007)." *Australasian Pentecostal Studies* (2010) 87–133.

Singleton, Andrew, et al. "The AGZ Study: Project Report." ANU, 2019. https://sociology.cass.anu.edu.au/sites/default/files/docs/2019/10/AGZ_Report_FINAL_single_pages.pdf?mc_cid=14c978a7ff&mc_eid=6e02fe181f

Stolow, Jeremy. "Religion and/as Media." *Theory, Culture & Society* 22 (2005) 119–45.

Stratton, Jon. "Whiteness, Morality and Christianity in Australia." *Journal of Intercultural Studies* 37 (2016) 17–32.

Thompson, Roger C. *Religion in Australia: A History*. Australia: Oxford University Press, 2002.

Ward, Pete. *Celebrity Worship*. London: Routledge, 2019.

Weng, Enqi. *Media Perceptions of Religious Changes in Australia: Of Dominance and Diversity*. London: Routledge, 2020.

———. "Through a National Lens Darkly: Religion as a Spectrum." *Journal for the Academic Study of Religion* 32 (2019) 3–26.

16

Grounded yet Wandering

*Church Architecture,
Space, and Place*

Elizabeth C. Culhane

"You'll never believe it!" my friend whispers. "I think I've met God. I entered a church, and the sheer beauty of it all—soaring arches, light bent through windowpanes and galloping across the floors—well, it just moved something in me. Suddenly, I was overcome by a sense that God was here."

When this friend made a profession of faith and entered the church, I judged it a happy accident. With friend number two, a coincidence. With friends three and four, it was a pattern. It demanded theological investigation.

Yet scant help was found in recent Western Protestant discourse on ecclesial architecture, which seemed reticent to ascribe to it any considerable spiritual significance. At best, some lauded church buildings for their functional value in attracting newcomers and extending hospitality.[1] At the other end of the spectrum, some warned that church buildings, while necessary, are often distractions in time and money from the real work of disciple-making.[2]

---

1. E.g., Williams, "Shaping Sacred Space," 5–6, 65; Jones, "Christian Church Architecture," esp. 14.

2. E.g., "When the church is fundamentally a gathering of committed people, the

Following passages such as 1 Peter 2, the church can be understood as God's homeless people, a community that lacks material and visible contours as it wanders toward its true eschatological home. This is akin to what the French theorist Michel de Certeau terms "space" (*espace*)—that which is produced when its various elements converge.³ Space is produced by actions, and never in the same way due to fluxes in people, contexts, and time. In Graham Ward's rendering, "practicing belief" generates the space of the church.⁴ This vision of the church is likely familiar to many contemporary anglophone Protestants.

In this chapter, I will suggest that the church can be also considered as a part of a long trajectory of God realizing God's objectives by gathering together a people and grounding them in a place; that is, a bounded site in the order of creation. This will occupy the first section. Next, I will trace how church architecture can convey meaning and orientate people toward their maker. I will then illustrate this regarding St. Paul's Cathedral, Melbourne, Australia.

The Form of God's Objectives

Gathered and Grounded

According to William Dyrness, "God's Trinitarian purposes *necessarily* involve a social shape and a historical engagement."⁵ This is part of his argument that the church is a "social space"; it has distinct practices with a distinct historical tradition.⁶ Dyrness's claim is valuable, yet it incompletely articulates that the social-historical realization of God's purposes transcends ecclesial practices and their history. Accordingly, I will elaborate his claim by turning to the Scriptures and tracing in broad stripes how God's objectives take a communal form across salvation history. Here God's "objectives" refer to the Trinity's plan to be present in and work through creation, and for creation to acknowledge and respond to this presence of God.⁷ I have grouped my analysis into two categories: first, a gathered

---

place where the church gathers hardly matters"; Platt, *Radical Together*, 61.

3. Certeau, *Practice of Everyday Life*, 117.

4. The church is "the space for communal living"; Ward, "Certeau's 'Spiritual Spaces,'" 514.

5. Dyrness, *Poetic Theology*, 243. Emphasis original.

6. Dyrness, *Poetic Theology*, 226.

7. See Dyrness, *Poetic Theology*, 21–24.

community grounded in a place, and second, a community enveloped in Christ and wandering in the world.

First, a gathered community grounded in a place. In the Genesis creation narratives, God realizes God's objectives (to be present in creation and for creation to recognize this) by creating distinctive places and a people. Gathering is central to both. We read that God "gathers" (יִקָּווּ—*yiqāwû*) the waters in one place and thereby marks out the land (Gen 1:9).[8] God further distinguishes the land from the waters by distinct "vegetation" (Gen 1:11–13). Next, God brings together the first human community and grounds them in a place, a garden in Eden (Gen 1:26–30; 2:7–25). The river running through the garden generates four additional "places." One place is distinguished by its gold, bdellium, and onyx (Gen 2:10–14).

Despite the sin of the first human beings, God continues to realize God's objectives—to be present in creation and for creation to respond to this—in people and places. In Noah's ark, God gathers together the beginnings of a new human community and grounds them in a place, albeit a moving one. With Abram, God starts to gather together God's special people at Ur and Haran. Eventually, God gathers God's people around a tabernacle and a temple. As Hebrew Bible scholar John Walton and others highlight, the symbolism of these structures conveys an interwoven heavenly and earthly reality, rendering them a microcosm of the cosmos structured by God's precepts.[9] The symbolism acts as a signpost in two directions. It recapitulates the gathered people and place in Eden, and it previews a restored cosmos. For example, the lampstand or menorah points to the tree of life in Eden along with its counterpart in the renewed creation, as is indicated in later Scriptures.[10] From Noah's ark to the temple, the corporate and temporal (in time) outline of God's objectives for creation is reflected in material forms.

Enveloped in Christ and Wandering

In the incarnation, the communal and temporal form of God's objective to be present in creation becomes centralized in Christ's historical and ecclesial bodies: Christ's body that lived in time and Christ's body as the church. As Philip Sheldrake says, in the incarnation, God in Christ "commits" to the material, and in the resurrection, God celebrates it.[11] The Fourth Gospel

---

8. Root: קוה (*qwh*) "to assemble." All Scripture quotations are from the NRSV.

9. See, for example, Walton, *Genesis 1 as Ancient Cosmology*, 178–92; Levenson, "The Temple and the World," 275–98.

10. Taylor, *Theater of God's Glory*, 76.

11. Sheldrake, *Spaces for the Sacred*, 29.

shows the Son realizing the Father's objectives by becoming flesh and living among us, and making known the Father who has never been seen (John 1:14, 18). As Craig Bartholomew and others note, the four evangelists are careful to record the geographical places where the Son realizes the Father's objectives (to "be" in creation and for creation to recognize this), from Cana in Galilee to Jacob's well in Samaria.[12]

The people that Christ draws to himself in his historical body are enveloped in what can be termed his ecclesial body. As Colossians declares, Christ is "the head of the body, the church." Those "who were once estranged . . . he has now reconciled in his fleshly body through death" (Col 1:18, 21–22). My point is that the Christ in whom God realizes God's objectives in temporal existence is also the one in whom God realizes God's objectives in a people: the church. In this way, we can understand how Christ realizes God's objectives both corporately and historically. In Christ's ecclesial body, the gathered community is enveloped, conformed to his likeness, and wanders through the world as his hands and feet.

While these references to Christ's ecclesial body from Colossians do not pertain to church architecture, we can nevertheless appreciate the intimate connection here between the historical, material body of Christ and his ecclesial body in present temporal existence. There is an inseparable link between the fleshly God-man, the pinnacle visible "form" of God's objectives in time, and his ecclesial body in the present. Further, it is this ecclesial body that God uses in a unique way to realize God's objectives in the present reality.

From the preceding scriptural trajectory of God's corporate and temporal objectives, my argument is this: the church's visible form in the church building should point to the fact that the church is now the primary communal and temporal realization of God's intention to be present in creation and for creation to acknowledge this.[13] In other words, the church building should witness to the truth that the church is the main way that God realizes God's objectives in a community in temporal reality—and to the long history of this. To develop this claim, I will now outline how church architecture can express meaning and why this is a matter that deserves attention. My discussion will center on critical engagement with Premkumar Williams's comprehensive, academically rigorous, and self-consciously evangelical theology of church architecture (2005). It is important to note that what follows should not be taken to suggest that church

---

12. Bartholomew, *Where Mortals Dwell*, 93–94. See also, Brueggemann, *The Land*, 198.

13. Cf. Dyrness, *Poetic Theology*, 243.

buildings could communicate some new revelation contrary to Scripture or impart a saving power that is distinct from that found in Jesus Christ, the only mediator between God and humanity.[14]

Church Architecture and Theological Meaning

There are several different theoretical approaches to understanding how ecclesial architecture can convey meaning. Some focus more on the building while others center more on the human being's aesthetic experience of the building, including how their faith commitments, interpretive activity, and access to cultural meanings give rise to the building's "meaning." Still other approaches to meaning in church architecture consider both elements.

One school of approach is hermeneutical perspectives, which tend to center the human subject. In hermeneutical perspectives, meaning typically arises when a subject interprets their encounter with a visual form that transmits cultural meanings. For example, Lindsay Jones suggests that church buildings have no inherent meaning. Meaning is instead constructed in the "ritual-architectural event."[15] This is an encounter with a ceremonial building—a structure designed for the ceremony—during an occasion of this ceremony or ritual. It is an event in which both the person and the building participate.

Premkumar Williams extends Jones's account by highlighting the contribution of the architect.[16] The architect "semantically" conveys the liturgy in purpose-built structures.[17] This "gives form to function" so that the building becomes a metaphor, following Michael Polanyi's definition.[18] Polanyi outlined two aspects of a metaphor. First, the "focus," namely, the nature of the metaphor or what it is itself. Second, the "subsidiary," that is, the impact of the metaphor on the people who encounter it.[19] Concerning the church building, Williams argues that the metaphor's subsidiary (the liturgy) and its focus (architecture) together "present a tremendous spectacle to our imagination."[20]

---

14. See also, Begbie, "Future of Theology Amid the Arts," 149.

15. Jones, *Hermeneutics of Sacred Architecture*, 1:29; 2:19, 32, 125; in Williams, "Shaping Sacred Space," 80, 196.

16. Williams, "Shaping Sacred Space," 81.

17. Williams, "Shaping Sacred Space," 196.

18. Williams, "Shaping Sacred Space," 81.

19. Williams, "Shaping Sacred Space," 85–86; citing Polanyi and Prosch, *Meaning*, 78–99.

20. Williams, "Shaping Sacred Space," 85. Here Williams is quoting Polanyi and

Architectural meaning arises in this interface between visible structure and communicative power. During the church service, the community interpretively interacts with the building and receives its intended meaning. Further, Williams argues, borrowing terms from Jones, that the aesthetics of church architecture "allure" in order to influence or "transform."[21] The church building helps congregants notice its function. It underscores why they are at church and invites them to enter into this. In tandem with the liturgy, the building encourages the congregation to match their behavior to who they are: God's children. The meaning of the building thus encompasses "theological action"; it conveys the worship of God's people and facilitates it.[22] Finally, Williams draws on Kevin Vanhoozer to argue that through the liturgical actions and speech of God's people, the building is implicated in God's dramatic action among God's people.[23]

Given his goal to outline an evangelical theology of church architecture, Williams expresses understandable caution about any additional communicative ability of symbols beyond those outlined. For Williams, symbols are at heart forms that convey a function—liturgical worship—when interpreted by the gathered community. Yet he also proposes that "vernacular architecture" can communicate evangelical commitments to Scripture and mission due to its mutual commitment to "the values of creation (nature), community and culture."[24] There seems to be a paradox here. Vernacular forms are sufficiently neutral to impart theological meaning, whereas explicitly theological forms can only transmit theological meaning when they give form to a function (liturgical worship) and are interpreted by active participants in this function (worshipping community). In sum, the paradox is this: theological truths can be conveyed by everyday buildings without too much difficulty but only by church buildings in a very specific context.

This paradox illuminates three opportunities for further developing Williams's account, all of which are connected: first, additional detail about the ability of vernacular forms to express a contrary reality; second, an expanded understanding of the multitude of symbols that could be employed in church architecture; and third, an enlarged vision of the meaning and audience of

---

Prosch, *Meaning*, 78.

21. Williams, "Shaping Sacred Space," iv, 30.
22. Williams, "Shaping Sacred Space," 197.
23. Williams, "Shaping Sacred Space," 99, 197; citing Vanhoozer, "The Voice and the Actor," 64, 81, 85.
24. Williams, "Shaping Sacred Space," 29.

church architecture. I will briefly address each in turn to illuminate more fully how church buildings can communicate meaning.

First, any apparent communicative potential of vernacular forms (due to "shared" scriptural values) is dramatically relativized by their ability to express a non-Christian or anti-Christian reality. Perhaps this negative ability is underemphasized by Williams because many secular symbolic forms seem neutral in that they do not seem to convey an explicitly non-Christian agenda. It is also overlooked by Williams since he applies the relationship between form and function to the church building but not to vernacular architecture. This is evident in Williams's apparent belief that the form of vernacular architecture could be adopted in distinction from its accompanying function altogether. An inconsistent separation between form and function is also evident in the notion that ecclesial use trumps any contrary communicative power of vernacular architecture. Resources to challenge such beliefs are already found in hermeneutical approaches to meaning in architecture, where subjects receive culturally-mediated meaning/s through interacting with a form and its attendant function. Stated differently, a black, metal, pointed object does not cease entirely to signify "gun" when painted with flowers and placed in a museum.

Reservations about the ability of vernacular forms to convey non-Christian truths are confronted by some recent developments in church architecture. By erecting churches that resemble shopping centers, evangelicals may have reinforced what these symbols have been designed to cultivate: materialism and hedonism.[25] The evangelical church complex provides a complete range of tailored services within a single mammoth, rectangular compound. In Stanley Hauerwas's words, the individual can thus "satisfy their need for intimacy yet identify with a large successful enterprise," all while remaining free from being subsumed into a single group and its program.[26] There are no significant markers of entry; people simply drift in and out as they please. Within the church complex's whitewashed and uniform regions, it is easy to lose track of time. The structure also seems politically and religiously neutral in its lack of any distinctive political or religious imagery and slogans.

Second, there are more symbols available for use in church architecture than simply those that give form to its liturgical function. We have seen this in the negative communicative potential of vernacular architecture, but there are additional potential symbols; indeed, the number may be almost

---

25. Smith, *Desiring the Kingdom*, 90–131. See also, Kilde, *When Church Became Theatre*, 101–222.

26. Hauerwas, "What Could It Mean for the Church," 2 n. 2.

limitless. One means of accounting for the multitude of potential symbols, particularly symbols of theological truths, is to point to an emotional or affective impact on human beings when they encounter representations of created realities (symbols). This is an effect of the love that underpins both the "gift and giver of creation," as Dyrness calls it, following Augustine.[27] This response occurs whether the human being recognizes its divine origin or not. The affective impact on the person can help shape their will. As Augustine suggests, the will of the human person is informed by what they love. In the rendering of a contemporary book title, we are what we love.[28] John Calvin developed Augustine's account by identifying that the responses of human beings to God's glory in creation are aesthetic responses. People are captured by the "divine art" of creation—that is, the "visible splendor" and "insignia whereby [God] shows his glory to us, whenever and wherever we cast our gaze."[29] Our wonder at the divine "workmanship" engenders "admiration of the Artificer."[30]

Significant here is the idea that the impact of creation on human beings includes an impact on our desires and will. Contemporary Protestant teaching often seems to emphasize the opposite, namely, that sufficient knowledge and/or willpower is the means by which God shapes what people love.[31] Thus, the phenomenon of the believer who knows about penal substitutionary atonement and Spirit-enabled sanctification but loves incessantly acquiring new clothing. Perhaps the incomplete attention to the multiplicity of communicative and transformative symbols contributes to this and points to a potential site of remedy.

Third, the potential meanings and audiences of church architecture are not limited to communicating the liturgy to receptive worshippers during a church service. This was indicated in the opening example, where a nonbeliever stumbled into a church building and had an affective, transformative experience. Williams's account requires an enlarged vision of the function of ecclesial architecture. Church buildings should witness to the cosmic scope of God's reality in its communal, temporal particularity. They should point to the historical engagement of a God who also transcends creaturely temporality, as will be detailed further in what follows. Both believers and non-believers can be impacted, given the universal affective potential of

---

27. See Dyrness, *Poetic Theology*, 25.
28. Smith, *You Are What You Love*.
29. Calvin, *Institutes*, 1.5.1–2; in Edwards, "Artful Creation," 68–69.
30. Calvin, *Institutes*, 1.5.1–2; in Edwards, "Artful Creation," 68–69.
31. See Smith, *Desiring the Kingdom*, 70–71. Cf., Turley, "Practicing the Kingdom," 136–42.

symbols of created realities. This is true despite the noetic effects of sin and the need for a transformed character to understand the full scope of the theological truths to which the symbols point.

Another lens that illuminates the wide scope of meanings and audiences of ecclesial architecture is that of aesthetic experience. In this perspective, the aesthetic experience of architectural forms elucidates theological truths in a new or different way. It helps the recipient catch sight of something that needs further theological elaboration or gives them a new angle on a cherished theological truth. In his studies of music, Jeremy Begbie has traced how musical forms cultivate a sense of suspended tension that ultimately gives way to a feeling of resolution.[32] This experience of longing that moves to satiation, or of a pledge that proceeds to realization, could help expand theological understandings of time. In particular, it could illuminate "the prefiguring of the eschaton in the coming of Christ and the giving of his Spirit."[33] For Begbie, the artistic form is a type of channel through which God works within the worshipping community.

Going beyond Begbie, other perspectives on aesthetic experience allow for a wider audience and a greater range of aesthetically-mediated meanings. In these perspectives, architecture embodies and displays theological meaning that exceeds normal human reason. This meaning is grasped by the subject in a sensory and affective aesthetic experience. As Frank Burch Brown highlights, this meaning is intrinsically aesthetic; it cannot be gained from some other conceptual source.[34] If the meaning were not inherently aesthetic, one would simply discard Bach or Mozart, to borrow Brown's examples, once their theological meaning had been ascertained.

Still others expand the potential meanings and audiences of church architecture by considering the impact of beauty on behavior. Kevin Vanhoozer argues that glimpsing something of beauty moves a person outward, beyond themselves.[35] It engenders a shift in awareness toward the other and toward a reality that transcends the individual. This occurs in an encounter with art because art, regardless of medium, conveys a meaningful pledge, idea, or activity that makes a claim on the viewer and demands a response. Vanhoozer explains that artwork expresses the Heideggerian "mood" (*Stimmung*). This is situational knowledge about three things: about the viewer's position vis-à-vis their setting, about themselves and their potential, and about the points of

32. Begbie, *Theology, Music, and Time*, 127; in Brown, "Aesthetics and the Arts," 533.

33. Begbie, *Theology, Music, and Time*, 127; in Brown, "Aesthetics and the Arts," 533.

34. Brown, "Aesthetics and the Arts," 536.

35. Vanhoozer, "Praising in Song," 113, 117.

interconnection between the two.³⁶ A receptive posture is needed to receive such knowledge, contra the self-absorbed, defensive, and desperate clinging to one's own position of the *incurvatus in se* (curved in on oneself). The receptive posture is characterized by a hunger to know more about that to which the claim points, along with a readiness to act accordingly.

Vanhoozer observes that any experience of beauty is permeated by a lingering sense of incompletion, the sense that it is not fully realized. Experiences of beauty thus point to the consummation of all things.³⁷ This recalls Eberhard Jüngel's comment that "the beautiful . . . carries within itself the promise of truth to come, a future *direct* encounter with the truth . . . the beautiful is a *pre-appearance directed to a goal*."³⁸ Vanhoozer proposes that eschatologically-complete beauty was manifested in Christ's resurrection and exaltation.³⁹ In the present, the Holy Spirit is the sign and seal of this eschatological beauty. The Spirit gives a foretaste of its richness in Christians' citizenship of the glorious kingdom and the associated impact on their thought and action.

Next, Vanhoozer highlights the power of the imagination in orthopraxis. To see what God is doing in Jesus Christ, one must be able to see a complex totality. This is precisely the ability associated with the imagination.⁴⁰ The creative arts facilitate the development of the imagination because they convey a vision of the meaningfulness of something regarding the wider whole.⁴¹ Indeed, the Holy Spirit has been termed "God's imagination let loose . . . in the world."⁴² The Spirit helps one to see the reality of God's truth in the world.

Finally, Vanhoozer identifies that beauty and the imagination are connected by wisdom, the virtue that informs all others. The notion of "fittingness" is implicated in all three elements (beauty, imagination, and wisdom).⁴³ The wise person has fitting attention to how the various aspects of something come together; namely, they engage in an appropriate use of the imagination. Consequently, they know how to act in a manner that is fitting both to the present moment yet also to the ordered beauty of created reality. The link to

36. Vanhoozer, "Praising in Song," 114.
37. Vanhoozer, "Praising in Song," 116.
38. Jüngel, "'Even the Beautiful Must Die,'" 76; in Begbie, "Future of Theology Amid the Arts," 149. Emphasis original.
39. Vanhoozer, "Praising in Song," 116.
40. Vanhoozer, "Praising in Song," 113, 115.
41. Vanhoozer, "Praising in Song," 114, 117.
42. McIntyre, *Faith, Theology and Imagination*, 64; in Vanhoozer, "Praising in Song," 116.
43. Vanhoozer, "Praising in Song," 115.

artistic mediums such as architecture is that such mediums communicate the ordered whole and develop the imagination's powers in noticing things about the present moment that are hidden to the bodily senses.[44]

We have seen several ways in which architecture conveys meaning. Symbols are prevalent and powerful, whether in representations of created entities or in churches that resemble shopping centers. Church architecture participates in social meanings, points to a particular vision of the whole, and facilitates some kind of response. The crucial issue is therefore to seek to express in the church meeting space the Christian reality rather than an alternate one. I will now investigate how this occurs at St. Paul's Cathedral in Melbourne, Australia.[45] I will highlight how the various elements of the Cathedral building signify a community that is both gathered in a place and enveloped in Christ to wander in the world. My hope is that imaginations will be inflamed with the possibilities of how this could apply in each Christian community. The point is not for every church to look like a cathedral, but to contemplate how the aesthetic elements of a church meeting place could witness to the Christian reality, even in temporary settings such as church plants.

Gathered and Grounded

Central to God's work of gathering a people into Christ is each person's encounter with Christ. Some, like the apostle Paul, encounter Christ in an overpowering radiance. At the Cathedral, this is communicated by the vast stained-glass entry doors, whose epicenter depicts a beam of light that stretches in all directions. This stained-glass "light" refracts the external rays of light so that they dance upon the floor. Others encounter Christ through his four evangelists. This is also conveyed in the doors of St. Paul's, which include the symbols of each evangelist as a border around the rays of the light. Of course, encountering Christ entails encountering the Triune God, which at St. Paul's is communicated by the trinitarian symbol of a three-in-one face in the entry narthex screen.[46]

This God transcends all earthly realities. This is symbolized by the Cathedral nave that stretches into the distance, arches that soar toward the heavens, and spires that lift the gaze still higher to that beyond human sight. As Philip Sheldrake notes, cathedrals are traditionally designed as

---

44. Vanhoozer, "Praising in Song," 113, 115.
45. Consecrated 1891 after eleven years of active construction.
46. "Explore—St. Paul's Cathedral Melbourne Website."

a "microcosm of the cosmos."[47] The grandeur of the transcendent realm exists harmoniously in the present. This means that the Creator who surpasses all created things is pointed to in the intricacy of each object.[48] In other words, the Cathedral conveys both God surpassing creation in its towering arches and so on, but also God the Creator, present in creation in the Spirit, in the dense complexity of each item.

Those who encounter Christ are gathered into his body, the church. This occurs through baptism. Accordingly, one cannot get far into St. Paul's (or most churches until recently) without chancing upon a baptismal font. The baptismal font is cruciform in shape, signifying that those who are "baptized into Christ Jesus [are] baptized into his death," in the words of Romans 6:3. Nearby is an eight-pointed star, a symbol of baptism and renewal. Its proximity to the Cathedral entry underscores that God gathers a people through baptism into Christ, like the eight people saved through the water in Noah's ark, and the countless gathered into Israel by circumcision on the eighth day, following 1 Peter 3:20–21.

Enveloped in Christ and Wandering

Like the community gathered in Noah's ark, the community baptized into Christ is enveloped in the hull of a ship as they wander toward home. At St. Paul's, this is signified by the ship-like central region where the congregation is seated. Appropriately, this region is designated the "nave," from the Latin for "ship." Its nautical confines envelop those present into a single group, reinforcing that God's people are one body, though many members (1 Cor 12:12–13). Above, the vaulted ceiling recalls the hull of a ship.

The community gathered into Christ is his body in the world, wandering through time. This body is conformed to his likeness by following Jesus' steps in ministry toward the cross. At St. Paul's, these key events in Jesus' life are depicted in the lower windows, so that they are impressed upon perambulators as they tread along the straight path of the nave. On the opposite wall, scenes from the life of Paul further reinforce the life pattern of ministry.

Like the apostle Paul, the church is to hear the gospel and take it to all people. Accordingly, the Cathedral's brass lectern, from which the Bible is read, is underpinned by an eagle on a sphere. This eagle, carrying the gospel on its back, thus symbolizes the gospel going out into the world.

---

47. Sheldrake, "Placing the Sacred," 247.

48. Sheldrake, *Spaces for the Sacred*, 26, 30. See also, Haecker, "Gothic Analogy of Being," esp. 23.

At the Cathedral, those walking up the nave soon discover that they are tracing the shape of the cross. At the end of the nave, the floorplan branches out on either side, like the crucifix crossbar. This vantage illuminates that one's path up the nave has followed the center "pole" of the cross. Those on this cruciform journey are not abandoned by the light of God, a biblical symbol of God's presence and power. At St. Paul's, this is conveyed by a lantern overhanging the crossing area. Its stained-glass sides depict a circle within a square, a symbol of God's presence in created reality. Overlaying this circle is an eight-pointed star, again expressing the rebirth of those in Christ.

Next, the communion table. Here the various temporalities of the Christian story collide and impress upon the gathered community. As they remember Jesus' death, they anticipate his future return and celebrate his current presence with his people.[49] Past, future, and present combine. Fed by Christ, they wander back down the nave and out into the world.

In this way, the Cathedral points to the church's dual reality as at once wandering and grounded. God's church is a wandering, peripatetic community that lives out God's ways. As I have argued, the church is also the people God gathered together in temporal existence to realize God's objective to be present in creation. This should be reflected in the church's visual contours, namely, the church building or meeting space. Several theoretical perspectives have explicated how the church building can signify this truth, including the modified hermeneutical approach of Premkumar Williams and accounts of aesthetic experience. The church, then, is wandering, but it is also grounded.

Bibliography

Bartholomew, Craig G. *Where Mortals Dwell: A Christian View of Place for Today*. Grand Rapids, MI: Baker Academic, 2011.
Begbie, Jeremy S. "The Future of Theology Amid the Arts: Some Reformed Reflections." In *A Peculiar Orthodoxy: Reflections on Theology and the Arts*, 145–65. Grand Rapids, MI: Baker Academic, 2018.
———. *Theology, Music, and Time*. Cambridge Studies in Christian Doctrine 4. Cambridge: Cambridge University Press, 2000.
Brown, Frank Burch. "Aesthetics and the Arts in Relation to Natural Theology." In *The Oxford Handbook of Natural Theology*, edited by John Hedley Brooke et al., 523–38. Oxford: Oxford University Press, 2013.
Brueggemann, Walter. *The Land: Place as Gift, Promise, and Challenge in Biblical Faith*. 2nd edition. Overtures to Biblical Theology. Minneapolis: Fortress, 2002.

---

49. See Cavanaugh, *Theopolitical Imagination*, 14–15.

Calvin, John. *Institutes of the Christian Religion*. Edited by John T. McNeill. Philadelphia, PA: Westminster John Knox, 1963.

Cavanaugh, William T. *Theopolitical Imagination: Discovering the Liturgy as a Political Act in an Age of Global Consumerism*. London: T&T Clark, 2002.

Certeau, Michel de. *The Practice of Everyday Life*. Translated by Steven Rendall. Berkeley: University of California, 1984.

Dyrness, William A. *Poetic Theology: God and the Poetics of Everyday Life*. Grand Rapids, MI: Eerdmans, 2010.

Edwards, L. Clifton. "Artful Creation and Aesthetic Rationality: Toward a Creational Theology of Revelatory Beauty." *Theology Today* 69.1 (2012) 56–72.

"Explore—St. Paul's Cathedral Melbourne Website," February 25, 2016. https://cathedral.org.au/cathedral/explore/.

Haecker, Ryan. "The Gothic Analogy of Being: An Investigation of the Sublime and the Infinite," 1–30. Unpublished conference paper, 2015.

Hauerwas, Stanley. "What Could It Mean for the Church to Be Christ's Body?: A Question without a Clear Answer." *Scottish Journal of Theology* 48.1 (1995) 1–21.

Jones, Lindsay. *The Hermeneutics of Sacred Architecture: Experience, Interpretation, Comparison*. 2 vols. Cambridge, MA: Harvard Center for the Study of World Religions, 2000.

Jones, Trestae M. "Christian Church Architecture across the United States: How the Rhetoric of the Building and Its Appointments Speak to the Doctrine and Practices of a Church." MA Diss., California State University, Long Beach, 2011.

Jüngel, Eberhard. "'Even the Beautiful Must Die'—Beauty in the Light of Truth." In *Theological Essays II*, edited by John B. Webster, 59–81. Edinburgh: T&T Clark, 1995.

Kilde, Jeanne Halgren. *When Church Became Theatre: The Transformation of Evangelical Architecture and Worship in Nineteenth-Century America*. Oxford: Oxford University Press, 2002.

Levenson, Jon D. "The Temple and the World." *The Journal of Religion* 64.3 (1984) 275–98.

McIntyre, John. *Faith, Theology and Imagination*. Edinburgh: Handsel, 1987.

Platt, David. *Radical Together: Unleashing the People of God for the Purpose of God*. Colorado Springs: Multnomah, 2011.

Polanyi, Michael, and Harry Prosch. *Meaning*. Chicago: University of Chicago Press, 1975.

Sheldrake, Philip. "Placing the Sacred: Transcendence and the City." *Literature and Theology* 21.3 (2007) 243–58.

———. *Spaces for the Sacred: Place, Memory, and Identity*. Baltimore: John Hopkins University Press, 2001.

Smith, James K. A. *Desiring the Kingdom: Worship, Worldview, and Cultural Formation*. Cultural Liturgies. Grand Rapids, MI: Baker Academic, 2009.

———. *You Are What You Love: The Spiritual Power of Habit*. Grand Rapids, MI: Brazos, 2016.

Taylor, W. David O. *The Theater of God's Glory: Calvin, Creation, and the Liturgical Arts*. Grand Rapids, MI: Eerdmans, 2017.

Turley, Stephen Richard. "Practicing the Kingdom: A Critical Appraisal of James K. A. Smith's Desiring the Kingdom." *Calvin Theological Journal* 48.1 (2013) 131–42.

Vanhoozer, Kevin J. "Praising in Song: Beauty and the Arts." In *The Blackwell Companion to Christian Ethics*, edited by Stanley Hauerwas and Samuel Wells, 110–22. Blackwell Companions to Religion. Malden, MA: Blackwell, 2004.

———. "The Voice and the Actor: A Dramatic Proposal About the Ministry and Minstrelsy of Theology." In *Evangelical Futures: A Conversation on Theological Method*, edited by John G. Stackhouse, 61–106. Grand Rapids, MI: Baker, 2000.

Walton, John H. *Genesis 1 as Ancient Cosmology*. Winona Lake: Eisenbrauns, 2011.

Ward, Graham. "Michel de Certeau's 'Spiritual Spaces.'" *The South Atlantic Quarterly* 100.2 (2001) 501–17.

Williams, Premkumar D. "Shaping Sacred Space: Toward an Evangelical Theology of Church Architecture." PhD Diss., Trinity Evangelical Divinity School, 2005.

17

Grounded in Work as Christians

Kara Martin

Paid work takes up the majority of our waking lives, yet is often overlooked as a subject of preaching, teaching, or discipleship in church or theological colleges. In the Western mindset, "work" usually connotes paid work, even if the plain dictionary meaning is about physical or mental effort to get a result. This means that in casual conversation, a mum or dad at home or a retired person will often say that they "don't work."

When we widen our understanding of work to include anything we do with intent or purpose, then it becomes an even more significant portion of our lives, yet with scant attention from sources of biblical reflection and spiritual guidance.

This chapter will consider what it means to remain grounded as Christians in our work, taking as its starting point that the first mentions of work in Genesis literally deal with the ground, a significant metaphor.

Consideration will be given to the varieties of work that we may be drawn to through our lifetime; and particularly the changing nature of work. Women's work will be briefly considered. When looking at resources and examples of remaining grounded at work, current research in spiritual formation for workplace Christians is presented.

Grounding Our Work in God's Work

In Genesis 1 we see God the worker, creating the world, bringing things into being, through his words, powerfully creating things from nothing.

He creates three kingdoms in the first three days: light and dark (vv. 3–5), sky and sea (vv. 6–8), and the earth with its flowers and plants (vv. 9–13). In the next three days he establishes rulers of these kingdoms: the sun and the moon (vv. 14–19), the birds in the sky and the fish in the sea (vv. 20–23), animals and, finally, human beings (vv. 24–31).

So, the material world has been brought into being, and it is pronounced good by God. In fact, by the end it is declared very good (v. 31). The sense of "good" here is of everything being as it should be—the right thing, pleasing to God, an outworking of his will and character. God takes delight in his work as a good thing.

Regent College's R. Paul Stevens says,

> God not only authored work but he himself was a worker (Genesis 1, 2; John 5:17; Revelation 21:5). Throughout the Bible, we see different images of God as a worker namely, shepherd (Psalm 23), potter (Jeremiah 18:6), physician (Matthew 8:16), teacher (Psalm 143:10), vineyard-dresser (Isaiah 5:1–7) etc. God is as active and creative today—creating, sustaining, redeeming and consummating—as God was when this five billion light year universe was begun.[1]

God Gives Us Work to Do

Very quickly in the Bible we get to a critical description of how God wants to invite humankind to join him in the working.

> Then God said, "Let us make mankind in our image, in our likeness, so that they may rule over the fish in the sea and the birds in the sky, over the livestock and all the wild animals, and over all the creatures that move along the ground." So God created mankind in his own image, in the image of God he created them; male and female he created them. God blessed them and said to them, 'Be fruitful and increase in number; fill the earth and subdue it. Rule over the fish in the sea and the birds in the sky and over every living creature that moves on the ground (Gen 1:26–28).[2]

---

1. Stevens, "Theology."
2. All Scripture quotations in this chapter are from the NIV unless otherwise

This is the "creation mandate" for humankind, to be involved in the ongoing work of imagining, laying out, ordering, filling in, and being abundant with all the resources God has given us.

Many of the words that are translated here in the passage may have negative and sinister overtones: rule, subdue, multiply . . . but that may well be a consequence of how we have abused our role as vice-regents with God.[3] Peterson talks about dominion[4] as a responsibility in *The Message* paraphrase,[5] which hints at the idea of stewardship, perhaps a more helpful term.

This invitation in Genesis 1:26–28 to become involved in God's work is offered explicitly to both men and women. This is why ideas of "women's work" may be too reductionistic; certainly being in "the home" is not the predominant arena for women's use of their gifting.

This idea of cultural stewardship—our role as vice-regents caring for all of God's creation and continuing the filling in or culture-making[6]—is exemplified by the wise woman described in Proverbs 31. Many translations use the word "noble" in Proverbs 31:10, but "valiant" is a better translation.[7] We have here a warrior woman. "Bringing food from afar" in v. 14 has connotations of hunting down prey. In v. 18 her trading is "profitable," not from good luck, but because she has worked so hard. She is brave and strong and industrious and courageous.

Our understanding of the Proverbs 31 woman is strengthened by comparison with Psalm 111, which is also a heroic poem, but about God, yet we see similar characteristics. Just like the Proverbs 31 woman, the LORD is celebrated among the elders. The LORD is gracious and compassionate, provides food, and is faithful and just and trustworthy. God's work and the woman's work are correlated.

---

indicated.

3. There is a debate about the terminology which is appropriate to describe humanity's authority and role; this is summarized well by McKim, *Christian Theology*, especially pages 175–76.

4. For a more thorough discussion of dominion, see Kline, *Kingdom Prologue*, 43: "Man is made with the glory of an official dominion, a dominion that is holy, righteous and true in its ethical character, a dominion that has promise ultimately of a perfected manifestation in the luminosity of human glorification." Humans will rule all the other rulers.

5. Peterson, *The Message*.

6. See pages 327ff in Crouch, *Culture Making*, where there is the additional consideration of our responsibility to steward proactively for justice.

7. For a discussion of the semantics and its description of women and work, this article by the Theology of Work Project is excellent: Waltke and Matthews, "The Valiant Woman."

This aspect is often underplayed about the Proverbs 31 woman; that she is being celebrated for her working, and for all aspects of her working. There is wife-ing, mothering, caring for the poor, sewing . . . but perhaps the most surprising element is the entrepreneurial activity commended here. This woman is involved in commercial transactions involving land, and trading in markets: "She considers a field and buys it; out of her earnings she plants a vineyard . . . She sees that her trading is profitable" (Prov 31:16–18). An extremely broad range of work is described here as appropriately undertaken by a woman who is praised by all.

God Works with Us

Being involved in working *with* God is played out further in Genesis 2. In v. 5, God laments that there is "no one to work the ground," so we see that human beings were actually created to work with God in the garden.

In Genesis 2 God invites humankind to join him in the work that needs to be done: "The LORD God took the man and put him in the Garden of Eden to work it and take care of it" (Gen 2:15), He tells Adam to work or "till the ground" and to "keep the garden."

He then invites Adam to join in the naming of the creatures: "Now the LORD God had formed out of the ground all the wild animals and all the birds in the sky. He brought them to the man to see what he would name them; and whatever the man called each living creature, that was its name. So the man gave names to all the livestock, the birds in the sky and all the wild animals" (Gen 2:19).

Familiarity with the passage may obscure the significance of this invitation to name what God has created. Names in the Bible invoke identity. Abram becomes Abraham—ancestor of a multitude; Jacob becomes Israel—one who wrestles with God. To name something, you must know it intimately and have authority over it. In effect, Adam was giving each creature its essence.[8] Gerhard Von Rad explains it slightly differently: "Language is seen here not as a means of communication but as an intellectual capacity by means of which man brings conceptual order to his sphere of life."[9] So naming a creature is understanding it and imagining it as part of life.

---

8. A discussion of "naming" can be found in most Old Testament background texts. Iain Provan helpfully outlines naming as part of the creation process, assigning roles and functions, building on the work of John Walton. See Provan, *Discovering Genesis*, 90–91.

9. Von Rad, *Genesis*, 83.

Note that the first work was tilling the ground—that is, physical work. This second sort of work is intellectual and creative work. In both we see God working with us, God choosing to work with us. In fact, looking back at Genesis 2:15, the roots of the Hebrew words for work the ground and keep the garden, *avad* and *shamar*, are actually also the words used later for serving God and keeping his commandments (see the duties of the Levites described in Numbers 3:7–8, 4:23–24, 26).[10] In our work we honor God and show him our obedience.

Gordon Wenham points out that humans were created from the land and have a relationship to the land. There is a play on words between *Adam* and *adamah* which means ground. "He was created from it; his job is to cultivate it (2:5, 15); and on death he returns to it (3:19)."[11] However, the human is not just a piece of dust (*afar*) shaped by God; he has life breathed into him by God (2:7).[12]

In fact, human beings are invited to work in relationship with God, with the land, and with the creatures to bring forth even more good, beautiful, and admirable works and wonders. Humanity is the vice-regent of the divine king, and unlike the myths of other Near Eastern nations is "a slave neither to the gods nor the environment, but a ruler who images the creator."[13]

What is more, our work should have an aesthetic dimension. God is generous and a lover of beauty. God makes things that aren't just inherently good, useful, functional, but also beautiful: "trees that were pleasing [or a delight] to the eye and good for food" (Gen 2:9). As Trible notes, the semantic range of *avad* and *shamar* means that "to till" is to work with respect, to serve, and "to keep" is to tend and protect, and "since Eden is a place of delight, to till and to keep it is to foster pleasure."[14]

Hence, human work is elevated from negativity and drudgery, but it is also holistic. Physical, mental, and emotional work flows from our spiritual connection with God. As John Bergsma says: "There is no division of secular and sacred service for the first man: there is a unity of work and worship, as all his tasks in the garden constitute part of his priestly liturgy."[15]

---

10. For a further discussion on this link, see Oswalt and Ross, *Genesis*, 46.

11. Wenham, *Genesis*, 59.

12. Note: gender is often assumed as male, but as Phyllis Trible points out, at this point "grammatical gender is not sexual identification," and sexual identity is created later, so "earth creature" is a preferred description Trible, *God and Rhetoric of Sexuality*, 80.

13. Wenham, *Genesis*, 67.

14. Trible, *God and Rhetoric of Sexuality*, 85.

15. Bergsma, "Creation narratives," 24.

Our Ongoing Work with God, Serving God and Others

Al Wolters in *Creation Regained* describes the ongoing significant work that human beings must do following on from the creation narrative:

> This is not the end of the development of creation, however. Although God has withdrawn from the work of creation, he has put an image of himself on the earth with a mandate to continue. The earth had been completely unformed and empty; in the six-day process of development God had formed it and filled it—but not completely. People must now carry on the work of development: by being fruitful they must fill it even more; by subduing it they must form it even more. Mankind, as God's representatives on the earth, carry on where God left off. But this is now to be a human development of the earth. The human race will fill the earth with its own kind, and it will form the earth for its own kind. From now on the development of the created earth will be societal and cultural in nature. In a single word, the task ahead is civilization.[16]

Work is not simply a means to get an income, it is about stewardship, productivity, fruitfulness, relationships, for the good of the world and the glory of God. As Richard Middleton says, Genesis 1–2 "depicts God as a generous creator, sharing power with a variety of creatures (especially humanity), inviting them (and trusting them—at some risk) to participate in creative (and historical) process."[17]

However, most of the world's population need to work to live, rather than live to work, and for them work is a constant struggle. It is much easier for those of us in wealthy countries to see that work is good, since it is the source of much meaning and purpose for us. We need to remember that for us choice is a precious thing; it is a luxury.

Finding Ourselves Ungrounded in Work

However, it is easy for us to become disconnected from this view that work is a good gift from God. There are lots of synonyms for "work" and most of them are negative: toil, exertion, slog, drudgery, grind, "hard yakka," travail, labor . . . It may be that we have become overwhelmed by working. Whatever our work is—housework, schoolwork, study, paid work, voluntary work—we

---

16. Wolters, *Creation Regained*, 41–42.
17. Middleton, *The Liberating Image*, 296–97.

find that it is always coupled with difficulty. None of us needs to be convinced of the reality of sin and its connection with work.

For many in Western countries, our view of work is summed up by these lines by Ogden Nash: "If you don't want to work you have to work to earn enough money so that you won't have to work."[18] In other words, people will work hard to save up money so that they will not have to work. Of course, Nash's assumption is that no one *wants* to work!

How can we see work as good when we feel weary, overwhelmed? When our workplace is toxic? When we are fighting with someone at work? Or when we are not even sure we are making a difference?

The "Curse of Work"

In chapters 1 and 2 of Genesis work is seen as a good thing—part of being made in the image of God—and God invites human beings to work with him, completing the filling of creation. But in chapter 3, everything begins to go horribly wrong. Working is directly impacted as sin enters creation.

Eve and Adam disobey God by eating the fruit they were instructed to leave alone. Adam blames Eve and God, and Eve blames the snake. Sin has entered the garden; relationships are broken with each other, with God and with creation. Then, dramatically, God pronounces the consequences. He starts with Eve and her primary work of childbirth, which will become painful and difficult. Notice the process is cursed, but not the child. Next comes Adam, and his primary work of cultivating food. Notice here, too, that work itself is not cursed; rather, the ground is cursed (v. 17), which means that it is the process of working that is impacted.

Work will be harder and more painful, "through painful toil . . . " (v. 17). The arrival of thorns and thistles will mean that we are not as productive or fruitful as we hope to be (v. 18). We will sweat with the effort to do things that were simple before (v. 19).

This is reality as we know it: all the frustrations and disappointments of work. Working is more difficult than it should be. Working has become unpleasant. Working is liable to failure and unintended consequences. The fruits of your housework do not last; it seems so difficult to simply keep things clean and ordered. Or study is hard because knowledge does not stick in your brain; you are surrounded by distractions and it is an effort to understand what you are reading. Or you are overwhelmed by the needs of work. There is always more to be done, and it is hard to establish who or what to focus on. Then your computer crashes, and you have to redo all that work.

18. From his poem, "More about People," in Nash, *Hard Lines,* 69.

Then there is the obvious sin that surrounds our working, when people deliberately use their work to harm others. This may not be a common experience for everyone, but can be a temptation in our highly competitive world.

In the very next chapter, Genesis 4, we read about Cain getting jealous of his brother Abel's work, and killing him. Work has become a source of competition, selfish ambition, and conflict. Again, this is something we see around us; we simply don't work together very well. The image of "sin crouching at the door" (v. 7) is resonant; there are many temptations to behave in the workplace in ways that are out of character with Christian values.

Then in Genesis 11 we hear the chilling account of the Tower of Babel, where humans work hard to try and reach heaven in order to make a name for themselves. Work can so easily become an idol and our means of impressing God. In its rightful place, work is an act of service, an offering to God. It should never be about bringing fame to our own name. Instead, our sincere hope is that by our good work, others might give honor to God (Matt 5:13–16, 1 Peter 2:12).

Cursed in Process, but Still Some Good

Despite these many challenges, we need to remember that work itself is not cursed. Even in the Cain and Abel story we see some good. The brothers are working to provide for their families, and they are seeking to offer the results of their work to God. In this we see the action of *avad* and *shamar* (Gen 2:15), worship and obedience, as Cain and Abel offer the fruit of their work in worship (Gen 4:3–4).

Sometimes it is easy to see the good in our work, and the more you are aware of working with God, the more good you will see. I have heard a teacher describe the change in a child when he gave them some focus and care. I have heard an aged care worker describe the impact on a family when she treated their mother with dignity and respect. I have heard a senior government worker describe the impact of her work in drafting legislation that will have a positive influence for a generation.

Nonetheless, sometimes we are overwhelmed by the difficulties of work, and Christians are not exempt. My Masters students were asked to survey their church congregations about the greatest challenges they were facing with work:

- Number one was stress: Christians feeling stretched and overwhelmed, struggling to find balance.

- Number two was ethical challenge: Christians trying to navigate the murky waters of our work.
- Number three was conflict at work: Christians conscious of the call to be peacemakers yet facing the reality that it is difficult for people to get along.

Timothy Keller describes the impact of sin in our working this way:

> We will be able to envision far more than we can accomplish, both because of a lack of ability and resistance in the environment around us. The experience of work will include pain, conflict, envy, and fatigue, and not all our goals will be met. For example, you may have an aspiration to do a certain kind of work and perform at a certain level of skill and quality, but you may never even get the opportunity to do the work you want, or if you do, you may not even be able to do it as well as it needs to be done. Your conflicts with others in the work environment will sap your confidence and undermine your productivity.[19]

We are sinful people living in a sinful world, where things do not work as they should. However, we should never let sin have the last word on work.

The Apostle Paul was not immune to the impact of sin in his working. In 2 Corinthians 11:23–28 he lists the following extraordinary litany of working hardships:

> I have worked much harder, been in prison more frequently, been flogged more severely, and been exposed to death again and again. Five times I received from the Jews the forty lashes minus one. Three times I was beaten with rods, once I was pelted with stones, three times I was shipwrecked, I spent a night and a day in the open sea, I have been constantly on the move. I have been in danger from rivers, in danger from bandits, in danger from my fellow Jews, in danger from Gentiles; in danger in the city, in danger in the country, in danger at sea; and in danger from false believers. I have labored and toiled and have often gone without sleep; I have known hunger and thirst and have often gone without food; I have been cold and naked. Besides everything else, I face daily the pressure of my concern for all the churches.

We can learn from the attitude he displays in the very next chapter: "For Christ's sake, I delight in weaknesses, in insults, in hardships, in persecutions, in difficulties. For when I am weak, then I am strong" (2 Cor 12:10). We need

---

19. Keller, *Every Good Endeavour*, 90.

the same eagerness to serve and obey, to honor God and work alongside him, that we saw demonstrated in Genesis 1 and 2.

We can also live in light of the hope of the New Creation. The whole earth is groaning for release as we read in Romans 8:22–23, and we share in that awareness of bondage to decay, and the desire for what is to come. As Paula Gooder says, "We are not the only ones who wait with eager longing for the new age, the whole of creation waits with us, yearning to be transformed."[20] She argues that all of creation is awaiting final release from sin into the fullness of the new creation, where Isaiah 65 reassures us that good and productive work awaits.

Re-grounding Our Work in God through Christ

With all the frustrations, temptations, and hardships we experience in work, is abiding until heaven and the future hope of good and productive work, the only way to move forward?

A Word on the Metaphor of Dirt

To ponder that question, it is worth considering more deeply the metaphor of dirt and ground and its significance for us. Many of us are far removed from dirt and any relationship with it. As city-dwellers, dirt is dirty. Food magically appears in the supermarket, many do not even garden anymore, as the move to apartments, or outsourcing household chores, increases.

This separates us from our relationship with creation, but also from our responsibility as stewards and the relationship between our work and the ongoing sustenance of God's creation.

Diana Butler Bass talks about her own journey of reconnecting spiritually with God around these ideas in her book *Grounded*. She points to Paul Tillich, a German military chaplain who was devastated by what he witnessed during the First World War. He lost his sense of God, and in his reflections after the war he sought a more dependable theological basis for faith. Finally, he proclaimed God as the "Ground of all Being"; it is God who grounds us.[21]

---

20. Gooder, *Body*, 69.
21. Bass, *Grounded*, 17–18.

Bass describes this as a move from a focus on the transcendence of God to his immanence. She describes this as a move from seeing God as only inhabiting heaven to One entwined with all of creation.[22]

Our lack of appreciation of dirt, and our lack of grounding in God, is linked by Bass to a lack of respect for the vocation we were given at creation:

> We humans wilfully disregarded our vocation to protect and keep the earth, choosing instead to do violence upon it. Thus, soil may be either blessed or cursed by our activity. Soil is good but may become bad, something sacred and fertile ruined into what is profaned and hardened. Our problem is that we hardly understand our own involvement in the degradation of the ground.[23]

As we struggle to retain God's perspective on our work in the here-and-now, the metaphor of "being grounded" can be really helpful. We remember that the first work we were invited to do by God was to "till the ground." We are made to interact with creation—with people and things. We are made to get our hands dirty in the messiness and difficulty of everything. We are made to restore order to chaos and to bring reconciliation to relationships. And we do all this in the power given to us by the dying and rising Christ.

This is brought home to us in Colossians 1:15–20. I love Eugene Peterson's paraphrase in *The Message*:

> We look at this Son and see the God who cannot be seen. We look at this Son and see God's original purpose in everything created. For everything, absolutely everything, above and below, visible and invisible, rank after rank after rank of angels—*everything* got started in him and finds its purpose in him. He was there before any of it came into existence and holds it all together right up to this moment. And when it comes to the church, he organizes and holds it together, like a head does a body. He was supreme in the beginning and—leading the resurrection parade—he is supreme in the end. From beginning to end he's there, towering far above everything, everyone. So spacious is he, so roomy, that everything of God finds its proper place in him without crowding. Not only that, but all the broken and dislocated pieces of the universe—people and things, animals and atoms—get properly fixed and fit together in vibrant harmonies, all because of his death, his blood that poured down from the cross.

---

22. Bass, *Grounded*, 25.
23. Bass, *Grounded*, 58.

Jesus' sovereignty and rule on earth is expressed through human beings imaging God's character. Much of this is explicitly through the work of the church and Christian organizations. As N. T. Wright says, "Jesus went about feeding the hungry, curing the sick, and rescuing the lost sheep; his Body is supposed to be doing the same. That is how his kingdom is at work."[24]

Our work is thus a part of the process of helping to fix "all the broken and dislocated pieces of the universe" (Peterson's paraphrase). Whether it is through medicine, or plumbing, or mothering, or counseling, or as a police officer, we are used by God to mend and solve and rescue. These images are familiar to Christians who have tended to prefer the helping professions as vocational choices.

However, our work is also part of finding purpose in Christ. Our work helps to bring meaning to everyday, ordinary activities. This meaning may be more personal—making beautiful art, or building a house that has capacity to be a home—or it may help to make meaning known to others as we give them glimpses of what it means to honor God and serve others through our work.

Furthermore, work itself can be grounding because it is inherently "soulful," connecting our bodily activities with our deepest sense of identity, meaning, purpose, and our yearning for God.

As articulated by David Benner, "a spirituality that is not attentive to the call of soul leaves us ungrounded in some fundamental way, and a journey of soulfulness that is not responsiveness to the call of the spirit leaves us self-encapsulated."[25] Benner suggests the easiest way to picture this is the spirit as a kite wanting to soar, but the soul is the string that connects us to the ground. Without the string, the kite would fly off and be lost. Without the kite, the string would be limp on the ground.

Work helps to ground our faith in the reality of our bodily existence. Our faith can have heavenly ideals of the way life is meant to be, but our work reminds us that we deal with the messiness of this ordinary life.

Paula Gooder also makes helpful distinctions between soul and spiritual, pointing out that Paul in his letter uses "spiritual" to explain that every Christian is animated by the Holy Spirit; thus it is not a personal characteristic, but it refers to one who has received God's Spirit.[26] Her study of the Hebrew concept of the soul, *nephesh*, suggests that it is grounded in the body which has been animated by the breath of God.[27] Becoming more

---

24. Wright, *God in Public*, 161.
25. Benner, *Soulful Spirituality*, 42–43.
26. Gooder, *Body*, 79.
27. Gooder, *Body*, 35–36. For a full explanation of the semantic range of the Hebrew

aware of our bodies through our ordinary work, and how this is deeply connected to God and his work, ensures that we remain alive to God's work on earth while we yearn for the New Earth.

In my research on how to effectively equip workplace Christians, I have interviewed Christian doctors about their working and can illustrate the ways that work grounds their faith and makes a difference to those around them. Here are a couple of examples:

> Oliver[28] is at the forefront of working with difficult people, and his work is intense. He has this knack for being grounded and diplomatic. He doesn't set people off, even in a stressful environment. He is very considerate. He would never put someone down, in spite of the difficulties he often faces. He is always working to affirm others, making it a point to pay someone a formal compliment rather than a formal complaint. He could complain about doctors who are difficult. There was one colleague, a surgeon, who was particularly obliging, and Oliver made it a point to inform his department heads how this doctor made it easy for Oliver to get some work done. The department heads talked about the compliment, commenting that it was the sort of behavior that should occur in the workplace. Oliver transformed the workplace by highlighting the positive.

> A patient was dying, and the family were being aggressive towards medical staff. Xanthe was a target, but she responded helpfully. She encouraged the staff to work together to deflect rather than being defensive or aggressive. They showed great self-control. Xanthe understood that anger is part of the grief process. In the end the family apologized for their behavior.

In these kinds of ways, we enter into the messiness of our workplace and our working relationships, marred by sin, just like Jesus entered into the messiness of our humanity (1 John 4:2).[29] Just like Jesus, we seek to bring a new way of perceiving (the real meaning of "repent"/*metanoia*[30] as used by Jesus

---

and Greek words for soul and spirit, see pages 13–14.

28. Names have been changed to protect the identity of individuals

29. Jesus became tired (Matt 4:11), thirsty (John 4:7), needed to escape from crowds and be alone (Luke 5:16). He had emotions including frustration (Matt 26:40), anger (Matt 21:12–13), sorrow (John 11:35), and amazement (Luke 7:9).

30. For a thorough discussion of this topic, see Boda and Smith, *Repentance*. They posit the term used by the Gospel writers and Paul within the cultural context of the term, particularly its usage in the writings of Josephus where it refers to "a fundamental change of thinking that is often accompanied by a fundamental change of living." (89–90)

in Mark 1:15) to the established patterns around us. Instead of responding to hostility with hostility, we find creative ways of bringing new hope:

> Finn does not respond to hostility with hostility, since that leads to relationship breakdown. He doesn't try to change the person but accepts the person and seeks to protect himself. By understanding where they come from, he builds a road to forgiveness, and protects himself from bitterness and resentment and anger. He is then able to show hospitality, kindness and care, in spite of the hostility received.

Even simple acts can make a big different to our working environments:

> Queenie is always sharing food. She makes people feel included and part of the team. She is different by not complaining all the time. She tries to make the workplace better rather than bitter.

Remembering the power of work to become an idol, like the Tower of Babel, we must also guard ourselves against the spirit of overwork that defines the privileged of our age. Derek Thompson, writing in *The Atlantic*, reports:

> Today, it is fair to say that elite American men have transformed themselves into the world's premier workaholics, toiling longer hours than both poorer men in the U.S. and rich men in similarly rich countries.
>
> This shift defies economic logic—and economic history. The rich have always worked less than the poor, because they could afford to. The landed gentry of preindustrial Europe dined, danced, and gossiped, while serfs toiled without end. In the early 20th century, rich Americans used their ample downtime to buy weekly movie tickets and dabble in sports. Today's rich American men can afford vastly more downtime. But they have used their wealth to buy the strangest of prizes: more work![31]

He reports that this ethos has spread beyond the rich, that there is an epidemic of workaholism fueled by a search for identity, purpose and meaning in the work itself.

Such a temptation can be resisted by Christians, and for two reasons. First, our identity, meaning and purpose are found in Christ,[32] not

---

31. Thompson, "Workism."

32. Ephesians 2:1–10 asserts that we were once dead in our sin, but we have been made alive "in Christ" as new creations (2 Cor 5:17). Three times in this passage Paul reminds us that we are "in Christ" (6, 7, 10), and 12 times in the letter of Ephesians. The concept is repeated multiple times in every letter Paul wrote, and it is his most common description of the new identity of believers.

in work, though we can worship God through our work and find meaning and purpose in it being aligned with God's purposes. Second, we can lead the way in modeling the rhythms of work and rest established by God in Genesis 2, and reinforced through the Ten Commandments (Exodus 20). We need to take care of our bodies. Paula Gooder points out that when Paul calls the body a "temple of the Holy Spirit" (1 Cor 6:19), then what we do with our bodies matter, "but also that God's Spirit, by its very nature, brings life. If we abuse our bodies in any way (by overwork, not resting enough, ignoring what our bodies tell us about our wellbeing) then we are not allowing the Spirit to work fully within us."[33]

Conclusion

Remembering the origins of work, and our relationship with the God who works, can ensure we stay grounded in our ordinary, everyday work. Our work is good, marred by sin, but able to be redeemed and a tool of redemption. It is an act of worship to God, and enables us to give others a glimpse of the New Creation, when our work will be freed from the bondage to decay, and we will again enjoy a productive and flourishing working relationship, serving God. In the meantime, we are willing to get our hands dirty, serving God and others, enacting the sovereign rule of Christ, and modelling healthy rhythms of work and rest.

Bibliography

Bass, Diana Butler. *Grounded: Finding God in the World—A Spiritual Revolution*. Reprint edition. New York: HarperOne, 2017.

Benner, David G. *Soulful Spirituality: Becoming Fully Alive and Deeply Human*. 1st edition. Grand Rapids, MI: Brazos, 2011.

Bergsma, John. "The Creation Narratives and the Original Unity of Work and Worship in the Human Vocation." In *Work: Theological Foundations and Practical Implications*, edited by R. Keith Loftin and Trey Dimsdale, 11–29. London: SCM, 2018.

Boda, Mark J., and Gordon T. Smith. *Repentance in Christian Theology*. Collegeville: Liturgical, 2006.

Gooder, Paula. *Body: Biblical Spirituality for the Whole Person*. London: SPCK, 2016.

Keller, Timothy. *Every Good Endeavour: Connecting Your Work to God's Plan for the World*. London: Hachette UK, 2012.

Kline, Meredith G. *Kingdom Prologue: Genesis Foundations for a Covenantal Worldview*. Eugene, OR: Wipf & Stock, 2006.

---

33. Gooder, *Body*, 86.

McKim, Mark G. *Christian Theology for a Secular Society: Singing the Lord's Song in a Strange Land*. Eugene, OR: Wipf & Stock, 2008.

Middleton, J. Richard. *The Liberating Image: The Imago Dei in Genesis 1*. Grand Rapids, MI: Brazos, 2005.

Nash, Ogden. *Hard Lines*. 1st edition. New York: Simon and Schuster, 1931.

Oswalt, John, and Alan Ross. *Genesis, Exodus*. Wheaton, IL: Tyndale, 2017.

Peterson, Eugene H. *The Message: The Bible in Contemporary Language*. Colorado Springs: Navpress, 2002.

Provan, Iain. *Discovering Genesis: Content, Interpretation, Reception*. Grand Rapids, MI: Eerdmans, 2016.

Rad, Gerhard Von. *Genesis*. Revised edition. Philadelphia, PA: Westminster John Knox, 1972.

Stevens, R. Paul. "A Theology of Work in 8 Easy Steps." ELO Network blog, February 8, 2014. http://www.entrepreneurialleaders.com/blog/22/.

Thompson, Derek. "Workism Is Making Americans Miserable." *The Atlantic*. Last modified February 24, 2019. https://www.theatlantic.com/ideas/archive/2019/02/religion-workism-making-americans-miserable/583441/.

Trible, Phyllis. *God and Rhetoric of Sexuality*. 2nd edition. Philadelphia: Augsburg Fortress, 1986.

Watke, Bruce, and Alice Matthews. "The Valiant Woman (Proverbs 31:10–31)." Online Bible commentary. June 10, 2012. https://www.theologyofwork.org/old-testament/proverbs/what-do-the-proverbs-have-to-do-with-work/the-valiant-woman-proverbs-3110-31.

Wenham, Gordon John. *Genesis 1–15, Volume 1*. Edited by David Allen Hubbard and Glenn W. Barker. Grand Rapids, MI: Zondervan, 2014.

Wolters, Albert M. *Creation Regained: Biblical Basics for a Reformational Worldview by Albert M. Wolters*. Grand Rapids, MI: Eerdmans, 1985.

Wright, N. T. *God in Public: How the Bible Speaks Truth to Power Today*. London: SPCK, 2016.

18

Tethered between Reality and Aspiration

Grounding and Formative Practices for Australian Leaders

MONICA O'NEIL

WE LEADERS ASPIRE. WE aspire to better, to stronger, to calmer, to livelier. We aspire to wiser. We aspire to be good. We aspire for and with our communities and our teams for a good day and a good way. What might a good day and a good way look like? How can we reach toward it and simultaneously ground ourselves with a gutsy grip on reality? What practices help us harness the wonderful tension between the two and fuel our transformation?

There are both possibilities and difficulties raised by these questions. In this chapter I explore the nature of a good worth aspiring to, examine some key challenges in tethering our aspiration and reality, and offer foundational practices that can foster life-long grounding in both reality and aspiration.

A Good Worth Becoming

If the positive psychologists are correct, "goodness" in virtually all cultures has been characterized by a relatively small set of virtues.[1] In biblical reflection this is also the case. At the core of the biblical vision of what it means to

---

1. Dahlsgaard et al., *Shared*, 203–213.

be a good person stand the twin ideals of the *imago Dei* and Christlikeness. To live the "good" life is to bear the image of God in this world; the good life is to be like Jesus Christ. In Jesus' devotion to God and his love for others, in his life and death, in the spirit of the Beatitudes, we have a clear representation of the good to which we are called. In terms of our aspiration, and the task of tethering reality to aspiration, the aspiration to a truly excellent life consists in *being* a certain kind of person—that is, a *good* person. Good leadership and the values we choose to inculcate as part of our formation must reflect and embody this good. Can we be more specific?

A number of biblical ethicists identify love and justice as the central good in the life and teaching of Jesus, and define them as both responsive dispositions and as individual and communal actions. They are human responses to the love and justice that God has dispensed in Jesus' death and resurrection,[2] and both the Great Commission and the Great Commandment flow from them.[3] These two central biblical themes are encapsulated in the Hebrew term "shalom." This shalom is,

> Peace of a certain kind: a just peace (each man sitting under his own fig tree, says Micah), a liberating peace (the children dancing in the streets, says Zechariah), a peace in which all enjoy the bounty of God and honor him thereby. Our highest end is to glorify God and enjoy him forever.[4]

According to William Spohn,

> Scripture answers the moral question "What ought I to do?" by replying "Love others as God has loved you in Jesus Christ." Christian moral life has the character of response because God's love comes to us first and our actions correspond to the character of that love. Christian love finds the motive and norm for loving others in the story of Jesus which defines the way God continues to love each of us.[5]

This responsive goodness is situated in the individual and in the life of their community. The community is called to live in response to Christ, and its actions are to reflect their orientation to follow him as their complete exemplar. This is a true orientation for the realization of the human identity in Christ.[6]

---

2. For further discussion of these two themes in Jesus' life and in ours, see Stassen and Gushee, *Kingdom Ethics*, especially chapters 16–17.
3. See Matt 28:18–20 and Matt 22:38–42.
4. Holmes, *Ethics*, 53.
5. Spohn, *Saying*, 94.
6. See Cahill, *Character*, 3, and Harrington and Keenan, *Jesus and Virtue Ethics*.

Stanley Hauerwas argues that virtues depend "upon an account of the historical nature of being human that defies all attempts to develop an ethics of virtue abstracted from society's particular traditions and history."[7] He urges us to engage in goodness that is tethered to Scripture, to the person of Jesus, to the history of the church, and to our current reality.

Such goodness constitutes both our human *telos*, our aspiration point, as well as our duty-bound moral obligations. It calls us to be leaders who are grounded in peace and who live prophetically in love and justice—in attitude of heart and in action—bearing witness to the gracious reign of God in our wider, now global, communities.

My work on virtue formation, personally, as director of our leadership center and as a supervisor of other leaders, called for a memorable, succinct, and tailored formation brief; a charter of formation. When reflecting on our practice, in personal interactions or in strategic development discussions, we were wrestling with competing values in the Christian culture around us as well as within our own habits and decisions. Competing streams in both leadership theory and spirituality were jostling for preeminence. Was a strategic approach inherently more or less good than an organic church or servant leadership approach? Was it more deeply good to orient into a social justice tradition or a monastic framework? Or perhaps a charismatic evangelical set of practices? I worked to develop a virtue-based framework that allowed both deep and quick reflection and therefore practice decisions. It needed to be memorable and able to be weighed in a single breath and in a deep and long consideration. The charter is designed to weigh intention and action in personal and ministry life.

This "charter of good" has three shades (mercy, humility, and endurance) and each shade has three hues.

Mercy

> We who have received mercy will show mercy in acts of liberation to others (Matt 18:23–35; Luke 10:30–37).

Displayed as Kindness

"Kindness as a posture of life and a practice that characterizes the people of God might just be sufficiently disarming to offer a glimpse into the new

---

7. Hauerwas, *Virtue*, 252.

creation."[8] In our pursuit of mission, we will prize liberating acts of generosity. Ruthlessness is rejected as foreign to the grace of the gospel. Trampling on others as we rush to our ends is a reflection of deep self-centeredness, which Jesus warned against in Matthew 18.[9]

Displayed as Forgiveness

When sinned against in any form, we will offer the forgiveness we have been given. We will be mindful that all have sinned and fallen short, and that the same forgiveness we have received is to be extended to others. We will seek progressive wholesome restoration where possible.

Displayed as Wounded Healing

Acknowledging our own frailty, we will walk as pilgrims engaging in healing work. Our posture is one of humility; we heal as ones who have been, and are still being, healed by the goodness of God. We will keenly recognize the error of trying to save others in our own strength, or of treating others as though we are better than they. We will not believe those who seek to magnify us for this service.[10]

Humility

> We who have received so much will serve others with respect, gratitude and humility (John 13:1–17; Phil 2:1–11; Rom 11:33–36).

Displayed as Teamwork

God did not create the body of Christ as a uniform community, so we will prize and guard our differences, valuing them as a reflection of the divine nature seen in the inter-relatedness and unity of the Trinity. We will gratefully acknowledge and make room for one another.

---

8. Pohl, *Kindness*, 11.
9. Pohl, *Kindness*, 10.
10. Olsen, *Burnout*, 304.

Displayed as Stewardship and Servanthood

That Jesus called his followers to serve one another is clearly demonstrated in his teaching as he washed his disciples' feet. We follow Christ who "made himself of no reputation, taking the form of a servant" (Phil 2:7). Therefore, we eschew the pursuit of power and status. Leonardo Boff has written of the manner in which the church might follow in the way of Jesus:

> He repudiates subordinationism as error, advocating equalitarian standing for all humanity regardless of gender, race, economic standing and so on. Any exclusion and nonparticipation in any aspect of life, any forms of marginalization or oppression deny the image of God in the other and reject the communion which the Trinity calls us to.[11]

Any authority we gain is a gift given that we might better serve as a steward of the grace of God and an under-shepherd of Jesus Christ.

Displayed as Learning

As Jesus' disciples we will diligently seek to understand what the way of God's kingdom is, in our time and context. We commit to being life-long learners and to personal growth, attending to God's voice in Scripture—by the Spirit and through his people historically and in our time.

Endurance

> We who have received freedom in Christ will offer our lives in disciplined service. (Jas 1:1–25; Acts 20:17–35; Heb 11:1–12:3; 2 Tim 2:1–13)

Displayed as Adaptability

Following the pattern of Jesus, and of Paul, we will lay down our habits and station—our ways, our comforts, our programs and methods, our status quo—for the sake of the gospel. Compelled by and responding to the Spirit, we will go and adapt, accepting that loss may be ours.

---

11. Boff, *Trinity*, 115.

Displayed as Strength of Will

We will endure disciplines for the sake of the gospel. We will labor and go without in obedience to Christ. Anchored in the hope of the gospel, we will seek wisdom from God, yielding and building towards a place of maturity and wellbeing for ourselves and our communities.

Displayed as Steadfastness

We resolve to persevere, by God's grace, in the face of trials and temptations. We will accept the responsibility of being strong in the Lord, holding faith and withstanding evil. We will hold course through adversity, championing shifts and corrections in our own hearts and behaviors and those of our communities.

A Problem and a Proposal

As we seek transformation to the good, being tethered to reality and aspiration has several challenges. These problems can exist within our person and our context. The first is personal, the interplay of Spirit and flesh in our transformation. The life the Spirit gives is strong and rich, enlivening our agency as we are called towards the Spirit's work. While we press toward transformation, we find another force tussling against our movement into Christ-reflecting life. Life from the Spirit and the drag of sin are at war within us. The writer of Romans expressed it like this:

> So I find this law at work: Although I want to do good, evil is right there with me. For in my inner being I delight in God's law; but I see another law at work in me waging war against the law of my mind and making me a prisoner of the law of sin at work within me (Rom 7:21–23).

I resonate with this personal and (so far) lifelong tussle between Spirit and flesh, as do many of the leaders and ministers I have had the privilege to walk alongside. Thankfully, the Spirit, empowering our new creation selves and communities, is irrepressibly at work sprouting the good in and among us.

There are also contextual forces which untether the leader from a grasp of reality. These include a human predilection to make overly positive or overly critical reports to those who have power in our context. Consider the first, the overly positive report. We honor (at its best), ingratiate (selfish and usually political), and self-preserve, giving versions of the truth that are designed to secure our position or to avoid harmful retaliations. Often benign and subconscious, it is a barrier to knowing the truth. People often map the veracity, actions, and motives of their peers and line managers, yet do not map these things for those who are not perceived as threats; the subordinate, the irrelevant, the powerless, the lesser-positioned "other." Pats on the back after a speech or effort, or words of affirmation, have their place as genuine encouragement. But care is required before appropriating them as truths whenever we hold power in relation to those giving them. In leadership contexts they are more abundantly offered, along with spin concerning situations and data, presented to soothe a leader's ego or anxiety. It is often an attempt to be positive and avoid harsh truth. This dynamic is complex, floating us further from knowing where we are, really. We should not believe our own press. If we want to know the truth, we are going to have to seek it out.

The cousin of a hyper-positive spin offered to leaders feels much darker to the receiver. This cousin is criticism, by others and self, which denies gifting and achievement and challenges a legitimate calling. Ronald Heifetz ably offers the analogy of leaders as lightning rods.[12] Standing visible as ready targets, we experience the attribution to ourselves of others' frustrations and anger. While at times we will have earned it, the phenomenon of receiving more than our earned portion is real. If we neglect weighing those critiques well against reality, they will embed and shape us, perhaps even "deform" us.

The hyper critique can also come from within. "Imposter Phenomenon" exists where a generally high-performing person expects that eventually, someone with gravitas will find out that they have arrived by accident into any fortunate position or achievement milestone. Redirecting achievement into such a framework has a complex etiology that is still being explored.[13] It appears that women more commonly wrestle with a sense of not being worthy of their position or achievement than their male peers do. While these women will energetically consider their worthiness and lean towards the "found wanting" verdict, the men appear to be more comfortable accepting their position and achievements as legitimately achieved. Women face extra challenges, regardless of their sense of worthiness, in the culture surrounding them. These gender differences are being explored further in organizational and positive psychology research and, while they are not a focus of this chapter, the knowledge emerging is helpful to those who work with this phenomenon either internally or in the

---

12. Heifetz, *Leadership*, 226.
13. Flora, *Fraud*, 75–76.

psyche of those around them.[14] Grounding in the truth of how hard work, ability, and good fortune have contributed to our achievement can reduce unjustified timidity. It seems a shame to crumble in self-doubt and lose sight of the rich deposits within us and our communities, and to needlessly shrink back from our full contribution.

At best these factors slow down our formation towards being and giving the most good in our lives. At their most insidious, they deform us.

Acknowledging the dangers that prevent us from knowing reality, we still encounter the merciful nudging of the Spirit towards living in the *imago Dei* and the likeness of Christ. The process is exactly that—a process.

Transformation as Process

Transformation has recognizable progressions over a lifetime, and in repetitive, shorter, more immediate cycles as we seek mastery of particular practices, vocational competencies, and presence. While different models each espouse a variety of taxonomies and named stages, learning theorists do recognize progressions.[15] If we are to become what we aspire to, then that progress will likely have a form found commonly in others.

Peter Senge, for example, proposed a simple taxonomy for progression in formation. In it, learning starts as a novice acquires the foundational practices, theory, and knowledge of their profession, and practices them until competence is achieved.[16] For example, we might take an incident or practice moment to supervision or to prayer, reflect on our practice, and plan new ways of practice for the future. Learning, doing, reflecting, or examining-learning, doing again, and so on.

Gradually (for Senge), principles are learned as one begins to understand the why, as well as know the how, of the discipline.[17] The ability to apply these principles is clumsy at first and begins in a simple range of circumstances. In time, however, new cognitive and linguistic capacity with the principles behind these practices are learned. This new capacity will later facilitate communication and problem-solving frameworks. As facility develops in practice, Senge's novice becomes principled. They act from new rules as old assumptions loosen, and are able to apply their craft in an

---

14. See, for example, Welbourne, "Double-Bind"; Correll and Simard, "Research"; and Snyder, "Abrasiveness."

15. For example, see Carroll, *Supervision*, 40–41.

16. Senge, *Fifth*, 383–84.

17. Senge, *Fifth*, 384.

increasing range of contexts, experimenting and problem solving the applications in a widening range of complexities.

They draw on their understanding of the principles, now as points of reference. Creative tension is harnessed, providing impetus to move from a well-examined reality to their vision of the matured self. What is this creative tension and where does it come from? Senge proposes that the juxtaposition of vision and current reality generates creative tension.[18] This tension is energy; a force to bring reality and vision closer together. When fostered, and not derailed by playing to unacknowledged emotional tension, it unlocks delayed gratification, the exercise of free will, and continued aspiration. Creative tension is renewed by continually clarifying what matters and tethering it to current reality. As such, it is deeply energizing for those who aspire to keep clarifying what they aspire to and grounding themselves in today's reality.

Learners devote their attention towards refining their practice and developing the ability to explain these practices and principles to others. This signals movement from being a novice to becoming a principled self.

With continued principled practice, Senge proposes that an essence develops, a personal mastery characterized by a "state of being that comes to be experienced naturally by individuals or groups with high levels of mastery in the discipline."[19] Operating from their values and increasingly unconscious assumptions, the mature practitioner displays core strength of practice, generating new ways and expressions of their craft. They adapt rules and speak in their own voice. I find Senge's schema useful as I companion leaders in formation, because it normalizes early clumsiness, the "gangly" stage of principled practice, and helps us to not label "being" as our state and stage prematurely. It encourages transformational change as a mature way of living.

Transforming Practices

Joseph Kotva argues that a "virtues" approach to formation should "Seek to identify and understand the habits, practices, images, and relationships that might help us to acquire or strengthen those virtues."[20] Kotva proposes that learning to pray, attending to friendship (community), and cultivating goodness in our soul in the routine and mundane aspects of life, will lead to the formation of a virtuous life. Moral trainers Kohlberg and Rath

18. Senge, *Fifth*, 132.
19. Senge, *Fifth*, 384.
20. Kotva, *Formation*, 290.

developed a framework for use in values formation in educational environments and argue a secular process to sustain the formation of values. Their guiding elements are alternatives, consequences, and freedom; their process involves choosing, prizing the chosen, and acting on the basis of what was chosen and prized.[21]

Christian leaders have adopted similar approaches which, without biblical, communal, and reflective practices, are threatened by a peculiar reworking of psychological approaches to moral formation, individualism, and cultural blindness.[22] Foundations and method that are not based in prayer, community, and theological reflection may be weakened by these appropriations and prove insufficient for an *imago Dei*, Christlikeness aspiration.[23] Richard Foster and Dallas Willard argue, quite differently, that we are formed into the image of Christ, a kingdom goodness, when we practice the spiritual disciplines.[24]

Prayer Habits

Kotva's first pillar for formation in virtue is prayer. If virtues are embedded into character through practices, then, for the Christian leader, the practice of prayer is chief among them. He suggests three key elements. First, it is to be a joint and cooperative activity as we learn to pray from others and with them. In so doing, we attend to God, the author of our aspiration, and the one who is truth. Second, the attentive and responsive nature of this form of prayer is more than simply petition for goods, blessings, or happiness. It is primarily adoration, worship, listening, and answering. When I have led clusters of leaders in prayer, I have encouraged requests for formation and resources to be offered by the one seeking them, aloud, and in the company of their peers. On our knees with others seeing, hearing, and joining in affirmation, and in combined request with us, it becomes a place of deep worship and a forming act of humility.[25] Third, I also encourage spiritual exercises such as *lectio divina* or the Ignatian practice of *examen* among my leaders as they offer a grounding counterweight to the pragmatism and politics that crowd a leader's soul. The resources are many, whether Benedictine, new monasticism, and so

---

21. Casement, *Values*, 131.

22. For more on Kohlberg and the formation question see Scholl, "Contributions," 364–72, and Hunter, "Psychotherapy," 5–17.

23. For a firm critique of the limits of this process see Casement, *Values*, 130–40.

24. Foster and Willard have written numerous works on this subject. For two introductory works, see the listings in the bibliography.

25. Kotva, *Formation*, 273–74.

on. We can examine them and appropriate them freely, searching and finding those that tether our hearts to honesty and aspiration.

Friendship Habits

Goodness is formed and tested in communities. The life of the community becomes a kind of greenhouse for character formation. While goodness must be original rather than cloned, it is still first learned by copying, individualizing, and internalizing within community.[26] Practices such as welcome and hospitality, sharing and support, are modeled and exchanged in community living. Goodness is modeled, experienced, and fostered in strong, honest, engaged friendships. Breaches and challenges to goodness are experienced together, allowing pathways of forgiveness, reconciliation, mercy, and justice to be tried and retried in the grounding reality of being seen consistently and deeply.

Aristotle was not the last human to see friendships as useful.[27] There is a need, however, to venture beyond his utilitarian ethos of friendship. Friends do change us, challenge us, help us, and encourage us. Finding and cultivating deep friendships that exist as rich subsets of our wider community is crucial for a leader. To be more deeply known, seen, loved, and forgiven by a few faithful souls is deeply grounding. Cultivating community life and deeper friendships that are not heavily curated as projections of role and image are valuable for grounding both the novice and the experienced.

Bible Habits

Regular, conscious deliberation on daily matters of life in the light of the Gospel narratives grounds us in kingdom vision. According to Spohn, we cultivate dispositions "anchored in the Gospel that guide the moral agent to recognize action which is consonant with the biblical exemplar. Those same dispositions provide the motivation to carry that discernment into action."[28]

Spohn's focus on the function of the biblical narratives in Christian formation is valuable. In the formation of goodness, the teachings of Jesus, particularly the Sermon on the Mount and the parables, are a primary resource. Of the parables, McKnight says,

---

26. Lawler, *Virtue*, 449.
27. Aristotle, *Nicomachean*, 220–47.
28. Spohn, *Saying*, 107.

> In those stories, the current world of Jesus—and ours too—is subverted. Our sense of power, our sense of passion, our sense of success, our sense of how to live—all these things are turned inside out and upside down ... A disciple is someone who is lost in the Kingdom dream of Jesus.[29]

Jesus' teachings generate a fresh vision of kingdom of God goodness.

What must also be said is that this deliberation takes place best in the company of a community of fellows who share a common commitment to learn the way of the kingdom together. Kotva wants them learned by regular application in the mundane things of life. They are to be practiced, become our principles, and eventually our posture as they are embedded in the ordinary affairs of each and every day. Grounding requires prominent attention to theological, gospel-centered reflection on the daily matters of life in order to nurture the virtues and values that shaped the life and ministry of Jesus, whose likeness is our primary aspiration.

Intentional Relating Habits

The life of faith and its offspring, the formation of reproductive faith in others, is core to Christian formation. The requirements of leadership also include difficult social demands, loud consumer appetites, and attention to both internal and external accountabilities in governance and professional practice. The systemic complexity of leadership practice is profound, and discerning what is good is not always easy.[30] Christian Scharen therefore calls for rigorous inquiry to be developed as we engage this very human task of faithful service, a faith lived out in our practices.

> Vitality of Christian faith today does not—and does—depend on us ... How do we understand the complexity of this beautiful and broken world? My argument is that the task of understanding requires a careful, disciplined craft for inquiry—a craft I call fieldwork in theology—if one seeks both to claim knowledge of divine action and to discern an appropriate response.[31]

Where and how can Scharen's craft of inquiry take place? Clear, early expressions of structures and accountabilities, and of relational development of emerging leaders, occur in the New Testament. Jesus' dialogues include reference to religious and governmental responsibilities and their

---

29. McKnight, *Full*, 57-58.
30. Headley, *Systems*, 1–8.
31. Scharen, *Fieldwork*, 5.

relation to the spiritual life as do the story of the emerging church and the letters.[32] We have records of intentional development and accountability structures and relationships in ministry through eras and across cultures and streams of spirituality.[33]

While the New Testament does not use the term specifically, the craft of supervision has emerged as a wonderfully companionate and rigorous relationship intended for formation of best practice and best selves. It is grounded in reflection on practice and seeks to develop the practitioner from novice to master. It provides a continuity of humble reflection on practice—a disciplined craft of inquiry. It is joint, relational, and firmly grounded in what is actually happening, as well as what may be desired or required for the good of others.[34] Leach and Paterson root the practice in discipleship, defined as "a relationship between two or more disciples who meet to consider the ministry of one or more of them in an intentional and disciplined way."[35] Pyle and Seals define it simply as "a process of integrating self-understanding, cognitive data, and practical skills in the practice of ministry."[36] Beyond this simplicity, Snorton points to transformational learning theory, personality understandings that embrace cultural bridging, and a theology rooted in the liberation of individuals and communities as vital for supervision to meet the rigor of our complex leadership landscape.[37]

Supervisory conversations foster awareness of self, especially of one's emotional state in practice, which is key to the change in meaning structures. Critical theological reflection is engaged as essential to transformative learning. It is a practice designed for the relentless pursuit of tethering reality and vision together. The longer contractual nature of supervision offers opportunity for deep change to belief structures and ways of behaving.

Conclusion

> I don't know any profession in which it is quite as easy to fake it as in ours. People need to be reassured that someone is in touch

---

32. See, for example, Matt 18:15–18 and 20:20–28, where Jesus instructs his disciples concerning norms for community life among the disciples, or Paul's instructions to Timothy in 2 Tim 2:2. See also Lewis, *Mentoring*, 42–67.

33. An outstanding example of such structures is seen in the catechetical practices of the ancient church. See Kreider, *Patient*, 133–84 for an overview and discussion of these practices.

34. Carroll, *Supervision*, 44.

35. Paterson and Leach, *Pastoral*, 1.

36. Pyle and Seals, *Experiencing*, 141.

37. Snorton, *Looking*, 122.

with the ultimate things. If we provide a bare bones outline of pretense, they take it as the real thing and run with it, imputing to us clean hands and pure hearts.[38]

Christian leadership is fraught with temptation to pretense, to a theatrical performance of a clerical version of a self, and to ambiguity regarding the nature of servanthood. We need help to "arrest the drift, drawing us back to our most noble intentions, our deepest connection with God, our most perceptive insights, our most gracious dealings with others and our most Spirit-filled service."[39]

Grounding our notions of what is a worthy vision for ourselves and our communities, of the truly good, is our calling to reflect the *imago Dei* and becoming like Jesus Christ. We set out to ground ourselves in a truth-rich view of reality. The practices of prayer, friendship, Bible reading, and supervision are key formative habits. As strong ropes they tether us between reality and our aspirational future. They harness the tension this produces and tie us to the impetus of the Spirit. We typically progress in our transformation through early clumsy practice, into a principled way of being, and hopefully towards a posture of rest in the grace of goodness.

I therefore invite us, as leaders, to move deliberately towards being those who can hear the truth when it is inconvenient and to recognize falsehood. That we avoid being drawn into deception and obfuscation, both overconfident and self-deprecating. That we would be grounded leaders who actively tether reality to our vision of what might be. And that a vision of what might be is grounded in a framework of the good news of justice and love, and springing from the work of the Spirit enlivening the *imago Dei* and drawing us to be like Christ.

Bibliography

Aristotle. *The Nicomachean Ethics*. Oxford World's Classics. Oxford: Oxford University Press, 1980.
Boff, Leonardo. *Holy Trinity, Perfect Community*. New York: Orbis, 2000.
Cahill, Lisa Sowle. "Christian Character, Biblical Community, and Human Values." In *Character and Scripture: Moral Formation, Community, and Biblical Interpretation*, edited by William P. Brown, 3–17. Grand Rapids, MI: Eerdmans, 2002.
Carroll, Michael. "Supervision and Transformational Learning." *Psychotherapy in Australia* 14.3 (2008) 38–45.
Casement, W. "Values Clarification, Kohlberg and Choosing." *Counseling and Values* 27.3 (1983) 130-140.

38. Peterson, *Working*, 6.
39. Lewis, *Mentoring*, 11.

Correll, Shelley J., and Caroline Simard. "Research: Vague Feedback is Holding Women Back." *Harvard Business Review*, April 29, 2016. https://hbr.org/2016/04/research-vague-feedback-is-holding-women-back.

Dahlsgaard, Katherine, Christopher Peterson, and Martin E. P. Seligman. "Shared Virtue: The Convergence of Valued Human Strengths Across Culture and History." *Review of General Psychology* 9.3 (2005) 203–13.

Flora, Carlin. "The Fraud Who Isn't." *Psychology Today* 49.6 (2016) 70–88.

Foster, Richard J. *Celebrating the Disciplines: The Path to Spiritual Growth*. San Francisco: Harper, 2002.

Harrington, Daniel J., and James F. Keenan. *Jesus and Virtue Ethics: Building Bridges Between New Testament Studies and Moral Theology*. Lanham, MD: Sheed & Ward, 2002.

Hauerwas, Stanley. "Virtue." In *Readings in Christian Ethics Volume 1: Theory and Method*, edited by Robert V. Rakestraw and David K. Clark, 251–56. Grand Rapids, MI: Baker, 1994.

Headley, Tom. "A Systems and Developmental Perspective on the Seasons of Pastoral Life and Ministry." *Psalm* (2007) 1–8.

Heifetz, Ronald A. *Leadership without Easy Answers*. Cambridge: Harvard University Press, 1994.

Holmes, Arthur Frank. *Ethics: Approaching Moral Decisions*. 2nd edition. Contours of Christian Philosophy. Downers Grove, IL: IVP Academic, 2007.

Hunter, James D. "When Psychotherapy Replaces Religion." *National Affairs; The Public Interest* 43 (2000) 5–17.

Kotva, Joseph J. Jr. "The Formation of Pastors, Parishioners, and Problems: A Virtue Reframing of Clergy Ethics." *Annual of the Society of Christian Ethics* 17 (1997) 271–90.

Kreider, Alan. *The Patient Ferment of the Early Church: The Improbable Rise of Christianity in the Roman Empire*. Grand Rapids, MI: Baker Academic, 2016.

Lawler, Michael G., and Todd A. Salzman. "Virtue Ethics: Natural and Christian." *Theological Studies* 74.2 (2013) 442–73.

Lewis, Rick. *Mentoring Matters*. Oxford: Monarch, 2009.

McKnight, Scot. "The Full Disciple." *Neue* (2011) 56–58.

Olsen, David C., and William M. Grosch. "Clergy Burnout: A Self-Psychology and Systems Perspective." *Journal of Pastoral Care* 45.3 (1991) 297–304.

Paterson, Michael, and Jane Leach. *Pastoral Supervision*. London: SCM, 2010.

Peterson, Eugene. *Working the Angles: The Shape of Pastoral Integrity*. Grand Rapids, MI: Eerdmans, 1997.

Pohl, Christine D. "Recovering Kindness: An Urgent Virtue in a Ruthless World." *Christian Century* 129.22 (2012) 10–11.

Pyle, William T., and Mary Alice Seals. *Experiencing Ministry Supervision: A Field Based Approach*. Nashville: Broadman and Holman, 1995.

Scharen, Christian. *Fieldwork in Theology: Exploring the Social Context of God's Work in the World*. Grand Rapids, MI: Baker Academic, 2015.

Scholl, Doug. "The Contributions of Lawrence Kohlberg to Religious and Moral Education." *Religious Education* 66.5 (1971) 364–72.

Senge, Peter M. *The Fifth Discipline: The Art and Practice of the Learning Organization*. London: Random, 2006.

Snorton, T. "Looking Toward the Future of Pastoral Supervision." In *Courageous Conversations: The Teaching and Learning of Pastoral Supervision*, edited by William R. DeLong, 119–27. Langham: University Press of America, 2010.

Snyder, Kieran. "The Abrasiveness Trap: High-Achieving Men and Women are Described Differently in Reviews." *Fortune* blog, August 26, 2014. https://fortune.com/2014/08/26/performance-review-gender-bias/

Spohn, William C. *What are They Saying about Scripture and Ethics?* Revised and expanded edition. New York: Paulist, 1995.

Stassen, Glen H., and David P. Gushee. *Kingdom Ethics: Following Jesus in Contemporary Context*. Downers Grove, IL: InterVarsity, 2003.

Welbourne, Theresa. "The Double-Bind Dilemma for Women in Leadership: Damned If You Do, Doomed If You Don't." Catalyst research paper, 2007. https://www.catalyst.org/wp-content/uploads/2019/01/The_Double_Bind_Dilemma_for_Women_in_Leadership_Damned_if_You_Do_Doomed_if_You_Dont.pdf.

Willard, Dallas. *The Spirit of the Disciplines: Understanding How God Changes Lives*. San Francisco: HarperCollins, 1988.

19

Grandmothers of Intention

Women in Australian Theological Academia (1883–2003)

JILL FIRTH

CHARLENE JIN LEE INVITES womanist scholars to inscribe "mothers and grandmothers, names and geography, earthly details and painful lament" into their scholarly work.[1] Many of us may not be womanist theologians, but we can benefit from becoming more aware of how our scholarship is grounded in our gender, ethnicity, time, and place, and can build on the heritage of our grandmothers, mothers, and sisters in Australian theological scholarship.[2] Mary Andrews, Eva Burrows, and Barbara Darling are household names to some Christians, but the wider tradition of women's theological scholarship in Australia is little known to many of us. Most can name only a few Australian women who have preceded us, and yet we are surrounded by "a great cloud of witnesses" of women who studied at home, in their community, or in missionary colleges, giving their lives in daily service to church, the community, the needy, or in foreign fields, women who were admitted to the theological colleges and obtained diplomas and degrees, and women who taught in theological colleges or who wrote articles and books.

1. Lee, "I Come from a Place," 34.
2. Paris, "Katie Cannon," 18.

There is a growing body of research on women in ministry and leadership in Australia, but women's theological study has been less investigated. This chapter began as a few paragraphs about the first Australian women theological students and lecturers, originally destined for the introduction to this book, but so many were identified that a separate chapter was needed. The data were obtained mainly through crowd sourcing, and are necessarily incomplete.[3] Around one hundred women are included in this chapter, their information gleaned from denominational and institutional histories, dictionary articles, college records, newspaper clippings, and some specialized studies on women's history. This introduction is neither systematic nor comprehensive, but rather a collection of snapshots in a gallery of women's theological scholarship in Australia. It is a preliminary sketch that can be expanded in future writing to include many other significant women and institutions, and women's theological publications. In some cases, we only have names, and more detailed investigations of these women's lives and contributions would be welcome.

The women presented here are from every state of Australia, and the Northern Territory.[4] The colleges include Anglican, Baptist, Congregational (later in the Uniting Church), nondenominational or interdenominational, Pentecostal, and Salvation Army.[5] The period 1883–2003 begins with the opening of the Salvation Army College in Melbourne and concludes with the appointment of Dawn Cardona as first Indigenous woman Principal of Nungalinya College in Darwin.

We will firstly consider Australian women studying theology, and then turn to meet some lecturers.

---

3. Thank you to the many people who contributed names and information for this chapter. We owe many of the early names to Megan Powell du Toit, who researched the ACT archives for students in ThA, ThL and ThSchol. Others who contributed names, information, or leads included: Monica O'Neil, Michael O'Neil, Jacqui Grey, Alanna Nobbs, Lyn Kidson, Janet Paterson, Glen O'Brien, Murray Seiffert, Charles Sherlock, Anthony Brammall, Anthea McCall, Len Firth, Anne Kennedy, Brooke Prentis, Naomi Wolfe, Louise Gosbell, Kara Martin, Rosalind Gooden, Kylie Brown, Joanna Cruickshank, Jean Thompson, Bronwen Speedie, Lynne Parsons, and Erin Sessions. Thanks also to others unnamed but not unappreciated.

4. A few references to New Zealand are also included.

5. Unfortunately, I did not gain a response about some institutions I would have liked to include. Future research could also include, e.g., Catholic and Orthodox scholars.

Women Studying Theology

In earlier years, women's theological education in Australia often took place outside the theological colleges in homes or in the community, in missionary training centers, or in special women's departments. Many Indigenous and non-Indigenous women did not have access to formal training, including the gifted Aboriginal leader, linguist, and missionary, Angelina Noble (1879–1964).[6] Angelina Noble was born in Queensland but kidnapped as a young girl by a white stockman. She was rescued by police in Cairns, and in 1902 married James Noble, an Aboriginal leader born in the Gulf Country in Queensland, near Normanton. Together, they worked in ministry and mission at Yarrabah in Queensland, Roper River in the Northern Territory, Forrest River in Western Australia, and Palm Island in Queensland. Angelina spoke over five Aboriginal languages, which she used in evangelism and as a translator. After James Noble's death in 1941, Angelina continued in ministry for a further twenty-three years at Yarrabah.[7]

The 1860s saw itinerant women preachers such as the "well read" Serena Thorne Lake,[8] who emigrated from the U.K. to Queensland in 1865 to establish a Methodist Connexion, and later preached in the Adelaide Town Hall, filling it to its capacity of 1500 during her three-week mission.[9]

Marion MacFarlane was ordained as an Anglican deaconess in Sydney in 1884.[10] I am not sure how she received her training, as this was before deaconess training was established in Sydney or Melbourne.

The chronology of women's access to formal theological education in Australia can be compared with women's admission to universities. The first woman to take an Australian university degree was Bella Guerin, with an Arts degree in 1883 from the University of Melbourne, then in 1885, Edith Emily Dornwell graduated from Adelaide University in science, and Isola Florence Thompson and Mary Elizabeth Brown graduated from the University of Sydney.[11] Australia followed the U.S.A., where degrees were granted to women by the 1850s,[12] Canada, where Grace Annie Lockhart received a BSc in 1875,[13] New Zealand, where Kate Edger was awarded

---

6. Kociumbas, "Noble, Angelina."
7. Kuan, "James and Angelina Noble," 161–75.
8. Jones, "Lake, Serena."
9. O'Brien, "Christian Church Workers."
10. O'Brien, "Christian Church Workers."
11. Alison Mackinnon, "Early Graduates"
12. Harwarth, DeBra, and Malin, *Women's Colleges*, 3–4.
13. Reid, "Grace Annie Lockhart."

a BA in 1877,[14] and the U.K. where the first degrees for women were in 1878.[15] Women graduating with research degrees became more common in Australian universities in the 1980s.[16]

Aboriginal women were even later in gaining access to university study. The first Aboriginal person to graduate from an Australian university was Margaret Williams-Weir, a Bundjalung woman, who in 1959 graduated from the University of Melbourne with a diploma in Physical Education. She later achieved a BEd, Masters, and PhD. Margaret Valadian was the first Aboriginal person to graduate with a bachelor's degree. She received a Bachelor of Social Studies from the University of Queensland in 1966, and went on to postgraduate studies.[17]

From 1892, women were trained for missionary service in centers such as the Missionary Training House in Kew established by Dr. and Mrs. Warren, Angas College in Adelaide,[18] Marsden House in Sydney, and St. Hilda's Women's Training Home in Fitzroy (1902–1963).[19] Eliza Hassell (1834–1917), granddaughter of Samuel Marsden, established the Marsden Training Home for Missionaries in Ashfield in 1893. Her first student, her niece Amy Isabel Oxley, became a missionary to China in 1896.[20] Charlotte Jessie Shoobridge trained at St. Hilda's. Having been newly ordained as Tasmania's only Anglican deaconess, from 1893 she led the work at the Mission House in Launceston. The Mission House was a refuge for unemployed servant girls, "fallen" girls, and battered wives, as well as offering evangelistic activities, a sewing class, and a boy's class.[21] Minnie and Eliza Clark received four months' training at St. Hilda's (Minnie in 1904 and Eliza in 1906), before serving for forty years in China.[22] The sisters had already completed several years' training as Sunday School teachers, and in 1898 were placed equal first in the Melbourne Diocese's Sunday School teachers' exams.[23]

From the late 1890s, women could enroll for a lay certificate (Associate in Theology) with the newly established Australian College of

---

14. "Kate Edger."
15. Carter, "First Women."
16. Mackinnon, "Early Graduates."
17. Cromb, "5 Indigenous women who didn't get the credit."
18. Parker, *Top of the Mount*, 6.
19. Kuan, *Foundations*, 212. St. Hilda's was merged into St. Andrew's Hall after 1963.
20. Sherlock, *Anglicans Remember*, 11–12. Marsden House later became part of the work of the Deaconess Institute in Newtown.
21. Tkaczuk, "Mission House"
22. Kuan, *Foundations*, 194.
23. Kuan, *Foundations*, 193.

Theology.[24] Women approved by their Anglican diocese studied remotely for ThA exams from 1898.[25] In the first five years after the opening of the ACT (1898–1903), twelve women received the ThA. One of the earliest was Florence Emily Green, Armidale (Grafton Diocese, 1898), who graduated with first class honors.[26] Florence Green was one of the first women to sign the matriculation register at the University of Melbourne, but she did not graduate. A sister of Bishop Arthur Green, she was headmistress of Trinity Church High School until 1889, and in 1895 she was first headmistress of the New England Girls' School, later acting as caretaker headmistress of Firbank Church of England Girls' Grammar School.

Other early ThA graduates included three Tasmanians: Laetitia Weatherhead and Winifred Emily Weatherhead, Launceston (Tasmanian Diocese, 1900),[27] and Charlotte Tarleton, Longford (Tasmanian Diocese, 1901).[28] Victorian women in this period were Mary A. Holloway, Hawthorn (Melbourne Diocese, 1898), Eleanor Eddington, Ballarat (Ballarat Diocese, 1901), and Flora Emerson, Kilmore (Melbourne Diocese, 1901). There were two women ThAs from South Australia, Annie Collins and Mabel Hornabrook, Adelaide (Adelaide Diocese, 1902), and three from NSW, Winifred Docker, Woollahra (Sydney Diocese, 1899), Lydia Frances Davison, Clarence (Grafton Diocese, 1900), and Emily C. F. Ford, Haymarket (Sydney Diocese, 1903).[29] The ACT holds a mark book from 1906, and in the first recorded results for the ThA, the class was topped by Emily Olive Burvill, Prahran (Melbourne Diocese, 1906).[30]

The ThL (Licentiate in Theology) was a basic qualification for men's Anglican ordination, with compulsory Greek, taught over two years with external examinations. Women could sit the exams, but could not be ordained in the early years. In the first five years of women graduating (1923–1927), eight women graduated from the ACT with the ThL, including Dorothy Edna Genders MBE (Deaconess House, Sydney, 1925). Dorothy Genders served at St. John's Mission House at Launceston from 1912–1917, with Charlotte

24. An outline of these older ACT awards can be found in Treloar, "Three (or Four) Identities," 103–7.

25. Notes on the ACT records of minister's names suggest that some supervised students' exams in their parish.

26. Grose and Robin. "Green, Florence Emily."

27. Laetitia Weatherhead was entered then withdrawn in a later year, so there is a question mark over her graduation, though she is in the ACT master list for 1900.

28. Charlotte Tarleton is not on the ACT master list—probably an oversight.

29. Australian College of Theology Records.

30. Australian College of Theology Records. Emily Olive Burvill was daughter of William Burvill, the headmaster of Daylesford Grammar; see "Burvill."

Shoobridge,[31] before moving to Sydney in 1917 to study at Deaconess House and Moore Theological College. In 1929, "Sister Dorothy" moved to Perth, where she trained aspiring deaconesses as well as founding a refuge for deserted women and children, battered wives and prostitutes, and visiting hospitals, jails and courts. She is commemorated by the Genders Library at Meath House, the Genders room at Wollaston College, Mount Claremont, and the Dorothy Genders Retirement Village, Mosman Park.[32]

Other early ThL graduates were Violet Dennis (Trinity College, Melbourne, 1923), Jennifer Innes, (St. John, Morpeth, 1923), Hilda Burden (St. Francis College, Adelaide, 1924), Adrienne Novice and Patricia Novice (Tasmanian Diocese, 1926), Sadie Ayre (Deaconess House, 1927), and Frances Winston (Melbourne Diocese, 1927).[33] When the BTh replaced the ThL, the first women to graduate were Eleanor Godman, Marilyn Haycock, Sandra Luxford, and Lynne Robertson from BCV (1978, now MST), Joan Gray from Moore College (1978); and Catherine Clark and Valerie Stilwell from Ridley College (1978).[34]

The first woman to graduate from the ACT with the ThSchol (Scholar in Theology) was Winifred Merritt (Ballarat Diocese) in 1956. In the previous year, Merritt was awarded the Frank and Elizabeth Cash Essay Prize, under the set topic, "The Relation of the Church to the Kingdom of God." She had received her ThL in 1947 as a candidate from Ballarat Diocese.[35] The ACT MTh was developed as a research award in 1975, and the first woman to graduate was Sheila Pritchard (BCNZ, 1982).[36] The introduction of research awards helped to foster a research culture within the ACT.[37]

The Melbourne Salvation Army College was established in 1883, and the Sydney College in 1921. Mary Anderson graduated from the Melbourne Training College in 1901, and went on to give outstanding service to women in the police courts. Marjorie Scobie entered the Melbourne Training College in 1932. After distinguished war service as a nurse, she received a scholarship to study for a Diploma at the Army's International College in London

31. Tkaczuk, "Mission House."
32. Birman, "Genders, Dorothy Edna."
33. Australian College of Theology Records.
34. The MCD (now UD) replaced their LTh with the BTheol in 1973, and the ACT BTh was inaugurated in 1975. Information from Charles Sherlock.
35. "ACT Winifred Merritt Fellowships."
36. Australian College of Theology Records.
37. Treloar, "Three (or Four) Identities," 108–9. From the records of the Australian College of Theology, the ACT's MTh was first awarded in 1977; the ThD from 1965, but the second ThD wasn't until 1980; the DMin was awarded since 2004; PhD awarded since 2015.

in 1956. Eva Burrows, who in 1986 became General of the Salvation Army, earned her BA at Queensland University (1950), and completed postgraduate studies at London University. She was Principal at the International College in London (1970–1975).[38]

Morling Theological College (the Baptist Theological College of NSW) opened in 1916, with ten male students in a ministerial stream of three to four years' study.[39] In 1918, Effie Steed graduated after one year of study and subsequently became a missionary to India. Effie Steed was Morling's first female graduate, and was later honored by having the women's block at Morling named after her.[40] According to historian Graeme Chatfield, Effie's father, Rev. D. Steed, "was a member of the NSW Baptist Theological College Board from its commencement in 1916, and special concession was made to allow his daughter to attend the college... The college charter was amended in 1918 to allow for training of Foreign Mission candidates."[41]

Winifred Kiek was the first woman to graduate from the Melbourne College of Divinity (MCD, now University of Divinity), receiving the BD in 1923.[42] She was the first woman to be ordained in the Christian ministry in Australia (June 13, 1927, in South Australia) to the Congregational Union of Australia (now in the Uniting Church in Australia).[43] She had earned a BA from the University of Manchester (1907), winning the university prize for logic, before emigrating to Australia with her husband and three children. She later graduated with an MA in Philosophy from the University of Adelaide (1929).[44] Kiek was later a lecturer at Parkin College, and was a well-known preacher and public speaker and an advocate for women's publishing.[45]

The Sydney Missionary and Bible College (SMBC) Women's Department opened in 1928, under the oversight of Mrs. F. D. Jackson. The first woman to enroll was Miss Morris, who "soon left to get married, and for a couple of months our faith was tested, in that no other students joined us."[46] Elizabeth Morris and Frances Abbot were the first women to graduate,

---

38. "Notable Salvos."

39. Kent, "Responding in Faith." The curriculum of the ministerial training is outlined in Chatfield, "Approaches," especially pages 52–54.

40. Robb and Chatfield, "Morling College," 4.

41. Author email correspondence with Graeme Chatfield, March 25, 2020.

42. Phillips, "Kiek, Winifred."

43. Lee, "Kiek, Winifred."

44. Phillips, "Kiek, Winifred."

45. Pitman, *Prophets and Priests*, 253.

46. Author email correspondence with Anthony Brammall, March 19, 2020.

with a two-year diploma, in November 1928. Graduates in 1930 included Doris Floate, Dorothy Kirton, Doris Wheat, Phyllis Bishop, Amy Thomson, Margaret Littlejohn, and Jean Cawley.[47] Prior to the opening of the women's campus accommodation, some women had studied by distance.

Lillian Ethel Livingstone (Hayman, 1914–2002) "outshone most of the men at the United Faculty in her academic work," though, due to her gender, she missed out on residential college experience at the Camden Theological College in Glebe (now UTC).[48] She completed a four-year theological program after graduating with a BA from the University of Sydney.[49] She was ordained in 1943 in the Congregational Church in Sydney.[50]

The first women to receive a ThL from Ridley College in Melbourne were Hebe May Martin and Violet Mills (1947), Hilda Kent (1948), Frances Northrop (1950), Marjorie McGregor (1959), Lucy Murray (1960), Mary Walker (1963), Shirley Bagster (1964), and Norma Nickson (1971).[51]

Brisbane School of Theology (formerly QBI) opened in 1943, and the first female student was Doris Wedd (née Ovens), who graduated in 1949. Doris and Reg Wedd were appointed as caretakers at a difficult time in the college's history in 1949.[52] Betty Christie (Black) entered QBI in 1953, completing her studies with excellent grades in 1955. She studied linguistics with SIL, then Arabic in the Sudan. With her husband, Keith, she translated Scripture in the Nuba Moro language and prepared reading primers, trained teachers, and worked in literacy. She later learned French and the Mesme language, and wrote a grammar of the Kanure language.[53]

Alphacrucis College was originally named Commonwealth Bible College (1948–1993), then became Southern Cross College (1993–2009), and AC's current title dates from 2009.[54] Prior to the opening of CBC in 1948, Pentecostal students studied in other colleges, such as the Sydney Bible Training Institute (1914–1957), which had been established for non-ministerial students in 1914.[55] In 1944, Pentecostal students Vena and Esther Wong Yen, daughters of missionary Mary Yeung, were accepted at

---

47. Brammall, *Out of Darkness*, 84–85.
48. Pitman, *Prophets and Priests*, 244.
49. Pitman, *Prophets and Priests*, 244, 389.
50. Pitman, *Prophets and Priests*, 244.
51. Australian College of Theology Records.
52. Parker, *Top of the Mount*, 29.
53. "Betty Black."
54. "AC History."
55. Robb and Chatfield, "Morling College."

SBTI, and in 1947, also Merle Smith and Joan Selby from Queensland.[56] CBC opened in Melbourne in 1948, offering a three-year course of biblical studies.[57] In the inaugural class of 1948, there were fifty-one students, including thirty-four men and seventeen women.[58] CBC opened a campus in Queensland in 1948, and students in 1949 included Indigenous woman Mary Edwards from Innisfail.[59]

Aboriginal Bishop Arthur Malcolm's wife, Colleen, graduated as a Church Army Officer, probably from the Church Army College near Newcastle, where Arthur Malcolm graduated in 1952. They ministered at Yarrabah in Queensland, where there was a powerful revival.[60]

Aunty Jean Phillips and Aunty Erica Kyle were Aboriginal students of the AIM (Aborigines Inland Mission) Bible Training Institute, Singleton, in the Hunter Valley, in 1954.[61] Miss Jean Phillips graduated in 1955 and arrived at Perch Creek to help in the spiritual work at Woorabinda in Queensland on May 16, 1956. Over one hundred adults and children attended the welcome picnic.[62] Aunty Jean Phillips was in ministry with the AIM (Aborigines Inland Mission, renamed Australian Indigenous Ministries in 1998), and has served many Aboriginal communities.[63] She was a deaconess in the Uniting Church, and Aunty Erica Kyle worked on Palm Island.[64] Aunty Jean Phillips and Aunty Erica Kyle were founders of Wontulp-Bi-Buya College in Cairns, where many Aboriginal students have studied. Aunty Jean was a founder of many Aboriginal Christian movements and organizations, including the Aboriginal Evangelical Fellowship, the UAICC, and the Grasstree Gathering, established in 2012. Aunty Jean has educated many non-Indigenous ministers and pastors of many denominations in her over sixty years of ministry which continues today. Aunty Jean is encouraging the next generation of Aboriginal and Torres Strait Islander Christian Leaders, many of them women, to undertake theological studies and actively participate in ministry.[65]

56. Austin, *Our College*, 32.
57. *Austin, Our College*, 55.
58. Austin, *Our College*, 41–42.
59. Austin, *Our College*, 52.
60. Ganter, *The Contest for Aboriginal Souls*, 217 n. 29.
61. Photo, *Australian Evangel* 20.9.
62. Press Cutting, *Woorabinda News*, 1956, see also, Photo *Australian Evangel* 30.9.
63. "Aunty Jean Phillips."
64. "Aboriginal Protestors."
65. Uniting Aboriginal and Islander Christian Congress. Information from Brooke Prentis. Also, see "Empowering," and Phillips, "Interview."

Vose Seminary (formerly Baptist Theological College of WA) opened in 1963 with six male students. Two women "private students" joined them in the next couple of years, but they were not on the ordination path.[66] Ruth Snell (Sampson) held a BA (Hons) and had been tutoring in linguistics and anthropology at UWA and Curtin. She attended as an audit student at BTCWA in 1970, while enrolled for the Melbourne BD. She married and transferred to Whitley College in Melbourne, where she also audited, while completing her BD. Ruth was the first woman to become a Senior Pastor in a Baptist church in Australia when she was appointed to Kew Baptist (1995–1999).[67]

Betty Roberts and Dinah Garadji were early students at Nungalinya College, which opened in Darwin as a joint Anglican and Catholic project in 1973 (the Uniting Church later joined). Betty and Dinah, sisters from Ngukurr, began their residential study at Nungalinya in 1979. In 1980, they took a full-time course in English as a second language, and they completed a Diploma in Theology over the next three years. They were ordained as the first Anglican Aboriginal deaconesses in 1984.[68] Nancy Dick, another Nungalinya graduate, was the first Aboriginal woman in Australia to be ordained as an Anglican deacon, in 1987, at Kowanyama in Queensland.[69] Yulki Nunggumajbarr from Numbulwar, who also trained at Nungalinya, was the first Aboriginal woman to be ordained as an Anglican priest in the Northern Territory, in 2009.[70]

Women as Theological Lecturers

From 1930, Winifred Kiek (née Jackson) lectured at Parkin Congregational College in Adelaide (now UCLT), where her husband was Principal. She had graduated from the MCD (now University of Divinity) in 1923.[71]

The inaugural 1948 staff of Alphacrucis College, originally Commonwealth Bible College (1948–1993), included Principal Frank Sturgeon, Assistant Principal Inez Sturgeon, who taught classes such as homiletics and church history, Mildred Thompson, who taught music and child

---

66. Chidgzey, "Fifty Years," 104–5.
67. Siggins, "Experience of Women," 124–27.
68. Seiffert, *Gumbuli*, 263.
69. Seiffert, *Gumbuli*, 269.
70. Seiffert, *Gumbuli*, 269.
71. "Kiek, Winifred," *The Australian Women's Register*. See above for Kiek's academic and ministry record.

evangelism, Joyce Jolly, who taught English, Alice Wright, the Registrar, and visiting lecturers.[72]

Hilda May Abba (née Blackham) was the first woman in Australia to be ordained as a theological lecturer, in 1951.[73] She held a BA (Hons) in History (Sheffield, 1943) and a BD (MCD, now UD, 1951). From 1948, she was a tutor at the Camden Theological College at Glebe (now UCA),[74] where her husband was the warden,[75] and she was a lecturer in Church History in the UFT (now UD) at St. Andrew's College, University of Sydney, from 1952. Hilda May Abba was a member of the Society for Old Testament Study (UK) and the Fellowship for Biblical Studies (Australia).[76]

Mary Andrews became the Principal of the Anglican Deaconess Training College in Sydney (1952–1975) and a leader in women's ministry and training in Sydney and beyond.[77] She completed a two-year diploma at SMBC in 1936, and then sailed with the Church Missionary Society for China in late 1938, returning in 1951. "The main emphases at SMBC were the primary importance of prayer and the unity of Christians from different denominational backgrounds. For Mary, prayer and interdenominationalism would be paramount throughout her life. Prayer was at the core of Mary's being."[78] The Deaconess Training College in Sydney, which was opened in 1891, was renamed in her honor after her death in 1996.[79]

The first Macquarie University woman staff member specifically in the area of Early Christian and Jewish studies was Judith Lieu, who established the MA program in the 1960s. Alanna Nobbs has taught and researched in the area since her appointment in 1970. Ros Kearsley also taught and still researches in the area. The first MA in Early Christian and Jewish studies was Deslee Campbell, who went on to complete a PhD in Sydney. The first woman PhD in the area was probably Erica Mathieson, whose book on Christian women in the papyri was published in 2016.[80]

---

72. Austin, *Our College*, 43.
73. "Blackham, Hilda May."
74. "Abba, Hilda May."
75. "Woman Cleric."
76. "Abba, Hilda May."
77. Brammall, *Out of Darkness*, 281–89.
78. Margaret Yarwood Lamb, *Going it Alone: Mary Andrews--Missionary to China 1938 to 1951* (Sydney South: Aquila, 1995), 26–27, quoted in Brammall, *Out of Darkness*, 102.
79. "About Mary Andrews."
80. Author email correspondence with Alanna Nobbs, April 3, 2020.

Miss Rosemary Skilton, who graduated as Dux of QBI (later BST) in 1971, was appointed with some lecturing duties in 1971,[81] and as Women's Superintendent (1972–1974). Miss Denise Scott was a tutor (1970–1976) as well as Dean of Women (1972–1976).[82]

Helena Stretton was the first woman to be appointed to faculty at BCNZ (later Laidlaw College) in 1972, where she was Student Dean and Lecturer in Christian Education (1972–2005), and English Language Teacher in the School of English Language Studies (1998–2005). Helena Stretton held a BSc (University of Adelaide, 1960), a Dip Ed (University of Adelaide, 1965), and PhD in Agricultural Science (University of Adelaide, 1973). She completed an LTh at BCNZ (1969) and a Dip RE through the MCD (1966–1967).[83]

Barbara Darling was the first woman on tenured faculty at Ridley, where she served for fourteen years. She held a BA and a Diploma in Education from the University of Sydney, an MA from the University of Melbourne, and a ThL with first class honors from Ridley College (1977).[84] She worked as a high school teacher and librarian in Sydney, then moved to Melbourne in 1975 to study under Leon Morris at Ridley College. After her ThL graduation, she accepted some short-term lecturing, which led into a faculty position.[85] She was ordained deacon in 1986, priest in 1992, and was consecrated as the second Anglican woman bishop in Australia in 2008.[86]

Robin Payne was on faculty at Ridley College lecturing in Old Testament (1984–1996) and then at BCQ (now Brisbane School of Theology) in 2003–2004. Robin held an MA (University of Sydney, 1967), Dip Ed (University of Sydney, 1968), BD (University of London, 1976), Dip RE (MCD, 1979), MTh (ACT, 1986), and DMin (Fuller, 2001). She was ordained as deacon in 1987 and priest in 1992. From 2005, she has been a theological lecturer in Central Asia.

Sylvia Collison was Acting Principal at BCSA (1989–1990), then Vice-Principal (1991–1995). She had been appointed Lecturer/Director of Studies (1981–1989), following Cynthia Hawke. She studied theology with a BA (Hons) from the London School of Theology (1973–1976), and held an MEd (Sydney, 1987) and a PhD (Murdoch, 1999).[87]

81. Parker, *Top of the Mount*, 74.
82. Parker, *Top of the Mount*, 96.
83. Author email correspondence with Stretton, March 11 and 26, 2020.
84 "Australia: Barbara Darling," *The Episcopal Church*.
85. Henningham, "Darling, Barbara."
86. Schwartz, "From Rookie."
87. Author email correspondence with Sylvia Collison, March 10, 2020.

Rosemary (Rose) Weir was the first woman on Morling Faculty (1996–2004). Rose Weir was also Lecturer in the Master of Counselling Program, Graduate School of Counselling, Wesley Institute, Drummoyne, NSW (1996–2013). She graduated with a Morling Award in theological studies (1994), a BMin (ACT, 1995), and an MA (Theol) from the ACT (1997). She also held a Master of Education (Adult) from the University of Technology, Sydney (1998), and a Master of Counselling (University of New England, 2000). Rose Weir started a PhD through University of Tasmania but transferred to a DMin with ACOM.[88]

The first woman to hold a permanent position on faculty at Vose Seminary (formerly Baptist Theological College of WA) was Evelyn Ashley, who began as a sessional lecturer, teaching introductory New Testament (2003) then as permanent faculty, also teaching Greek and exegesis.[89] Honorary tutors and lecturers in the 1990s included Ruth Galloway, Lucy Twining, Sylvia Collison, and Genevieve Milne.[90]

Dawn Cardona was the first Indigenous woman Principal of Nungalinya College in Darwin (2003–2007), following Larrakia man Wali Fejo, who was the first Indigenous Principal of the College (1996–2002).[91]

The NAIITS program based at Whitley College in Melbourne is a new initiative in Indigenous learning, with input from Aunty Jean Phillips, Brooke Prentis (CEO of Common Grace), Naomi Wolfe, an Australian Aboriginal lecturer at Australian Catholic University, and many other lecturers from around Australia and internationally.[92]

Some recently founded centers for women's studies merit attention. The ACT's Angelina Noble Centre is for women undertaking Masters research projects and higher degree research in cross-cultural missions. The Centre is named after the gifted Indigenous leader, linguist, and missionary, Angelina Noble (1879–1964).[93] *When Women Speak . . .* is a network of Christian women scholars and practitioners in mission to Muslim women, led by missiologists Dr. Cathy Hine and Dr. Moyra Dale.[94] We would also like to know

---

88. Author email correspondence with Rose Weir, March 13, 2020.

89. Siggins, "Experience of Women," 134–35. Monica O'Neil was appointed as director of Vose leadership in 2007.

90. Siggins, "Experience of Women," 130; author email correspondence with Monica O'Neil, April 7, 2020.

91. Seiffert, *Gumbuli*, 269.

92. Payne, "Breakthrough." See also, Yunkaporta, *Sand Talk*; and Deverell, *Gondwana Theology*.

93. Kociumbas, "Noble, Angelina."

94. *When Women Speak . . .*

more about women staff and students in Chinese Departments such as at MST, and other language specific programs around Australia.[95]

Concluding Thoughts

Australian women's scholarship does not occur in a vacuum. As Korean scholar Kooyong Kim comments about developing Asian perspectives, "It would be unwise ... to study the Bible as if for the first time."[96] Australian women scholars share in the international tradition of women's and men's scholarship leading back to biblical times.[97] We also have our own heritage of Australian scholarship from women and men, both Indigenous and Settler, many giving their lives in missions, ministry, and service to the community.

Some of our "grandmothers" received a formal theological education, resulting in a degree. For others, especially in the early years, training was more informal. "Necessity was the mother of invention," and their intention to love, serve, and become like Christ led them to gain knowledge and skills in whatever way they could find access. We honor them for their commitment, and for becoming "grandmothers of intention" for us.

Australian women theological scholars today are blessed with opportunities for study and belonging to a cohort of women scholars. We can remember those who blazed the trail for us and look forward to ourselves contributing to future students. We will benefit from reflection on Australian history, Indigenous culture and wisdom, and insights and approaches from multicultural Australia. Deepening relationships between Aboriginal and Torres Strait Islander people and other Australians will enrich our ability to be grounded in the body, in time and place, and in Scripture. We look forward to research by women and men that brings the names, stories, methods, and knowledges of more Australian women scholars in Bible and theology to our attention.[98]

---

95. Wang, "Chinese Perspective," discusses male lecturers in three Chinese programs within Australian theological colleges.

96. Kim, *1 Samuel*, 9.

97. Gooder, *Phoebe*; Cohick, *Women in the World*; Cohick, *Christian Women*; Taylor and Choi, *Handbook*; Benckhuysen, *Gospel According to Eve*; Taylor and Weir, *Women in the Story*.

98. For some current women scholars, see Hill and Barker, "160+ Australian and New Zealander Women."

Bibliography

"Abba, Hilda May." *HerStory Archive*. N.d. https://wmoa.com.au/herstory2017/woman/abba-hilda-may

"Aboriginal Protestors." Getty Images website, February 7, 1991. https://www.gettyimages.ae/detail/news-photo/aboriginal-protesters-deaconess-jean-phillips-of-brisbane-news-photo/1079982360

"About Mary Andrews." https://www.mac.edu.au/about-mary-andrews/

"AC History." https://www.ac.edu.au/about/history/

"ACT Winifred Merritt Fellowships—Female Research Fellows." https://www.actheology.edu.au/act-winifred-merritt-fellowships-female-research-fellows/

Atkinson, Judy. *Trauma Trails, Recreating Song Lines: The Transgenerational Effects of Trauma in Indigenous Australia*. North Geelong: Spinifex, 2002.

Austin, Denise. *Our College: A History of the National Training College of Australian Christian Churches*. Sydney: Australian Pentecostal Studies, 2013.

"Australia: Barbara Darling Named Assistant Bishop for Melbourne." *The Episcopal Church*, April 27, 2008. https://episcopalchurch.org/library/article/australia-barbara-darling-named-assistant-bishop-melbourne.

Australian College of Theology Records. Unpublished data from the ACT archives, accessed by Megan Powell du Toit, March 10, 2020.

"Aunty Jean Phillips." https://www.commongrace.org.au/naidoc_aunty_jean_phillips

Benckhuysen, Amanda W. *The Gospel According to Eve: A Women's History of Interpretation*. Downers Grove, IL: InterVarsity, 2019.

"Betty Black." *Connect* 13 (2018). https://bst.qld.edu.au/wp-content/uploads/2019/07/BST-Connect-Summer-2018.pdf.

Birman, Wendy. "Genders, Dorothy Edna (1892–1978)." *Australian Dictionary of Biography*, Volume 14, 1996. http://adb.anu.edu.au/biography/genders-dorothy-edna-10289.

"Blackham, Hilda May." *HerStory Archive*. https://wmoa.com.au/collection/herstory-archive/blackham.

Brammall, Anthony C. *Out of Darkness: 100 Years of Sydney Missionary and Bible College*. Sydney: SMBC, 2016.

"Burvill," *The Argus*, March 29, 1881. https://trove.nla.gov.au/newspaper/article/5988899.

Carter, Philip. "The first Women at University: Remembering 'the London Nine.'" *Times Higher Education*, January 28, 2018. https://www.timeshighereducation.com/blog/first-women-university-remembering-london-nine.

Chatfield, Graeme. "Approaches to Ministerial Training Among New South Wales Baptists: Initial Lines of Enquiry," *The Pacific Journal of Baptist Research* 2.1 (2006) 39–62.

Chidgzey, Aaron. "Fifty Years of Students: The Changing Demography of the Vose Student Body." In *Vose Seminary at 50: "Preach the Word" to "Come, Grow,"* edited by Nathan Hobby, John Olley, and Michael O'Neill, 103–119. Preston: Mosaic, 2013.

Cohick, Lynn H. *Women in the World of the Earliest Christians: Illuminating Ancient Ways of Life*. Grand Rapids, MI: Baker, 2009.

Cohick, Lynn H., and Amy Brown Hughes. *Christian Women in the Patristic World: Their Influence, Authority and Legacy in the Second through Fifth Centuries.* Grand Rapids, MI: Baker, 2017.
Cromb, Natalie, "5 Indigenous Women Who Didn't Get the Credit." *NITV*, July 12, 2018. https://www.sbs.com.au/nitv/article/2018/07/12/5-indigenous-women-who-didnt-get-credit
Deaconess House. *The Vision Unfolding: Deaconess Institution 1891–1991.* Newtown: Deaconess House, 1991.
Deverell, Garry Worete. *Gondwana Theology: A Trawloolway Man Reflects on Christian Faith.* Reservoir: Morning Star, 2018.
"Empowering Aboriginal & Torres Strait Islander Christian Leaders." *Grasstree Gathering* website. https://www.grasstreegathering.org.au.
Ganter, Regina. *The Contest for Aboriginal Souls: European Missionary Agendas in Australia.* Canberra: ANU Press, 2018.
Gooder, Paula. *Phoebe: A Story.* London: Hodder and Stoughton, 2018.
Grose, Kelvin, and A. De Q. Robin. "Green, Florence Emily (1862–1926)." *Australian Dictionary of Biography.* http://adb.anu.edu.au/biography/green-florence-emily-7046.
Harwarth, Irene, Elizabeth DeBra, and Mindi Malin. *Women's Colleges in the United States: History, Issues, & Challenges.* National Institute on Postsecondary Education, Libraries, and Lifelong Learning, U.S. Dept. of Education, University of Michigan, 1997, 3–4.
Henningham, Nikki. "Darling, Barbara." *Encyclopaedia of Women and Leadership in Twentieth Century Australia.* http://www.womenaustralia.info/leaders/biogs/WLE0282b.htm.
Hill, Graham Joseph, and Jen Barker. "160+ Australian and New Zealander Women in Theology You Should Know About." December 13, 2019. https://theglobalchurchproject.com/australian-new-zealander-women-theologians/.
Jones, Helen. "Lake, Serena (1842–1902)" In *Australian Dictionary of Biography.* http://adb.anu.edu.au/biography/lake-serena-13037.
"Kate Edger." *New Zealand History.* https://nzhistory.govt.nz/people/kate-edger.
Kent, Gayle, "Responding in Faith to Our Changing World." *Eternity.* https://www.eternitynews.com.au/australia/responding-in-faith-to-our-changing-world/
"Kiek, Winifred (1884–1975)." *The Australian Women's Register.* http://www.womenaustralia.info/biogs/AWE3708b.htm.
Kim, Koowon. *1 Samuel.* Asia Bible Commentary Series. Carlisle: Langham Global, 2018.
Kociumbas, Jan. "Noble, Angelina (1879–1964)." *Australian Dictionary of Biography.* http://adb.anu.edu.au/biography/noble-angelina-8533.
Kuan, Wei-Han. *Foundations of Anglican Evangelicalism in Victoria.* Australian College of Theology Monograph. Wipf & Stock, 2019.
Kuan, Wei-Han. "James and Angelina Noble: Pioneer Australian Anglican Missionaries." In *Making the Word of God Fully Known: Essays on Church, Culture, and Mission in Honor of Archbishop Philip Freier*, edited by Paul A. Barker and Bradly S. Billings, 159–77. Eugene, OR: Wipf & Stock, 2020.
Lee, Charlene Jin. "I Come from a Place: Reflections on Katie Cannon's Womanist Classroom." *Interpretation* 74 (2020) 31–37.

Lee, Ruth. "Andrews, Mary Maria." *The Encyclopedia of Women and Leadership in Twentieth-Century Australia.* N.d. http://www.womenaustralia.info/leaders/biogs/WLE0137b.htm.

———. "Kiek, Winifred." *Encyclopaedia of Women and Leadership in Twentieth Century Australia.* N.d. http://www.womenaustralia.info/leaders/biogs/WLE0126b.htm.

Mackinnon, Alison. "Early Graduates." *The Encyclopedia of Women & Leadership in Twentieth-Century Australia.* http://www.womenaustralia.info/leaders/biogs/WLE0432b.htm

Martin, Kara, Megan Powell du Toit, Jill Firth, and Moyra Dale. "Women in Theological Education in the ACT in 21st Century Australia." in *Theological Education in Australia: Foundations, Current Practices and Future Options,* edited by Andrew Bain and Ian Hussey, 160–74. Eugene, OR: Wipf & Stock, 2018.

"Mrs. H. M. Abba Ordained a Minister," *Sydney Morning Herald,* October 9, 1951. https://trove.nla.gov.au/newspaper/article/18234237

"Notable Salvos." Salvation Army website, updated 2020. https://www.salvationarmy.org.au/about-us/our-story/our-history/notable-salvos/

O'Brien, Anne. "Christian Church Workers." *The Encyclopedia of Women and Leadership in Twentieth-Century Australia.* http://www.womenaustralia.info/leaders/biogs/WLE0033b.htm.

Parker, David. *Top of the Mount: The Story of the Queensland Bible Institute,* Brisbane: Queensland Bible Institute, 1981.

Paris, Peter J. "Katie Cannon's Non-Canonical Canon." *Interpretation* 74 (2020) 17–22.

Payne, Kaley, "Breakthrough on teaching theology through Indigenous eyes." *Eternity,* April 9, 2019. https://www.eternitynews.com.au/australia/breakthrough-on-teaching-theology-through-indigenous-eyes/.

Phillips, Walter. "Kiek, Winifred (1884–1975)." Australian Dictionary of Biography, Volume 9, 1983. http://adb.anu.edu.au/biography/kiek-winifred-7099/text12069.

Phillips, Jean. "Interview with Miss Jean Phillips and Rev Graham Paulsen," (1989) https://myrrh.library.moore.edu.au/handle/10248/8826

Pitman, Julia. *Prophets and Priests: Congregational Women in Australia 1919–1977.* Unpublished PhD diss., University of Adelaide, 2005.

Pitman, Julia, and Peter Bentley, "AN UPDATE Julia Pitman and Peter Bentley1"

Porter, Muriel. "Second Female Bishop Barbara Darling Broke Ground in Anglican Church." *Sydney Morning Herald,* February 26, 2015. https://www.smh.com.au/national/second-female-bishop-barbara-darling-broke-ground-in-anglican-church-20150226-13p9lg.html.

Press Cutting, *Woorabinda News,* 1956.

Reid, John G. "Grace Annie Lockhart." *The Canadian Encyclopedia,* April 1 2008. https://www.thecanadianencyclopedia.ca/en/article/grace-annie-lockhart

Ridley College. https://www.ridley.edu.au/

Robb, Ron, and Graeme Chatfield. "Morling College—A Brief Summary of Its History." *The Baptist Recorder* 93 (2006) 1–11. http://www.baptisthistory.org.au/journals/tbr/tbr93_jan06

Schwartz, Barney. "From Rookie to Melbourne Bishop, Meet Barbara Darling." *The Age,* April 26, 2008. https://www.theage.com.au/national/from-rookie-to-melbourne-bishop-meet-barbara-darling-20080426-ge7oc9.html.

Seiffert, Murray. *Gumbuli of Ngukurr: Aboriginal Elder in Arnhem Land.* Brunswick East: Acorn, 2011.

Sherlock, Charles. *Australian Anglicans Remember*. Mulgrave: Broughton, 2015.
Sherlock, Charles. *Uncovering Theology: The Depth, Reach and Utility of Australian Theological Education*. Hindmarsh: ATF, 2009.
Siggins, Karen. "The Experience of Women in Theological Education: From the Fringes Towards the Centre." In *Vose Seminary at 50: "Preach the Word" to "Come, Grow,"* edited by Nathan Hobby, John Olley, and Michael O'Neill, 120–39. Preston: Mosaic, 2013.
Taylor, Marion Ann, and Agnes Choi, eds. *Handbook of Women Biblical Interpreters: A Historical and Biographical Guide*. Grand Rapids, MI: Baker Academic, 2012.
Taylor, Marion, and Heather E. Weir, eds. *Women in the Story of Jesus: The Gospels Through the Eyes of Nineteenth-Century Female Biblical Interpreters*. Grand Rapids, MI: Eerdmans, 2016.
Tkaczuk, Basil. "Mission House." All Saints Network blog, 2018. http://www.stjohnsac.net.au/index.php/mission-house/
Treloar, G. "The Three (or Four) Identities of the Australian College of Theology, 1891–2016." In *Theological Education in Australia: Foundations, Current Practices and Future Options*, edited by Andrew Bain and Ian Hussey, 101–118. Eugene, OR: Wipf & Stock, 2018.
Wang, Wally. "A Chinese Perspective on Theological Education." In *Theological Education in Australia: Foundations, Current Practices and Future Options*, edited by Andrew Bain and Ian Hussey, 148–59. Eugene, OR: Wipf & Stock, 2018.
Welch, Ian. *Australian and New Zealand Missionary Training Homes*. Working Paper, September 2014. https://openresearch-repository.anu.edu.au/bitstream/1885/12034/1/Welch.pdf.
Wingard, Barbara, Carolynanha Johnson, and Tileah Drahm-Butler. *Aboriginal Narrative Practice: Honouring Storylines of Pride, Strength and Creativity*. Adelaide: Dulwich Centre Publications, 2015.
When Women Speak . . . https://whenwomenspeak.net/
"Woman Cleric." *The Courier Mail* (Brisbane), 9 October, 1951. https://trove.nla.gov.au/newspaper/article/50241965.
Yunkaporta, Tyson. *Sand Talk: How Indigenous Thinking Can Save the World*. Melbourne: Text, 2019.

Epilogue

Saam 151
Carol Robertson

Song blanga wi laif, hau wi jidan tudei
Carol bin raidemdan dijan song blanga ola komyuniti

Shainiwan God,
Haulong pipul garra jidan langa det dakbala en weitabat blanga yu?

Yu sabi melabat laif holot,
insaidwei en hau had melebat hat.
Pipul jidan nogudbinji, nomo sabi wanim blanga dum.
Dei rekon ol detlot ting dei dumbat meik olabat gubinji, bat najing.
Olabat stil luk sadwan autsaidwei.

Wan ting mising la olabat laif.
Samtaim pipul hu wandi beptais jidan gubinji ba lilbitaim,
bat bambai, olabat gowei brom yu,
en melabat luk olabat nogudbinji igin.

Nomo libum melabat!
Kaman gulijap langa melabat pipul.
Dumaji wen yu jidan gulijap la melabat,
melabat fil seifwan, en jidan gudbinji.

Album melabat ba kigon trastimbat oni yu na,
dumaji yu na det truwan lait, en yu shainwan God
hu gin tjakidawei ola dakbalating langa dijan wel.

Wi gibit yu preis en teingks
dumaji yu na det lait weya bin kaman langa dijan wel
en yu shain langa ola pipul langa ebri kantri.
En wi sabi yu gin shain iya du.

Psalm 151
Translated from Kriol by Kate Beer

Song about how our life is today
Carol wrote this song about/for all the communities

God of glory,
How long will people be in the darkness and waiting for you?

You know our entire life,
our inside thoughts and how hard our hearts are.
People are unhappy and don't know what to do.
They think all the things they do make them happy, but nothing.
They still look sad on their outside.

One thing is missing in their life.
Sometimes people who get baptized are happy for a little while,

But after a bit, they go away from You,
and we see them unhappy again.

Don't leave us!
Come near to our people.
Because when you are close to us,
We feel safe, and are happy.

Help us keep trusting only you,
because you are the true light and the glorious God
who can throw away all the darkness in this world.

We give you praise and thanks
Because you are the light that came into this world
And you shine to people in every country.
and we know you can shine here too.

www.ingramcontent.com/pod-product-compliance
Lightning Source LLC
Chambersburg PA
CBHW061428300426
44114CB00014B/1588